# CHILDBIRTH & MARRIAGE

*Other Avon Books by*
**Tracy Hotchner**

PREGNANCY & CHILDBIRTH

# CHILDBIRTH & MARRIAGE

## THE TRANSITION TO PARENTHOOD

## TRACY HOTCHNER

Foreword by Walter Brackelmanns, M.D.

AVON BOOKS ◆ NEW YORK

CHILDBIRTH & MARRIAGE is an original publication of Avon Books. This work has never before appeared in book form.

AVON BOOKS
A division of
The Hearst Corporation
105 Madison Avenue
New York, New York 10016

First Avon Books Trade Printing: October 1988

*for Frank, with love*

# Acknowledgments

I am grateful for the enthusiastic encouragement I got for this book from many groups and professionals who provide services for new parents. My thanks to all of you, but in particular:

Ann Adalist-Estrin, Nancy T. Bachelder, Jay Belsky, Elizabeth Bing, Karen Blanchard, Amy F. Cades, James Cameron, Susan Cappone, Barbara Carlson, Cynthia G. Cavallo, Jean Illsley Clarke, Jan H. Clayton, Fran R. Cogen, Sara Coleman, Barbara Levy Daniels, Rosemary Diulio, Arlene Dulsky, Karen Farber, Sandy Feinberg, Glory Fox-Dierker, Lynne Friedman, Aviva Gershweir, Margaret Hallett, A. Dawn Hallman. Cynthia L. Harbach, Susan Host, Elizabeth Jacob, Eldor Kaiser, Joyce Kaser, Nancy Kleckner, Ellen Kleiner, Vicki Lansky, Jo Anne Lattiak, Michele Lauer-Bader, Carolyn Lewis, Helen Maxwell, Jennifer McComas, Marian McDonald, Madeline Molis, Donna Newton, Lorraine Norwood, Donna M. Noyes, Tandy Parks, Lynn E. Pooley, Paul Reinelt, Elinor Renfield, Fretta Reitzes, Carolyn Rose, Jerry Sachs, Elizabeth C. Salin, Lucy Scott, Joan Slanina, Nancy Smith, Sheila Tishler, Betsy Weaver, Jackie Dubey Weintraub, Barbara Williams, Marion Wilson, Holly Zwerling.

My thanks also to the generosity of friends who shared their experiences and advice about parenting with me: Mickey Astor, Karen and Norman Fell, Stephen Foreman, Allan Metzger, Peggy Pollock, Lynn Povich, Elinor Pullen, Mary Willis, and Stacey Winkler. Dikla Peebles' enthusiasm went so far that she read each chapter as it poured out of the computer, not only giving me wise comments, but inventing new ways to tear computer paper!

Special thanks to Daphne Astor, a port-in-the-storm to other adoptive parents and an incomparable friend who has steered me and cheered me right through this book—and my life!

Peggy Penn has been a gift in my life, loving me as though she was my mother.

Kate Korshak has shown me the joys of loving someone as though she was your own daughter.

My eternal gratitude to Ron McDevitt for the understanding he has given me about human emotions, which has helped me to empathize with other peoples' needs and problems.

Many thanks to my editor, Judith Riven, for her intelligent and caring contributions to this book—and for my good fortune in having an editor I would choose as a friend.

My love and thanks to my agent, Robert Lescher, who has made the Publishing Experience a pleasurable adventure for me over the last decade.

I can never repay the hours Tom Polizzi spent making my computer "user friendly," and then his infinite patience in making emergency house calls when the "user" needed reprograming!

My thanks to Janice Foster for helping to organize the appendices to this book (and many other areas of my desk)!

And thanks to the people at the Burlington Book Shop in New York City for their enthusiastic assistance in researching this book.

Finally, no writer could wish for a life partner more loving, supportive and unselfish than Frank Yablans.

This book was born under a lucky star: I had the incredible good fortune to meet Walter Brackelmanns, who agreed to be the medical advisor. Dr. Brackelmanns' background could not have been more perfectly tailored to the subject matter of CHILDBIRTH & MARRIAGE: his medical training was in child psychiatry, which he practices, but he has also become a renowned couples' therapist. Walter Brackelmanns is not only a compassionate and skilled psychotherapist, he has the rare and additional qualities of being a kind, gentle and smart man. This book has been enhanced by his involvement—and I have been personally enriched by knowing him.

# Contents

# List of Charts

# Foreword

## by Walter Brackelmanns, M.D.

There are many books written on the subject of relationships. This is a very special one. A child is born. This brings much pleasure to the lives of the parents; they are happy, anxious, confused, and stressed. There is so much that they do not know about this new life and how it will impact on their marriage and them as individuals. This book is a must for all new and old parents. What Tracy Hotchner has done is quite remarkable: she has written a work that is easy to read and comprehensive.

As an adult and child psychiatrist, psychoanalyst, and couples' therapist, I found this book full of useful and practical suggestions. It gives the reader an understanding of all aspects of the parent-child relationship as well as the husband-wife relationship. There are several philosophies throughout this work that deliver what I consider to be some of the most valuable messages a medical or mental health professional can offer. Probably the most important theme is that *parents should appropriately turn to books and professionals for help, but never at the sacrifice of their own intuitiveness and personal judgment.* I believe that parents should prepare for the birth of their child by reading everything they can get their hands on, and then when the child is born, throw the books away and raise the child by the seat of their pants. I am exaggerating to make the point. I do believe that encouraging people to respect themselves and their own talents and skills is essential. Tracy Hotchner accomplishes a blending of valuable and at times even critical information while encouraging self-respect and self-confidence. She tells you to trust your instincts. I agree.

A second significant point that is made over and over in this book is *to take care of yourself.* Adopting or giving birth to a baby is a miracle and full of joy and wonder. It is also an incredible stress. The newborn infant is a bundle of energy and at times a source of insatiable demands. There is a tendency on the part of the parents to be self-sacrificing; they are often willing to give up themselves in the interest of the baby to the extent that they become raw, jangling nerves. Tracy Hotchner makes the point that the parents must preserve their physical and mental strength. This is the only way to have a healthy child, marriage, and family. The author offers many practical ways that this can be achieved.

*Parents should give themselves permission to be human.* This is a third principle of child rearing. If you do something wrong or things do not go as well as you would like, forgive yourself. Try to remember that you are well intentioned and conscientious. Nobody is perfect. Raising a child is a difficult, important, and challenging job that requires flexibility, creativity, and a willingness to tolerate the process of trial and error. Mistakes will be made and your child will not only survive but thrive if you are accepting of yourself and your foibles and pratfalls. Tracy Hotchner has much to say about this and she says it so well. When you read this book, you will not only learn useful facts; you will learn to be more comfortable with the interactional process between you and your child.

Tracy Hotchner is a very positive person—it was a pleasure to work with this knowledgeable and enthusiastic writer. After every encounter with her, I came away feeling a warm, pleasant glow. This emotional tone pervades the book. The reader feels optimistic and encouraged, chapter after chapter. She clearly delivers the message that parenting and marriage can comfortably co-exist and flourish.

The last principle I want to underline has to do with a subject close to my heart: *It is essential that parents maintain an effective and empathic line of communication with each other.* The art and skill of talking and listening is not taught to any of us in our long years of education and experience. We must pick it up by ourselves. It is this skill that enables us to problem-solve and to develop a close, intimate relationship with our mates, and later with our child. Tracy Hotchner underlines the importance of this capacity to establish a dialogue of intimacy and gives us many practical suggestions as to how to accomplish it.

The book is virtually an encyclopedia of child, parent, and marital material. No matter where you open it, each section provides a concise, useful, and thorough discussion. There are ideas about what to expect from your baby, as well as much insight into what a marriage experiences with the entry of a baby into the family. The author has much to say about what the new mother and father can do to enhance and enrich their own personal lives and also encourage growth of the evolving marriage. Marriage is like an organism—it is constantly changing and growing. The parents must never forget that there is a marriage. The presence of a new family member should not detract from the husband and wife concentrating on improving and developing their love relationship. This is perhaps the most important message of this book.

I strongly recommend that all potential and new parents read *Childbirth & Marriage*. Learn its facts and its sage messages and let it help you to be free of some of the anxieties of new parenthood. Let it help you to be more comfortable with your new baby. A child is a great joy and is meant to enrich the life of you and your spouse. Here is the most useful guide I know to help you achieve this goal.

WALTER BRACKELMANNS, M.D.
Los Angeles
October 1987

# Introduction

You may already know me from *Pregnancy & Childbirth*. I feel as though I know many of you: many readers wrote or called to ask questions or let me know how that book enhanced their pregnancy and birth. I feel lucky to have been some small part of your lives—but I couldn't just let it drop there. I saw so many couples struggling with their marriages during the transition to parenthood. Even while they were overjoyed to have a child, couples were frazzled, frightened, and depressed. They seemed so caught up in the intensity of the transition to parenthood that they'd lost their perspective, sense of humor, and even a sense of priorities. I thought, "There must be a way I can help. It doesn't have to be this hard and lonely."

As a word of explanation, I am not a doctor—not an obstetrician-gynecologist, a psychiatrist, a sociologist, a pediatrician, a family therapist, or a social worker. I researched this book as a consumer advocate, which was the same position I took in writing *Pregnancy & Childbirth*. The text is an amalgamation of wisdom I gathered in interviews with many representatives of the above-named specialists. I also conducted interviews with countless parents of all ages who were wonderfully generous in opening up their lives to me.

This book is for you and your partner; it is not about

raising your child and how to make him smarter or develop sooner. This book is in part a reaction to all those baby-care and child-rearing books. It seems as though everyone is so excited about infants who can swim the length of an Olympic pool and two-year-olds who play the cello while reading flashcards that we've forgotten about the man and woman who made all this possible. What about Mom and Dad?

I am here to raise some issues that people have been ignoring in the mad rush to produce Super Babies. What happens to the two of you when you become a threesome? How does a child affect your marriage? What does a baby do to a couple's relationship? What kind of lovers and partners will you be once you become parents?

I wanted to help couples preserve and improve the quality of their relationship after they became parents. I hope you'll come away from reading this believing that you can have it all—it takes some hard work and there will be rough spots, but people can be good parents and still be personally fulfilled as individuals and life partners.

The book is meant for both the new mother and father, so the style goes back and forth between addressing you separately and together. There may be times when the emphasis may seem slanted toward the woman's point of view, but that is not my intention.

I hope *Childbirth & Marriage* gives you and your partner the information you need to achieve your full potential once a child enters your lives. I've tried to emphasize how important it is to meet your individual needs while giving your child the best possible life: be true to yourself, trust yourself, and above all, enjoy the adventure of parenthood.

Tuscany, Italy
October 1987

# 1

# Getting your house in order

There are many things you might want to think about and plan for before your baby is born. (It's still worth giving some thought to the issues in this chapter, even if you're already holding your gurgling baby in your arms!) Fore-warned is forearmed, as the saying goes, and nothing could be truer about bringing a child into your life. The more you know about yourself and your mate, and the more infor-mation you have about what to expect, the smoother your transition from couple to parents will be.

## WHY DO YOU WANT TO BE PARENTS?

You and your mate probably have quite different reasons for wanting to have children. It may be a goal you've had for years or a recent decision. It may be something you feel certain about or you may have doubts. In any case it can't hurt for you to analyze what has influenced your decision. It will probably be helpful to gain some insight into what is motivating you.

It can ease the adjustment to parenthood if a couple takes the time to talk about what attracts each of them to having a child. By doing this, parents-to-be may find that it helps them to become a unified team for going through pregnancy, birth, and then integrating the baby into their

1

lives. A child is going to demand a great deal of time, energy, patience, and money from both of you. The strain might be less if you understand why you each wanted the baby in the first place.

***Examine your childhoods.*** One reason that frequently motivates people to have children is their pleasant memories of their own childhoods and their relationships with their parents. There are also many people who think of their childhoods as having been unhappy, yet they are eager to be parents. One reason why a person with an unhappy childhood may want a child is because s/he identifies with the child. The baby becomes them and they become their parents: by having a child they can finally be taken care of in the way they've always wanted. Either way, you may find it constructive to recognize these influences rather than letting them have an effect on you of which you aren't aware. (*Chapters 3, 4,* and *5* go into more detail about the effects of your parents and your childhoods.)

***Free-associate with your partner.*** In order to gather your early memories it can help to talk freely with your spouse. Find a quiet time to talk together in a relaxed, unpressured setting that will encourage you to call up memories. Together you can discover what it felt like for each of you to be a child; you can reminisce about your memories of how you were treated. You will probably learn things about your mate that you never knew before—and you may uncover things about yourself and your past that will surprise you.

If a couple talks in an unpressured, nonjudgmental way about the dreams and disappointments of their own childhoods, it creates a new kind of bond between them. What you learn together will enable you to understand what in your past is influencing your desire to be parents. It will also be an indication of how both your early experiences may affect the kind of parenting you will give your child. These discussions can open up a couple to be better, more understanding partners as well as parents.

Discuss which aspects of your childhood are positive in your memories. Try to recall what decisions your parents made for you that you feel good about. What did they do or how did they behave that made you uncomfortable or angry? If you take the time to look back at yourselves as children, you may realize where you developed the hopes and dreams you have for your child. You may also discover that you have unrealistic expectations for yourself or your mate as a parent or you may have expectations of your child that may be unfair because you're imposing your own hopes on him.

*Two charts follow.*   Although these are not listed in any order of importance, the charts cover many of the reasons that people give for wanting to have children. There are no "right" or "wrong" reasons for the decision, but it is possible to say that there are positive, healthy reasons for choosing to become parents and other reasons that—taken by themselves—are less good. You will probably find factors on both lists that may apply to one or both of you. The point of these charts is not to judge you as "good" or "bad," but just to help you think about what is influencing you.

## THE FINANCIAL REALITIES OF PARENTING

Money can be a major source of friction in a marriage: finances are often cited as a primary cause of conflict between husbands and wives, with fewer funds causing more fights. Finances are of particular concern to new parents who were accustomed to two incomes and often find themselves suddenly supporting *three* people on *half* the income they had before.

*Money can be symbolic of other issues.*   The way that the two of you handle your finances can function as a yardstick for your marriage; it can be an example of how you cope with other aspects of your life and relationship. As can happen with any argument, fights about money often aren't really about money. They are about feelings that run

### Some "Good" Reasons for Wanting a Child

- To experience pregnancy and childbirth
- Wanting to create a family, and all that it entails
- Reaffirmation of feelings and commitment to your mate; greater permanence to your marriage
- You think you'll be a good parent
- Perpetuation of yourselves through children; a sense of immortality and ties to the future
- Stimulation, novelty, fun: the energy, noise, and activity that children bring to a home
- To add meaning to your lives: a child can make life seem more worthwhile, give it a purpose
- Fear that you'll be sorry later on if you don't have a child now
- Birth allows people to re-experience the wonderful, magical feeling of being in love

### Some "Not So Good" Reasons for Wanting a Child

- Validation of adult status and social identity (the social system values people with children)
- Sense of control: you'll have power and influence over the child
- Self-esteem gained by this ego gratification
- Achievement of moral values: you're doing something "good" by having and caring for a child
- Feeling of pride in producing a child: a demonstration of achievement, competence
- Social competition, comparison with peers (all your friends are having babies)
- A child can achieve all you haven't
- You can give a child all the things you didn't have
- To improve a troubled marriage
- Proof of a man's virility or a woman's femininity
- An heir to carry on the family name, business, or dreams
- Pressure from your parents to produce a grandchild
- Because you can't figure out why you don't have one

deeper, about the things that money can represent: power, competition, self-esteem, anger, guilt, or love. Of course, financial arguments can also genuinely be about money. We live in a society where "more" is perceived as "better." Worries about money can overtake you when you begin to think that the things you cannot afford are the answers to your happiness.

*Talk about money.* The more you're able to discuss your finances, the less you may argue about how you spend the money. An open discussion gives you a chance to exchange ideas about money and budgeting, to express your attitudes and fears to each other. It is important that you learn each other's underlying feelings about money so that together you can learn how to handle it. You will probably each have different views on loans, investments, savings accounts, credit cards, and trust funds for the child's future. Your opinions will have been formed, at least in part, by your own upbringing and by the attitude toward money of each of your families.

*It can be hard for couples to talk about money.* You may be afraid to confront your financial condition and admit that there are things you cannot afford. But you might have to force yourselves to discuss money, even at the risk of an emotional scene. Many people have a wide range of negative feelings when their funds are inadequate: depression, anxiety, and anger are just some of these feelings. But it can be better to face the reality and the emotions together, rather than to hide your heads in the sand.

*Arguments about money are going to happen.* Don't imagine that something is wrong with you or your relationship just because you have heated discussions about finances; arguments are normal and happen in many marriages. However, you can make these discussions constructive if you remember that you are partners, not adversaries. If you each really listen to your mate and make an effort to understand and accommodate the other person's needs and feelings, you'll be way ahead of the game.

If you have discussions *now* it might defuse pressure and avoid an explosion later on. Letting off steam as it builds up is a great habit to develop in all aspects of your life as new parents. You can even teach yourselves to avoid having huge blow-ups on any subject. You just have to get into the habit of dealing with issues when they happen. If you can make the time to talk about it when a disagreement begins, you may be able to keep it from escalating into a nasty, heated argument.

*Money problems can invade your entire relationship.* Money may not buy happiness, but a lack of it has been known to bring a lot of **unhappiness!** A lack of money can affect a marriage by undermining confidence, trust, and openness. If you are struggling with financial worries, one way to protect your relationship from the strain is to rearrange your priorities so that leisure time becomes a top priority. If you have problems with money, it isn't just the lack of ''goods and services'' that affects you. You are also affected by pressure, anxiety, and the feeling that you can't afford leisure time. But if you don't have ''time off,'' you can become so burnt out that you don't work effectively or have quality time together.

If your budget is tight, don't make the mistake of making material things more important than yourselves. Leisure time should be at the top of your list, right below food and shelter. Your emotional well-being is worth a lot more than a new washing machine.

*Change your expectations.* You may have more peace of mind about your finances if you expect to have somewhat less once you have a child. You'll probably have to control or suppress your desire to have it all—to have all the material things or services that you might want. The new operative word in your lives may become **''compromise.''** It isn't such a terrible thing! You may not be able to afford to have a baby-sitter, go out to dinner, *and* see a movie. So you make an adjustment and make a choice: either you just see the movie or just have dinner.

Expensive vacations, clothes, or entertainment may no longer be part of your lifestyle. However, if you do not *expect* these luxuries, if you can stop depending on them as a measure of your happiness, then you won't feel disappointed. If you have been operating on the premise that you will be consistently moving up the financial ladder, you may have to revise that expectation. Then you won't be bitter when you see other people buying things and going places that you can no longer afford.

To reorder priorities, it will help if you can sit down together and talk through what you both expect to be able to afford. As a result, you'll probably have to revise how often you can buy a new car, eat out in restaurants, or go skiing. If you can be realistic and modify your goals and dreams, you'll experience less friction and frustration. If you do not lower your expectations, you might get into credit problems, charging things you cannot pay for; in the long run you're asking for financial and emotional stress.

***Grandparents may be a source of financial aid.*** You may have already accepted help from your parents or in-laws in the past. Was there any "price" to pay for their generosity? Do you both feel all right about taking the help? Do the grandparents who give you money have more influence or control over your lives than the other set of grandparents who may not have been willing or able to help out?

If you have never taken money from your parents or in-laws before, they may offer it (or you may need to ask) now that you have the baby. You and your partner should talk about what ramifications there may be. Will either of you be uncomfortable with feelings of being dependent or beholden? If so, it might be a good idea to plan your budget and see if you can manage without the grandparents' help. You might feel better accepting their generosity if they put money in a trust fund for the child's education.

### FIGURE OUT HOW MUCH
### YOUR BABY IS GOING TO COST

Once you determine your costs, you can look for ways to cut those costs. There is no doubt that the costs of giving birth and raising children in America have become astounding. Some studies show that at 1988 prices the birth of a baby averages around $7,000. That figure does *not* include the possibility that you may have to move to accommodate the new family member. It also doesn't take into account the lost salary of a mother who temporarily or permanently gives up her job. Other statistics show that it costs an average of $100 a week to raise a child to the age of 18. This comes out to about $80,000 (which also doesn't take into consideration the lost salary of a parent who may give up a job to raise the child). By anybody's standards that is a staggering amount of money!

*Every home situation is different.*   Costs will vary depending on where you live, the kind of schooling and extracurricular activities you choose, and so on. But regardless of your style of life or the choices you make for birth and child rearing, there are certain unavoidable costs that everyone has to meet. If you and your mate are prepared for these expenses, you will probably have fewer arguments and misunderstandings about finances. There are going to be many surprises and a lot of adjustments to make as new parents: protect yourselves from the shock or burden of unexpected costs by planning ahead.

*The following chart may help you.*   This is a list of the unavoidable costs of childbirth and the baby's first year. The chart will be followed by suggestions on some ways to reduce the costs so that the baby's arrival isn't too much of a financial strain on you.

---

### Costs of Birth and the First Year

- *Obstetrician's bill* for prenatal care and delivery
- *Hospital charges* for normal delivery and average 3-day stay
- *Pediatrician's bill* for hospital examination, 6 routine follow-up visits, and the required immunizations
- *Maternity clothes*
- *Baby clothing and bedding,* including towels, diapers, bibs
- *Nursery equipment:* car seat, crib, stroller, bathtub, changing table, toiletries
- *Baby-sitter,* or full-time nanny, day care or other child care
- *Baby food,* including cereals, juice, formula for nonbreast-fed babies (some breast-fed babies get supplementary bottles, too), bottles, pacifiers, teething aids

---

## SUGGESTIONS ON HOW TO TAKE CONTROL
## OF YOUR FINANCES

***Figure out your budget.***     The first step is to determine your monthly overhead. You have to budget the necessities; any money left over afterwards is what you've got to play with. You should decide as a team what your priorities are for this available money. Will it be used for better housing now, or will you save it for preschool or private schooling later on? Do you want to spend all or most of this discretionary income on your child? It might be a good idea to be prepared to do so, making adjustments later if your income increases. What follows is a simple chart of the items you have to include when you are budgeting your basic necessities.

---

### A BASIC BUDGET

- *Rent or mortgage*
- *Insurance and taxes*
- *Utilities:* electricity, gas, water, telephone
- *Food:* groceries and eating out
- *Transportation:* taxis, bus, train and/or car (including gas, repairs, insurance)
- *Entertainment:* guests at home, movies, etc.
- *Child costs:* **everything** on the previous chart!

---

***Sit down together to make these lists.***     The way you handle your finances is probably going to have to change now that you have more responsibilities and expenses. But in order to change, it helps to look at the way you have handled money in the past. Is one partner in control of the decisions? Does one partner earn more (or all) and does that give him or her more control or power? How are financial decisions and payments made (who writes the checks? whose responsibility is it to keep you within your monetary limits?)? Does one partner spend more on him- or herself than the other?

***Make a list of every expenditure.*** Do this for your costs during one week, listing items in order of importance. The expenses that come at the bottom of the list can either be eliminated or indulged in less frequently. This exercise can be difficult or upsetting. If either one or both of you have gotten used to taking for granted certain luxuries like wine with dinner, weekends away, impulse buying, and other indulgences, it may be a shock to have to answer for every penny you're going to spend. Bill-paying time can become tense and argumentative unless you make these decisions together on how to accommodate your new expenses. Keep a perspective: your cash outlay in the first months is going to be highest because of the costs of birth and the initial one-time purchases.

## SUGGESTIONS ON WAYS TO CUT COSTS

### WAYS TO LOWER HOSPITAL AND HEALTH-CARE EXPENDITURES

***Cut the costs of hospital birth.*** This can usually only be accomplished in low-risk, normal deliveries. Of course there is much less expense in giving birth at home, but since financial considerations should not be the motivating factor in choosing a home birth, I am not including it as a way to save money.

***Remain in the labor room for delivery.*** This cuts out the charges of the operating room and personnel. Some women also find it much less disruptive if they aren't moved to another room and rearranged on another table when the baby is ready to be delivered. However, this option is only possible in low-risk pregnancies that remain low-risk during labor. (You might want to read the relevant section in my *Pregnancy & Childbirth* to inform yourselves more fully about this option.) Before you go into labor you'll need to discuss delivering in the labor room with your obstetrician and find out whether the hospital's policies are flexible enough to allow it.

*Use an ABC (Alternative Birth Center).* This option is now offered in more and more hospitals and usually represents a savings over normal hospital deliveries. But you must remain low-risk throughout your labor and delivery or you will be transferred to the hospital's regular birthing facilities—and obviously you have no way of knowing this ahead of time. Also, it can be a problem if you budget for an ABC birth and cannot have it. ABCs are usually available on a first-come, first-served basis: another couple may already be occupying the room when you go into labor. In addition to what you will save compared to regular hospital charges for the birth, ABC births are normally accompanied by Early Discharge (see below), which saves even more.

*Early discharge also saves money.* This option is usually automatic with an uncomplicated ABC birth, but anybody delivering in a hospital can request it. It means that instead of the usual three-day postpartum stay (with sky-high charges for everything from sanitary napkins to Tylenol to the television), you can leave with your baby 6 hours after delivery. However, this is only possible in hospitals that offer it, and then only in unmedicated births with no complications during a 6-hour postpartum observation period. In addition, you'll need to figure in some expense for professional care at home during the first days.

*Low-cost baby care is often available.* There are ways other than using a private pediatrician to take care of your child on a limited budget. You can find Well-baby clinics through hospitals and medical schools, through the Public Health Department, women's clinics, and free clinics. These are usually only for routine checkups; they don't treat sick babies but can refer you to other facilities if necessary. There may be a charge but it will be low compared to a private doctor. The drawbacks are that there may be a long wait and you will probably see a different doctor every time you go. The Department of Health also gives free immunizations to infants.

*A Public Health Nurse can make home visits.* Call the Department of Health to find out if they do have this service available in your area. If so, it is free of charge. The nurse does routine checks on you and the baby, which can be reassuring especially if you haven't seen a doctor since the baby was born. She can be a sympathetic listener with practical suggestions; she also may know of other services for new parents in your area. The nurse can usually come back as often as you need her, for as long as a year. And don't worry what your house looks like: these ladies know what a mess a newborn makes of a previously neat house!

*Health insurance can save you money.* But in almost every case the policy has to be active before you get pregnant. Review your policy before you get pregnant if at all possible. Find out what costs are payable. Does your policy cover maternity care? Baby care? The following four areas are the ones you must investigate:

### 1: PRE-EXISTING CONDITIONS CLAUSE

- If you move or change jobs, you may get caught by this clause. Most policies don't cover conditions that existed before the policy took effect. Therefore it is not wise to move to another state or change your job during the time you are pregnant: this will mean changing to another insurance carrier. Even if the woman has her own insurance coverage, the baby's father should also wait to change jobs during the period of pregnancy and birth. You will probably lose more in health benefits than you'll gain in a job move. Don't forget, *both* your policies can pay for the costs on one claim.
- There may be a waiting period. Many insurance companies are arbitrary in their rulings. Check your carrier's policy if you plan a pregnancy within the first year of your coverage. Some companies require that a year must elapse from the date the policy took effect and *then* they will cover a pre-existing condition.
- Once you are pregnant (which is the "pre-existing condition"), you cannot get a better insurance policy because of this clause. Therefore you'll be paying out of your own pocket.

## 2: BENEFITS COVERAGE

* Most insurance companies have a scale showing how much each medical service is "supposed" to cost. This is based on the charges in a broad geographical area. If you live in an urban area with a high cost of living, the insurance company will not take this into account; the services you need will probably cost more than they allow.
* You will therefore not only have to pay your 20 percent of what they determine to be "fair and reasonable costs," but you will have to pay the entire difference between their pay scale and what doctors and hospitals **actually** charge.
* Check ahead of time to avoid the shock of finding out how much the insurance does not pay. Get a pre-registration packet from the hospital you intend to use and take it to your personnel department. Also take a statement of your doctor's fees. Find out beforehand how much your insurance will cover. You may want to consider changing your hospital or doctor if the difference is too great.
* Nontraditional birth options (home birth or a birth center outside a hospital) may not be covered by insurance. Check first whether your insurance will accept the birth center you may have chosen (home birth is rarely covered).

## 3: CO-INSURED PAYMENTS

* A typical insurance policy covers 80 percent of the medical charges and the "co-insurer" pays the other 20 percent. If you only have one policy in your family, that means that you are the co-insurer.
* If both of you work and have comprehensive health policies, the man's insurance company can pay the co-insured portion. Sometimes his policy will also pay the woman's deductible, which is usually around $200 a year. However, the preceding information about "benefits coverage" still applies: some expense of the cost won't be paid by either insurer.

## 4: FAMILY POLICY PLAN

* If the coverage you have is only for the individual

named on it, you should convert it into a family policy before the baby is born. This change is usually at
your expense.

- Most people's medical coverage **does not** cover their
baby's expenses, in or out of the hospital. It is critical
that you check on this ahead of time.

- Family coverage is absolutely **essential**. God forbid
that your baby should need it, but just the cost of an
intensive-care nursery can be $1,000 a day. But pro-
tect yourselves from ever facing medical complications without full insurance coverage.

## HOW TO CUT THE EXPENSE OF
## CLOTHES AND SUPPLIES

It can be surprisingly easy to lower your costs on baby
things. The first step is to control your impulse to be a Super Consumer! If you can tell yourselves that there's no
reason to clutter up your life with an accumulation of baby
stuff, it's easier to resist the endless temptations. Buying or
borrowing used clothing and equipment is nothing to be
ashamed of: it makes good economic sense. Don't worry
about what the baby thinks, either. She won't resent you
because her clothes didn't come out of a new box with
fancy price tags (you have years to go before she's a teenager)!

*Use hand-me-downs.* You can save a great deal by getting much of your maternity and baby clothes and equipment from friends and relatives. Whenever you have the
urge to buy some embroidered sweater that you can't afford, remind yourself the baby doesn't know the difference.
He doesn't care what he's wearing as long as he's comfortable. There is very little that you actually have to buy. Some
stretch suits, receiving blankets, a sleeping bag if it's cold,
and maybe a baby towel with a hood are all you really need.
Anything more is just "consumeritis"!

The two essentials you'll need in the early months
are a car seat (if you have a car) and a front- or backpack. A
tiny baby doesn't need a stroller, which you can get when
the baby outgrows the baby carrier (or your back gives out,
whichever comes first). These are items which you can get

through friends or find in garage sales or even through parent/child groups.

***Look for garage sales.***   Either make a note of signs as you drive around or look for notices in local giveaway newspapers. These sales are an inexpensive way to buy used toys and equipment.

***A baby shower can save you a fortune.***   This was the traditional way to get a new mother the things she needed, or the extravagant items she wouldn't buy for herself. You might want to make a list with the hostess in order to avoid receiving four crib quilts as gifts and no T-shirts. By discussing it ahead of time, the hostess can tell guests what's on the list and they decide what they'd like to give.

***Newborns do not need toys.***   The toy industry may not like me to say this, but they'll get their chance as soon as your baby grows up a little. It won't be long before your child is bombarded with advertisements on television to BUY, BUY, BUY, so enjoy the early uncluttered months and save some money.

Despite what books tell you about gadgets that raise a baby's I.Q., the most that a very young baby can relate to is a mobile hanging over the crib. You can even *make* a mobile if you're at all handy. When the infant gets a little older there are many ordinary household objects that give a child as much pleasure as something purchased. You've probably heard parents tell about the time they bought some fancy toy, only to find their child was more interested in the box it came in. Use plastic cups, measuring spoons that are joined together, wooden spoons, and so on.

*WARNING: Be sure to check the safety of anything for the baby that you receive or buy secondhand. The same is true for any homemade toys. Are all the parts too large to be swallowed? Does it have any sharp edges? Any toxic paint? Remember: a baby puts everything in his mouth.*

***Baby-sitting can be a money-saving gift.***   However, you may have to suggest it to people who might not think of this as a present. They can either give you a baby-sitting "gift-certificate" by offering their own time as sitters or they can give money to cover the cost.

## WOMEN'S FEARS ABOUT FINANCES

There are certain fears about money that are particular to married women after they have children. Of course men have fears of their own—about being the provider, having increased responsibilities, and so on (which will be dealt with later, in *Chapter 4: The Father's Needs and Problems*). Women have special fears once they become mothers, particularly those women who worked before the baby was born and have now given up their jobs. They have also given up a salary and independence.

*Motherhood often means half as much income.* Reducing your income by 50 percent as a couple will undoubtedly have impact on you together and separately. You may see yourself in a new light as a mother, and if you've given up a job you'll have to adapt to having less outside stimulation in your life. At the same time you have to learn how to run your household with less income and higher expenses. Your husband has to take on more responsibility and also deal with your fears and doubts about your new life. It may help both of you to deal with this transition if you know some of the fears and problems that new mothers can experience.

*Fear of something happening to the baby's father.* You may worry that your husband will die or leave you. You may feel afraid that there will be no one to provide for you and the baby; this can happen to women who have never had this kind of worry before. Motherhood may be the first time that you find yourself financially dependent on your mate.

Life insurance and wills are something you should both attend to, preferably even before the baby is born. There is nothing morbid about making plans for your assets if you were to die—it can give you both a certain peace of mind to know that you have put everything in order. At the same time you should review in whose name your assets, bank accounts, and investments are held. Consult with a tax attorney or investment counselor about whether any changes should be made.

*Is the man's income "his" money?* If you stop working in order to raise your child, you may become worried about what is rightfully yours to spend. Is your mate's money "his" or can you spend it as freely as you used to with your salary?

A new mother often leaves her job or lowers her salary by downgrading her position or hours. If you decide to do this, you may find you are uncomfortable about the resulting financial arrangements. You may be on the defensive, pointing out the various things you paid for before (your own clothes or gifts, household furnishings, the down payment on the house, etc.). You may feel vulnerable and weak without a financial base of your own.

The fear of "having to ask" for money can be unpleasant for some women. You may find it degrading or that you're the inferior partner when you have to "ask Daddy" for an allowance. Try to remind yourself that your contribution to the partnership is a commitment to the marriage and raising the children. It's all too easy for people to view this investment as *less* valuable than the money your mate contributes. We live in a society that often seems to prize money more than almost anything else. You may suffer less financial anxiety if you're able to step outside that value system and recognize the incalculable value of raising a child and making a home.

*Keep cash around the house.* There are at least two ways to help solve the problem of a mother at home not having income she can call her own. One solution is to keep $100 or more in cash in the house that either of you can use for gifts, petty expenditures, etc. When it's running low, you tell each other and replenish it (although there's always the risk that one of you will say, "What? It's gone already!").

The other solution that works well for some couples is that each partner gets a weekly allowance. This amount should be as much as you can afford and is money you don't have to answer for. You may find it relieves pressure and tension between you about other issues if you have a bit of money to spend however you want.

***A women should express her feelings.***   If you're feeling fearful or disoriented about money, it may be a good idea to let your spouse know your feelings. However, you need to be prepared for your mate to respond with his feelings. There really isn't any point in your being open and forthright unless your spouse can feel free to be as honest in his reaction as you were in your presentation. In order to come to terms with the shift in your personal sense of financial equilibrium, you may have to give up your false pride or what might have been fierce independence. The new interdependence between you can be a positive bond that draws you closer together if you can first recognize and then let go of your fears.

***Fear of having too little money.***   This can be a problem if you're taking a leave of absence or staying but working part time. The first thing that may help you see your situation in perspective is to recognize that this is a short-term situation (a few months to a few years). But if you give up your job or cut back on your salary, it doesn't necessarily mean that you have to cut back on the way you want to live.

***Motherhood may mean going into debt.***   You may decide that you want to live beyond your means, at least while your child is young. There are times in life when people decide to go into debt, usually to get through college, graduate, or professional school. New motherhood may be one of those times for you.

The first question is whether you can manage to live on less income. Remember that when you aren't working you will have lower child-care costs and less need for clothing, but your rent/mortgage, car payments, and so on, won't change. Then figure out whether you have enough money saved to get you through this period, or whether you have equity against which you can get a bank loan (your home, life insurance, etc.) or parents who will give you a loan.

***Do not live off credit cards.***   However you decide to handle your finances, do not make the mistake that has created nightmares for so many people. Plastic money can destroy you insidiously: it is almost painless to build up a large balance that is "invisible." It's too easy to ignore that mountain of debt when "all" you have to do is pay the interest. But don't be fooled: credit cards charge astronomical interest rates of up to 20 percent. The safe way to live beyond your income is to determine approximately how much you need and borrow it in a lump sum, from the bank or your family.

## MOVING YOUR HOME

***Moving may seem logical.***  It can seem necessary and practical to move when you're pregnant or once the baby is born, but it's actually a terrible idea! You will already have the stress of the physical and financial burdens of new parenthood. The last thing you should do to yourselves is to further complicate your life with the pressure of relocating your home.

***Moving doesn't necessarily improve your life.***  You may think that you are opting for a better life by moving. You probably *will* get more spacious living space and perhaps a neighborhood more suited to children, but you will also probably be trading off this "better" life for a depleted bank account and the considerable work and upset of resettling. Although a too-small house or apartment can cause tension and confusion with the baby and all her paraphernalia, there are many ways to minimize feeling cramped in the first year without having to move. The chart that follows, The Baby's Space, has some practical suggestions if you don't have an empty room for the child.

***Insufficient space isn't as big a stress as moving.***
Some couples blame their marital stress on having too-small living quarters. It is easy to convince yourselves that one of the reasons for problems you may be having is that you don't have enough space. You imagine that "bigger, better" living quarters will improve your relationship. However, you may be underestimating the stress and hard work involved in moving. The pressure can be magnified if you are moving from an apartment to a house. If you have never

## THE BABY'S SPACE

- The baby doesn't need a separate room for at least the first 6 months to a year.
- Some spaces you may be able to convert to a baby's area: dining room, darkroom, office, or workshop, or make an alcove out of a closet or built-in bar
- Use a movable screen to partition part of a room as the baby's area
- Do not buy too much stuff: storage becomes a problem when all the baby really needs is a place to sleep, get changed, and have a bath
- Avoid a full-size crib in the beginning: use a Porta-crib, bassinet, or carriage
- A dresser/changing table is useful, but if you don't have room you can get a small vinyl mattress (or cover a piece of foam with vinyl or a plastic table-cloth) and put it on a table, the floor, or bed when needed (and out of sight otherwise). CAUTION: Once the baby starts to turn over at 3 to 4 months, it is dangerous to use this pad anywhere but on the floor
- It's better not to share your bedroom with the baby (except in the early months when having her there is easier for night feedings). You need a sense of privacy as a couple and the baby's noises during the night interrupt your sleep
- Keep bassinet or carriage partitioned in your room or an adjacent room so that both of you aren't awakened for nighttime feedings

owned a house before you may discover that the costs and responsibilities of buying a house can be equal to those of having a baby.

We read about all the new parents moving to the suburbs as they begin a family. What we don't hear about are the couples who move back! There are couples who put their new house back on the market, take the baby under their arm, and return to apartment living. They discover that there is too much negotiation, arguing, and exhaustion over the constant chores and problems of homeowning. It can be a burden to clean a larger space when you are exhausted and have less time. There is always something that needs fixing in a house. The idea of a house with a backyard may look cozy and romantic on paper, but in real life you may find that an urban area has more conveniences. There is also easier access to friends and other established relationships that can be helpful during the stress of early parenthood.

*A house can demand a lot of a man's time.* What are your priorities as new father? How do you want to spend the time you have at home? Do you want to do the chores that are traditionally considered the male domain (mow the lawn, fix the drainpipes, put up a new light fixture) or would you prefer using your time to take more than a traditional involvement in infant care? There are only so many hours in a day and a house demands a lot from both partners. You might want to ask yourselves whether the house is going to rob you of time and energy that you'd rather spend with each other and the baby.

### WHERE YOU LIVE AFFECTS HOW YOU LIVE

There are a number of questions you can ask yourselves before you make a decision about whether to move, and where to move. It isn't just a question of gaining floor space; a move also has an impact on many other areas of your life.

1. How much upkeep is required in the new house?
2. How long a commute will you have to work, to shopping, or to entertainment?
3. How close is the house to public transport?
4. How far are you from friends and relatives? Will you feel isolated or be unable to take advantage of their help with the baby?
5. Are child-care services available nearby?
6. How does the move affect any live-in or day help that you already have?
7. Are stores within walking distance if there is no public transportation and you don't have a car?

8. How far are doctors, dentists, and other professionals you may need?

Once you realize how many things are at stake when you decide to move, you can make a thoughtful decision that will be best for your relationship and your family's needs.

## WHAT ABOUT YOUR PETS?

*Your pet(s) are affected by the baby.*   Sometimes new parents don't realize that they need to consider their pets when they bring a baby into their home. I'm not presuming to be a cat or dog psychologist, but animals have to make adjustments, too. And you can be affected by the modification in your living arrangement because a pet can often have a special place in a couple's relationship.

*Your dog or cat may have been a surrogate child.* The birth of a child can alter your pet's place in your lives and can cause problems between you or in the household. The animal can remain a close and integral part of your new family or you may find that your attitude toward her changes; the pet goes from being a companion to being "just an animal."

You may have noticed that your pet was a "trial run" for you as "parents": as a couple you may have learned to negotiate issues such as discipline, affection, and responsibility. An animal often provides a chance for a couple to practice parenting skills together and learn to adjust to each other's style and attitudes.

*How will your pet react to the displacement?*   You may have wondered how the baby will affect your pet, who now has to adjust to the fact that he has to take second billing. You may also want to make changes in the pet's routines, such as where he eats, sleeps, etc., which can be upsetting to him. Some pets demand attention from whoever is with the baby. The high-pitched voice you may use for the baby can be similar to the one you used for your pet, which can confuse him if he comes to you in response to this tone of voice and then you reject him.

*A pet may go into a depression.*   A pet can be so confused or feel so displaced by the commotion in the household that he changes his behavior or goes into a depression. Sometimes an animal will withdraw in reaction to the baby: the pet may stay in a corner or outside, ignoring everything. You can try to reassure the animal that you love him by encouraging him to take part in your new life.

*It can be harder if you have been very close to the pet.*   If you have been very affectionate with your pet and he's spent a great deal of time with you, there can be difficulties when the baby comes into your lives. Some people find that all the attention they gave to the animal is now transferred entirely to the baby. This can create a problem for your pet, who may feel abandoned. It may also make you feel guilty for "betraying" your pet. Even if you still have time and affection for him, you may feel a conflict in how to handle the situation.

*There are ways to ease the pet's adjustment.*   You may want to help the pet feel that he is not being abandoned in favor of the new baby. When the mother and baby first come home from the hospital it can ease the transition if the Mom gives the pet a big welcome. You might want to encourage him to come close and see the baby, praising the animal and speaking in a soft voice. One way to handle your pet when you have a baby is to treat the situation as you would sibling rivalry. It can make a big difference if, for the first few days, everyone in the house gives the pet some extra time and special treats.

*There can be problems if one of you isn't close to the animal.*   If both partners are equally attached to the pet, then working out a new arrangement can be something you share in together. You both can understand the pet's needs and try to accommodate them while welcoming your child into your home. However, if only *one* of you was close to the pet it can create arguments and tension because the nonanimal-lover may not be sensitive to the pet's predicament (or to the mate's concern). That insensitivity can disappoint or anger the pet-loving partner, who is already feeling torn and perhaps guilty.

There is no right and wrong here. This is more an emotional issue than a rational one, but it will help if you can both try to be supportive of each other and suspend judgments on whether the other partner is being "neurotic" or "cold-hearted." Reassure the pet of your love and try to de-escalate competition, especially in the beginning.

***Some pets cannot adjust to a baby.*** It may be a question of your pet's temperament, the way you've handled the situation, or probably a combination. Some pets develop a psychosomatic illness, destroy things in the house, "forget" they are housebroken, or even go into a depression, as mentioned. If a pet cannot adjust to sharing your love with a baby, you may have to give the animal away. This is a highly emotional decision that can tear people apart, but you have to decide whether a dog or cat "acting out" a rebellion is worth the trouble and strain it causes you. Your veterinarian or pediatrician may have some helpful suggestions.

***There can be problems with the pet and the baby's things.*** You may find that your dog wants to chew the cuddly stuffed animals your baby receives as gifts. One solution is to buy a new toy or two for the dog to play with. You may also have a cat who wants to curl up in the baby's crib, a common desire for cats. It is not healthy or safe to allow a cat to do this. As a substitute, you can give the cat a basket with an old towel or blanket in it, but the animal may have to be banned from the nursery.

***A pet can be wonderful for a child.*** Just as an animal can be a loving companion for an adult, the pet can also be a great addition to a child's life. A baby can get a lot of pleasure watching and touching animals, most of whom love the contact, too. Some dogs turn into Lassie overnight and become devoted and protective of the baby, alerting you to the littlest cries.

*Are animals unsanitary?*   Pet hairs and friendly licks may concern you but they usually won't harm the baby. All the same, one parent or the other can become so nervous about the animal's germs that s/he wants to ban the pet from the house or any proximity to the baby. Talking to your pediatrician may alleviate some of those fears.

*There are hygienic precautions that you must take.* Despite the advice offered above, there are some hazards to babies from pets. For example, worming your pet is absolutely essential. Children can go blind from roundworms. Also, you must keep your pets free of fleas with flea baths, dips, sprays, etc., because a toddler who spends a lot of time with a flea-infested animal can also get bitten. WARNING: *Flea collars can be dangerous to young children, who may suck on them.*

*Pets should be there to enhance your life.*   If the pleasures outweigh the problems, then you know where you stand. Sometimes a couple cannot predict how they will feel about their pet until the baby arrives. You and your mate should talk ahead of time about how you'd like your pet to fit into your new family. However, until the time comes, you won't know how you (and the pet!) will feel. It is best not to make any rash, hasty decisions. Let things fall into place. But also remember that as new parents your aim is to do everything you can to promote harmony in your home.

# 2

# Changing expectations

The American family is in trouble, partly because we expect too much. Many people expect their marriages to be fulfilling, interesting, and satisfying all the time. You may have these unrealistic expectations (although you aren't aware of it) even if it sounds foolish when you see them in black and white. The "pursuit of happiness" seems to be fundamental to our beliefs about what life "should" be like. This uniquely American idea doesn't exist in other countries. Perhaps our forefathers gave us a legacy that makes us pretty unrealistic in our expectations! This can be especially true when you become parents, a process that demands so much of you and your relationship.

***We get our expectations from stories.*** Our ideas about life were influenced by the happily-ever-after fairy tales we heard as children and the television shows and advertisements we grew up with (adult fairy tales). They didn't show the ordinary, boring part of life: the normal drudgery of people doing their best to get through each day. They didn't show the divorces of people who became disillusioned when false expectations were confronted with reality.

The women's movement also left a lot of confused and frustrated people in its wake: some women were shocked to find that "having it all" (family and career) left

26

them feeling like a sponge squeezed dry; other women worried they were inadequate because "all" they wanted to do was run a household and raise a family. Perhaps there would have been less trauma to women and their families if everyone's expectations were practical instead of theoretical.

## CHANGING PERCEPTIONS OF EACH OTHER

You may have a new view of your partner after you become parents: you may feel more admiring or more critical. Seeing your mate in this new role is quite different from relating to each other alone; becoming a parent may be complimentary to your image of your partner or discordant. When someone becomes a parent, new qualities will emerge, or you'll see facets that weren't evident before the baby was born.

*The most important relationship in the family is the couple.*    Before you had a baby, did you perceive yourself as an individual or as a couple? If your identity was primarily as an individual, then how does a baby fit into this sense of yourself? If you were couple-identified, how does a baby change your relationship and your self-image as a "couple"? A baby is a wonderful addition to your life, but don't lose sight of the building blocks that are the foundation of a healthy family. In order of importance, you are (1) a person, (2) a couple, and (3) with your child you form a family.

The health of your family depends on both of you as parents supporting each other, whether it's toward outsiders or your own children. If one parent sides with the child, it weakens the bond with the other parent and makes a strong one-sided bond with the child. This can happen even when the baby is two days old and you disagree over using talcum powder or picking up a crying baby. One of you becomes the baby's protector; this stance can create major confrontations over "what is best for the baby." Perhaps because there are basic unresolved conflicts between you that have nothing to do with parenting, you are fighting through the baby. If you continue this pattern, your child will become a helpless victim in a triangle.

*The perception of yourselves as Mommy and Daddy.*
This new self-image can work against your relationship as
a couple. It can mean that you lose sight of your adult roles
and needs. You can become so wrapped up in what you
think is appropriate parental behavior, doing what you
imagine you are "supposed" to do as parents, that the baby
becomes the center of your existence. If you give all-
consuming importance to your child, it can mean that you
deny adult needs like sex, privacy, touching, and nonbaby
conversation—or you "postpone" them to a later time in
your lives.

*Trying to live through the child can hurt your
relationship.* You can allow yourself to become so
wrapped up in the child that you confuse your own needs
for personal development with those of your child. When
this happens, parents lose sight of themselves and their relationship. You try to grow **through** your child. You sub-
limate your needs and self-expression, hoping to accomplish
or experience things by living vicariously through your
child. Pushing a child to play the piano or compete at sports
denies you **and** your child the right to be yourselves. Although this doesn't happen until your baby is older, beware
early on that you may be setting the stage for it.

*You are going through a metamorphosis.* You are
changing from a two-person to a three-person group. Your
success in making this enormous adjustment is what will
give your life quality as a couple and a family. Whether you
can make the adjustment—or how well you manage it—
depends on your frame of mind going into the new situation about each other and your baby.

*Try to focus on the positive aspects of the change.*
In order to adapt to your changed roles vis-à-vis each other,
it helps if you can relax and try to enjoy this transitional
phase of your life together. Birth, child rearing, and the
stress of changing relationships in your family affect your
image of yourselves. The daily battles and pleasures of living together are what help form your perceptions of yourself and your partner. You need to give yourselves plenty

of time to settle down and understand your new roles, without giving up who you were before.

You are two individuals who have been joined by a baby. Until your child was born you may have had two fairly separate lives, going along on separate tracks and checking in with each other. Your baby changes your relationship by giving you a shared task and dream. Even though there is hard work in parenting, it can be uplifting to have this new vision of your life with your partner: you are sharing a lifework together. This sense of sharing can strengthen your relationship. It may even override problems you've had together and make them seem petty now.

*A baby brings out many facets of your personalities.* Before your child was born, you may not have known all aspects of yourself, and you surely couldn't have known all facets of your partner. During this experience of growing into parenthood, new sides of your personalities will blossom that you may not have known you had—earthiness, maturity, patience, warmth, playfulness. You will undoubtedly discover deficiencies in your characters, too. The stress, demands, and long hours of parenting mean that you cannot hide from yourself: your strengths and weaknesses will be fully exposed.

A baby teaches you selfless love. This may be something you've read about in the Bible or in classical literature, but having a baby may be the first time you experience pure, unselfish love. This new awareness may spill over into your relationship. Love for the baby can release love for each other in your new roles as parents. A baby is a gift not just because of his own presence, but because he brings you so many surprises about yourselves and the world around you.

*Parenthood may change your partner entirely.* It is not unusual for a man who was a ''liberated'' husband to become ultraconservative when he becomes a father. It can come as a shock if you married a liberal, progressive man who, when the baby is born, suddenly behaves as though he's living in a re-run of *Father Knows Best!* Don't panic, don't wonder whether you've been duped; it is normal for new parents to have a knee-jerk reaction, falling back on familiar images and role models that influenced them when they were growing up (there is more on this in *Chapter 4: The Father's Needs and Problems*). A woman may also retreat to a more traditional role and turn into a bossy mother hen or become conservative, uptight, or matronly.

Regardless of how fair and equal your life was before, you may find that the democracy you were enjoying turns into a dictatorship. Your mate may display authoritarian attitudes that you've never seen in him/her before. S/he may make statements like "no wife of mine will ever . . ." or, "I refuse to allow my child to . . ." Your best defense is a sense of humor. Poking fun at their pomposity (which probably comes from insecurity) is going to get you a lot further than making a heavy issue of it.

***There can be a shift in the power balance.*** After the baby's arrival the balance in your relationship may change in a way that can be hard on the father. In most relationships the man is the dominant force . . . until the baby is born. Then all bets are off. The woman is now working longer, harder hours than the man and expects recognition for it. The man is used to coming home and getting attention, maybe even pampering. Now his wife wants to *get* it, not give it! This is an extremely difficult adjustment for a man to make, as it changes his perception not only of his wife but of his marriage (see *Chapter 4*).

***A dependency existed between you before you became parents.*** The dependency between you and your partner can be a crucial issue in how you perceive each other after the baby arrives. It is common, for example, for a husband and wife to have been attracted because, on the surface, they were very independent. However, each of them also has a dependency need and is looking for someone to take care of them. This can lead to conflict because each of you expects the other to be the strong one and you may be disappointed.

In other cases, a very dependent male is attracted to a strong independent female, or vice versa. This may be a natural choice to complement your own degree of independence, and to fit in with how fully you have made the separation from your "family of origin" (which is the clinical term for the family you grew up in). In such a case, however, one of you may only *seem* to be different on the surface. Psychotherapists have found that often both partners are actually dependent, but manifest their dependency in different ways.

***Every couple has a certain balance of dependence and independence.*** This equilibrium is maintained until something enters the system that causes stress: work problems, in-law friction, or the birth of a child. A baby has overwhelming needs that require constant attention. Adult needs must be postponed. The spouse who is more dependent feels threatened by this baby, whose demands mean that her parents have to put aside *their* dependency needs.

The more dependent parent may also feel inadequate if s/he cannot get satisfaction and pleasure from meeting the infant's enormous needs. Try to avoid preconceived ideas about how your spouse will react to the demands of his/her new role. Even your partner, someone you know so well, may surprise you when s/he becomes a parent.

***The more independent spouse can form a closer bond with the baby.*** The more dependent partner may not be as comfortable getting close to the baby because the infant's needs are a personal threat. The close bond between the baby and the independent parent can make the more dependent spouse feel further alienated.

This can present a dilemma for the independent mate, who is in a difficult bind: bonding with the baby may cause a rift with the other parent. It can also be overwhelming to try to satisfy the dependency needs of *two* people, the baby and the more dependent spouse.

***Some women feel defensive and vulnerable as mothers.*** If you feel an increased dependence on your mate once you become a mother, it may make you uncomfortable. This can be especially true if you've had your own income and suddenly have to depend on your mate financially (for more on this subject, see *Chapter 13: Career vs. Full-time Motherhood*). Or you may feel diminished by your dependence on your mate. Today's women put a high premium on being strong and independent. This is a phase you are going—and growing—through. Allow yourself to have those feelings.

*A woman may resent her mate's demands.* If your husband expects the same time and attention that he got from you before the baby was born, it can make you angry. You may even feel conflicted because you wonder whether you *should* still be catering to your spouse. Are you first a wife or a Mom? There can be nasty arguments over whether the woman should respond to the man's needs or those of the baby. These are things that cannot be dismissed or ignored—you have to talk them through.

It can be infuriating if your mate becomes childish, expecting you to continue to take care of his needs as you did before. You may perceive him as a spoiled brat and it can lower your respect for him. If you begin to view your mate as a baby, it can make you feel bitchy: your anger can come out in arguments over unimportant details. You may find yourself annoyed at some of your spouse's idiosyncrasies that never bothered you before. By trying to understand how the dependency/independence issue can affect a relationship, you may be able to avoid unnecessary strife. Both of you have to recognize that **interdependence** is a positive aspect of growth in a relationship.

*Doubts and ambivalence are normal reactions to becoming parents.* Are you ready, do you really want the responsibility and sacrifice necessary to be the parent of a newborn? These negative feelings can be frightening, even though you've been told they are common. If you participate in a parent support group you may find reassurance in talking about your ambivalence in a supportive setting.

A baby can be the "end of the honeymoon" or simply a turning point in your life together. Suddenly you see flaws in each other that were invisible before. Have you made a mistake? Who is this person you married? The stress of adjusting to the baby can cause an escalating series of unresolved arguments between you, usually about petty issues. This often happens as a way to avoid dealing with your own fears about becoming a parent; instead, you focus on trivial aspects of your mate that you've discovered you can't stand! Doubts about yourself as a new parent can make you wonder whether you should be married at all, much less to that person. (More on this in *Chapter 10: Bad Feelings*.)

## OLDER PARENTS

Nowadays many couples are waiting until their 30s and even early 40s to have children. Studies show that the more years you are married before having children, the greater the odds of a marriage lasting (statistics also show that marriages last longer if people are older when they marry). Some experts feel that there is less chance of divorce if couples wait to have kids until after they have made the jolting personal transition into their 30s.

What follows is a look at both the pros and cons of being older when you become a parent.

### SOME NEGATIVE ASPECTS OF BEING AN OLDER PARENT

*You may feel you have to prove yourselves.* Sometimes older parents think they have to show they're as good as (or better than) younger parents. You may feel determined to succeed, to prove to doubting friends, relatives, or society-at-large that you will be great parents. If you feel this pressure to be perfect in your new roles, your expectations may be even further from reality than those of very young parents.

*You might be embarrassed to say you're pregnant.* Some older couples are afraid of criticism they might get, or comments like "Was it a mistake?" Although there is a trend toward delaying child rearing, there may also be a social stigma about having a baby if you're nearing 40.

*You might hear "We told you so" from others.* You may imagine that other people are watching or judging you as new parents—even if they aren't, you may still feel you're being scrutinized. Especially if people were unsupportive of your decision to have a child, it can be hard for you to admit just how rough parenthood can be.

Older parents are often so deeply grateful to have a

child enriching their lives that they don't feel free to complain about the exhaustion, depression, and irritations of having a baby. It can be equally difficult to air your feelings about having shattered your previous life in order to have a baby. Instead of sympathy, the listener's reaction may be "I told you so!"

***It can be tougher to break old habits.*** As an older parent, you've had more years getting used to certain freedoms and amenities. Parenthood may disturb some of these rituals and indulgences: as an "old dog" it can be harder to learn new tricks! Older couples may expect privacy and peacefulness in their daily routine. For instance, you may be accustomed to having some quiet time every morning to read the newspaper. A newborn doesn't always (ever?) allow that.

You may be used to a degree of independence and control over your own life. You're probably used to having time and money to yourself, to use at your discretion. It may be harder for you to tolerate mess, chaos, interruptions, or broken sleep. You may also be used to feeling a sense of competence and mastery at what you do. Having a baby will probably change all that, even if you're fortunate enough to have full-time help.

***Did you delay motherhood by choice?*** Later motherhood is often chosen because a woman has doubts about whether motherhood is for her (unless infertility problems forced the long wait). You may have avoided childbearing, made a conscious choice to put it off, perhaps terminated a pregnancy or been ambivalent in pursuing getting pregnant. Just because you've finally become a mother, it doesn't mean that you've automatically resolved whatever fears and doubts you may have had about your career, financial security, the strength of your marriage, etc. Those conflicting emotions still remain: if you don't address them it can interfere with your transition to parenthood.

***Older women usually have careers.*** A woman who has waited to have a child has often been pursuing a career and committed a good part of her life to developing her skills and reputation. If you fit this description, you may discover that you want to escape back into your career after the baby is born. Motherhood can make a career woman feel overwhelmed by the loss of control over her own life and the loss of tranquility and of what she perceives as productive time.

***You may worry about being isolated.***   Perhaps few of your friends have children, or they had them when they were younger and the kids are grown now. You may worry that none of these friends will be interested in your child or new life. You may also wonder whether you'll be able to relate to younger couples who are having babies. This concern about isolation is a real problem; each couple has to solve it according to their individual circumstances.

***You may not think you have the strength for parenting.***   You may be afraid that you'll tire easily and not have enough energy to keep up with a baby or play with her when she gets older. You may be concerned that you'll have less patience for the interruptions, noise levels, and messiness that a child brings into a home.

***Do you have children from a previous marriage?***   If either you or your partner were previously married, you may be anxious about how the older child(ren) will relate to the baby. There is no general advice that can fit all situations, except that it's safe to say that the new baby's step-sisters or half brothers are bound to have many feelings about the infant, ranging from jealousy and rivalry to infatuation and enjoyment.

***Are you afraid of the effect of a baby on your marriage?***   Older parents have often been married before. If your previous marriage ended in divorce, you may have conscious or unconscious fears that the pressures of a new baby may lead you to another divorce court. Although every situation is different, you're probably already taking good care of your marriage if you're reading this book and developing an awareness of how a baby can affect a relationship.

***You may have fears about dying.***   Older fathers, in particular, may worry whether they will live to see their child grow to adulthood. If your contemporaries have had heart attacks or bypasses, or if friends of yours have died, it can make you feel vulnerable. These fears can make you feel additional pressure to provide financial security for your wife and the baby "in case" something should happen to you. It will be easier on you if your partner is sympathetic to the fears and pressure you're feeling.

### Some Positive Aspects of Older Parenting

*You may feel a greater capacity for giving.* You may have already accomplished much of what you wanted so that it's less important for you to prove yourselves in your career(s) and you can devote more energy to your child. As older parents you may feel more ready to give to your child than you would have been at a younger age and less threatened by the necessary sacrifices.

*You accept the burdens of parenthood.* If you've delayed childbearing, then you probably recognize the sacrifices you may have to make in raising a child. If you've waited until your mid-30s it may be because you know that a child is going to be take a lot out of you; you've probably postponed parenthood for good reasons. You may have had second thoughts and misgivings about being a parent that surfaced during the pregnancy. These doubts may reappear in the postpartum period. Your feelings are normal; you can even look at them as a good sign because it means that you're being realistic in assessing the road ahead of you.

*You have more financial security.* You probably have more money and can handle the expense of child rearing more easily than you could have when you were younger. Older parents may have more to offer their children in the way of education, travel, and other advantages because they have had more years to save and invest their money. Although you may have less energy and patience than younger parents might, you can offer a child the fact that as parents you are settled and secure.

*You probably didn't sacrifice career advancement.* As an older parent you probably don't feel that a child is keeping you from reaching your career goals because you've probably already accomplished a fair amount: you won't have as much need to prove yourself in your work. In most trades or professions, the ages between 25 and 35 are crucial. If you have waited until after this growth period to have a child, you haven't sacrificed either the satisfaction or financial rewards of advancement in your work.

*You know each other really well.* The better a couple knows each other, the easier their transition to parenthood will probably be. Older parents have been together longer, or are mature enough to have self-knowledge and a deeper understanding of their partner than they might have had when they were younger. It can be hard on a couple to have a baby when they don't yet know each other well. If you have to deal with surprises about each other, it can be tougher to handle surprises from the baby.

*You have better communicating skills.* Older parents who have been around (and been together) longer may have more skills for coping with problems. You probably have more practice dealing with difficult situations than your younger counterparts. Young couples often haven't faced problems and pressures before, so they haven't yet developed the skills for dealing with adversity.

*A baby can be rejuvenating.* Although as older parents you may suffer from the physical demands of caring for a newborn, there is also a compensation. Having a baby can be exhausting but it also can put you in touch with the child inside yourself, can give you a new perspective on life and make you feel younger. Older parents are often deeply grateful for their child because of the way he can transform their outlook on life.

*You may accept a baby on her own terms.* Because you are mature, you may have a generous acceptance of your child as an individual, separate from you. Younger parents may not have that perspective or openmindedness. Older parents may be more able to encourage a child to develop at her own pace, in her own style.

*You may have a greater appreciation of time.* A baby can make older parents aware of how valuable time is, and how important it is to fully enjoy the time they have left ahead of them. Older parents may feel they are set in their ways and that it's hard to give up habits of their previous lifestyle. However, a baby can give you the realization that you only have so many years left to enjoy; that can mean that you live every day more fully.

*A baby can give you a perspective about priorities.* Having a child when you are older can make you aware that time is passing: you may recognize that it's not important to worry about trivial problems. A baby can put day-to-day conflicts in a better perspective. You can learn to ignore (or let pass) the minor irritations between you and your partner and focus on what is positive in your mate and your relationship.

*You may have a bittersweet feeling of time passing.* You are no longer the two young (or younger) people who fell in love and married. However, you may now have a new sense of depth and maturity to your relationship, an increased feeling of closeness and sharing a purpose in life. More mature parents may feel their youth has gone forever, but they may discover that a baby brings new energy and love into their lives.

## EXPECTATIONS OF YOUR MARRIAGE AFTER CHILDBIRTH

*Life has changed.* After the baby's birth you have a new reality. You have to learn to accept your new life and find your own way to get comfortable with it. New parents often make the mistake of trying to return things to the way they were before the baby was born. But life has changed for you: things will NEVER be as they were before. Couples who keep hoping to get things "back to normal" are missing the whole point. *This* is your new normal!

*Your expectations of marriage may be too high.* In any intimate relationship there are going to be difficult, confusing, frustrating, and painful times. Of course that intimacy can also be wonderfully rewarding. But a relationship can flare up and burn out unexpectedly. As the Beatles once said in a song, "Love has a nasty habit of disappearing overnight." Many couples don't realize this or do anything to prevent or ease the strain.

***Be honest as to what your marriage is about.*** Did you marry because you admired your partner's potential parenting qualities? Did you marry for financial security? Did you marry your mate because of his/her stability or maturity? Did you pick your partner partly because you appreciated his/her organizational abilities or nurturing side? If you made what can be considered a "sensible" union, for example, then don't expect sexual fireworks or romantic intensity.

***A marriage can be complicated and fragile after the baby is born.*** At the very least, your relationship will be inexorably changed. And although parenthood creates a sense of intimacy between you, it also gives you a sense of being isolated from the rest of the world. Turning your relationship into a working partnership is going to take hard work. Who is going to do what? Who nurtures whom? There are three tasks facing you as new parents: to nurture yourself, each other, and the baby. In order to develop self-esteem and confidence, all three of you need an environment of love and protection.

As you raise a child and build a family you are both growing, too. Parenthood is an important part of becoming a grown-up. The first year of parenting is the toughest, so be kind to yourselves. Recognize that you're in a growth process; then you'll accept that there are going to be physical demands, painful times, and anxiety when you don't know how to do things.

***Marriage within parenthood needs special care in order to flourish.*** Don't imagine that your relationship is something you can take for granted: you cannot treat your marriage like an old shoe that will always fit just because it's taken the shape of your foot. You've got to feed and nurture your marriage, like any other living thing.

One good way to understand the fragility of your marriage is to compare it to a baby that suffers from what is clinically called "failure to thrive." This can happen to infants who are institutionalized and don't get enough personal attention; it can also happen to the children of mothers with serious postpartum depression who cannot interact with them. These babies are fine physically: they are fed and bathed and kept warm. But it has been found this isn't enough. If the babies' emotional needs are not met, they suffer what is called a "failure to thrive." If someone doesn't hug and cuddle and talk to them, they don't grow at a normal rate; they don't respond to love . . . they wither emotionally. The same thing can happen to your marriage if you don't take care of it.

***The rhythm of your relationship can get lost.*** After the baby arrives, it can be hard to recapture your rhythm if you aren't aware that it is in jeopardy. By rhythm, I mean the special ways that you have fun and enjoy each other, the ways that you have learned to give each other pleasure and comfort. You need to think about this issue right from the baby's birth. Otherwise, in all the excitement and adjustment it can be six months or more before one of you notices that "something is missing" between you. At that point it can be hard to reconstruct what you have lost.

The rhythm of your relationship is made up of the habits and patterns between you that you've probably taken for granted. Now you have to think about these things so they don't get lost in the shuffle. Before the baby, did you go out to dinner often or have quiet evenings at home alone? Did you entertain friends or business associates frequently and get positive feedback about yourself from socializing? Did you play cards or other games? Watch sports or movies on television? Go out to movies, sports, or cultural events? How did you make each other feel good? Did you buy little presents, leave notes, call each other, take baths, use a special vocabulary or way of talking with each other? Give each other massages? Share a bottle of wine and fall into bed? Parenthood doesn't mean giving up these things: you have to try to recreate these feelings and activities in the new context of parenthood.

*A baby is not a threat to a marriage.* A baby cannot jeopardize a relationship that welcomes him with open arms (although the situation can be complicated if one of you doesn't want a child). However, a baby is going to require things of you—call on resources—that you may not even know you have. There are going to be continuous, intense demands on you that are unlike anything you have ever experienced. Some people say that parenthood requires sacrifices; perhaps it's more positive to call them trade-offs. You give a lot but you get a great deal in return.

The results of various studies show that most parents find new parenthood difficult, but despite the problems they would still choose to have children. Many of them feel sorry for childless couples, even though they may envy certain aspects of a child-free existence. Having children gives them so much joy (along with the headaches) that if they had a chance to turn back the clock, most would do it all over again.

*You may feel disappointment about parenting.* If you feel let down by your new life, it can be hard to admit or talk about. Having a child is "supposed" to be miraculous, wonderful, and thrilling—which it is. But child rearing is also exhausting, frustrating, and anxiety-provoking. You may also see parenting as a constant test of your ability to solve problems and feel you aren't succeeding.

*You have to make time to talk.* Ask yourselves what elements of your relationship are important to you: what makes your marriage tick? If you wait until you are resentful and disappointed, you may have already lost your intimacy. By directing all your energy to the baby you can lose interest in each other. Be aware that one or both of you may withdraw; resentment drives people apart. It takes patience, determination, and hard work to keep a marriage going.

*Tell the truth about your unmet expectations.* Try talking to your mate, or even to other parents, about how awful you may be feeling. There are other mothers who may share your feelings but never admitted them. Your partner may be grateful to know what has been bugging you, or glad to have a chance to air some of his/her own gripes. If you don't talk about your feelings, you may imagine that there's something wrong with you, that "other people" don't have your misgivings and bounce back more quickly after their baby is born.

***Try talking about your deepest fears.*** If you can discuss your doubts about parenthood, you may find out what is *really* behind these changing perceptions of each other. Maybe one or both of you hasn't yet shown all the facets of your personality, good or bad. You may have been hiding aspects of yourselves, perhaps without knowing it. Some people are afraid to reveal their whole or true self for fear of being rejected, even by a loving mate. But the strains and intensity of new parenthood can strip away the masks. You may also learn how to pull together and solve your problems. These normal doubts and fears are usually temporary but they may come from basic marital problems that you've ignored. Now you have a chance to confront these issues. **GET PROFESSIONAL HELP BEFORE TOO MUCH DAMAGE IS DONE.**

A realistic view of your partner's parenting abilities may save you a great deal of frustration and heartache. We all know the qualities we'd like in an "ideal" co-parent, but it is important to understand and accept real-life limitations—both yours and your mate's. A man may not want to be involved in infant care; he may not feel comfortable relating to a tiny infant. Some mothers feel the same way. Don't try to force the baby down each other's throats. Give one another the time and room to discover a personal way to relate to the new arrival.

***Disappointment in your partner can be insidious.*** You can become disappointed and even disillusioned in your spouse if you have resentment toward him/her that you don't express. These suppressed feelings, anger in particular, can build up and reverberate in your relationship for years to come. If you feel your mate has let you down, try to talk about it using some of the communication techniques discussed in *Chapter 10: Bad Feelings.*

***Don't wait for your relationship to get into trouble.*** Anticipate that it's going to be a rocky road for a while:

prepare yourself with good emotional shock absorbers! The overwhelming changes in a marriage caused by a baby (joined with the couple's expectations that everything is going to be pretty much the same) are what lead, in part, to the high divorce rate for couples with small children.

***Did you expect "more" out of life?*** Couples used to be content if they could get by financially and raise a family. Today, children are often a crisis point in a couple's development. "Is this all there is?" people seem to ask. Instead of examining their problems and looking for solutions, they blame each other for their unhappiness or restlessness. Discontented couples often blame sex, thinking, "If only we had more (or better) sex, everything would be okay." What they may be bemoaning is the fact that real life isn't living up to their projected fantasies.

***Do you expect to have no conflict in your life?*** If you think that marriage is going to be all sweetness and romance, then you are going to have a shock when problems do arise. Your disillusionment may lead you to fear that you're falling out of love. However, your bitter disappointment doesn't mean there's anything wrong with your marriage; it highlights the fundamental error of having impossible expectations. Difficulties are part of life, and part of the natural process of marriage.

***Having problems is not a danger signal.*** If your marriage isn't going well, you may think that is a bad thing; you may think it means you're in trouble and have to fix it immediately or end it. This comes from that American idea of wanting to be happy all the time, which means that you feel betrayed by your spouse if you aren't. Many of us expect our relationship to always be nurturing, intimate, and smooth—and we panic if it isn't.

Non-American couples usually accept the ups and downs of marriage with either a stiff upper lip or a laissez-faire attitude. Our high divorce rate in America (roughly one divorce for every two marriages in the U.S., and one divorce for every marriage in California) show that we are confused about what a marriage should be and feel like.

*You may try to deny marital conflict.*  If you expect to have a life without conflict, then when it occurs, you are forced to sweep the problems under the rug to avoid a fight. This can happen if you perceived your own parents as unhappy or they got divorced. You may be afraid to threaten your own marriage by confronting problems—but the very act of avoidance will create a distance between you and your spouse. The fear of confrontation can be much worse than actually sitting down to have a discussion. I hope you will discover that it's possible to have constructive, nonhostile talks about whatever may be bothering you. This kind of interchange doesn't have to break a marriage, it can be what makes it strong.

*All marriages go through ups and downs.*  A successful marriage isn't one without conflict, it's one in which the partners learn to roll with the punches. You have a chance of building a strong marriage if you can learn to ride the waves, to tough out the difficult times. This doesn't mean that parenthood is *necessarily* going to be rough for you, but your relationship is definitely going to change. All marriages go through stages: becoming parents is undoubtedly the biggest adjustment of them all.

*Unrealistic expectations can lead to divorce.*  The statistics on when people get divorced are chilling: the highest divorce rates are for women at age 30 and men at age 33. As you can see, this means that many people are splitting up with very small children—and perhaps as a result of the unreasonable expectations they may have had.

*Love is going to change.*  Metamorphosis is the nature of love, it is constantly changing. The love you two have after your child is born can be intense and satisfying—but it has a different quality. Especially if your relationship is new (see below) and at the romantic stage, be prepared to shift gears. Otherwise you may feel cheated by the baby, whose arrival and demands signal the end of romantic, selfish love as you have known it.

*If you are in the early, erotic stage of your marriage, a baby may pose a problem.*  It is said that the first six to eight months of a relationship are the "erotic or passionate" stage. Experts feel that the all-consuming love and passion of the early stages of a relationship are not compatible with new parenthood. This means that women who get pregnant "on their wedding night" are going to have more to deal with in their marital relationship.

A baby too soon in a marriage can sadden you both over the loss of the romantic, intense early stage of love. If you have a baby right away and nip the romantic rose in the bud, it can leave you with deep resentments toward the child or each other. A baby cannot help but force a different kind of relationship on you when you may not be ready for it. If you are in this situation, then being aware of the special strains you have to deal with can help you to make the best of it.

***Try to wait two years before you have a baby.*** There are marriage counselors who say that the honeymoon is often over about six months after you marry (time spent living together before the commitment of marriage does not count here). It is thought that the period from six months to two years is a critical one in a marriage. During this period a couple establishes their bond: they learn how much they can give up of themselves, and how to negotiate and compromise in order to get their needs met. This is the stage when a couple usually spends a lot of intense time together learning how to communicate—developing their talking and listening skills and discovering how to understand and empathize with their mate. In the first two years you have a chance to find out what the conflicts are between you and begin to work on them, a process which the birth of a baby would not permit you to do.

## EXPECTATIONS OF EACH OTHER AS PARENTS

***Expectations of your spouse come from your childhood.*** What you expect from yourself and your mate as parents comes from your experience in your own family as a child. How your family functioned when you were a child (attitudes toward baby-sitters, parental interactions, etc.) forms your ideas of what a family is. There are some things you'll want to repeat in your life now, and other things that you may want to do in an opposite way from your parents.

Although it helps to try to be aware of this influence on what you expect now, these motivations are unconscious. You probably won't be fully aware of what you expect your mate to be like until you sit down together and talk it out. Talking over unrealized expectations—or ones that may be unrealizable—can strengthen your marriage.

*Conflict and stress are inevitable.* It is normal (and temporary) to have tension between you when you become parents. Many of us have been taught to think of conflict and stress as "bad" when actually they can help build your family's strength. Your attitude toward stress is the key to handling it well. Working together to reduce and handle stress is actually good for your relationship: it can strengthen that relationship and give you resiliency as a family.

Problem solving from this perspective requires you to be honest about your feelings; it demands patience and flexibility toward your partner. Adapting your life to include a child is a challenge: you have to learn to share child care, reorder priorities, and redistribute your time. There are three basic transitions you have to make as new parents: physical, emotional, and social. This means that the possible areas of conflict are multiplied by three! You should give yourselves credit for using positive tactics to handle this new and demanding situation.

*Expectations about parenting and the reality are quite different.* You may wonder whether society expects you to be loving and reasonable with your kids all the time. Are you always supposed to feel good about them? Is being a parent supposed to make you feel content and fulfilled?

In the early months you may expect to be perfect parents and perfect mates. However, the exhaustion will catch up with you. Reality will hit you before long and you may be shocked to be snarling at each other over nothing. You would never have expected to go berserk because you discover there are no bottles of formula ready and no clean clothes!

*Unrealistic expectations can cause stress.* New parents often underestimate the time and work involved in caring for an infant. You may not realize the extent to which a baby disrupts your life and routine. You can also overestimate your mate's nurturing abilities and romanticize parenthood.

If you expect too much from each other as parents, it can be a major cause of problems between you. Your individual images of parenting are going to be different, and if you haven't had a chance to discuss this ahead of time it can create tension and anger. It is important not to confuse your partner's different style with a lack of involvement or less of a commitment to parenting.

You may criticize or belittle your spouse's efforts if they don't fit your expectations (this is usually directed at a new father by his wife). You may be interested in every little detail about the baby and expect your mate to share your fascination (usually the woman does this to her husband).

*Respect each other's feelings.* Try to avoid judging your spouse based on that ideal image in your fantasies. Some women have been known to start building a case against their husbands' noninvolvement even before the baby is born. If your partner isn't interested in playing patty-cake with the baby, don't make a federal case of it. In a few years he may be delighted to take the tot to the zoo . . . or he may not. But there's nothing you say or do that will make your mate into the parent you want him to be. It's out of your control, so let go of it.

*Many new fathers refuse to go to parent groups.* Some men see these groups as a tea-party waste of time (this is so common that many parent organizations have cancelled evening postpartum groups for couples). In actuality, these gatherings can be a genuine benefit to new parents, but if your mate doesn't like the idea of spending his time that way, so be it. It is helpful to be realistic about the kind of support and involvement you can expect from your mate. Then, work with what you've got.

*Your partner's habits may suddenly irritate you.* If you can let go of your notions about how your mate should be a parent, you can learn to accommodate his or her idiosyncrasies. You may have tolerated your spouse's personal habits before, but now that you are parents you may find you resent sloppiness, absentmindedness, spending habits, energy levels, and so on.

You need to find a way to compromise. You may find that certain of your habits really do need to change after you have a baby, whether it is the way one of you spends money, invites guests over unexpectedly, or is disorganized. However, just because *your* feelings have changed as a parent doesn't mean that your partner is obliged to fit your expectations. It is really only useful (and fair) to focus on those personal habits that affect your daily survival!

## FALSE EXPECTATIONS AND "END OF THE DAY BLUES"

*The "end of the day" is often a big shock.* Once you have a baby, you may discover that your fantasies of what your evenings will be like are far from what actually transpires. It is just these kinds of unrealistic expectations that can make the transition to parenthood so much more difficult than you ever imagined. If you are prepared for the realities, the adjustment can be easier on all of you.

*Your husband's return home at night may be the first disappointment.* Many new mothers feel that this is the worst moment of the day, simultaneous chaos and demands. There can be a conflict between a Dad who comes home and wants to be involved with his baby, and a Mama who has spent hours trying to settle the baby down. The child is finally quiet when Dad comes home and wants his "quality time" with the baby. The mother then has to deal with the shrieks of a tired and hyped-up baby while she's getting dinner ready.

*You may have been waiting all day for adult companionship.* Your spouse may think you'll be so pleased if he's affectionate toward the baby, so he bypasses you and heads for the child. Your feelings may be hurt: being ignored can make you think that he's taking you for granted and giving all his attention to the new addition to the family. Then your husband may want restorative time to put his feet up and be with you: he's flush with news of his work and the outside world, and you may feel inadequate with only mundane trivia about the house and baby to report.

Worst of all, you probably aren't going to express these feelings directly (you're also delighted that he loves the baby). But even though you swallow your emotions, your husband can feel the chill coming off you like an open refrigerator door. He doesn't know what's wrong, but the tension is there between you.

**Dinnertime can be another disappointment.** Many new parents have idealized visions of what mealtimes will be like when they are parents. You may imagine that the baby will be asleep by 7:30 and you'll whip up a lovely little dinner over which you and your husband can get in touch. Some people have angelic babies that do fit right into adult schedules. Some people have full-time help to take over. But for most women this is the hardest part of the day.

Have you anticipated having to relearn cooking with only one hand? You may have to chop and stir with one hand while holding a fussy, tired baby in the other arm. Have you noticed the skill required of a mother who has to cut and eat food one-handed while holding a crying baby? When you planned the menu, did you take into account what the meal you've prepared will taste like *cold?* A fussy baby often only lets her father get one hot bite before she cries and he has to get up (the same syndrome as crying halfway through your lovemaking)! Many new parents do not get to sit down and eat an entire meal together for months.

## EXPECTATIONS ABOUT YOURSELF AS A PARENT

**Traditional parenting roles can be a trap.** Many of us have unconscious expectations that our lives will fall into the pattern of Mom as Housewife and Dad as Breadwinner, especially if our parents played those parts. However, in today's world even the most traditional couples find that they want to share some aspects of parenting and may feel limited by traditional pigeon-holing. If the father is viewed exclusively as the "provider," and the mother is viewed exclusively as the "nurturer," both partners may resent the burden of those roles. You may feel deprived of the opportunity to realize other aspects of your personalities in defining your relationship with your child.

***Change your expectations of yourselves as parents.*** You want to be good parents and do the right thing. You may find your job will be easier if you can acknowledge right up front that you are not in total control of your life. The unknown quantity of the baby has entered the equation of your life: that means your actions and reactions will be completely different. You are bound to fail if you don't give yourselves room to make mistakes.

If you have unrealistic expectations of yourselves, you may have to change your self-image. You may never have thought of yourself as a woman who would still be in her bathrobe at noon, or who would go all the way to a store and forget what she needed. Once you are able to recognize your limitations, you can alter your expectations. You may never have thought of yourself as a man who would argue with his wife in front of the child—or you may have thought your children would never fight with each other. Once you drop your unrealistic ideas, you'll probably be able to deal with arguments (and everything else) more easily because you'll accept the problems as just being part of life.

***Being a parent means being imperfect.*** Parenthood will give you many opportunities to make mistakes—to have successes and failures, both small and large. Your spouse will have just as many chances to mess up as you do—although sometimes you may think s/he is more talented at being wrong!

To make life better for both of you, you'll have to forgive mistakes, let go of your preconceived ideas, and try to appreciate the efforts that your spouse is making. It is counterproductive to have arguments about the right or wrong way to dress, feed, or educate your child. Both of you are learning and growing as parents: support each other. Once you become a parent you may even find some of your ideas and philosophies about life will change—give yourselves room to evolve.

***If you expect to be perfect, you're guaranteed a sense of failure.*** If you expect perfection from yourself or your partner, you may feel you are falling short as a parent. If you aren't living up to your standard of being perfect, you'll feel guilty or like a failure for not managing your life better. Eventually this unrealistic expectation can pervade your whole life so that you feel deficient not only as a parent or spouse, but as a worker, friend, etc.

***Child-rearing experts can raise your expectations.*** If you allow yourself to get caught up in the whirlwind of theories about child care, you will have to constantly worry whether you are doing things "right," in the prescribed fashion. And which expert will you choose as your guru? (More on "experts" in *Chapter 3: The Transition to Parenthood.*) One child development specialist will declare that the first 36 months of a child's life will determine her future achievement. There are special-interest groups which advocate breast-feeding until a child is three (never mind the teeth!). Another expert claims that damage is done by leaving your child with anyone else in the first three years. Other theorists demand that you give your baby only all natural, homemade food, organic toys, and no television.

If you subscribe to any theory lock, stock, and barrel, you're probably buying impossible expectations for yourself at the same time. Try to believe in yourself and your mate and make decisions about your child to fit your life, rather than allowing yourselves to become vulnerable to current theories. For example, at least half of the mothers of small children work: where do the idealistic theories of the experts leave these women?

***Do you expect a perfect child?*** The idealization process about your child begins long before your baby is born (or adopted). These expectations include how the child will look, his intelligence, and the way he'll interact with you. Your ideals are based in part on your own childhood experiences, hoping to recreate the good aspects and correct the bad ones. They are also based on your ideas about what is "right" and "wrong" behavior in a child and ideas about what parents "should" do.

If you take the advice of experts and add to it your own lifelong fantasies of being perfect parents, it's possible to come to the conclusion that you can raise a superior, perfect child. It's easy to imagine that if you offer enough motor development toys and cognitive development books, your child is going to be a winner. And God help her if she doesn't measure up! The big trap is in believing that the only way to judge yourself as a parent is by your child's personality and behavior. This expectation is a sure ticket to failure. Kids are not perfect, either because of their personality or the parenting they receive.

**Don't expect yourself to be a "Gerber Baby Mama."** Some parents are shocked when their infant doesn't look like the chubby-cheeked cherub in the baby-food ads—you may be upset if you don't look and feel like the serenely smiling parents in those ads. Advertising has more influence on what we expect of ourselves than we realize. The more you believe the images in the ads, the more disappointed you'll probably be with yourself and parenthood.

In printed advertisements and television, the baby is beautiful and the parents look wise and calm. I have never heard a new mother say that she feels dewy and Madonna-like but the models in those ads are 24 and don't even have the responsibility of a goldfish to look after! Many new mothers feel dumpy, frumpy, frightened, confused—only on rare occasions do they feel pretty and brilliant.

**Lower your housekeeping standards.** Many new mothers get stressed because of the mess and lack of cleanliness in their home in the early months. A baby's paraphernalia seems to be everywhere (before long, so does the baby). Try to have realistic expectations: more clutter, a bit of dust, slightly wrinkled shirts, and lots of take-out food containers. If you can do that, you'll probably be able to relax and enjoy your new life. Forget the spanking-clean floor of TV commercials; regardless of what your grandmother said, it is *not* important to have a toilet as clean as a teacup or a kitchen floor you could eat off. That's why you have mugs and plates.

***Parenting is a new skill that requires practice.*** Both of you may feel awkward as parents in the beginning, but this doesn't mean you are inadequate. Even feeling comfortable holding your child is something you need time and experience to learn. The same is true for feeding, whether it is bottle or breast; this routine takes a while to establish comfortably. Despite popular myth, feeding an infant isn't a skill that "comes naturally."

There are so many questions that you can answer only through trial and error with your own baby. What should you do when the newborn cries? It's so hard to know what the baby is feeling and how to comfort him. How long does a bath take, or a feeding? How many diaper changes will you have to do each day, and how many loads of laundry? How many hours will *you* be awake when it's your partner's turn for the night feeding?

***Parents need time to warm up to their baby.*** Your adjustment to parenthood will probably be less stressful if you don't expect to have an intense interaction immediately with the baby. Give yourselves time. A man can be slower than a woman to get involved with a newborn, often because there isn't much feedback from the baby. If you can accept the fact that fathers often bloom later, this acceptance may mean there will be less friction and strain between you.

***"Woman's intuition" is a fraud!*** An anxious, frustrated father of a crying baby may hand her over to her mother and say, "Use your intuition." Guess what: there's no such thing! The father's guess is as good as the mother's. Both parents are equally equipped to stop a baby's crying.

***A mother may think she has to be a saint.*** Some mothers think they have to live up to the image of the self-sacrificing, all-giving mother. Although this devotion is rarely acknowledged by the outside world, you may think it is "expected" of you. On the other hand, if a new father does even the littlest bit of child care he is deluged with feedback: friends and relatives extol his wonderfulness and even expect the new mother to acknowledge how lucky she is to have such a great guy!

## SUGGESTIONS TO MAKE LIFE A LITTLE EASIER

***Have faith in each other.*** If your mate's reactions or behavior seem strange to you, it's not always necessary for you to understand. If you can trust each other, you'll be able to accept the premise that some things are instinctive, not rational. With the intense and fundamental issues that arise around parenting you often just have to let things happen rather than try to control or even understand them.

In general, it's healthy to talk things through with each other, but there are times when it's better not to demand any explanation. Before you intrude on your mate to get answers for what you see as bizarre behavior, ask yourself: "Does it really matter whether I understand? Or am I just being controlling and nosey?" Be honest with yourself: is there something genuinely unhealthy happening, or do you just feel left out? Wait it out if you can. If you have faith in your partner, you can allow the space that can give him/her a chance to work things out. There are times when patience and hands-off are much better than confrontation to get you through a shaky or confusing time in your relationship.

***Give yourselves credit.*** Make it a point to compliment your mate—and yourself—for the things that are well done. It's equally important to give each other credit for the attempts you may make as a spouse or parent that are well intentioned but perhaps don't succeed! Try this as a formula: For every criticism that you make (of yourself or your partner), find a word of praise for something you have accomplished, however small.

Here is a chart of some reminders to help with your outlook. You can Xerox it and put it on the refrigerator door (as people do with diet reminders). You can embroider it in needlepoint on a pillow. Or you can forget about it and find your own cheery little phrases to help you through the night.

## HELPFUL LITTLE CLICHÉS

* Roll with the punches
* There is no right way to parent
* You are going to make mistakes
* So is your partner
* Laugh, accept, forgive, LIGHTEN UP!
* Look for solutions, not blame
* Conquering a problem doesn't mean it will stay resolved
* Resolving one problem can create another stress or conflict: it's a risk worth taking
* The key lies in attitude: some parents remain content, even calm, in difficult situations
* The above is hearsay. I've personally never met a new parent who was that relaxed!

## SOME "REALITY TESTING" TO CONSIDER

1. A child changes your relationship.
2. Neither of you is going to change: your personalities are pretty much set. What you see is what you get!
3. Your differences are part of what attracted you. The differences between you are not going to diminish; they may even increase over time.
4. Your marriage is going to have ups and downs. Your union has a better chance of enduring if you don't expect perfection or demand "happy endings" to every encounter.
5. You're probably going to fight about money at some point. The argument may be a sign of problems with dependence, self-esteem, or power, but the conflict will arise.
6. You are probably going to fight about relatives and other in-laws.
7. Sex won't always be great. Sometimes it may not even be so good. Sometimes it may not be at all. That's life.
8. One person can't fulfill all the needs of another. You

will both need outside relationships and activities so that you don't put the impossible burden on your partner of being everything for you.

9. You don't have to do everything together or enjoy all the same things. Some separateness is healthy.

10. Your spouse is not a mind reader. Love has nothing to do with being a psychic. You have to spell out what you are thinking and feeling.

# 3

# The transition to parenthood

SURVIVAL *is the operative word in the first few months.* You may think I'm making too harsh an assessment of what it's like when you bring your baby home, but I think it's better to prepare you for the worst possible scenario (and hope for the best!). Many couples do experience the transition to parenthood as a stressful upheaval. Many couples have said that the biggest problem was that the difficulties were so unexpected: they wish someone had levelled with them about just how tough it can be.

*Realistic expectations can make all the difference.* If you have realistic expectations of this period in your lives, you'll be better equipped to handle the changes. If you *expect* the hard work and total change in the rhythm of your life that come with a baby, it will probably make the adjustment easier for you.

New parents often need to be relieved of the idealized, romantic notions that surround a baby's birth. These unrealistic fantasies can be harmful because they are usually followed by the dreadful shock of reality. ''Why didn't anyone tell us?'' is a complaint heard from many new parents in the early days of their baby's life.

It is baffling to try to figure out why no one tries to prepare expectant parents for the difficulties of parenting.

It seems as though no one tells you what to *really* expect. You can take a Red Cross class or play with your sister's baby. You can read Dr. Spock until you have whole sections memorized. You can believe you are prepared. But there's one little hitch: you still won't know how to parent! Nobody does, not until the arrival of their baby forces them to learn.

It can be very hard for new parents to envision how much time and emotional energy a newborn baby requires. You may be pragmatic and realize that your daily routine is going to change. However, most new parents cannot imagine **how much** their lives will be altered until they actually live through the first sleepless months. If your baby is colicky or there are other problems, it can take even more out of you. It helps if you can acknowledge these possibilities before the baby arrives; if it comes as a shock, it can cause unpleasantness between you and your mate.

***Think of the first six weeks as boot camp.*** Just imagine that you and your spouse have joined the Marines together! If you think this way, you will have a very good idea of what to expect of new parenthood. You're going to be run ragged—the food will be lousy—you'll be awakened for duty at all hours—you'll be forced to go until you drop . . . and then a little further. Get the idea? I'm not trying to scare you, I'm here as a friend—an honest friend. I'd hate to see you go off to boot camp like Private Benjamin, with distorted expectations!

***Parenthood is an endurance test.*** It can be useful to think of the early postpartum period as a test of your endurance. The first couple of months are the hardest physically: you don't get much sleep and in addition you have to constantly learn new skills. Everyday tasks like diapering, bathing, changing the baby's clothes, and nail clipping are major undertakings until you get comfortable with them. If, like most new parents, you haven't had much experience with infants, you are going to underestimate the time and energy that a new baby demands.

There is a lot of work and not much rest. Perhaps hardest of all is the lack of a predictable schedule: you cannot determine what your days and nights are going to be like in the beginning. Most of us are used to living our lives by the clock and having control of our time. New parenthood is going to demand many adjustments from both parents; there is no way to predict how you will respond. What follows are some insights into the early postpartum adjustment that may help both of you to cope with your partner's feelings and your own.

## THE EMOTIONAL EFFECT
## OF YOUR BIRTH EXPERIENCE

The way you feel about yourselves and your child is influenced by the birth experience you had. It is a good idea to evaluate what you both felt about the baby's birth so that you can reconcile what you had **imagined** it would be like and what you actually experienced. This is considered part of the process of forming an attachment to the baby.

*Avoid viewing the birth experience as a competition.*    It is not unusual for new parents to compare their labor and delivery with other new parents and find themselves competing: who had the ''best'' birth? With the current trend toward taking classes in childbirth preparation, there is the possibility that some couples may view their baby's birth as a performance that will be evaluated.

*New parents may feel like failures.*    If you can't report that your child's birth was a peak moment in your lives, you may feel you have failed compared to other couples you know. Although it's wonderful that there's a trend toward couples preparing for birth together, it's important not to lose sight of the fact that what really matters is that you give birth to a healthy baby. The rest is gravy. For some couples the birth experience is truly fabulous, but for many others it's an experience they are glad to put behind them. So if ''the earth didn't move'' for you, or if labor and delivery were miserable for you, *it's okay!* Don't get caught up in comparing notes or competing with other new parents. If other couples want to display color photos of their all-natural delivery on their coffee table, don't let it become your problem.

***You may be angry, disappointed, or sad.*** If you have these feelings about the birth experience, it may help to come to terms with them. If you don't recognize and understand these emotions, they may undermine the start of your new family life. You and your spouse probably had different expectations of the birth and have different expectations of the baby. You may feel you were a failure or inadequate. You may feel your mate let you down. It's important that you talk honestly about these feelings.

***Does a disappointing birth reflect on your ability as parents?*** If the birth experience falls short of your expectations in any way, you may see it as an early indicator of the kind of parents you will be. If you judge yourselves by how you handled the birth, you may feel inadequate. The way that caregivers treated you during the birth may have a lasting effect on your perception of the birth, especially if anyone made negative remarks or interfered.

If you feel sufficiently uncomfortable about things that the doctors, nurses, or midwives did or said, you may get some relief by calling or writing to these people (or to hospital/patient relations). You can explain how they offended or disappointed you. Your comments may improve their care-giving style for the next couple they attend to; it may also be good for you to get it off your chest.

***You may prepare for natural childbirth but accept medication.*** If you have a "failure" of natural childbirth, it can make you angry and cause you difficulties in your adjustment in the early weeks. The media and couples who are "successful" with natural childbirth (who go through it without medical intervention) glorify drug-free labor and delivery. But there are various medical and emotional reasons why childbirth doesn't always finish that way, despite the couple's best intentions. However, if you haven't lived up to your mate's (or other people's) expectations in this area, you may feel isolated, blaming yourself and becoming alienated from your partner.

***The mother is usually more prone to feeling like a failure.*** When a couple has prepared for natural childbirth and then medication is required, the woman often feels she has failed, although her husband can be angry with himself for not having been more supportive or more demanding of his wife.

There can be the additional problem that, afterwards, a man may not be sensitive to what his wife went through in labor or her possible feelings of guilt. If a woman hoped to have a drug-free birth but accepted medication, it can be devastating if her spouse tells other people that the labor and delivery "weren't so bad." A woman is obviously the only qualified judge of her labor pain, but you can feel like such a failure that you won't say anything to contradict your spouse. Your harsh criticism of yourself may mean you don't feel entitled to your anger, and therefore you won't tell your mate that his attitude makes you feel betrayed by him. However, your anger can remain and can seep insidiously into your relationship.

All of this is a breeding ground for the kind of volatile, repressed feelings that can explode into misplaced arguments. You can't afford to let that dynamic develop at this time in your lives; you need to be partners in the true sense of the word. One way to avoid bottled-up feelings about the labor and delivery is to tell each other what the experience meant to you: how you wish it might have been different, without placing any blame. That will give you the emotional freedom to begin the next phase of the adventure—your attachment to the baby and to accepting the new concept of yourselves as parents.

## THE EMOTIONAL ASPECTS OF THE EARLY WEEKS

***The adjustment to parenthood can be an emotional roller-coaster ride.*** In the blink of an eye you can go from exhilaration to rage, from awe and enthusiasm to fear and frustration, from desperation to laughter. This is disconcerting, to say the least, but it is *absolutely normal*. It is common for people to have depression that alternates with euphoria—the feeling of hopeless overload and anxiety that is replaced by feeling peaceful and high. Don't worry, you haven't turned into a manic-depressive; you've just become a parent!

*Babies evoke intense emotions from their parents.*
Your baby will probably make you feel loving and protective, but also angry and resentful. Being angry at a baby is a frightening, embarrassing, even humiliating experience. You actually know that the baby is only a baby, doing the things babies do, and none of it done purposely to irritate you. But that sort of rational thinking goes out the window when you haven't slept for days, the house is a mess, and just when you thought the baby was finally down-and-out you hear wails from the crib. Anger is too mild a word for the way you can feel!

*You are not alone.* No matter what kind of emotional seesaw you find yourself on, it should give you some comfort to know that other new parents have been through the same wringer. Many women have felt crazy, resentful, even paralyzed in the early weeks. Many men feel their life is over, they've lost their wife to a tiny tyrant, and will never again be able to watch a football game in its entirety. When you feel this way, remind yourselves: You are not alone. It will get better. You will love your baby. You will even love yourself again.

*The fourth-week "blahs" are common.* This is an emotional phenomenon that nobody tells you about . . . so here I am again, the bearer of bad tidings! Of course, you may not get these "blahs," but if you do, you'll know it's a normal phase that will pass. It's very hard to stand back and get a realistic perspective when you're feeling down. If so, your partner may have to read this and help you through it.

What often happens between approximately the third to sixth weeks postpartum is that reality settles in. You have fewer visitors, a routine is establishing itself, and the practical realities of having a baby can hit home. The mother may feel trapped at home and find it takes too much effort to get out with the baby or get away from the house for a break. The father may be bored by his wife's recounting of the trivia of the baby's day, combined with her lack of interest in the trivia of *his* day.

For some women, a sense of hopelessness hovers like a cloud at this time. The baby's schedule seems to give you no rest, no sleep, no solitude, and no privacy. It can feel as if nothing will improve. You feel fat, there's no sex, the baby won't sleep at convenient times, you are wiped out, and there's no light at the end of the tunnel. You feel defeated and lose your perspective. If you understand that things will change, that they'll get better, you can cope more effectively with these "blahs."

*Feeling forgetful and stupid is common.* Some new mothers have this problem as another by-product of adjusting to their new role. There are many women who feel like "airheads" in the first few months: they can't complete simple tasks, they can't remember things. It is entirely possible to find yourself going out to the car, forgetting the keys (perhaps locking yourself out of the house at the same time), taking a wrong turn driving to the store, and then forgetting what you needed to buy. You pick out a few things anyway, but when you reach the cashier you discover that instead of your purse you have taken the sewing basket!

Some women go through a period like this during their pregnancy, but somehow it seems more charming then. A pregnant woman can be forgiven all sorts of idiosyncrasies. But a mother is supposed to be a competent, capable person, not some weirdo with rancid formula on her blouse, wandering around a market carrying a sewing basket!

There's no point in fretting about it if you find yourself being forgetful and dumb. It's only a reaction to the stress, fatigue, and distractions of new motherhood. It comes from the natural tendency of a new mother to put her total focus on the baby to the exclusion of everything else. Don't be tough on yourself about it. Try to connect with your sense of humor, do the best you can to cheer yourself up with the knowledge that this, too, shall pass.

*A father may lack understanding.* If a man cannot sympathize with his wife's life in the early weeks, it can create problems. A new mother's situation may not look so terrible from the outside, especially to a man who's been gone all day at a tiring, demanding job. It's pretty hard for a man to conceive what it is like to be at the beck and call of an infant. A man arrives home having had a day full of pressures and frustrations; it's hard for him to relate to the emotional price that a woman can pay as she adjusts to motherhood.

A woman may try to describe her day to her husband. You can try to explain how you feel out of control because your day is dominated by the erratic, unpredictable schedule of a newborn, which allows you to get nothing else done. You can explain that your days are one long waiting game: waiting for the baby to sleep, then wake up, then eat, then nap. You may feel like a handmaiden to a capricious little creature whose whims leave a mother feeling she isn't in control of her own time.

One solution to this dilemma is that a woman not even try to make the man understand or empathize with her situation, so that neither of you will feel frustrated. Another solution is for a mother to take one day off while the father takes over child care for a day. This is a remedy that can work wonders with a father who says, "I don't see what's so tough about taking care of that little guy." Leaving the baby with his Dad is an effective way to foster fatherly understanding when a man may not be able to comprehend what a day with an infant is like. It is preferable not to conduct this exercise in a nasty, "Here, you take the little brat and see how *you* like it!" sort of way. The point isn't to teach the baby's father a lesson, but rather to bring the two of you closer together in understanding and supporting each other.

## ATTACHMENT TO THE BABY

Your attachment to the baby is a process which can happen quickly or slowly. It is an essential part of the emotional adjustment of the early weeks. Accepting the fact that the baby "belongs" to you (coming to terms with the reality that you are parents now) is the first step in forming a relationship with your child. This sounds more obvious and easy than it is. Many parents do not immediately feel this attachment to their child and it can be a painful source of anxiety.

***You can feel similar or dissimilar to the baby.*** The degree to which you feel alike with your infant is an important part of the attachment process, whether the child is adopted or natural. Feeling closeness or distance from the baby often depends on whether the child reminds you of yourself or seems very different. Some people have strong ideas about being a better parent with one sex or the other. If the child has qualities in her personality that you dislike in yourself, your mate, or other relatives (cranky, hyper, shrill, fussy), it can create a distance between you and the baby. The child's appearance can also influence the way you feel. See the section on "FLKs"(Funny-Looking Kids) in *Chapter 16: Problems with the Baby*.

These feelings of affinity or dissimilarity are normal: you are not a "bad" person for feeling this way. These are emotions you may be able to dispel once you're aware of them. Another impediment to your attachment to the baby can be a hired baby nurse or relative who is too helpful with the baby in the beginning. It can slow down the process of attachment if someone intervenes too much and comes between you and the baby, or is too capable compared to the new Mama.

*A lack of early bonding can occur.* This can happen when the parents and child are separated at birth and don't have time to "bond" to each other, which can create a sense of failure. There can also be problems if the first meeting with the child is not a fabulous emotional experience: you can convince yourselves that the relationship is off to a bad start. For whatever reason, one partner can also blame the other for interfering with the initial bonding/attachment process, which can add another unnecessary emotional burden on the parents.

These feelings of failure can lower your self-image and put you into a depression that you may not understand. Feeling depressed and lousy about yourself can actually keep you from reaching out to your child emotionally. It's essential to know that maternal-infant bonding, as the process is called, is not an instant or magical formula. Like so many other theories, we have given it too much importance. If you don't have immediate early contact with your baby it doesn't mean your relationship is going to be any less good. Neither does a wonderful first hour for the parents and baby guarantee that they'll form an early, strong attachment. You are going to have a lifetime with your child—there's no rush. Try to let things unfold naturally.

***The attachment can remind you of your mother***. During the attachment period some new mothers try to re-create an exaggerated closeness that they felt with their own mothers. As a child you had an exclusive relationship with your mother; having a baby can recreate that bond. You may embrace the intense closeness without realizing the possible negative effect on your marriage. The very nature of this kind of bond is that it excludes other people; it may interrupt your attachment to your husband for a while. But just as you eventually detached from your own mother, you will loosen your exclusive bond to your baby and return to your marital relationship. This phase is nothing to be pre-occupied about; like so many other adjustment problems, it will pass.

***Phobias about the baby are common in the beginning***. They are similar to the fears that some parents also experience during pregnancy. A baby can make you feel very vulnerable, fearful of harm that can befall the child, you, or your mate. Whenever you fall in love or make an attachment it can make you aware of the possibility of losing that love object. A totally dependent, tiny baby only heightens these feelings.

It is common to fear for your own safety for the child's sake. Many new parents give up sports that had a high risk—motorcycles, swimming alone in the ocean, diving or surfing, hiking or jogging alone in remote areas. Others find that they develop a fear of flying, or even of crossing busy streets. Some parents are afraid to take their child in a car, imagining possible dangers and accidents around every corner.

Sometimes the phobia is about being separated from your mate. It is not unusual to have fantasies of the other parent being in an accident or dying. The reaction to this variation of phobia can be to try to stay very close because you're afraid to let the other parent leave you. Unconsciously you may think that if you stick together, nothing bad can happen.

For other people, the phobia is that harm will come

to the baby, that someone will grab her from the carriage and run off with her. Other parents fear that siblings will injure the baby: sometimes they have horrible visions of the older child throwing the baby out the window or smothering him. In this case, the parents have not only the fear, but the guilt for thinking something so terrible about the sibling! An older child will often have anger toward the younger one, but this is usually converted into a positive, loving, helpful attitude. This process is called reaction formation.

The phobias will pass. Don't judge yourself for having them—you're not crazy. You're also not a clairvoyant. Don't get yourself even more worried by imagining that the frightening visions you have are going to come true. Just give yourself time and the fears and nightmares will subside before long.

**You may develop an aversion to the baby.** You may not want to be near the baby, or have other serious problems adapting to her. This happens to some parents and can be a result of problems bonding to the baby in the early days. It can also happen if you have a colicky baby who is screaming all the time. You can also develop an aversion to a highly sensitive infant who becomes easily hysterical, for instance every time you change a diaper.

A danger with aversion to the baby is that if you give in to the feeling and remove yourself from close contact with the child, there is the risk that you may never form a bond with her as closely as you might have. It is important to take corrective action immediately.

**Get professional help as soon as you recognize the problem.** The following chart may help you be aware of the signs of aversion, which can become intensified and complicate your relationship with your child if you don't seek help. What follows is a list of the symptoms that would indicate you may have problems bonding with your baby. These can be indicators that you haven't accepted her. If you have several of these symptoms and they persist, this is a problem rooted in your past emotional history and you should seek professional counselling as soon as possible. The longer you allow this situation to persist, the harder it may be to form a healthy attachment to your child.

---

#### SIGNS OF AVERSION TO THE BABY

- No eye contact
- No physical contact
- No cooing or talking
- You see the baby as gross, ugly, disgusting
- You can't stand the smells, noises, and activities of the baby
- You feel you're living with an enemy

---

***Possessiveness about the baby can interrupt your marital relationship.*** This problem is the opposite of aversion to the baby, but can also disturb your growth as a family. If the process of attachment to the baby turns into possessiveness for either parent, it can create a rift between them. One partner may take the attitude, "I'm the only one who can take care of the baby," and will try to push aside and criticize the other parent's efforts with the child. It is not just mothers who become possessive and territorial, racing to the crib first when the baby cries or criticizing the other parent's driving habits. Fathers, too, have been known to have this distorted form of attachment, which drives them to push other people away from the baby. This behavior obviously creates problems in the couple's relationship and is a destructive pattern.

## INFATUATION WITH THE BABY

***Infatuation with the baby can create serious problems between a man and woman.*** This expression of feelings is quite different from the healthy attachment process of a mother and child. Infatuation occurs when you have overpowering feelings for the baby, not unlike the first blush of a romantic love affair.

These feelings can make you feel confused or disloyal if you have never had intense, adoring emotions like these for your husband. You may feel guilty and ashamed for carrying on a "secret love affair" with the baby. Your husband may suffer all the pains of a jilted (or cuckolded) spouse. If you don't understand what is happening to you, infatuation can affect your marriage the way an extramarital affair would.

***The intensity of your love can be overpowering.*** The love parents feel for their children is so deep and powerful that it is hard to describe. But when this love overwhelms you, so that everything else in your life pales by comparison, it can upset the balance of your life and marriage. The intensity of the feelings can be frightening. It can make you afraid of smothering your child with love. Women who are not used to such intense emotions may feel threatened by the power of these feelings. Anyone who has been in love knows how powerful it can feel, that it really *can* be a dangerous condition that takes control of your life!

***You may dream about raising the baby alone.*** Sometimes a woman will fantasize about having the baby all to herself, often imagining a divorce so that her mate cannot come between her and the child. A man's needs for attention, food, clean clothes, etc., can just seem too much after a long, demanding day with an infant. A father can also have the fantasy of keeping the baby to himself. This often happens when the baby is a man's first son, particularly if he has had only daughters in this or a previous marriage. In fact it is common for one parent to have a disproportionate attachment to the exclusion of the other parent.

***Your self-image can be damaged by your crush on the baby.*** You may think less of yourself because your emotions are immoral or unnatural. They are not. It is wonderful to love your baby and it is quite common for new mothers to feel intensely. There is nothing wrong with you. Your feelings can appear more distorted if your mate is having trouble or is slower in forming an attachment to the baby; this only makes your intensity seem greater than it is.

***You may feel guilty for having this obsession.*** If you have obsessive feelings and try to conceal them from your spouse, it is a natural response to feel guilty. At the same time, if you act in a secretive way it can also be threatening and confusing to your mate, who will sense that something is wrong. A man will tend to pull away in reaction to such feelings.

***Try to admit and talk about your feelings.*** If you aren't able to be open about your infatuation and discuss it with your mate, it can create a barricade between you. If you try to hide your feelings, your partner may feel betrayed and begin to doubt your relationship. It will help to discuss your feelings, even if you're afraid that this will make the baby's father angry or jealous. It can be much worse for him to feel that you are hiding something from him. If you don't deal with it honestly, your crush on the baby can be overwhelming, distressing, and destructive to your relationship.

***The baby's father can help his wife deal with her feelings.*** If your husband can meet you halfway in struggling with your infatuation, it can make a world of difference. You may be more disturbed and frightened by your love affair with the baby than he is! It really helps a woman if she has her mate's support and understanding during this intense stage of adjustment.

Part of being a good partner and parent is to be unselfish, to strive for a nonjudgmental acceptance of the developmental stages that your spouse and children will go through. A woman experiencing a powerful crush on her child creates a complex situation in her marriage. It only becomes more complicated if her mate is critical of her, or feels injured or allows his ego to get in the way.

***The intensity of the infatuation should lessen over time.*** Usually the initial outpouring of devotion cools down, just as it does in infatuations or crushes between adults. However, if the intensity does not let up, the partner who is *not* over-attached—usually the man—needs to sit his wife down for a talk. You should tell her as calmly and rationally as possible that an attachment to a baby cannot replace an adult relationship. You might want to point out that for some women this is a normal, temporary phase of motherhood. However, if you aren't able to help your wife get over her infatuation, you may reach a point where you're at the end of your rope and might want to consider getting professional help.

## OBSESSIVENESS ABOUT THE BABY

***Obsessiveness about the baby goes one step further than infatuation.*** Obsession is usually a mother's problem, although fathers can suffer from it, too: it means that almost 100 percent of your time and energy is directed toward the baby, whether he is asleep or awake. For instance, you might constantly be worrying whether the baby is dressed correctly, whether he is eating enough, growing properly, if he's sleeping too much, etc. This mental over-attention is probably a way for an insecure mother to feel that she's in control. Invariably, it backfires. The more that you obsess, the more you worry: worrying makes you feel anxious and out of control. It is a vicious cycle that only you can break.

***A new father's obsession can seem like criticism of the mother.*** Some men want charts and demand businesslike information about what the baby ate and did all day long. This can be a man's way of trying to feel that he's in charge, or is involved in the infant's care. However, his need for information can put his wife on the spot. If a man comes home from work and wants a precise rundown of the baby's day, a woman can interpret this as criticism of her, checking up on her. Of course every case is different, and some fathers who want detailed information about the baby may just be interested or sad to have missed so much of the day with the infant.

***Obsession can become paranoia.*** For some women, their fixation on the child can translate into a frantic fearfulness about leaving the child or allowing anyone else to touch it. You are suffering from this syndrome if you freak out when a friend, your mate, or a grandparent lovingly takes the baby out of your arms. You may not say anything but you feel as though you have been violated, as though a piece of your own body has been torn off. You may find yourself doggedly following the person holding the infant, fixated on *your* baby in *their* arms, desperately waiting to get back what belongs to you. As you can imagine, this attitude makes it hard for the baby's father to get close to his child or feel close to you.

Mothers usually get over their unwillingness to be separated from their baby gradually. Eventually you'll feel all right leaving the child with your mate for short periods. Later on you will be able to leave the baby with a friend or sitter. Finally you will reach the point where you will want some time on your own . . . when this will happen depends on how deep your obsession is.

The process of separating from your child is actually a two-way street—your baby has to learn to separate from you, too. The separation and individuation process is more subtle for the mother, however, and may be a replay of early experiences in her own life. There is a psychoanalytic school of thought which postulates that as your child reaches a certain age, you re-experience the conflicts and difficulties that you yourself had at that point in your development. This theory concludes that if you had difficulties with your parents when you were an infant, young child, or adolescent, you will experience those feelings again when your child reaches that age.

*Some parents become obsessive about the baby's temperature and clothing.*   Some couples have passionate debates about whether the baby is warm enough, or too hot. Many pediatricians recommend dressing the kid in the same weight clothing as you dress yourself, on the theory that if you are comfortable, the child will be. Unfortunately this doesn't always solve the problem with obsessive parents because a man and woman can have different personal thermometers—so which parent's "thermostat" will determine the right wardrobe for the baby? This means there will be lots of taking clothing on and off, probably accompanied by shrieks from the child each time you disrupt his comfort, until you can get control of your obsessing.

*There are ways to break the habit of obsessing.*   One good way to start getting over obsessive behavior is to laugh at yourself. The process that follows is a method that can be used in psychotherapy for *anyone* who is obsessive/

compulsive; it can help you to get a perspective and to get a grip on yourself.

For example, when you find yourself in a panicky dither about whether to take off or leave on the baby's sweater, say to yourself: "It is a life-and-death decision. If I am wrong, this child will be damaged for life." Another example would be if the baby's diaper leaks down her leg and all over your new skirt, say to yourself, "This is proof of how inept I am. I can't even put on a diaper, I'm not fit to be a mother."

This system of breaking the habit of obsessing will only work if *you* say these things, preferably out loud, and hear for yourself how absurd they sound. It can be helpful to actually hear what you may have been saying to yourself silently, perhaps unconsciously. On some level these are the assumptions behind your obsessiveness. You are judging yourself severely (and/or imagine you are being judged) over every little aspect of parenting.

**Breast-feeding is a common topic for obsessiveness.** Because obsessive people worry even more about things they cannot measure or control, the amount of breast milk a mother produces can be a subject for intense concern. Some new fathers display their obsessiveness by asking the mother to keep a chart of how often and long the baby was at the breast, or they make a graph of the baby's weight. A new mother may find herself becoming crazed over whether she has enough breast milk for the baby. One sure way to interfere with your milk production and let-down reflex is to work yourself into a nervous sweat about how much milk you have. Try the method of poking fun at yourself by saying aloud, "Babies in Biafra survive on their mother's milk, but I am so deficient that my baby will be the first one in my neighborhood to suffer from malnutrition."

**Your spouse cannot use this method on you.** These paradoxical statements only work if a person says them to him/herself; it's a process that may give you the perspective to laugh and stop what you're doing. However, it isn't effective if the statements come from another person. If you try to use this ironic tone on your wife, it will probably make her angry at you. It may even boomerang and make her more convinced of the need to be obsessive!

***You have to decide you want to stop obsessing.*** Apart from trying to gain perspective with the previous suggestion about paradoxical thinking, you are going to have to force yourself to be strong mentally. You have to make a conscious effort to believe that your baby is going to be fine. Try to trust that everything will fall into place, while recognizing that you cannot **make** it happen by hovering 24 hours a day. Think about the babies in the Mexican earthquake: they survived for days on end without food or milk, without anyone to hold or talk to them. Nature is interested in the survival of the species—babies are tremendously resilient creatures.

***Try to let go of your need to be in control.*** See if you can experiment by not trying to be in charge for a moment. You will undoubtedly find that your child will develop her own schedule—and you'll be the first to know about it! Like all babies before her, this remarkable little being will learn to communicate whether she is comfortable or not—and you will learn the signals. She will teach you how to meet her needs. This will happen as part of the natural order of things. If you cannot believe in yourself, at least you can trust that your baby hasn't had a chance to become neurotic, yet!

***Force yourself to pay attention to your own needs.*** Although your needs may seen unimportant in the midst of your obsession, you have to think about yourself. To some extent, your well-being depends on taking time off from your child and spending time with adults in order to replenish and redefine yourself. You are still a separate individual, with a mate and other people who care about you and depend on you. Your obsessiveness can be terribly difficult for the people in your life, your spouse particularly. If you aren't motivated to break out of your obsession for yourself, at least do it for your mate.

***Preoccupation with the baby can be an escape.*** Don't overlook the possibility that parents may be fixated on their child as a way of avoiding intensity with each other. For example, you may be constantly worried and involved with the child, always putting the child first, refusing ever to leave her to go out. This may be a way of avoiding dealing with your mate and his/her feelings.

The nonobsessive parent may think your total preoccupation with the baby is not only unnecessary but is also a rejection of him/her. Objectively speaking, one can see the point! The obsessive parent may think the other should be equally mesmerized by every detail of the baby's existence. Objectively speaking, it's a lot harder to agree with *that* point! Don't deceive yourself or your mate. If there are problems in your relationship that you haven't confronted, don't hide behind your obsession with the baby. A child can be a defense against looking at marital conflict—for as long as 10 to 20 years. (This is why "the cover" is often blown on a rocky marriage when the child reaches adolescence and the parents split up.)

## THE PROBLEM OF ISOLATION FOR NEW PARENTS

*Isolation is a common problem in the modern family.* If you are too cut off it can lead to postpartum depression (see *Chapter 7: Postpartum Depression*), or being alone can just take a lot of the fun out of your early life as a parent. **DON'T TRY TO DO IT ALONE!** You need to share ideas with people going through the same experience as you are. You need reassurance from people who have been parents before. You need as many nonjudgmental, supportive people in your new life as you can possibly gather.

*Most newborns are relatively unresponsive.* During the first month your baby is apt to sleep, eat, and cry with little feedback to your interaction with her. If you feel alone and without adult companionship, it can be more difficult to cope with this early period; it can be harder to wait patiently for the baby's first smile. If you are simultaneously dealing with learning new skills as a parent, including how to communicate with the baby, this can intensify your feelings of isolation.

*Your partner may be your greatest ally.* During the early adjustment to parenting you may be friends with your spouse . . . or not. It is up to you whether you let yourself feel isolation or closeness with each other. Some women are worried about burdening a hardworking man with either their doubts or their excitement about their new life with the baby. A new father may not want to go to his wife with his troubles. But if you cut yourself off from your spouse it can lead to depression or an uncomfortable distance between you that is hard to bridge. Keep talking; keep listening. A partner is someone who is there for you during the stressful times in life: parenthood is a test of that alliance between you.

*Parents are developing along with their babies.* In order to flourish as parents it helps to have moral support, practical help, and the companionship of peers. The way that you feel about yourselves as parents can make a difference in your growth as adults and in the way your child will develop. You are going to have to make or discover new support systems in your life. You'll need someone to baby-sit. Someone for advice. Someone to lend clothes, share the highs, and help with the lows.

*You still need people other than your mate.* There are various ways to get the support systems going, but keep in mind that only you can make it happen. New parents often suffer from isolation simply because they withdraw, waiting for other people to call them. You have to take the initiative, whether it's striking up a conversation with a stranger who has a child the age of yours, or picking up the phone and telling friends that you need them. You have to surround yourself with people who will reinforce your belief in your own strengths. Try to avoid those outside influences (whether doctors, visitors, books, etc.) that encourage your self-doubts.

*Some suggestions on how to make new friends.* There are several ways to bring new acquaintances with babies into your life. You can take the baby for walks in your neighborhood and stop to talk to other mothers on the street, in stores, or in playgrounds. Try to seek out people whose child is within a few months of your baby's age. It takes courage to reach out to strangers, but you will be pleasantly surprised at the positive reception you will get most of the time. The other parents will probably be grateful that you took the step they may have wanted to take, but may have been too shy or insecure to attempt. You can also put up a card on a local bulletin board saying, "Do you want to meet other new parents?" or, "Do you feel isolated with your new baby?" This is how family centers or parent groups often begin.

***Family is very important, too.*** Even if relatives live far away you should make an effort to write or call them. This is a time in your life when you may want to mend fences and attempt a closeness with relatives that you haven't maintained before. This is particularly true of your parents and in-laws, who are discussed in depth in the section on Grandparents in *Chapter 11: Outside Relationships*.

***Don't rule out old friends who are childless.*** It is important for you to maintain adult relationships in which you can talk and enjoy yourself as something other than a parent (more on this in *Chapter 11*). Sometimes it can make you feel jealous to see friends who are active and childless; perhaps it makes them jealous to see you with your baby. For many friendships it is worth it to talk this through and try to overcome these perceptions of each other. You need those friendships now. However, don't expect friends to read your mind; they may think you want time alone when in fact you are feeling lonely.

Another reason that childless friends are important is that although it can be riveting to discuss babies, it can also be oppressive. Many new parents talk obsessively about their infants, focusing solely on that subject until it is suffocating. They are known as "baby bores." There are couples who began this pattern of single-mindedness during pregnancy and carry it over into parenting. It is possible to want a child and love her to pieces, but not want to talk about her all the time. Too much baby talk can make you feel out of touch, as though you are missing things in the "real" world. Friends without children can help you maintain that connection.

## TRANSITIONS ARE NEVER EASY

*Change is frightening.*   This is true whether the adjustment you have to make is to a new job, to marriage, or to
becoming parents. The difference in the transition to parenthood is that it also requires inner change. There are a
couple of observations that can make your journey into parenthood go more smoothly. Although few generalizations
will hold true for all couples, there seem to be two things
that usually hold true:

1. The first six weeks aren't going to be what you expect.
2. The adjustment will probably make some waves between the two of you.

*Parenthood puts your marriage to the test.*   Not all
couples view this transition as a crisis, but the intense stress
in the beginning is tough on even the best partnerships.
Studies have shown that couples who participate together
in the preparation for labor and delivery make an easier
adjustment later. Perhaps in sharing that intense experience
you learn to be sensitive to each other and to pull together
under stress. These are precisely the skills you'll need as
new parents.

   You may have had a lot of outside support for birth,
but many couples discover that other people give very little
help for parenting and the postpartum adjustment. Studies
show that the strain of becoming parents is less for couples
who have approached parenthood together: they've taken
childbirth classes, read books, and talked about plans for
the baby's future. Facing the pressure of new parenthood
as a team can lighten the load for each of you.

*A weak, troubled marriage will be in trouble.*   If your
marriage has been shaky, you are in particular jeopardy
when you have a baby. The pressure of the transition to
parenthood often brings problems to the surface, particularly in a marriage with serious problems, a fundamental
disharmony. However, it is natural for even the most hap-
pily paired couple to experience tension and misunderstandings in the first months.

   If you find yourselves squabbling or snapping at each

other, this doesn't mean you need to panic about the future of your marriage. You probably don't even need to spend time figuring out why you're not getting along. Some couples feel they have to look for something to "blame" for those tensions—maybe you'll wonder if the problem is that you need a bigger place to live, or that the grandparents are meddling, or you'll question whether you should have had a baby at all. Tension between new parents is usually just a normal reaction to the stress they're experiencing.

***New responsibilities create pressure.*** It's not unusual for new parents to feel they've got the weight of the world on their shoulders. There is a different quality of commitment in parenthood to that in any other relationship: once the baby is born, you realize that you now have total responsibility for the physical and emotional welfare of that child.

    The commitment of parenthood is greater than marriage, even of the most loving and devoted relationship. To put it bluntly: you can always get a divorce but parenthood is forever. This fact can make a couple feel frightened, inadequate, pressured, or overwhelmed. However, these increased demands can be more of a burden for some new parents than for others; one parent may feel more anxious than the other. Neither of you is "right or wrong," or "weaker or superior" in the way you handle your realization of this new commitment and responsibility.

***Your feelings are normal.*** If you can accept your reactions to being a parent, it can give you a chance to come to terms with your emotions at your own pace. If you can't condone your heightened emotions (or those of your partner), they can boomerang and cause friction between you.

    Many couples are unprepared for the intensity of the baby's needs. Along with that adjustment you have to undergo the abrupt change from a two-person to a three-person unit. The baby's arrival is a real test of your partnership; you were dependent on each other and now there's this child who depends so much on both of you. The early weeks of parenthood are the first time that you are face to face with the reality of your increased responsibilities. Try to be gentle and generous about any feelings you may have.

***A baby puts your relationship in a new perspective.*** No matter what may happen to the two of you from this time forward, you will always be connected through that child. When you think about your lives in this new context you may find that previously insignificant issues take on much more importance. Suddenly your reaction to your mate's habits and attitudes is magnified: you are joined to this person for life now that you are parents together. This new perception of your relationship is normal and something you will adjust to in time. Couples who aren't aware of this may overreact to little things and create big problems.

Parenthood changes the ground rules of your life together—yet at first you don't even know what exactly is different. You aren't relating to each other the way you were before the baby was born, but you haven't yet established new rules and patterns. You may feel you've lost the equilibrium you had and turn against your mate. As we discussed earlier, change is upsetting and disorienting. On the one hand you may be afraid that your relationship is going to change; at the same time you may be anxious that it *won't* be able to make the necessary adjustments.

## THE ROLE CHANGE TO "PARENT"

The role change you both have to adjust to can create conflicts between you that you may not understand. Some of these issues were considered in *Chapter 2: Changing Expectations* (your identities as a mother and father are looked at in depth in *Chapters 4 and 5*). In this section we'll look at some elements of the role change to parenthood that can affect you in the early weeks.

***You think of yourself as a parent for the first time.*** When you become a parent, you have to deal with your initial conception of what "mother" and "father" mean to you. You have to adjust to a new identity, bringing with you a lifetime of experiences, beliefs, and myths about what it means to be "a parent." Each of you will have a different sense of timing in your own change to being a parent. It may take you a week (or a year) to make the change; your partner may need a day (or three months) to evolve toward a sense of self as a parent.

***Each partner has expectations of the other.*** The hopes you have may lead to misunderstandings and disappointment between you: if you have specific expectations of your mate it can trip you up if you aren't prepared to handle the reality. For example, a man may overestimate a woman's mothering ability—this is especially true with a first child. Or a woman may expect a man to be a more involved and helpful father than he turns out to be. Or a career mother may feel resentful or uprooted when she gives up her job for motherhood.

There can also be problems when one partner or the other changes dramatically as a result of becoming a parent. For example, a man who may have always seemed liberal and nonchauvinistic in his attitude toward women may become resentful if his wife does not give up her career to raise their children. You have no way of knowing how you will feel until you become a father yourself; you may be surprised to discover that you expect your wife to devote her life to your children and are angry if she doesn't do it. Another climatic change can be that an easygoing, softspoken woman becomes bossy, demanding or rigid when she becomes a mother.

***Dealing with each other's emotional adjustments can be hard.*** When you're struggling with your own feelings about what it means to be a mother or father (and how it affects everything in your life), it's hard to reach out to your partner. It is hard enough to cope with your own needs and reactions. Although in the best of all possible worlds you want to respond sensitively to your mate, it may seem impossible now. You may be feeling so needy yourself that you just don't have the strength to help your mate with his or her reaction to parenting.

It can make matters even worse if, when you finally do find the time to sit down to discuss your feelings, you are totally disappointed in your mate's reactions. You may be surprised or angry to find out that your partner's impressions of parenting are completely different from yours.

New parents often assume that they are both experiencing similar feelings about this pivotal time in their lives. It is easy to resent the fact that your mate has different moods, perceptions, and concerns about the baby.

*Idealization of yourselves as "super parents."* Without even realizing it, you can fall into the trap of feeling you have to be "super parents" with a "super baby." This is a mental process that may begin years before you even get pregnant. Almost everybody has expectations about what it will feel like to be a parent, and dreams of how a child will interact with them. These ideas come directly from your own experience growing up—the way your family of origin (as it is called) functioned is pretty much what forms your concept of what "a family" is.

Some people take these ideas and images from their past and develop idealized expectations of what parenthood and their child will be like. If you are like most people, you may not be aware of the power that your past has over your present-day ideas and expectations. You may be operating on the theory that you have to be a "perfect" parent without even knowing what that means to you.

Some people approach parenting as another test in their lives: they want to get an "A." For them, performing "perfectly" as a parent becomes a way to get reassurance about their self-worth and adequacy. However, what this actually does is make a physical and emotional wreck of them and the people in their life! Making mistakes is part of being alive; it's how we learn and grow.

Think of it this way: it takes hard work and practice to master any skill. If you could sit down at the piano and play a sonata perfectly right off the bat, there would be no artistry in music and there would be no concert pianists. The **process** of becoming a good parent—hitting sour notes, having to practice—is what it's all about. If you are a perfectionist, then becoming a parent may give you a chance to allow yourself to be human. Try to be generous and forgiving with yourself. First you need to give yourself "permission" to make mistakes and then (just as important) you must forgive the errors you do make. Once you learn to extend this kindness to yourself, you may discover you don't have to be so tough on yourself. You can ease up and show the same generosity to your mate, child, and others in your life.

***You should be aware of the "super baby syndrome."*** You should avoid projecting your unrealistic expectations onto your child (or help your mate to avoid doing this). It is a no-win situation, unfair to your child and certain to create hassles between you as parents. It is natural to want to recreate happy aspects of your childhood and/or rewrite unhappy ones through your child. However, if either of you is expecting a "perfect" child or hoping to mold her to conform to your fantasies, you are putting an enormous burden on a tiny, defenseless baby.

Most people have firm ideas about what are "good or bad" personality traits in a child, "right and wrong" behavior. But problems can arise when you're not able to differentiate between what you'd *like* a child to be, and the *reality* of the unique individual who is your child. This can lead to an unhappy child and disappointed parents, quarrelling with each other without really understanding why.

***The parent-as-martyr syndrome.*** Some people sacrifice everything else in their lives to prove themselves as parents. They believe that if they do it "right" they will get validation from the outside world, along with eternal gratitude from their spouse, their parents, in-laws, or children. Fathers and mothers both make this assumption, often unconsciously. For many parents this "martyrdom" to their children will be a root cause of feeling unfulfilled and unappreciated in their lives.

In the demanding early months of the baby's life it's easy to lose sight of the fact that you and your marriage are important, too. The baby may become the center of your universe for a while, but it isn't a good idea to let that disequilibrium remain for long. Parenting *is* important work. However, you're building a house of cards if you make a child the be-all and end-all of your existence. Your marriage is one of the fundamental relationships in your life: don't take it for granted. If you nourish your marriage, everything will flow from that. If you put the child first and don't look out for your own needs and feelings, you're not going to be of much use to yourself or anyone else.

## WHO'S TAKING CARE OF THE GROWN-UPS?

*Adult needs must not be neglected.* You don't have to forget your needs or your mate's just because you're also fulfilling the baby's demands. A man may feel neglected if his wife is all wrapped up in the baby, to the exclusion of him. Conversely, a woman staying home with the baby may feel shut out as her partner reinvolves himself in the non-baby world.

Ignoring your own needs for rest, food, entertainment, and stimulation can push you to the limit. If you let yourselves get overtired and strung out you will feel more needy and less patient. There is the potential for damage to your relationship if you ignore the things that fed you emotionally and intellectually as a couple before you became parents.

*Both parents' needs are at a high level.* In the early months you need love, attention, validation, approval, help, and relief. It can help if you think in terms of "being good" to yourselves. You can protect yourself and your spouse by reminding yourselves that your needs are as important as the baby's. Forget any other people in your lives for now; nobody else's needs matter except the three of you (and other children you may have). At least for the time being, worry only about yourselves, not friends or relatives (for specific suggestions, see *Chapter 11: Outside Relationships*).

*Either of you may be feeling trapped.* Before you had the baby you may have known that "settling down" was part of parenthood; but you probably didn't expect to feel imprisoned! For most people, becoming parents means that you can't be impulsive any more, making last-minute plans to go to the movies or away for the weekend. You have to consider the baby in every move you make.

Be generous emotionally with your mate. Even if your partner's reactions seem strange, try to let it pass and avoid making an issue of it. Indulge each other's emotions. Don't make confrontations. Remember that either of you may be having intense emotions, like feeling trapped, which can explain bizarre behavior. Unless you recognize these pressures, you and your mate may express this feeling of entrapment by arguing with each other, which creates a new set of problems.

*Amuse yourselves.*   If you can't go out as much as before, get a VCR to see movies at home or get a cable TV service. You may be so exhausted from sleepless nights and the rest of the adjustment that you don't even have the energy to do the things you used to enjoy. Treat yourselves to new books, magazines, records, and special food or wine. Try to make it a point to get out of the house regularly, to get a break from the telephone, chores, and responsibilities, even if only for a little while. Have fun!

*Ask for help!*   When friends ask, "What can we do?" don't be shy, **tell them**. You'll be surprised—many of them will enjoy the involvement. You can ask visitors to bring food when they visit, either a meal they can share with you or something for you to freeze for a later time. You can ask friends to run quick errands, help address birth announcements, walk a colicky baby, and so on. Once you start thinking along these lines, you'll be amazed how much friends can contribute.

*Paid help can ease a lot of pressure.*   Especially in the early months there are a variety of services which can lighten your load. Once you make up your minds that you **deserve** the luxury of paid help, you'll probably have to make choices about which of the costly amenities are most important to you. Baby-sitters, car washers, laundry service, dog groomer or walker, house cleaner, even a take-out meal from a nice restaurant can all make your life easier.

You may have been taught that doing it alone is the "right" way to do things—but that's not going to make your life any easier as a new parent. Asking for help and getting feedback is very important for you now. There's no reason for mother- and fatherhood to be something you learn by being thrown into cold water to see if you'll sink or swim! Your adjustment to parenthood may be more comfortable if you can learn to tell your mate and other people what you feel and need. New situations and problems with the baby can cause you anxiety until your confidence builds as you learn the ropes. Having people you can turn to is a real comfort. It is a step toward getting your needs met and taking control of the new life you are beginning.

## FEARS ABOUT CHILD REARING

The job of raising a child in today's world is an understandable source of anxiety to new parents. There are few guidelines to help light the path; since most people do not have an extended family, they are also quite isolated. Many new parents haven't been around small children. They don't feel comfortable with everyday tasks, much less the more complex issues about the child's upbringing. It is not unusual for new parents to feel as if they are the blind leading the blind when it comes to raising a child.

*Philosophical differences about child rearing.* Arguments about how to handle the baby can create nasty problems for a couple. However, differences are natural—almost *any* two people will have different opinions about raising children. There's no use trying to eliminate disagreements or trying to prove your own point of view. The answer would seem to lie in *how you handle your differences.* Parenting is ripe with possibilities for frustrating conflicts. You can find yourselves in passionate arguments that leave you feeling alienated from each other, backed into a corner, and so angry that there's no graceful way out. The trick is not to box yourself in like that.

*Respect your mate's personal style.* Try to listen and acknowledge the validity of each other's viewpoints about child rearing. You're not doing yourselves any good by locking horns over issues that, in the long run, are not as important as the way the two of you treat each other. Listen to each other: don't just react emotionally, really try to see the other person's point of view. No issue about child rearing is more important than whether the two of you are compassionate with each other.

***"Right" and "wrong" child-rearing theories.*** There can be a vast difference in the degree to which either of you worries about the "right" and "wrong" way to respond to a child's needs and demands. Don't let yourself feel superior to your partner, imagining that your way of coping with the anxieties of new parenthood is "better."

For instance, your husband may not want to make a move without consulting his copy of Dr. Spock or Penelope Leach while you may believe in doing things by personal trial-and-error. Your husband may not care whether your child wears a sunbonnet, but he may be intensely concerned about when to pick up a crying baby. You may share his viewpoint on these issues, you may have different anxieties, or maybe you don't have any at all! Neither of you is a "better" parent because of your attitude. Try to allow room for each other's personal style without making a judgment about it. Keep in mind that you're each doing the best you can. Approach child rearing as a team and you'll be ahead of the game.

## BOOKS AND CHILD DEVELOPMENT EXPERTS

***Approach books and experts with caution.*** The child development authorities can leave you feeling more insecure and inadequate as a parent than you were before you read them. The very existence of these specialists reinforces the nagging worry that there *is* an absolutely right or wrong way to raise a child. These books can feed into your fear that everything you do will irreversibly affect your child. They can actually undermine your natural talents for parenting and turn you into a self-doubting worry-wart. If you don't believe me, just look at the conflicting advice of these experts: for every theory there is another opposite theory that contradicts it.

***New parents can overreact and distort child-rearing theories.*** It's possible to lose your rational perspective when you get caught up in paying attention to the "experts." You can compare this to the way that some expectant couples reacted to the "nonviolent" Leboyer method of birth when it was first popularized. Leboyer advocated a low-light, low-noise, warm-bath birth: it was a very nice idea. But there were some couples who insisted (almost violently) that they had to have a Leboyer birth or no birth at all. People drew the illogical conclusion that any child who *didn't* have the "nonviolent" birth experience was going to be psychologically damaged. This came, in part, from wishful thinking that if you could just give your baby the "right" start, you'd be assured of a good child. Overreactions to theories about child rearing can come from similar fears, hopes, and insecurities.

*You may be afraid of making a "mistake."*   The fear of making one mistake that will ruin your child for life seems to be a popular nightmare these days. It is a tremendous burden for parents who imagine that they are going to "blow it" with their child: they worry that a few slip-ups will leave lifelong scars on a youngster's psyche. Don't believe it! Children are remarkably resilient little creatures. They will grow into healthy, well-adjusted people in spite of the blunders of their well-meaning parents.

While we may feel we're under tremendous pressure to do every little thing "right" with our children (or "pay the consequences"), our parents and grandparents didn't have to function under this kind of threat. In great part because of Freud, today's parents live in a society that pays a lot of attention to the psychological aspects of our lives, with emphasis on the impressionable early years.

Many people can carry this intense focus too far, reading stacks of books on child development that rob the parents of their own common sense. In addition, some pediatricians have a condescending attitude toward nervous mothers who have lists of worries—which may only make them feel more inadequate. Children are constantly changing and growing. Perhaps the wisest experts are the ones who say that all a parent can do is create an environment in which change can occur.

Obviously I'm not referring to child abuse or other severe child-rearing problems. However, there are modern child-care theories floating around that can be frightening if misinterpreted. New parents want to do what's best for their child and are easily influenced by opinions they hear or read. For instance, some parents believe that if they don't literally respond **instantly** to a baby's cries, the child will never trust anyone or be able to form meaningful relationships later in life. Common sense gets lost in the desperate desire not to make a mistake.

***Don't become a victim of media pressure.*** No one can deny the importance of a child's early experiences and interactions, but that doesn't mean you have to jump on the bandwagon for every new theory that comes down the pike. Let's be real, as they say! Have we been so thoroughly manipulated by the media that glorifies these "authorities" that we have lost confidence in ourselves? Child development experts mean well, of course, but often they don't seem to acknowledge that parents are intelligent, compassionate people.

***New parents are not inept or stupid.*** What is it that makes so many parents perceive themselves as incompetent? I think it may be our lack of practical knowledge about baby care: most of us are cut off from the support of an extended family. I'm here to remind you that you and your mate are smart, caring people whose opinions about their children are as good as *if not better than* any expert's. The experiences you've had and the instincts you've developed are valuable assets for you as parents. Sure, raising children is a big responsibility. But trust yourselves. Don't give in to the social pressures that can make you fearful; don't underestimate your ability to cope. Turn to each other for answers and reassurance. Raising children is not a competitive sport.

***We are susceptible to trendy theories.*** Today's parents seem to extend exaggerated importance to books and classes like "How to Make Your Baby More Intelligent" . . . "How to Teach Your Child Morals and Ethics" . . . "How to Raise an Emotionally Balanced Child" . . . "How to Dress a Baby for Success" . . . , etc.

Does any sane person *really* think it's desirable or important for an 18-month-old baby to swim underwater? For a two-year-old to recognize flashcards? Or a three-year-old to play the violin? Have you heard about parents who are so intent on their toddler learning to read that they stick labels on everything in the house? The father comes home and the mother slaps a sign on his back that says "Daddy." Have you been to homes where they have those deadly serious collections of educational toys? Toys for motor development, toys for cognitive development. Whatever in heaven's name happened to **childhood** in the fever to create "super babies"?

# 4

# The father's needs and problems

Although this book is intended for couples, sometimes it may seem as though I'm speaking more to the new mother. I really don't intend to shortchange the new father, and this chapter is proof of that. When a baby joins a marriage, there are various issues that particularly affect the man. This chapter is an attempt to address the problems and changes that you have to cope with when you become a father.

## THE DIFFERENCES BETWEEN MEN AND WOMEN

There are basic traditional differences in how men and women are socialized that can affect the way they react to parenting. The differences between the way that you and your wife were raised give you a different outlook on yourself and other people. These differences may really come into focus when a child enters your lives.

The categories that follow are not meant to be all-inclusive or any kind of gospel truth. They certainly are not meant to perpetuate myths or prejudices about the sexes. These are just some broad generalizations that may help you see how the differences between the sexes can affect them as partners when they become parents.

## SOME THINGS THAT GIRLS ARE TAUGHT

*Girls are taught to be "nice."* Girls are usually trained not to express negative feelings, which is what people may mean when they say "be a nice girl." Boys are usually encouraged to be argumentative and challenge things.

*Girls are taught to always be there for people.* A woman is expected to be thinking of her husband and children all the time and always be available to them. She is expected to be on call, physically and psychologically (with support, advice, encouragement), all the time.

*Girls are trained to be social secretaries.* A woman is supposed to remember birthdays, buy presents, send flowers, write thank-you notes, and make social engagements.

*A girl is taught to take care of others before herself.* Girls are often raised to believe that they shouldn't ask for anything for themselves. If a girl needs something, she is trained to preface any request with self-effacing disclaimers like "If it's not too much trouble . . ." or, "Would you mind . . ." or, "When you have a minute . . ." A boy is taught to ask for what he needs, and usually expects to be waited on.

*A girl is encouraged to want and need intimacy in a relationship.* Men ordinarily desire only isolated moments of intimacy: they usually want that feeling only during courtship. Because most women have been socialized to want intimacy continuously, this can create a profound and perhaps insoluble problem at the foundation of your relationship.

*A girl is taught to be aware of nonverbal clues.* Men are not as sensitized as women are to facial expressions, body language, subtle comments, and other clues about feelings.

*Girls learn emotional self-expression.* Girls are taught to be open with their emotions; they learn to share personal information. Girls can also learn manipulative, circuitous ways of interacting. Boys are usually taught to be straightforward, to stand up to opposition, and to keep things to themselves.

## SOME THINGS BOYS ARE TAUGHT

***Men are generally less nurturing.*** Men are not as spontaneously giving or caring for others, although it's not known whether this is because of biological or learned reasons. It may be that men are not comfortable with dependency or with strong emotions. This would explain why a man may withdraw when his wife or child needs him.

***Boys are encouraged to be aggressive.*** Boys are taught to be comfortable with feelings of anger (which can be threatening to a woman). Boys are trained to show anger, to be territorial and combative. Although this is true, men also have trouble with anger and try to repress it, while women are generally more expressive of emotions.

***A man often has a need for power and control.*** This need, which is often instilled from boyhood, can cause problems after a baby is born. There can be a problem if you think (or you think your partner feels) that you are suddenly the less powerful one in the relationship. If you feel diminished as a father, then sharing tasks with your spouse can be a difficult concept for you, as can the feeling that the woman is in control of the household now that you have a child. You may not feel good about yourself if you have to accept a subjugated or equal position with your wife. If the change is gradual it will probably be easier for you to adjust.

***A man's self-esteem is often career-related.*** Your sense of yourself may be linked to your work: you may feel inadequate or incompetent as a man if your career isn't going as well as you'd like. Although it is common for wives to view a man's preoccupation with work as a rejection of them, it is usually untrue.

***Boys tend to be less expressive verbally.*** It can be harder for a man to put his feelings into words and share them. Often at the beginning of a relationship a man will be more verbally expressive, but for many men this is not natural behavior so they regress after the courtship. A problem can arise: a woman may think she's been duped or she may feel less loved afterwards. She may see the withdrawal of emotional expressiveness as an indication that you love her less, when in truth you may simply be returning to who you were before the courtship.

***A man can be more dependent on his marriage.*** Because men usually have fewer deep relationships or sources of emotional support, they may depend more on the marital relationship to feed their needs. However, it can be hard for men to talk about feeling vulnerable or hurt or lonely: they often get angry instead. You may get angry if you feel your wife has abandoned you emotionally after you have a baby. You may get angry just because you have threatening feelings that you can't fully understand. You will probably also be angry about having these dependent feelings and direct this anger at your wife, who is the "cause" of these feelings.

You may be shocked to find yourself striking out at your wife over what you've (unconsciously) perceived as her abandonment of you. If you get home and your wife isn't there, or she goes out and perhaps leaves you with the baby, you may find yourself saying, "Where the — have you been all day?" when she gets home. If you and your partner can appreciate the anxious feelings behind your anger, you'll understand that what you meant was "I missed you."

## YOUR IDENTITY AS A FATHER

***Your relationship with your own father affects your perception of yourself as a father.*** Pregnancy and birth may reactivate feelings about your own father and childhood. If you have angry, aggressive feelings toward your father, you may direct them at your child. This can happen even before she is born, if you're not aware of the possibility.

You may believe (perhaps unconsciously) that your

child will have the same feelings for you that you had for your father. If you have warm memories and love for your father, you'll anticipate a positive rapport with your own child. If you disliked your father (for any reason, including that he left the family or the way he treated you, your mother, or your siblings), you may unconsciously believe your child will hate you, too.

*If you never had a father, it can be more difficult for you to learn "how to father."* You may not have had a role model if you were orphaned in some sense: your father died or left your mother when you were small, or he was emotionally absent. Even without realizing it, you may have modelled yourself after an uncle, brother, family friend, or even your mother; you may be worried about your own ability to be a father. You may also have developed fantasies of what a perfect father should be, and expect yourself to become that idealized father. This is an enormous pressure on you as a new Dad.

*If your father is dead, it can complicate your emerging identity as a father.* First you'll probably feel sad that he can't see your baby and share your pride and pleasure. The flip side of that emotion is that you may feel resentful and angry that he's not here! If your father is dead, it may be much harder for you to develop a father image different from your father. It is common to idealize everything your Dad did once he is gone, and to feel disloyal for any critical thoughts you may have about his fathering. An awareness of this may free you from that constraint.

*Doubts about your image as a father are quite normal.* In particular, new parents (fathers especially) worry whether they'll be able to discipline their baby when he grows up. Many people are afraid of spoiling their child. If you have confusing or painful memories of being disciplined harshly or ineffectively, it can worry you even more.

You'll probably have different concerns depending on the gender of your child. If the baby is a boy, you may worry whether you will serve as a good role model and teach him the sorts of things a boy needs to know. Alternately, you may fear having a son because it will force you to re-experience some of the unpleasantness of your child-hood, although this is usually unconscious. This can be one of the reasons that a man would prefer to have a daughter. If the baby is a girl, you may worry about spoiling her, or fear that she and her mother will be two against one, and will have a special female bond that excludes you.

***You'll develop your own personal style of fathering.*** In order to come into your own as a father, you have to take the time to identify those elements of your past that may be constricting you. You have to make a separation between your present behavior and hopes you have for the future and any emotional injuries, loyalties, and regrets from the past.

## DIFFERENT KINDS OF FATHERING ROLES

***Do you want to be a father as your father was?*** Think back to your childhood and compare yourself to your father: try to imagine what his experience of fatherhood was. This can make you feel closer to him. You may also be more able as an adult to understand his absences or for-give things he may have done.

Men often declare that they want to be different from their fathers, that they particularly want to spend more time with their kids than their fathers did with them. Although you may *want* things to be different, it's quite easy to fall into your father's style of fathering. If you manage to be different from your father, more nurturant, for example, or less strict, there is an emotional price to pay. If you choose to be a different kind of father, that signifies a certain kind of disloyalty to your father or criticism of him. Being more nurturing can also make you wonder whether you are being feminine or are infringing on the mother's role.

***Society's definition of "father" is limited.*** From the time you were a boy you probably accepted society's de-scription of a father as a provider and disciplinarian. The common social attitude is that a man doesn't know how to take care of a child. You've probably heard critical com-ments (even without being aware of it) about the way a man takes care of a child.

Your workplace is probably inflexible about making time for your fathering. Teachers, pediatricians, and other professionals almost always assume that the mother is the primary parent and treat the father as inferior or deficient. Unless you are alert to the possibility that these negative social attitudes might influence you, they can undermine your desire to share care of your baby with your wife.

**What kind of father can you be?** In order to decide the kind of father you want to be, it might be interesting to know what some experts consider as the traditional fathering roles. These are either the "Authoritarian" or the "Breadwinner." The role model you got from your father is probably one (or both) of these. The newer male role of "Caretaker" goes against tradition: if you want to have this kind of involved relationship with your child, it may take determination to go against the grain.

**The Authoritarian father sees himself as a teacher or a disciplinarian.** You may adopt this familiar role with your child but it will probably isolate you from her. An infant cannot interact with you on this level. If you see yourself as a father who teaches morals and information, who is going to socialize and civilize his child, it means you'll have to wait for the baby to grow up before you can communicate with her. A newborn can learn things, of course, but until she's a toddler she cannot understand concepts you may want to teach her, like "right and wrong," "truth" or "lies." That doesn't give you much to do as a father for the first couple of years!

**Being a disciplinarian is an essential aspect of being an Authoritarian father.** By taking this view of fathering, you allow yourself only minimal involvement with the baby. Many men think of a father traditionally as being the parent who dispenses rules and discipline. But there is no place for being strict with an infant, who has barely formed a sense of herself as separate from the world around her. Of course children need discipline, but it's not relevant with an infant. If you withdraw and wait until the child is old enough to interact with you as a teacher/disciplinarian, you are, in a certain sense, waiting until then to become her father.

*WARNING: You had better stop and think about what's going on if you find yourself disciplining a baby. This is unhealthy for your family and can be dangerous for the child—it can become child abuse. You should talk to a professional or someone else who is objective about this.*

*The Breadwinner is another traditional role of the father.* Being the "provider" is still considered a major function of fathering, even though many women now share in a family's income. A new father can be so preoccupied about money that he can wind up resenting this responsibility. If you perceive this as your fathering role, you may worry frequently about your death and what would happen to your wife and child if you died. Meanwhile, you probably aren't getting any more pleasure from your baby than the Authoritarian father does.

*Being a Caretaker means being a pioneer.* The Caretaker or nurturant role is a way to explore new possibilities for yourself as a father. However, adopting a nontraditional fathering role may be more difficult than it sounds. The man's role used to be clearly defined: everyone knew what was expected of a father. With today's changing attitudes about shared responsibility between parents, there can be conflict and confusion about a man's role in his child's life.

*The traditional roles may be more comfortable.* You (and/or your wife) may feel more at ease following in the footsteps of your parents. If your father was a rigidly traditional father but you'd like to explore the possibility of being nurturant, this can create confusion for you. Your adult ideas about fathering are in conflict with the powerful role model your father provided as you grew up. In order to create new patterns and relationships for yourself and your children you'll need to really make an effort. A man has to be committed, remain aware of the influence of his childhood, and have his wife's support.

***You may have to change your self-image if you want to be a "Caretaker."*** If you do choose to be a nurturant father instead of a traditional one, don't be too tough on yourself about performance. A woman faces the same challenge as you do in learning to care for an infant. Child-care skills are not instinctive for men *or* women; infant care isn't something that women do better by nature. Don't worry about feeling like a clumsy oaf—everybody finds babies squirmy and slippery at first! Your wife may be as unfamiliar as you are with the daily tasks of caring for a baby. She may even hope that *you'll* help her figure it out.

It isn't difficult for a father to learn the skills of infant care: just like a mother, after a bit of bumbling it becomes easy. Even if you've never held a baby you'll be fine with your own child. It is only your fear of inadequacy, or the fear of making a fool of yourself, that can create a distance between you and your baby.

***A man's discomfort with his baby may be the result of his own childhood.*** The difference between men and women and the ease with which they adjust to child care often has to do with childhood experiences in caring for "other things" (younger children, pets, or dolls). If you were like most boys, you probably didn't have any, or many, nurturing experiences. Although things may be changing, boys have traditionally grown up without the valuable opportunity to practice child care directly since baby-sitting is usually not offered to them. A strong interest in younger children is considered acceptable for girls, not boys. Even a warm, loving relationship with a doll is usually forbidden. Your parents may have feared that playing with dolls would lead to homosexuality.

***Certain attributes can make you more suited to being a caretaking parent.*** There are certain aspects of a boy's childhood that can make it easier for him to adopt a nurturant self-image as a father. Obviously if your father was a love-giving, nurturant Dad, the style will come more easily to you. You got valuable practice if you were close to pets and looked after them, or if you took care of younger siblings or other relatives. You might feel more secure about child care if you did baby-sitting; even if you don't remember the actual skills, you gained confidence from those experiences.

## THE EARLY POSTPARTUM ADJUSTMENT

*Certain factors can ease your postpartum adjustment.* Couples who are able to discuss the issue of shared responsibility before the baby is born often have less stress in making the actual adjustment. One study of the adjustment period showed that men had an easier transition to fatherhood if the baby was in good health, there was support from the families, and supportiveness from fellow workers.

*Your attitude toward pregnancy affects your postpartum adjustment.* Studies show that nearly half of all men are affected by the "pregnant husband syndrome," in which they experience emotional or physical reactions to their wife's pregnancies. This kind of identification with the pregnancy process may be an indication of how much a man will throw himself into fathering. Experts say that a man who is involved in the pregnancy is likely to be an involved father, and that a man who was helpful during the pregnancy is likely to do the same postpartum.

*You may feel inadequate as a father.* If you are confused over your new life role and what it entails, you may feel unqualified as a father. Your sense of inadequacy can make you feel angry or bitter toward your spouse, who may have needs you feel you can't meet right now.

*A father needs a supportive environment.* You may feel inept at fathering in the beginning: it can make a big difference if there is an attitude of encouragement around you. Unfortunately, women around you may automatically criticize and put down your awkward first attempts at baby care (this may include your wife, mother, mother-in-law, and any baby nurse you have). If there are too many people around in the beginning it doesn't give you any time alone with the baby to find your way.

***The new mother gets all the attention.*** Once your baby is born, it seems as though public interest is on the new couple: the mother and baby. All the questions are about how the baby is, how the mother is feeling; no one asks you how you're doing. You may begin to feel, "Where do I fit in?"

***You may be confused or uncertain about being a father.*** The 1980s are a difficult time for men having babies. The vast majority of you have no role model from your own fathers for being active in child care. As you pave a new path for yourself and learn the required skills for infant care, try to go easy on yourself.

***Ambivalence toward parenting can drive you away.*** A child can highlight feelings that you may not have dealt with before. You may stay away from the house, take on extra work, or throw yourself into a sport to avoid dealing with your uncomfortable feelings. It is common for a new father who's feeling ambivalent to become a workaholic; you may say that you're doing this to earn more money, but it may be an escape hatch. This can lead to problems in your relationship because your wife may feel abandoned at this early stage, when she most needs your emotional and physical support.

## COMPLICATED FEELINGS
## TOWARD YOUR WIFE

***The mother-child closeness can be threatening.*** During the immediate postpartum period, your wife's main aim is to nurture the baby. A mother is usually the one most responsible for the baby, so she bonds more closely with him. You may feel left out, as though you are an unimportant part of this new triangle. Being an outsider may be a new and painful experience for you, especially if you and your wife were very close before the baby was born.

***Your wife may feel threatened if you are close to the baby.*** A woman may need her husband more than the baby needs his father in the early weeks. Some men are so intent on bonding with their baby that they don't realize that the well-being of the family depends on the bond between man and woman.

*Fears for your wife's welfare are also normal.* You may start worrying about what will happen should she die and leave you alone with the baby. But while your wife has the same anxieties and insecurities, *she* is socially "allowed" to express those feelings. A man in our society is not encouraged to talk about such feelings. What is it we're worried about? Are we afraid that if a man shows weakness his wife will be devastated to know he is just a human being . . . like herself?

*A mothering wife can influence your new identity as a father.* Many women mother men to some extent, but if this nurturing is at the core of your relationship the newborn is really going to upset things. If you're in a marriage with a very mothering wife, it may be because you had insufficient love as a child, or ambivalent loving, or had trouble making a separation from your mother.

If your wife is a particularly mothering woman, then the nurturing you got before the baby's birth probably met both your needs. Mothering women often want a little boy to look after. But this means that the balance in your relationship is disturbed when your wife gets a real child of her own.

*You may feel dependent on your wife.* Accept your own babylike qualities and needs. Wanting to be cared for does not make you less of an adult, less good a parent, less of a father figure, or less of a man. If you are intolerant of this normal (although perhaps unconscious) part of yourself, it can make you much less accepting of the baby's constant demands. This is true for the baby's mother, too. It is quite natural for both parents to identify with the child. Becoming a parent reawakens your desire for dependency and having your needs met; don't fight the feeling or judge yourself harshly for it.

*Envy of your wife can complicate the development of your identity as a father.* Some men wish they could be pregnant: carry a child, give birth, breast-feed, and generally nurture the baby as a mother does. This envy is normal—you may have dreams about being a mother. You may also become unusually creative as a way of expressing your desire to create something: art, carpentry, gardening, even raising dogs or cats are natural expressions of that drive.

Competitiveness with your wife, as opposed to sharing, is one way that you may express envy. Do you boast about your own skills with the baby and belittle your wife's abilities? This is obviously an unhealthy pattern that you need to look at. Another motive for this kind of competitiveness can be that your wife is having trouble adjusting to parenthood and you are overcompensating by turning it into a contest.

**You may have a problem with your wife's body postpartum.**   You may feel turned off by your wife's figure postpartum. After the baby is born she probably won't be able to fit into her regular wardrobe for a while so she'll probably be wearing those same old maternity clothes over and over. You may have expected or hoped that her body would return to normal right away. It can be a disappointment or a turn-off if your wife is still carrying the extra weight from her pregnancy.

However, part of your problem with her not looking young, slender, and sexy can be your own resistance to parenthood. You may see your wife's figure postpartum and feel like you've given up the pleasures of your happy-go-lucky youth, that life is no longer as it used to be, just the two of you. And you're right about that! Parenthood is a transition to another lifestyle and new images for both of you. As you get more comfortable in the role of father, and as the baby fits into your life, you'll probably be able to accept your wife (at whatever weight) more easily. At the same time, after she has adjusted to motherhood she'll probably be able to focus on her appearance and lose weight.

## COMPETITION WITH YOUR PARTNER

**Your wife may resist your attempts to be an involved father.**   You might have thought your spouse would be thrilled by your desire to be nurturant with the baby. You may be shocked to find she is resistant; this is an added burden while you're coping with the difficulties about feeling comfortable in your new role. Whatever you do, **don't give up!** Try to understand what is motivating your mate's negative attitude and then insist on being your own kind of father.

*Why would a mother be prejudiced against a father's involvement with his own baby?*  There are various common reasons for a woman's negative attitude. Some women don't know how to deal with a hands-on father. For instance, your wife's father may have been aloof and she may never have seen any other father sharing in infant care. She may not feel comfortable with this new kind of man. There are some women whose identity or self-worth may depend on feeling they are the most important person in their child's life.

*Your wife may want to be the primary parent.*  If you are a father who wants to take care of his baby, your wife may view you as competition for the role of primary parent. If you want to have a lot of involvement in child care, you may get resistance from your spouse. You need to discuss this issue so that you don't become adversaries. You don't want to get into a competition with your wife over who has the role of the primary parent. A new father needs encouragement, not criticism, for the new skills he has to learn if he's going to be actively caring for his child.

*Your spouse may be insecure in the role of parent.*
She may have such low self-esteem that she's afraid that if you do well with the child that means she is inadequate. She may feel if you turn out to be right about a decision, then that automatically makes her wrong. Her doubts about herself as a mother and the pressure she feels she's under to perform may drive her to claim ''her'' baby. Although your wife's attitude is probably unconscious, it's important not to let it rob you of the joys of parenting or push you into the position of being an outsider.

REASONS FOR MATERNAL RESISTANCE TO PATERNAL HELP

- She thinks that a father should only be a Breadwinner/Authoritarian figure
- She believes baby care is a woman's responsibility, that it's not "a man's place"
- She thinks men are clumsy to the point of ineptitude with babies
- She has a neurotic need to have the baby to herself
- She is reacting to the intense competitiveness that already exists in your relationship (and the baby gives her an edge)

*You need to establish that each of you has a separate relationship with the baby.* You can tell your spouse this or depend on your actions to make it clear that you intend to be an active participant in this baby's upbringing. If you can, try to show confidence in your own style of parenting (even if you don't feel it!).

If your wife has the need to constantly correct you and be "right" about baby care, try to ignore her without stirring up more friction. Relate to the baby exactly as you choose: stick to your guns and she'll get the message. If your wife comes to understand that you won't give in to her attempts to control or undermine your way of fathering, she will undoubtedly back off.

*Neither of you is an expert at baby care.* Try to approach new parenthood as a team effort, something fun you can learn together. Do not make the common mistake of letting child care become a competition over who does what task better. Your wife may have more experience or more confidence than you do; she may turn out to be a patient, enthusiastic teacher or a short-tempered taskmaster. You may have trouble asking for her help for fear that she is going to be unpleasant.

*Your wife may push you out without realizing she's doing it.* She may be more experienced or efficient with baby care so you step aside or she may shoo you aside and take over because it's faster and easier. Even if she believes that a man has no place in infant care, it comes down to the same thing: you are excluded from the center of activity, your baby's care.

***Don't give up on fathering because of your wife's attitude.*** You and your baby will lose out on developing a relationship and your marriage will also be diminished if you can't be the father you want to be. If your wife tries to take control of "her" baby, try to recognize that she doesn't know what she's doing. Her position is not a conscious choice but is most likely a result of her own childhood and the fathering role models she saw around her.

***Take the risk of telling your wife your feelings.*** If your mate puts you down, or treats you in a condescending way about your skills or interest in the baby, you have to take control of the situation. You've got to talk to her, make her see how unfair she is being. She has to realize that her obnoxious style will drive you away. She'll lose your involvement with the baby, as well as creating bad feelings between you. Let your wife know what is bothering you. It may help to remind her (and yourself) that you are not adversaries: you both want to be comfortable as parents and partners.

It's important to talk, but also to listen. Just because you brought up the issue doesn't mean you have the floor. Neither one of you should dominate the discussion, but you may want to make a ground rule that you can't interrupt each other until you've finished a thought. And don't use a conversation as a forum for criticism; look for compromise and solutions. (There is more on the topic of constructive discussion in *Chapter 10: Bad Feelings.*)

***Other women may interfere with your fathering.*** It may not be your mate who pushes you away from the crib; grandmothers and baby nurses are guilty of this, too. They don't realize (as you may not) how much your early involvement matters to your developing sense of yourself as a father. You may feel like they're squeezing you out even though you want to be a participant. A new father has to take a stand if he doesn't want to be bullied, bossed, shooed, patronized, or made to feel like a fool.

# COMPLICATED FEELINGS ABOUT THE BABY

***It's common to feel rivalry with the baby.***   You may feel that your position in your home and marriage has been usurped by the infant. You may be aware of your anger or you may have hidden rage that your baby has cheated you out of your wife's love and affection. This anger can make you withdraw sexually and emotionally from your spouse at a time when you most want to be close to her.

***Jealousy can come from an attachment to your own mother.***   When you were a child you eventually had to relinquish your close attachment to your mother. This comes for most boys when they accept their father's primary attachment to their mother (commonly known as the Oedipus complex).

   Marriage establishes a total and exclusive relationship between a man and a woman. The marital bond can be similar to the attachment that a boy had to his mother—that relationship is destroyed once again by the new baby, who disrupts your closeness to your wife. This can stir up jealousy and anger from the past, Oedipal feelings you probably didn't know you had.

***You may feel ambivalent toward your son.***   Although most fathers want a boy child, you may be surprised to feel distant toward your son and awkward handling him. You may feel especially uncomfortable touching your son's genitals. You may have difficulty watching your son breastfeeding. These feelings of irritation and resentment will probably pass. Every father sees a potential rival in his son: he will become a man as your physical and sexual prowess will be waning. But even though you may have uncomfortable feelings watching your son nurse, you'll probably also feel proud and wish for his success. There is nothing black and white about becoming a father; accept the feelings you have.

***Resentment of the baby can be a sign of a good marriage!***   If you have made an effort to keep romance and sexiness alive in your marriage, it can be especially hard not to feel resentful about the baby's intrusion. You may be used to having special intimate times together with your wife, dressing up and going out for a romantic dinner or just a walk in the moonlight. All of a sudden motherhood may have so absorbed and exhausted your sweetheart that she's collapsed in bed at 8:30!

*A fear of not being close to the baby is quite common for new fathers.* It is the same problem that a woman experiences when she doesn't have the intense feelings for the infant that she anticipated or thought she was "supposed" to have. You may be full of self-doubt: are you an unfeeling, unnatural man?

Parenting is a unique experience for each person. Some prefer infants, others toddlers, yet others school-age children. Some parents find infant care boring, burdensome, and a restriction on their adult life. This doesn't make you a bad father; you will grow to love your baby and find your own way of relating to her.

*There are external factors that can interfere with your enjoyment of the baby.* Certain conflicts can prevent you from feeling close to her. Financial problems and cramped living quarters can be a burden. Also, conflict with unsupportive parents or in-laws who don't agree with choices you've made about raising your child can undermine your parental desire for closeness with the baby.

*Some men have trouble relating to an infant.* You may prefer older kids with whom you can communicate. Fathers are often slower to get interested in the baby than are mothers. It often happens that a man really gets involved as his child matures and starts to be someone with whom he can interact.

Mothers seem to be able to make a relationship sooner with less feedback from the baby. This unequal development between a father and mother can lead to jealousy, resentment, or even fights between you. You may say to your wife, "You're spending too much time with the baby," while she says to you, "You're not giving the baby enough time."

It may be difficult for you to find ways to interact with your infant, especially if you are a verbally oriented person. New fathers sometimes feel guilty about not connecting with their baby: don't be hard on yourself. You might find things you can do with the baby that can be enjoyable, like bathing him or taking him for a walk, but don't rush yourself. Let your wife read this section if she is pressuring you to do too much, too soon. Reassure her that fathers do "catch up" eventually if you give them time and don't make demands on them!

***You may think that nurturing isn't masculine.*** You may feel awkward with your baby, unable to meet her needs or soothe her when she's upset. This discomfort may come from your deep inner conviction that warm, nurturant feelings are "feminine." The role of being an involved father may just not feel right to you, which makes it hard to relax and enjoy your baby. It may be helpful to recognize that some of your feelings about masculinity and fathering probably come from society's traditional definitions. It may just be a question of "daring to be different."

## YOUR INNER EMOTIONS
## ABOUT FATHERHOOD

***You may feel alone and pressured.*** Unfortunately it isn't uncommon for a new father to feel isolated. You feel responsible for the welfare of your wife and the baby, along with the increased pressure for financial success. At the same time you have personal needs—to be cared for, catered to, appreciated, made love to—which are often ignored in the early months.

***Talk about the pressures you're feeling.*** The pressures a man can feel when he becomes a father are significant. You have to talk about these emotions in order for your wife to understand what you're going through and give you the support and comfort you need. You'll need to find ways to express your feelings that will encourage your partner's sympathies rather than accusatory comments that may put her on the defensive. For instance, it's fine to say, "I'm anxious about having to support both of you now." However, it might be helpful to add, "But these are just my fears, it's no reflection on you."

*You may be caught between contradictory feelings.*
You might feel sadness and a sense of loss for the qualities you had in your marital relationship before the baby, but you can't express those feelings because a man is "supposed" to be strong, confident, and brave.

*You may feel guilty about your negative feelings.*
Many new fathers feel guilty about not doing more, and then they feel guilty for not **wanting** to do more! Guilt is a destructive emotion that you may be able to eliminate if you understand that your feelings are normal.

*You have the same emotions as your wife but nowhere to go with them.* A new father can experience the same bombardment of feelings as his spouse—guilt, stress, fatigue, failure—but it's hard to find somewhere to unload those emotions. Your wife has friends, her mother, or a parent group to listen to her, but most new fathers don't have an outlet for their anxieties. It's hard for you to turn to your partner with your feelings because she's going through similar stresses: it can be hard for her to give you support and sympathy.

*You may feel like your life is out of control.* It isn't unusual for a new father to have feelings of danger, that he is losing himself. You may get the feeling that your best years are behind you, which can be a big blow to your ego. You might feel unimportant, that no one cares about you any more, that you aren't in control of your life. If you were involved and supportive during the pregnancy and birth, the postpartum period can be an even greater letdown. Your feelings are normal and real, but don't try to pin them onto anyone else. Your wife is not to blame since she is not the cause of your disequilibrium.

*The strong emotions of fatherhood may freak you out.* Some men try to retreat from strong emotions. Parenthood is partly a test of how much you and your partner can trust and depend on each other. Rather than trying to pull away and isolate yourself from that emotional intensity, take a leap of faith (yes, another one!) and test it out.

***You may be embarrassed by your new emotionality.***
You may have intense feelings for the baby, plus some ambivalence as you see your wife's tenderness going to the
little intruder. If you feel shut out of the relationship between your wife and the baby, you may feel like the ultimate outsider: the baby grew inside her, she gave birth to
him, and now he's hers. In addition, you may feel inept in
your first attempts to take care of the baby: this might be
the first time in your marriage that you feel you can't perform adequately.

All these intense emotions can overwhelm you. Try
to roll with the punches, knowing that things will settle
down. Some men, instead of accepting their emotionality
as normal and temporary, may "act out." Some signs of
acting out might be if you have an affair (or think about it
seriously) or suddenly become accident-prone.

***Your need for affection may not be met now.*** It may
shock you or make you angry that you need nurturing but
your wife is equally needy right now. Both of you may be
uncomfortable with your own (or your spouse's) needy
feelings. You may feel embarrassed by your need for encouragement and appreciation now that you're a father—
especially because those feelings can make you feel like a
child again.

If you have any way to get stroking and attention
outside of your marriage, you might try to get those needs
met or subdued during the transition to parenthood. Short
of having an affair, you should find people and activities
that really feed you, that reinforce a good feeling about
yourself.

***You may feel dependent and want to be taken care
of.*** Although you may feel foolish for having these desires, they are a normal reaction to having a baby. New
mothers often have the same feeling. Experts describe the
psychology of this dependency as being "the child" inside
the man who wants the new mother (his wife) to take care
of him.

You may be aware of your wife's lack of time for
you and allow yourself to think that she doesn't care about
you. This can make you feel a rivalry with your baby. Al-

though you love your child and want to take care of her, at the same time you identify with the infant and are jealous of the attention she gets.

Your childishness may irritate your wife, who doesn't understand your neediness and wants you to be strong and supportive of her. She doesn't want another dependent, demanding infant in the house. You'll have to help your wife realize that you have increased emotional needs now—needs that you realize she may not be able to meet. If both of you can accept this as a normal phase it will be less worrisome and annoying.

***You may feel you have lost your power base.*** A baby creates chaos in the established power balance in your marriage. All relationships have a power balance, and in most cases the man is dominant. The mother usually adopts a more dominant role once a baby is born: she expects attention and appreciation from you that she probably didn't before. There's a good chance that you are going to feel threatened, betrayed, ignored, or angry, and there's an even better chance that you'll want the balance in your relationship back where it was before.

Do not blame your baby for the feelings you're experiencing; the baby doesn't deserve your resentment. In addition, once resentments are misdirected they can pollute the father/child relationship for life. You may hate the new power balance in your relationship so much that you throw a fit about it—and you may be entitled to a temper tantrum! Fatherhood means giving up more than you ever imagined. Try to reach acceptance, and even enjoyment, of your wife with her new strength and role. It can be a rocky road but it's worth the journey.

***PPD (postpartum depression) can affect men.*** For a thorough examination of this subject, see *Chapter* 7.

## CAREER VS. FATHERHOOD

***You may feel you're between a rock and a hard place between fathering and career.*** A new father often has to deal with the Superman Syndrome: you're supposed to spend time with your child, be sensitive to your wife, share in household maintenance, and still live up to an ideal of being a successful man in the work world.

***Guilt may enter the picture again.***   You may feel guilty about not spending more time with the baby, but if you devote yourself to fathering it can make you anxious about your job. There isn't much support for a man caught in this conflict: your boss may question your dedication if you put your family first, and vice versa with your wife. The media promotes the image of a "modern" father who's somehow supposed to provide for his children while making them a priority. If you find it hard to juggle work and family, you may think you are deficient: you may feel you've failed personally, or that your dedication to your family is abnormal. Try to step back and see that the bind you're in would be impossible for any man.

***The demands of your job may put you in conflict.***
Fatherhood doesn't eliminate job responsibility and demands—for many men, it increases them. However, the problem of performance on the job can make you feel conflicted about what you should be doing at home. If that is the case, discuss your conflicted feelings with your partner and then both of you can try to accept the situation. It is counterproductive to allow yourself to worry, feel guilty or frustrated.

***Earning a living doesn't mean you aren't being a father.***   Keep in mind that providing money **is** fathering. The current interest in men taking paternity leaves or assuming 50 percent responsibility for child care may sound intriguing but it's usually unrealistic. There is no way that the average man can be a full-time parent—nor should he expect to be.

It's unrealistic to think about making that kind of commitment to your child unless you can afford to give up a year of work. What's more, why should you? Being a provider is an essential part of being a parent. Creating a comfortable home is the foundation of a relaxed, nurturing environment in which a child can grow.

***You may worry about feeling exhausted all the time.*** A new father usually doesn't get a paternity leave; you usually don't even have the choice of taking a leave of absence from work. This may mean that you'll get very little sleep for the first weeks (months?) but still be expected to function as usual at your job. You may worry—and rightly so—that fatigue will hamper your job performance. This can be especially true for professions like trial lawyers, surgeons, or machine operators where other people's lives depend on your alertness and concentration.

One solution to this is to try to relieve some of the pressures you have at work. Talk about the problem with your boss and co-workers: you'll never get any relief if you keep it to yourself. You might be able to find a temporary solution, like a co-worker who can take on some of your responsibilities for a month.

***Fatherhood may give you a greater drive for success.*** Before you had a child you might have thought there was a lot of time ahead of you in which to achieve success. Once you have a baby, your perspective may change. You may find that being successful, especially in financial terms, can become very important. Whereas you once saw infinite possibilities ahead of you, becoming a father can give you more focus so that you zero in on a goal or increase your pace.

## TRYING TO ESCAPE FROM FATHERHOOD

***Nothing is ever enough.*** You may feel that everyone wants a piece of you and none of them is satisfied with what they get. Your wife, your baby, and your boss all have needs and don't seem to acknowledge the other demands on your time and energy. There are times when you may just want to shout "Leave me alone!" to all of them. This reaction is normal and human. Try to find a way to indulge your need for some peaceful time to yourself, even if it's only for 15 minutes at a time.

***You may feel panicky and trapped at home.*** Both new parents can feel suffocated by the demands of their new roles. Both you and your wife need to find ways to meet your own personal needs, whether at home or outside. You're not going to be content if you feel that parenting ties you down. Don't lose sight of the fact that your life is in your own hands. You have control over how you arrange it. Experiment with new ways to organize your life so that your needs are met and you can achieve the goals you set for yourself.

*"Workaholism" can be a form of escape.* For some men it's easier to throw themselves into their work rather than coping with the new demands and strains of fatherhood. This can rob your relationship of time and intimacy as much as if you'd had an affair—maybe more. Unless you and your wife recognize possible reasons for your workaholism, it can create angry, defensive feelings between you.

*Throwing yourself into a sport or hobby is another escape hatch.* Some men turn to extracurricular activities as a way to avoid facing the new demands of parenthood. Running, racquetball, working out in a gym, or taking up a new hobby with a vengeance can be ways to put off going home. Look at your reasons for the time you're spending at these outside activities, most particularly if they are new interests since the pregnancy or baby's birth. You may be throwing yourself into these endeavors because they are less overwhelming and threatening than your new paternal role.

*Your "rebellion against fatherhood" may not happen right away.* Some fathers don't have a negative reaction to their new role until the baby is six to nine months old, at which time a man may rebel against the demands and constrictions of fatherhood. This often happens in young or recently married couples, but it exists to some degree for all men, no matter how healthy or mature their relationships may be.

The impulse is usually a desire to escape responsibilities and return to the feeling of bachelorhood. Of course just because you have the impulse you don't have to act on it! Understanding what motivates your feelings can often bring them down to a manageable size.

*Your wife's reaction makes a big difference.* If you are having conflicted feelings about fatherhood, the effect on your relationship will differ depending on whether your partner's reaction is angry/hurt/offensive or sympathetic and easygoing. It will help your mate if you can let her know that your "rebellion" against fatherhood isn't directed at her but at the whole picture of your new life.

Your wife's degree of involvement with the baby and motherhood can also affect your feelings. If your wife is obsessed by the baby's health and progress, if her self-image has become that of the super homemaker, it can aggravate your rebellious feelings. You might like to come home to a woman who cares about you and the outside world, as well as the child, especially at a time when you are struggling with your own new role. Just keep in mind that being a father, husband, and productive worker can be confusing, aggravating, and plain hard work. Give yourself credit for what you're attempting to do, and look for validation from people who matter in your life.

# 5

# Your identity as a mother

The psychological realization that you are a mother can take days or weeks after the actual birth. Before your baby becomes a reality for you, you may even suffer a brief grieving period for the "lost" pregnancy and your previous identity. However, most women begin their preparation for parenthood during the pregnancy itself, as they develop a new perception of themselves in relation to their partner, parents, and so on. As you readied yourself for the baby, you were also readying yourself to be a mother.

## FEARS AND DOUBTS ABOUT MOTHERHOOD

*You may have apprehensions about motherhood.* Doubts about being a parent may have bothered you when you were pregnant, and may still worry you now that you're a mother. You ask yourself whether you want to give up so much for motherhood. You wonder whether you'll really be any good at it. These are perfectly normal concerns of pregnancy and the postpartum period: don't imagine there is something wrong with you for having such questions. As for the answers, don't worry about those, either. All you need to do is live through the experience, doing the best you can. Your doubts will be relieved as you get comfortable being a mother.

*You may fear that you lack maternal instinct.* This is a common concern for new mothers, but your doubts can make you wonder whether you're abnormal. You may feel terrible if you believe that all "normal" mothers have an immediate, overwhelming adoration for their baby and you do not. But these feelings come slowly for some parents, which is just as "normal."

*The caretaker role may feel awkward to you.* You may also question your ability to take care of someone, to be a mother. Recognize that you've taken care of things before, whether they were pets, plants, siblings, or a sick husband. It can undermine your self-confidence if you let your image of yourself as a nurturer be measured by your infant's day-to-day happiness. If you allow this to happen, it means that you'll feel fine in the mothering role as long as the baby is fine. However, once the baby becomes distressed and you can't comfort him, you'll feel helpless, frustrated, and inadequate. The baby's comfort should not be any proof of whether you're okay as a mother; sometimes your baby is going to feel lousy and there's nothing you can do about it.

*A mother is something you learn how to be.* It takes time to learn: you'll eventually feel comfortable once you get hands-on experience, asking for help as needed and easing into the new role. Your fatigue and self-doubt will probably lessen as you get used to doing the chores of bathing, nail clipping, dealing with the first crying fit, fever, rash, etc.

*It is a myth that women automatically know how to "mother."* A woman has to spend many hours with her baby in order to learn his personal patterns and temperament. The ability to pick up the baby's cues—his earliest form of communication—is something a parent learns by spending time with the baby. Sometimes a new father will feel proud of his wife for her ability to handle their baby, and then feel inadequate himself for not being more tuned in to the infant. If you feel inadequate as a mother, you're probably suffering from believing the same myth as the insecure father. Mothering isn't something that comes naturally, it isn't in your blood or your hormones: it's a skill that you learn by tuning in to your baby.

***It's a myth that you have to study parenting.*** There are plenty of people who are fine parents and have never read a word about infant development. We seem to be experiencing a current trend that makes new parents feel it is necessary to read books and study how to be a "good" parent or raise "good" children. Reading a stack of highfalutin books does not mean you'll be well equipped to be a parent. There isn't any assurance that the information you read will even be useful! Try to develop confidence in your own instincts and life experience to guide you through the demands of parenting.

***Caring for your baby may not be totally enjoyable.*** It's possible that you may feel bored, irritable, and exhausted by your new job as a mother. You may have a hard time dealing with these feelings because other people (friends, your mother, or mother-in-law) may enthuse about infant care. You may be having a miserable time taking care of the baby you love, while everyone is admonishing you to savor every moment. People seem to believe that the baby's first years are the best and pass so quickly that you should enjoy every minute—meanwhile you don't think that infancy can pass quickly enough!

You may doubt yourself as a mother for having such negative feelings. Don't worry about it. If you don't like infant care it doesn't mean you don't like your infant. The part of mothering you may enjoy is up ahead: so live through the early months by knowing that you can look forward to the next phase of motherhood.

***Frustration is part of parenthood.*** Don't believe that you aren't good parent material just because you're having a hard time being a mother. Anxiety and stress are part of real life as a parent. If you keep your fears and doubts to yourself, all you're doing is perpetuating the myths that parenting is (or should be) easy. If you don't talk about your doubts, about the burdens of being a mother, you'll wonder why it's so hard for you to be a parent and not for other new parents. You can do yourself and everyone around you a favor by breaking through the silence. Let yourself off the hook so you don't have to keep up the facade that "everything's peachy."

***Don't keep your negative feelings a secret.*** If you have negative feelings about being a mother, don't feel you have to hide those emotions (for more on this subject, see *Chapter 10: Bad Feelings*). It's easy to imagine that outsiders are judging your worth as a mother and a person by how happy you seem in your new role. Women seem to perpetuate this lie by rarely sharing their fears and disillusionment about motherhood with each other. Therefore you think you're supposed to be strong and self-reliant, adjust effortlessly, and leap into motherhood with total enthusiasm.

But what about ambivalence? How about the letdown, resentment, fears, and anger? Admit these emotions, let yourself be human and vulnerable. Somebody has to start being honest about how hard and trying motherhood is: it might as well be you! Tell other women that you have fears and frustrations, let yourself cry if you feel like it. You may be amazed to find other mothers who share your ambivalence but have been constricted by the conspiracy of silence that has grown up around motherhood.

If you feel you have to hide your negative feelings, it will create inner tension and pressure that can make you overreact to little things and feel even more negative. Holding feelings back can frequently make them seem more powerful. Once they are released it can free you to grow into your new role, accepting motherhood with all its good and bad points.

## YOUR RELATIONSHIP WITH YOUR MOTHER

***Your feelings about your mother and your experiences with her influence you as a parent.*** You may be determined to improve with your child on the parenting you feel you got from your mother. However, it's likely that you'll fall back on the model of motherhood that you received in your early life. This is especially true in times of stress. You'll be more like your mother than you expect to be. Even if you decide that you purposely want to do the opposite of what your mother did, this desire itself is proof of what a strong connection there is between you. Perhaps you'll want to resolve some of these differences.

**You may have trouble using your mother as a role model.** You may think of your mother as unaffectionate, perhaps as a woman who was uncomfortable with being nurturant. Another problem can arise if your mother is highly critical of you as a new mother, comparing you negatively to her, "the perfect mother." Yet another difficult situation is if your mother has always complained to you about how hard and unpleasant child care was for her and what a sacrifice she made for her children. Especially if you're enjoying being a mother, this discrepancy can make you feel disloyal to your mother or unsympathetic about her martyred complaining.

**Talk with your partner about your parents.** Discussing your parents can help you better understand their influence in your parenting. Which of their attitudes and behavior do you have positive feelings about; what things would you want to repeat with your own child?

If you discover that all you have is criticism and complaints about the way you were parented, stop feeling sorry for yourself and step back. You could not have turned out to be a pretty decent person unless you got *some* good parenting! Keeping a laundry list of complaints isn't going to do anyone any good: try to focus on what your parents *might* have done right and then be the best parent you can.

**Don't blame your childhood for your inadequacies.** It's liberating to realize that you are not crippled by your parents' shortcomings. You want to be a good parent and good partner, perhaps better than your own folks in various ways. But your parents did the best they could, given what *their* childhoods were like, the resources and education they had, their relationship as a couple, and so on. We are all human beings with our assets and imperfections; every one of us was "imperfectly" parented. Now you are setting out to raise the next generation. You feel strong, prepared with all the answers about the flaws in your upbringing and full of dreams, ready to make your own personal triumphs.

Instead of being so quick to blame your parents, keep in mind that you are about to begin a lifetime of making your own unique errors as a parent!

***Did your mother love another child more than you?***
If you grew up thinking your mother didn't love you, or that one of your siblings was the favorite, you should talk about it to your brother or sister today. You might be surprised to learn that they didn't feel well loved, either. A mother with problems from her own childhood was probably incapable of giving love fully to any other person.

***Do you think a grandchild will win your mother's love?***   If you've been craving your mother's love all these years, you might feel that a grandchild will finally win her approval. However, she probably doesn't have that love to give, any more than she did when you were a girl, although there are times when a grandparent can give affection to a grandchild while she could not give it to her own child. In order for you to move on and grow, you'll have to accept your childhood: you didn't get the love you wanted from your mother. Once you come to terms with this, it will free you emotionally to look for nurturing love from other people in your life.

***Avoid making judgments about your parents.***   You may have felt slighted as a child but this doesn't mean you had "bad" parents. It's even possible that from an objective point of view, no one else would think you had problems. However, if you felt there was neglect, lack of love or concern from your mother, this can affect your own capabilities as a mother. It can also create problems if you were given too much attention, were overprotected, and prevented from developing a sense of independence. Your memories may not be accurate but your feelings and perception of your childhood can have a powerful effect on you, right up to the time you become a mother yourself.

***What is your relationship like now with your Mom?***
Your relationship with your mother in the present has reverberations in your transition to motherhood. If you feel loving toward your mother and want to be close to her, it

can influence you to copy her mothering style. Strangely enough, even if you have anger or grudges against your mother (perhaps unconscious) you may still perceive her as being perfect. If your mother is dead, or very ill, it is especially true that you might feel an overwhelming need to be the kind of mother she was.

***Your attitude toward your mother may change.*** Becoming a mother yourself can change your outlook on your mother, either while you are still pregnant or once your own child is born. You may look back on your childhood, see things in a different light, and find you are more able to understand and accept your mother now. If motherhood makes you feel more independent, that may give you the freedom to be closer to your mother than you could be before. On the other hand, if you are especially fearful of your new role you may find yourself clinging to your mother and perhaps resenting that dependency.

***Your mother's attitude toward you may change.*** It's not unusual for a mother's attitude toward her daughter to change once she becomes a grandmother. You may have found that your mother began treating you with more respect once you were pregnant. Now that you have a child, she may view you as an adult for the first time, an equal with whom she has something in common.

***You may not want to be like your mother.*** Many women want to be different from their mothers. If you have mixed feelings about your mother, you may be fearful that you'll become just like her once you're a mother. As a parent you probably want to be understanding, compassionate, and loving with your child, and you may feel your mother didn't give you those things, or at least not enough. You may want to give your child(ren) an image of a mother as a competent, confident, and whole person, and you may feel that your mother lacked those qualities.

## THE SUPER MOM SYNDROME

*A Super Mom has to be everything for everyone.* She can never disappoint anyone. She has to be constantly doing, planning, and giving. If this is your credo in life, it probably won't be long before you are trapped in your own net. If you feel that you can never let anyone down—your husband, childbirth teacher, in-laws, child, etc.—then you'll make commitments that you cannot realistically keep. A mother who believes she can do it all, and be everything for everyone, is headed for a fall. By spreading yourself too thin you cause yourself maximum stress and will get a minimum of satisfaction for your efforts.

*Society glorifies motherhood.* This social pressure can create insecurity and guilt in women who feel uncomfortable or inadequate about their mothering abilities. The myth is that a mother is supposed to be an all-loving, all-giving, accepting woman who is without selfishness, ambition, anger, fatigue, or irrationality.

*You may expect sainthood of yourself.* Many women are taught that a good mother puts others first. Just to complicate matters, many men learn the same thing! If you learned this, you may feel guilty if you spend any time taking care of your own needs. There may have been a women's liberation movement but we still expect ourselves as mothers to have saintlike devotion and attentiveness to our children's needs.

The only way to break this pattern is for each of us to throw darts at this dangerously unrealistic cultural view of motherhood. Otherwise, how are we going to grow as individuals and allow our marriages to flourish? Taking care of yourself is essential to your psychological well-being and the health of your family.

*Social myths form your concept of what "mother" means.* These idealized images can make it hard to be a real mother in the real world. Your images were formed by your own mother plus stereotypes from children's stories, school books, television and movies, advertising, and so on. The negative image you may have learned is that a "bad" mother is overprotective, pushy, neglectful, and resentful. This kind of mother is usually seen as being responsible for all her children's neuroses and unhappiness. The mythological positive image of a "good" mother is one who is generous and kind, with Madonnalike patience, a woman who gives her life over to her children and is fulfilled by it.

***Do you think that a "perfect" mother can meet all her baby's needs?*** If you are a Super Mother, then you may set this goal for yourself. The truth is that you can't be everything to any person: you can meet some of their needs, some of the time. You may have expectations for yourself to be perfect that aren't necessarily conscious ideas but are put there by movies, books, the advertisements you see, and the messages you learned growing up. Try to get back down to earth and accept that "imperfect" parenting is the only kind that really exists.

***Do you believe that you can completely control your child's experience of life?*** Total responsibility for a "perfect child" is yet another destructive myth, the idea that a mother should have total control and responsibility for her child. The social pressure to produce a psychologically perfect, well-adjusted child can make you crazy! You can give to and do for a child constantly and still have a colicky, fretful, sleepless baby. Giving total attention around the clock cannot prevent your child from experiencing frustration, unhappiness, and the other normal range of emotions. *The baby is a separate person with needs and feelings—you cannot know nor can you satisfy all of them.*

***Trying to entirely protect your child can backfire.*** If you give yourself complete responsibility for your child's every action and emotion, instead of feeling like a Super Mom you may wind up a loser. If you let yourself think that your child's emotional welfare is completely in your hands, this can mean that your entire emotional investment in life is vested in your child. If you allow yourself to be a mother whose needs and expectations are this distorted, you may very well have a child who will one day come to resent and withdraw from you.

*A Super Mother is terrified of an imperfect child.* Some women torment themselves over the possibility that their child may be neurotic, insecure, not well rounded, delinquent, or socially unsuccessful. The fear that one mistake as a mother will result in a damaged child can be crippling. You have to keep a perspective: there are limits to how much anyone can be responsible for someone else's life and happiness.

*There are warning symptoms of the Super Mom Syndrome.* Fatigue is probably the greatest warning that you are overdoing it. Trying to do it all can lead to a physical or nervous breakdown if you don't pull yourself up short. A woman who tries to do it all—and perfectly, of course—had better learn to slow down and compromise before she collapses.

Another sign that you're overdoing it is if you feel resentful of the time you spend caring for others. You may feel annoyed or irritable without knowing exactly why. This is probably a sign that you aren't allowing enough time for your own needs.

### SOME REMEDIES FOR SUPER MOM SYNDROME

*Begin by accepting that you're just an ordinary human.* Most Super Moms are horrified at the very idea of being called "normal" or "ordinary." Guess what? You're just a plain ordinary mortal like the rest of us. Sorry about that! Because of that harsh reality, you only have so much energy, and so much emotion. That means you've got to face the terrible task of making compromises, thereby proving that you're just a normal human. Come down off your pedestal and give yourself a break.

*Accept the concept of "limitations."* It can be hard for a Super Mother to come to terms with the idea that she has to cut back in certain areas, but you cannot do it all. You can't have a satisfying career . . . and also be loving, compassionate, and sexy with your husband . . . and also give your child the time, affection, and stimulation she needs . . . and also run your household like a Swiss watch.

*Are you being neurotic about the goals you set?*
There are areas in which even the most laid-back mothers
are compulsive: as a Super Mom you probably have certain areas you're neurotic about. You may get yourself
crazy about how clean your house should be, whether
your baby is "ahead" of his age group, or whether you
use convenience foods. If you're really neurotic about
something, you may not be able to entirely change your
attitude but it can help to develop an awareness of what
really matters and how much you expect of yourself. You
can at least begin by reducing how much time and energy
you devote to certain things so that you feel less driven
and more in control.

*"Who else can do this?"* Super Moms aren't much good
at delegating authority and tasks, partly because they feel
that paying for help would mean they are lazy or inadequate. Also, a Super Mom gets some part of her identity and
self-image from being able to do it all herself. You may feel
that getting help is being self-indulgent, or you worry deep
down that you're not going to get credit for the tasks that
are accomplished by someone else.

   Remember the floor-wax commercials you watched
on TV when you were growing up, with the housewife
whose happiness seemed to revolve around how shiny she
could get the kitchen floor? Do you want to be that woman?
What about the TV homemaker who spends most of her
waking hours trying to see her reflection in her china, worrying about spots on plates from her dishwasher? Are those
women your role models? Is *that* the kind of validation and
feedback you need to feel good about yourself as a mother
and housewife?

*Reduce the demands you make on yourself.* Ask
yourself, "Is what I'm doing really, truly necessary?" If it
isn't, then eliminate it. Most Super Moms could do 50 percent less, still get a lot accomplished, but have some quality
time for themselves. There are three ways to reduce what
you expect of yourself: (1) pay someone else to do some
things; (2) eliminate some things; (3) don't volunteer to do
so many things at home, at work, or in the community.

***Treat yourself as well as you do the baby.*** You should make time for yourself to do adult activities on your own, just as thoughtfully as you plan recreation for your child. Make time for old or new hobbies, go to the library or bookstore, read, do crossword puzzles, watch a soap opera, have lunch with a friend.

If fresh air, exercise, and mental stimulation are good for your baby, what makes you think that you don't need them every bit as much? Super Moms often forget that they need to rest, eat well, and get exercise if they want to get any real satisfaction and pleasure from their lives. Also, by paying attention to your own selfish needs, you are counteracting the Super Mom Syndrome and getting yourself off that treadmill.

***You have options available to you at every step.*** Recognizing that you have options comes from the realization that you don't have to do everything yourself and some things don't have to be done at all. You also can exercise choice in your decisions when you acknowledge that your life is in your control.

For example, instead of giving the baby a bath, take a bubble bath yourself. Aha! Does the very idea of that sound like fingernails on a blackboard to you? If so, that's a telltale sign that you are deeply hooked on being a Super Mother. How about this: instead of cleaning the kitchen cupboards, put a mud pack on your face and a conditioning treatment on your hair (no, you can't fix the cupboards at the same time that you have on the beauty treatments, that's cheating!). Instead of folding laundry, take a nap. Little by little you may be able to make headway against the Super Mom super ego that doesn't give you permission to take care of Number One. (For those Super Moms who don't yet know who Number One is, run to the nearest mirror and say "Cheese"!)

***Working mothers run a high risk of being Super Moms.*** If you have a career, you're especially vulnerable to falling into the Super Mother Syndrome because you feel you have to make up for your absences. The danger is that having a family and a job means you're already operating at full capacity. There's no place you can go to recharge your emotional or physical batteries because you're going full steam. The end result is that you run the risk of being a runaway train unless you can put on the brakes right from the start.

***You may try*** ANYTHING ***to compensate for having a job.*** A working Super Mom secretly may hope that her husband and children don't notice she's working! One way to do this is to be such a blur of frenetic energy that you never stop long enough for the dust to settle. You may try to find a job that can be done around your child's schedule so that you never appear to be gone from the house.

A Super Mom would never cut corners by using convenience products or services. If you did that, it might mean you weren't a good mother, wife, or human being. You have to make meals from scratch, Halloween costumes by hand, and dress your children in clothes that require ironing.

***The media has helped create the Super Mom Monster.*** You didn't become so tough on yourself all alone: many of a Super Mother's ideas about what she "should" do come from magazines and television. Have you noticed how often the women's magazines have articles detailing exactly how to apportion your time so you can do it all? The writer tells you how to cook a nutritious (inexpensive) gourmet meal in 20 minutes: the truth is that it takes at least that long just to shop for the ingredients! Then you're told how to sew darling clothes for the kids or curtains for the powder room in 30 minutes: unless you're an expert seamstress, you might spend that much time just ripping out your mistakes! Then there's a long list of all the ways you can use the other 23 hours and 10 minutes of your day more productively (the magazine article was probably written by a professional journalist who may have had to cancel everything else in his/her life just to get the piece written by the deadline).

***Something has to give.*** Simple logic tells you that you cannot push yourself like a beast of burden and expect to make it to your 40th (50th?) birthday intact. It is not possible to be a full-time homemaker *and* worker. If you try to do both things "to the max," you are bound to wind up driven by inner demons that leave you frazzled and feeling like a failure.

*If you don't have a career it can be a burden, too.* A Super Mom who does not have work outside the home has different problems. You will probably try twice as hard to justify that you're doing one job instead of two. You may feel you have to fill every nook in your schedule to prove how Super you really are. You may take exercise or yoga or tennis or cooking classes, you may do volunteer or charity work, but one thing that's sure is that you'll overdo everything to prove your worth.

## A WOMAN CAN GET LOST IN THE MOTHERING ROLE

*You can get lost in the role of mother.* Being a mother is simply one of many challenges and roles in your life: daughter, sibling, wife, friend, worker. You can lose a sense of yourself and other facets of your personality if you totally immerse yourself in mothering. A baby does not "complete" you as a woman. In fact, the opposite can be true if you give up who you were, abandon yourself, to become somebody's mother. It probably won't even make you a very good parent.

*Are you trying to look like "a mother"?* Some women adopt a radical physical change when they become mothers. This can be an external manifestation of discarding the person you were and taking a new identity. Some women start to talk, walk, and dress "like a mother," adopting sensible shoes and hairstyle and conducting themselves in a self-consciously restrained manner. By giving up your personal style for motherhood you are sacrificing the sensuality, youthfulness, and spontaneity you may have had.

Becoming a mother doesn't have to be so serious—you don't have to wear your hair in a bun! By doing something as seemingly superficial as changing the way you look, you may actually be giving up your self-image and the dreams that went with it. At the same time you may lose the relationship you had with your mate, based on those attributes.

*You may be fearful of losing your previous identity.* Becoming a mother can make you feel as though your previous life and identity have been erased and you're expected to be a totally new person. But you don't need to give up personal qualities and interests that you've developed over your lifetime. Who you were before you became a parent will enhance you as a mother. You can want to be a mother and a nurturer and still be the person you were before. You may feel trapped, at first, between these two roles. It's just a question of slowly meshing the two identities, folding one into the other.

*Expecting the baby to give you an identity is a dangerous proposition.* If you're hoping that a child will fortify, justify, or prove who you are, forget it! If you're already insecure about who you are, that feeling will probably only get worse if you tie your identity to your child. A baby's personality and behavior are unpredictable: they are no reflection on who you are. You might as well erase yourself if being "Jacob's mother" is the sum total of how you see yourself.

*The most important person in your life must be you.* In order to remain mature and vital you need intellectual and emotional feedback from adults, your mate in particular. If you put yourself and your marriage in second place after the baby, you are going to lose contact with yourself as a woman. Once the initial glow of motherhood wears off, you may feel shallow and lousy about yourself. How would you feel if ten years down the road the only identity you had was as "Sally's mother" and "Harry's wife"? At that point, you really won't have an identity of your own.

*Your self-esteem can be increased by becoming a mother.* For some women, their sense of themselves is improved by motherhood. In many relationships there is a power shift: becoming a mother can help a woman to develop a stronger identity and greater self-worth. You may see yourself in a new light. You may even expect your husband to have an improved opinion of you!

This shift can affect your marriage; it is an especially

difficult adjustment if the man's ego was fed by being "top dog." If you discover newfound pride as a mother and greater self-esteem, it's very important that you present this change to your partner in a nonthreatening way. Your mate needs a chance to reorient himself, to overcome any possible jealousy or resentment he may feel so that he can also develop pride in your new strength and self-love.

***Motherhood can diminish your self-confidence.*** If you are anxious about your capabilities and fearful of the responsibility of being a Mom, you may lose self-confidence. Even a strong woman with a career can find herself calling the baby's father in desperation if she can't cope with a colicky, crying baby. It's normal for new parents to feel a need to share responsibility and depend on each other.

However, if you're making constant phone calls to your spouse at work, crying for help, he may become understandably resentful. Your calls are an interruption of business for a man who is trying to get ahead in his career, to provide increased financial stability for his family. Your husband can't handle that additional burden and it is not good for your self-image, either. If you find yourself leaning on your partner this way, it can lower your self-esteem. You may feel demeaned, envision yourself as a weak, dependent woman (perhaps like your mother?). This can lead to doubts about yourself as a woman and mother.

***Identifying with the baby can lower your self-esteem.*** It can be uncomfortable to feel like a baby yourself, seeking support and comfort. You may also feel that the baby is a way to nurture the child inside yourself—you can give the baby what you craved or missed in your childhood. This is one reason that a woman may want a girl as a first child: she can identify with her and wants to recreate or rewrite her relationship with her own mother.

***Becoming a mother does not "complete" a woman.*** Self-fulfillment through mothering is another part of our social mythology. It is true and wonderful that raising a child can give new meaning and intensity to your life and enrich you emotionally. But don't fall into the trap of expecting constant or total fulfillment from mothering: you aren't going to get immediate or constant gratification. Just as with any other relationship, the process of mothering has its ups and downs, its periods of growth and stagnation.

***Making a child happy cannot be a life goal.*** If you do not maintain some idea of your own needs, of what makes you happy, you will ultimately have nothing to give your partner and nothing to pass on to your child. You may end up an unhappy woman with no sense of herself, who has sacrificed herself needlessly.

***There is a danger in being nothing but a mother.*** Commitment and dedication to raising your child is an honorable and admirable intention . . . but you can run into trouble if that is your only ambition and purpose in life. There is some current social propaganda about making yourself a mother first, last, and foremost. There is some social pressure to be a mother above all, with the baby always coming first. The trend here is toward "total mothering"—the belief that a devoted, full-time Mom is "best," that she is a "better" mother than a working mother or one who also devotes herself to other interests and pursuits.

Twenty-four-hour loving care may be the way some women want to raise their children, but for others it can be a burden that wears them down. Full-time mothering can backfire: it can make you depleted, irritable, bored, resentful, and guilty about real or imagined "mistakes" you're making. Before you accept the idea behind total mothering, ask yourself if it's really best. Who does it benefit in your new family? What is the cost to yourself and your marriage?

Instead of the mothering that you fantasized giving to your child, full-time mothering may backfire on you. Depending on your personality and other interests, you may find that you would be twice the mother if you spent half as long at the job. If you embrace the belief system of total servitude to a baby, it can lead to a short temper, marital friction, and even forms of child abuse.

***A full-time mother gets very little social support.*** Raising a child no longer has the value that it used to, which is the ironic flip side of the total-mothering movement. You may have childhood images of Mother as the backbone of the family, the warmth at the center of the house. No matter how close you get to this image of perfect mothering, you may find little support for your efforts from the outside world. The message today often is, "You're less of a person for staying home with a baby—you probably don't have any ambition or talent." Your ideal image of motherhood can haunt you if you get no respect from society for giving up other aspects of your life to devote yourself primarily to nurturing your child.

*A career mother is no better off: she is in a double bind.* If you want to develop your career while raising a child, it puts you between a rock and a hard place. No matter how well you manage to mesh career and motherhood, social disapproval seems to be inevitable. Ambition, personal drives, and being a nurturant mother are often considered contradictory. You are going to hear judgmental tones every time someone asks you a question about how old your child is, how much time you spend with him, and how you feel about it.

The "good mother" image allows no room for ambivalence about baby tending—the assumption is that if you were really a good mother, you'd be with your child day and night. The ideal image of the successful businesswoman permits no distractions as you reach for the top. The presumption is that if you worry about your child's dentist or your husband's cold, you are showing a lack of seriousness or dedication to your job. The problem is compounded by the current social expectation that a woman should be able to do it all. (More on this subject in *Chapter 13: Career vs. Full-time Motherhood.*)

## GUILTY PARENTING

*Any and all guilt you feel as a parent is undeserved.* No parent who loves a child and does his or her best should feel guilt. And yet so many parents do feel guilty. The fear of failure as a parent is foolish—yet so many parents are foolish in this way. And it seems to be mothers who suffer "the guilts" the most. Loving your child and doing your best is all you can ask of yourself.

***Mothers demand too much of themselves.*** Today's mother reads much more on child rearing than her mother and grandmother did. You "know" too much, you have too much book learning. Many parents expect to be perfect and generally expect too much of the whole parenting experience. What can happen is that you wind up feeling guilty for not accomplishing more. You focus on what you haven't done instead of praising yourself for what has worked out well.

***Women feel more guilt than men.*** A mother tends to feel more guilty than a father does, perhaps from society's assumption that she can do it all. Your mother may have passed on beliefs about making food from scratch, keeping an immaculate home, and always being available to meet everyone else's needs.

***You cannot do and be everything for everyone.*** That may have begun to sound like an incantation in the course of this chapter, but it's a little chant you might hum to yourself when you're just trying too hard and feeling lousy about it. Repeat that phrase once an hour until the point sinks in. If you don't get it, you have a good chance of feeling disillusioned with yourself as a mother, crippled by guilt, and constantly worrying that you're coming up short.

***Guilt can come from feeling abnormal.*** You may wonder what's wrong with you if you don't take to motherhood like a duck to water. You tell yourself that millions of women for thousands of years have been mothers and managed fine. So what's your problem? You may feel guilty if you're already wondering "What's wrong with me?" You may have doubts about yourself as a mother, because you have postpartum depression, or because you can't do it all perfectly.

***Mother love is chaotic, irrational, and overwhelming.*** There is no way to explain the passionate highs and lows, the intense attachment and compulsiveness of being a mother. However, if you make a commitment to meet your baby's every whim, you will ultimately feel guilty for having failed him and he will become a controlling little prince.

Some mothers need protection from their own powerful maternal instinct. Out of self-preservation, as well as for your baby's sake, you have to take time for yourself. A natural love between a mother and her baby should optimally mean that the mother isn't afraid of losing her baby's love if she doesn't reinforce it every single minute. Have faith in the bond between the parent and child—it is a faith that's similar to the one that should exist between husband and wife.

A mother with these insecurities may also experience guilt. Yet if your child is well adjusted, she should feel secure about your affection without constant reinforcement. The loving way that you interact with your child is what enables her to love later on in life. Trying to be there for your child, continuously, under any circumstances, is an impossible task. Therefore, you're bound to fail and thus to feel guilty.

*Guilt comes from the myth of the Perfect Parent.* This view of parenting is that kids can be made perfect if they receive perfect mothering, especially in the early years. This goes along with the Super Baby Syndrome: parents feel it's proof that they're doing things right if their child can do things like tap-dance, play the violin, and read flashcards by age two. The inverse of this seems to be that you are not a groovy parent if your child can't do these dancing-bear routines. *However, there are no perfect children and no perfect parents.*

*Many child development specialists promote the myth of the Perfect Parent.* There are theories which imply that inadequate maternal caretaking can pretty much be blamed for most of a child's faults. The "continuity" of the relationship with the mother is what is stressed. Of course if you read any of this stuff, and aren't able to be constantly by your child's side, you're bound to feel you're doing something wrong about which you should feel guilty.

*Try to take the theories with a grain of salt.* Several renowned experts in child development have written extensively about the concept that the mother should not leave her child in the early years. There is no point getting you to feel any guiltier than you may already, but just so you know to whom I'm referring, three of the experts are Selma Fraiberg *(The Magic Years),* William Sears *(Creative Parenting),* and John Bowlby back in the 1950s *(Love and Attachment).*

The theorists suggest that if Mother is always there for baby's every little fussy mood, developmental transition, etc., the child will turn out great. These authorities and others suggest that if Mother has to be absent, the child will be imperfect and Mom will be to blame. Hence, **guilt.** These concepts filter into our social consciousness and are often distorted. One example of a distorted theory is the Leboyer birth method: he suggested that bright lights and brusque handling at birth meant a trauma that would scar a child for life. In fact, there is no one event that can undo all the cumulative good to a child of a loving, caring environment.

***Experts promote guilt.***   New parents rely heavily on advice from experts about how to raise their kids. We are all so cut off from extended family, from older women and those our own age, that we turn to the experts (Spock, Piaget, Leach, you name it) to get confirmation that we're doing a good job. Do you sometimes feel as though you're looking over your shoulder to see if someone has caught you doing it "wrong," being an imperfect parent? Relying on experts instead of on yourself is one way to wind up feeling guilty. There's sure to be a book somewhere to tell you how you're not measuring up as a parent.

***Parental guilt is seen as a virtue by society.***   Exhibiting guilt is considered proof of how much you care about your child. This is especially true with working parents, who get social encouragement to show how *good* they are by how *bad* they feel about being away from their child. The simple realization that you are in such a bind can release you from its grip.

***Many parents are guilt-ridden.***   You may feel guilty out of fear that mistakes you make will accumulate and somehow damage your child. What you do every minute of every day is not as important as who you are over the long run. Face it: you're not perfect, and you are not going to be a Perfect Parent. All parents are imperfectly good, each in his/her own way. Just try your best.

***Don't feel bad about what you don't do right.*** If you lose your temper, if you are moody, if you're inconsistent, if you don't like playing peek-a-boo 60 times in a row—join the club. There are other parents out there suffering the same imperfections. Give up the illusion of being a Perfect Parent and you may be able to let go of some of your guilt.

***Career mothers often have permanent guilt.*** If you work you may worry, "What if the kid needs me and I'm not there?" Your husband or other family members may not approve of your working and their comments can increase your feelings of guilt. You may also enjoy your work and enjoy the time you spend away from home and your child, which can *really* make you feel guilty!

***Working mothers blame themselves for any problems.*** A working mother is sure to feel at fault if her child has any problem like waking up in the night, toilet training, being temperamental when she leaves or comes home. It's so easy to feel that your job is to blame. Although your working is an easy answer to problems, in truth your job is only one part of your home environment.

***Career mothers may not be able to eliminate guilt.*** You may not even be able to reduce the guilt you feel, depending on how others in your life react to your working and how much time and energy your job requires. However, guilt requires a certain amount of emotional energy, which you may be able to rechannel. Instead of feeling paralyzed by guilt, try doing something to change the situation. Restructure your time and get up an hour early to have special breakfast time with your child. You may be able to cut down your travel time to work, you may be able to take your child along once in a while, or leave early and take work home.

# 6

# Practical concerns in the early weeks

The physical demands and problems of a new baby in the first six weeks require just as much from you as the more subtle emotional adjustments. There is a great deal for you to cope with and learn, yet you have limited time and energy. This chapter will outline some of the areas that may affect you, with suggestions on how best to handle them.

## THE FATIGUE FACTOR

*Fatigue is the number one complaint of new parents.* "You don't know what 'tired' means until you become a parent" is a common lament. The first six to eight weeks are usually the worst for parent sleeplessness. A newborn cannot differentiate between day and night; most require a couple of months to fit into a pattern of waking and sleeping. Keep in mind that a breast-fed baby eats every 2 hours; a bottle-fed child around every 4 hours.

*If you don't expect to sleep you won't be disappointed.* New parents should not count on getting a full night's sleep. This holds true even if your baby is the world's best sleeper, and even once the baby settles into a routine. You can expect to get up at least once a night for the first year. Some parents are not terribly bothered by this disturbance, while other parents do not feel they've had a decent night's rest during the entire first year.

***Sleep deprivation causes problems.***   Studies of interrupted sleep show that adults become irritable and disoriented if they do not get 6 to 8 hours of **uninterrupted** sleep. What can happen is that you fall into a "fatigue cycle," which means you have less patience to cope with problems that arise. It can also mean that you feel you aren't accomplishing enough and feel pressured to do unfinished chores that would not otherwise bother you. To compensate for feeling inadequate you try to do more, resulting in further fatigue. Feeling tense, irritable, and unable to relax are signs of overexertion and tiredness.

***Naps are very important.***   Lack of sleep will catch up with you eventually and you won't have the strength to get through the day. You have to try and pamper yourself, to "put yourself down" as you would do with the baby if she got overtired. Before you lie down, remember to do something about the telephone or it's sure to ring right as you're dozing off. You can smother the phone with a pillow, unplug it, or take it off the hook.

New mothers may have trouble resting for several reasons. For instance, the classic advice to "nap when the baby does" is good advice only if your baby stays down long enough for you to nap. If you have a child who doesn't sleep long enough, then you should get someone else to watch the child while you force yourself to rest. Also, you may view the baby's nap time as your chance to do housework, bills, phoning, or reading.

Naps can be especially hard for career women who have had a radically different daily routine before motherhood. Lying down in the middle of the day is an alien concept for them. If you are a career (or ex-career) mother, you'll have to reorient your entire perspective on the rhythm of your day and redefine what "time" (and how you use it) means to you.

***Reduce the number of chores you do.***   Doing less around the house is another way to cope with fatigue. Eliminate everything but the absolute essentials. If you and your mate can share tasks around the house, that's great. If not, it can be beneficial just to discuss with him what things can be left undone. This can be a way to keep in touch with each other's needs and feelings, which is essential to any good partnership.

*Sleeplessness can be a result of fatigue.* When you are overtired it can be difficult to fall asleep. Here are some suggestions on ways to cope with sleeplessness:

1. Eat well and take multivitamins
2. Don't eat heavily before bed
3. Don't drink caffeine or other stimulating drinks before bed—or, if you're sensitive to its affects, not after noontime
4. Stay calm and inactive for an hour or two before bedtime: no chores, work, bill paying
5. Get into bed early, before your "bedtime," and have a book, music, or TV to relax you

## What to Do About Visitors

*Visitors can be a blessing and a curse.* Of course it's wonderful to have company and to share people's enthusiasm about your baby. However, it is also disruptive and exhausting to have a parade of people coming through your house. Also, not all visitors are created equal; some will be calm and supportive, while others will give advice and interfere at a time when you may not have the patience to smile and ignore them. You and your mate are going to have to decide together how to handle visitors in general. You may want to make specific decisions about how to deal with certain difficult people.

*Limit visiting to family only for the first week or two.* Other than immediate family you might want to postpone most friends until you are settled in with the baby. Very often, visitors are showing up so soon **for your sake.** They want you to know how happy they are for you and share your happiness; they might even be afraid of hurting your feelings if they don't visit the first week. In fact, most people have pretty tight schedules and may be relieved to be told that they'll be more welcome a bit later.

***Make a priority list of visitors.*** If you have a lot of people who are eager to visit you immediately, it might be a good idea to make a list for yourself of which friends come first. It may be annoying or diplomatically difficult to make the list, but if you don't take control of the situation your house is going to be overrun with well-wishers.

***Don't feel guilty about turning visitors away.*** People can be quite aggressive and practically demand that you let them come see you and the baby. Each of them has his/her own reasons and personal needs for being so adamant about visiting. You have one obligation, from the moment your baby is born: to your new family. Everyone else comes second.

---

### RULES OF THUMB FOR VISITORS

* Visitors who ask "What can I bring?" should receive a definite answer like "Dinner!" (This is no time to be coy and say, "Just bring yourself.")
* Tell them beforehand that their visit is time-limited to, say, a half hour . . . and remind them when the time is up. Otherwise you'll be wiped out.
* You do not have to play hostess. A pot of tea or coffee is sufficient.
* It should be fun to have visitors. If it begins to feel like a chore, stop doing it.
* Cancel visitors at any time if you're getting exhausted. You two and the baby are the most important people right now. Friends will understand (and those who don't are probably going to be ex-friends soon!).
* You can head off visitors on the phone without hurting their feelings: just say, "The baby is colicky today and I'd rather you see him at his best."

### THE CURSE OF ALEXANDER GRAHAM BELL

***The telephone is another mixed blessing.*** The telephone gives you a way to get in touch with people without having them visit. However, the phone can also be a constant intrusion in your new life with the baby. You'll have to learn to pace yourself—you are going to be exhausted if you feel obliged to describe the labor and delivery to every caller. Of course it is wonderful to share memories of the baby's birth with a few special people, but *be selective*. You're going to wear yourself out if every time somebody politely asks, "How was the birth?" you launch into a minute-by-minute replay. Most people don't want that kind of detail and it only depletes your time and energy.

***Put an egg timer beside the phone.*** This is a good way to limit your time on the phone if you have trouble keeping the calls short. It is so easy to get trapped on the phone, afraid to hurt the caller's feelings but painfully aware of how limited your time is now that you have a baby. The telephone takes more time and energy out of the day than most of us realize.

***Get a phone answering machine.*** This is an essential investment that you should accustom yourselves to even before the baby arrives. If you already have one, so much the better. BREAK THE HABIT OF ANSWERING THE PHONE AUTOMATICALLY. You can use the phone machine to protect yourselves: either to ignore the phone completely (a good new habit to develop) or to screen calls and only pick up certain ones.

A phone machine is also useful to inform people who want to know all about your new baby if you can't speak to all your friends personally. Put a message on the phone machine that gives the vital statistics about the baby and says, "Please don't expect a call back right away because the three of us are busy settling in together. Janet or I will get back to you as soon as we can, but please be patient." And then don't return the calls until you really want to and have the time.

*Have anyone but the mother answer the phone.*   If you pick up the phone it can be tricky for you to get off again quickly without seeming impolite. When you have a new baby you'll be surprised how little time and energy you have for telephoning. Whoever answers the phone should say, "She's resting now," or, "Glad you called but . . ." or even, "I know she'd love to see you but the doctor said she shouldn't have visitors the first week." As new parents you'll be eager for contact with other people, but in the first week or two there will be days when you'll want to throw the phone against the wall.

## POSTPARTUM EXERCISE

*Exercise after the baby is born can be very good for you.*   It can relieve tiredness and sluggishness—so much so that women who suffer from postpartum depression are encouraged to exercise as a remedy. However, don't be too tough on yourself in this area. Physical exercise is of great benefit physically and psychologically but it's often realistically hard to find the time and energy when you have a small baby.

*Whatever exercise you can do is good enough.*   Although exercise is great, if you can't find the time or energy to do it don't fall into the trap of pressuring yourself because you think that you "should" do it. Don't make unreasonable demands on yourself: you may honestly not have enough time or motivation to exercise. Otherwise, what may happen is you'll "beat yourself up" emotionally for not doing it. There's no point in hating yourself for what you simply may not be able to do right now.

*Don't expect your prepregnancy body to come back by itself.*   Some women believe that at six weeks postpartum their old figure will simply come back, by magic. The truth is that you have to fight to get it back, and exercise is the best way. It doesn't matter whether you jog, swim, take exercise or dance classes, or go for long, brisk walks.

The cold truth is that if you are like most women, your body will probably never again be as it was. No amount of running, swimming, or dieting will bring it back.

Most mothers welcome their baby and say goodbye (to varying degrees) to the flat stomach, trim thighs, and high breasts they may have been lucky to have.

***How to do the Kegel (or pelvic-floor) exercise.*** The pelvic-floor muscles are the same ones you use to stop the flow of urine: you can get the feel of them that way. When you are urinating, practice stopping the flow. Once you are acquainted with these muscles, you can exercise them regularly during the day. If you drive or walk a lot you can practice doing Kegels every time you see a red light, or any other reminder that helps you.

***Kegel exercises are the most important "workout" you can do for your body postpartum.*** It is important to do them every single day postpartum, to tone your pelvic-floor muscles after the delivery both for your personal health and for your sex life. Do not underestimate how important they are: get in the habit of doing them every day, always.

Start by doing five at a time, holding for 5 seconds, and then build up to 50 at a time (which is the minimum recommended by experts for all women at all times). Doing them for a maximum of 5 seconds apiece is considered best—it is better to do more short ones because holding for longer than 5 seconds tires the muscles.

***Some hints about doing Kegels postpartum.*** If you've had an episiotomy, lying on your back or stomach will be most comfortable. It is better to keep your legs apart, not together; that way you won't contract only at the vaginal opening, or confuse thigh or groin muscles for those higher up in the vagina. Breathe in and out: if you hold your breath it encourages you to bear down rather than pulling the muscles in and upward. Be aware of the difference between the abdominal and pelvic-floor muscles: you cannot contract both at once, but you might mistake the abdominals for the pelvic muscles.

***There are ways to check your abilities.*** To see if you are doing Kegels properly, try to stop the flow of urine in midstream (don't try this first thing in the morning when your bladder is full—it's too hard). The better your control, the better the muscle tone. You can also check during love-making, by letting your mate tell you if he can feel the strength of your muscles increasing. He may be a better judge of your progress than you are!

## BREAST-FEEDING

Breast-feeding is an issue that affects not just the mother-and-child couple but the parent couple as well. The father may feel excluded or there may be problems with breast-feeding itself that may alienate the two of you. Breast-feeding is more complicated than just a "good way to feed the baby"; it isn't something the mother does exclusive of the father.

NOTE: I AM PLAYING DEVIL'S ADVOCATE HERE. This book is intended for couples, unlike child-care books, most of which lobby for breast-feeding. No intelligent person can question the nutritional content or the potential emotional benefits of breast-feeding. (If you have any doubts about where I stand personally on the subject, see that section in *Pregnancy & Childbirth*.)

This section is not intended as an examination of whether breast-feeding is better for your child. This book is dedicated to you as a couple, thus I am considering breast-feeding only as it affects your relationship. Although breast milk may be the best food for a baby, it can create problems for the parents. Most of these problems are temporary and surmountable, but it is important to recognize that nursing may not be comfortable for some people's lifestyles or compatible with their temperaments.

I'm here as a Devil's advocate, arguing the other side for you two as a couple. I want to help a new mother view her breasts as her own property, not something that belongs automatically to her baby. I'd like to help fathers understand that their feelings are important, too. People may try to pressure you into breast-feeding against your will or instinct, by telling you the terrible damage and disservice you'll be doing to your baby with a bottle. Keep in mind that your baby is going to thrive either way: the harmony in her home life is **at least** as important as what goes into her tummy and how it gets there.

Some of the following suggestions may sound contradictory, but that's because nursing is such an emotionally charged issue. The decision is not one that most couples can deal with in a light and easy way.

***Breast-feeding can be a big cause of conflict.*** Nursing can cause disagreements, either because one of you doesn't want the baby to breast-feed or because of the logistics of nursing. There is a current belief (based on a lot of evidence) that "breast-feeding is natural and therefore better." It follows from this that "good" parents will choose to breast-feed their child, while selfish or ignorant ones will bottle-feed.

***There is a social value placed on nursing.*** Some people believe that breast-feeding means you are "a real mother." This implies that there will be a stigma on you if you don't nurse your baby. However, you can be a good and loving mother and simply not want to nurse your baby.

***A new father may pressure his wife to breast-feed.*** A new father is influenced by the same social expectations that influence his wife: because nursing is the right thing to do in other people's eyes. Of course, a father may also think that nursing is the right thing for the baby. But if it's wrong for the baby's mother, then how can it possibly be right for the baby? The breast-feeding decision for a man is purely ideological; he has no way to comprehend the reality of nursing a baby, no experience that is equal to it. A baby's father shouldn't imagine that he can understand what breast-feeding means to the baby's mother, nor should she assume that he can.

***Your self-esteem depends on being true to yourself.*** It is important to your self-esteem that you respect your own feelings and not allow yourself to be swayed by social pressure, either inside your family or outside it. There is a price to pay for anything you do for the wrong reasons and that goes against your grain. If nursing causes you too much physical or emotional discomfort, or inconvenience, your resistance may cause you to fail at breast-feeding and you'll have to cope with the resulting guilt.

A new mother may decide to breast-feed primarily because she thinks other people or her mate expect it of her. Doing it to please your husband, your mother, or a pediatrician is an error. You have to want it yourself or the physical and emotional pressures will either lead to a nursing failure or complicate your marital relationship by creating deep resentments. They may also interfere with your attachment to the baby.

*A relaxed, happy home is your goal.*　Your happiness, a smooth transition to parenting, and your baby's well-being all depend on the **atmosphere** in your home. The quality of that environment is more important than your baby's feeding method and you're not going to be relaxed if you don't want to nurse. There can be a variety of reasons for your feelings: because of your career, because you can't stand having swollen and leaky breasts, because you don't like actually nursing, or because you're so utterly exhausted that you can do nothing else. Bottle-feeding may be the right choice for you.

*You should share the decision to breast-feed.*　Ideally, breast-feeding should be a shared decision and experience. If the father feels included he will be an invaluable ally if the going gets rough. When the nursing mother is discouraged or uncomfortable, the father's support can make the difference between success and failure. He can also give his wife emotional support if friends or relatives question her decision to breast-feed. By sticking together you can ignore other people's attitudes, such as negative reactions to mixing career and breast-feeding, to "mixed feeding" (using a bottle when breast-feeding), or to breast-feeding for either a short or long time.

*When in doubt, give it a try.*　If either of you is uncertain about whether to breast-feed, you might as well give it a try. You have nothing to lose from a short breast-feeding experience, whereas if you don't try it you may regret it later and it will be too late. Once you're involved, your doubts and feelings will be resolved. You can always stop, or combine breast-feeding and bottle-feeding. Be patient, don't jump to any decisions, and take it one day at a time.

***Bottle-feeding may be better for your family.*** Passionate advocates of breast-feeding may not want me to say this, but for some couples bottle-feeding may be more practical for their lifestyle or protective of their relationship. This may sound "selfish" to breast-feeding devotees, but it's important to understand that sometimes selfishness is a good thing. It certainly isn't a great idea for the *baby's* needs to take priority over everything else, because you are setting up a situation in which you are "teaching" him right from the beginning that he reigns supreme. The feeding decision should revolve around the precept that the baby is not the center of the universe and his needs aren't the only ones to consider.

***Breast-feeding may depend on the kind of relationship you have.*** For couples who are very connected and have gotten used to spending a lot of private time together, bottle-feeding may soften the transition to parenthood and having to share each other with the baby. Breast-feeding doesn't allow a mother much rest, or very much time for the relationship with her mate. A mother who bottle-feeds is going to be less tired.

Also, a couple's sex life may resume sooner because a woman's hormones return more rapidly to previous levels if she doesn't breast-feed. Your figure and sexual identity may come back more quickly. Finally, if you are bottle-feeding you'll be able to leave the baby for more than 2 hours at a time. This means you can have a social life with your husband, returning sooner to life in the outside world.

***The "second-week blues" are common.*** Even if they don't hit you hard, the blues are something to anticipate. The baby will be nursing energetically at this point and your nipples may be sore. Your milk is fully in and your breasts may be engorged and painful. This is a point at which you might question your decision to breast-feed and even feel you want to give it up. Hang in there: you've gotten through the hardest part of it. The second week is often the roughest. You shouldn't make any decisions when things seem bleak because you don't have the perspective you need.

*Nursing failure is a delicate issue.*   Breast-feeding is wonderful for those women who can and want to: it shouldn't be a catastrophic issue for those who cannot nurse or are not interested. Breast-feeding is not a test of womanhood or motherhood. Don't give in to outside pressure and try to nurse your baby against your own wishes, if you believe strongly that it's not for you. If you don't want to nurse then you won't have the inner conviction you're going to need when the going gets tough. Most women have some difficulties when they first breast-feed—it is their own determination that gets them through.

*Failing at nursing can feel like the end of the world.*   If you attempt to breast-feed and cannot nurse your baby successfully for any reason whatever, it can cause you terrible anguish. It is virtually impossible for anyone who has not experienced nursing failure to understand how deep and powerful that failure can be. As a new mother you are automatically vulnerable emotionally about yourself and the baby; the added burden of a nursing failure can be terrible.

   If you are unable to breast-feed successfully you are going to need a great deal of understanding and support, especially from your partner. He has to be sensitive to your pain and careful in the way he reacts to the nursing failure, otherwise the problem magnifies and becomes an area of disappointment and resentment between you. But a man should not think that he understands his wife's feelings just because he loves their child too and bonds with the child in various other ways. Nothing is like nursing. And nothing is like a nursing failure.

### THE FATHER'S REACTION TO BREAST-FEEDING

*Your husband may encourage you to quit nursing.*
If you have problems or doubts about nursing, your mate may encourage you to quit—or he may insist in a dictatorial way that you continue to breast-feed when you want to stop. He means well and only wants the best for you and the baby, but it is vital that you and your partner both

recognize that no man can fully comprehend what breast-feeding means to a woman. Once you realize that, you can accept your mate's help and support and he can extend them, knowing that no matter how sensitive he may be, he can't truly understand the experience of breast-feeding. He sees it as a nice, healthy way to feed the baby; he has no way to understand the depth of a woman's physical and emotional responses to nursing.

*Your husband will not be able to truly understand.*
If you are breast-feeding and have problems or doubts, your spouse cannot relate to the conflict that this creates for you. You are into breast-feeding emotionally on a level that he can't truly comprehend. For you, the idea of giving up nursing your baby, of "failing," is devastating.

*A father may have problems with breast-feeding.*
The father may feel isolated and, because of that, shut out of the early bonding his wife has with the baby. Being able to feed your baby, and especially to share the night feedings, may be more important to you as a new father than the benefits of breast milk. If you are taking a paternity leave and want to really share in feeding your child, as opposed to just giving an occasional bottle, then you might want to consider bottle-feeding. However, if you and your mate are willing to make the effort, she can express breast milk and refrigerate or freeze the bottles. That way you can feed the baby, who will still be getting the benefits of mother's milk.

*Here are some suggestions for how a new father can avoid feeling left out because the baby is breast-feeding:*

---

HINTS FOR A "BREAST-FEEDING" FATHER

- Acknowledge that you are feeling helpless and frustrated because you can't feed your baby
- Whenever possible, give the baby at least an occasional bottle of breast milk, formula, or water so that you can partially satisfy your desire to nourish him
- Recognize that the baby has many other needs you can meet: give him a bath, take him for a walk, play with toys
- Make time to be totally alone with the baby, away from everyone: you may find special pleasure in getting away from criticism and enjoying your fathering style on your own
- Try to learn to forget yourself and be unself-conscious when you're with the baby; discover all the ways you can be a father other than by feeding a bottle

---

*Any and all reactions to breast-feeding are legitimate.* Some new mothers make the fundamental mistake of being insensitive to their husbands' feelings about breast-feeding. Both parents should feel free to express their feelings without judgment from their partner.

*There is only so much a man can do.* Your wife may want to breast-feed but have problems and expect too much help from you. You can encourage your partner or help with household tasks but you'll probably reach a point where her dependence on you becomes a problem. Ultimately, a woman has to be responsible for her own body and its ability to feed her baby. Remember that the first two weeks are the most demanding (see "second-week blues" on page 149) and that the situation will improve.

## BREAST-FEEDING AND YOUR SEX LIFE

*Nursing usually affects a couple's sex life.* Your sexuality as a couple will probably be affected by breast-feeding. A nursing woman generally is not very interested in sex: her hormones don't return to prepregnancy levels until after the baby is weaned. Also, most of her energy is going to the child. Women often find that they have no passion or desire for their mate and are fearful that something is wrong with them.

***Your husband may be uncomfortable with your body.*** It is not unusual for a man to be afraid of his wife's large, leaky breasts or to be turned off by them. Or he may be turned on by her breasts but be uncomfortable having sexual feelings about his baby's milk supply! He may also feel intensely jealous, left out of a strong attachment that excludes him. Some men fantasize breast-feeding themselves; it is a perfectly normal reaction. **None of this is a crisis.** These are common feelings in the postpartum adjustment to breast-feeding. Unrealistic expectations are more of a problem than the difficulties themselves. Nursing is **temporary** and the disruptions will pass (for more specific information, see *Chapter 8: Sex and Romance*).

***Some women describe a sensual pleasure in breast-feeding.*** For women who were not particularly erotic or aware of physical pleasure before, these sensations can be exciting or frightening. Other women may be upset to find that their sex drive is reduced or nonexistent because of prolactin, the hormone a woman's body produces to make milk.

***Changes in your sexual appetite can be surprising or disturbing.*** Keep in mind that sexual pleasure is an involuntary response over which you have no control. It is normal to worry whether you are perverse for getting so much pleasure from your baby while not desiring your mate. Your guilt or confusion can make you pull away from your partner even more.

***A new father may worry whether he's lost his wife.*** Many men wonder whether they will ever get their lover back. At the same time, many breast-feeding wives worry whether they'll ever return to normal and want to make love again. The two of you may not have much patience left because of whatever sexual abstinence or adjustments you made in the end of the pregnancy. It may feel like years since you've had sex, but just try to be patient a little longer. Things will get better, little by little.

***A nursing woman can feel fat and unattractive.*** When you're breast-feeding, your feelings about your body can be a problem for your sex life. The pregnancy weight comes off very slowly, often not until the baby is weaned. If you are uncomfortable or disgusted by your large breasts and heavy body, you may begin to think of yourself as a fat cow—many women do. This self-image will not make you feel particularly sexy!

Your mate may find you attractive but if you feel bad about yourself you're not going to respond sexually; undoubtedly you will reject him if he wants to make love. This can create a vicious cycle at a point in your lives when you're both vulnerable emotionally. If you fall asleep during intercourse (breast-feeding is exhausting work) or spurn your mate's advances, he's going to have hurt feelings and doubts. Don't you find him attractive any more? What happened to the sexy woman he married?

**Your husband may feel lonely, angry, and frustrated if your rejection continues.**   How would you feel about being rejected over and over? He may have various reactions: his anger at you may come out at inappropriate times, or he may masturbate, or he may have an affair.

He may also become paranoid about you, especially if you were a sensual, sexual woman before you had the baby. Your mate may not be able to imagine that you'd want *no sex* at all, therefore he begins to fantasize that you must be having an affair. This may sound ludicrous to you, dead-tired, with swollen leaky breasts, but when a man feels needy and abandoned you can't expect his paranoia to be very logical.

**A woman's orgasms may change when she is breast-feeding.**   If you are a woman who experiences orgasm, you may notice a difference in the sexual climax itself. You may become less orgasmic or have less intense orgasms. During intercourse, having an orgasm may seem less important to you; if you don't have an orgasm your body may not stay in a state of excitement, as it normally might. If you used to masturbate you may not have any desire to do so while you are nursing: the bottom line is that sex just isn't very important to you now. These are things you should try to discuss with your mate so that he understands your lack of sex drive and doesn't take it personally.

***Where the baby sleeps can affect your sex life.*** If your baby fusses a lot or nurses for a long time at each feeding, the mother and baby may choose to sleep separately from the father so that he can get more rest. Even though this decision may seem like it is for a man's own good, it can create a distance between you as a couple that you can't afford right now.

Sleeping apart can highlight a basic conflict in your intimate or sexual life when you are nursing. The woman may be satisfied by her relationship with the baby, plus she is exhausted and has a low sex drive. The man needs warmth, reassurance, and sexual release. So before you consider sleeping apart, recognize the emotional effect it can have and discuss this with each other.

***A man may want to taste breast milk.*** It's quite natural for a new father to be curious about breast milk and want to see what it tastes like. This is not weird or abnormal, but for some couples it can create a conflict for either partner about sexuality and mothering. The breasts were initially part of a couple's sex life; their new function is to nourish the baby, albeit with some sensual pleasure for the mother.

If the father now wants to suckle at his wife's breast, it can be an emotionally charged issue for either of them, mixing together two contradictory aspects of their life. The best thing you can do is try to be relaxed about it. If a man is curious about breast milk, his wife should accept it as a healthy, normal desire and let him try it. If, on the other hand, he isn't interested in her breast milk, she has to respect his feelings and not expect him to try it.

## "ON-DEMAND" BREAST-FEEDING

***On-demand breast-feeding is a strain on a marriage.*** If you feed your baby every time he cries, it can be very difficult on both parents. What is referred to as "total breast-feeding" denies a woman's needs and subjugates her to the baby's whims. Maintaining an on-demand schedule is particularly disruptive to your life as a couple because the baby is at the breast more or less constantly, day and night. A mother also requires some time for herself, as a person separate from her milk-producing skills: "total breast-feeding" doesn't permit you to plan any individual activities for yourself.

Certain parents' groups espouse total breast-feeding, but they don't seem to think that a mother has individual needs that count as much as her baby's needs do. No one would deny that it's wonderful for a baby to have breast milk and a warm, close relationship with its provider. However, on-demand breast-feeding can become a ritual offering of a mother on the altar of breast-feeding.

There are logical limits on how frequently you should offer your breasts, unless you welcome the idea of suckling your child around the clock. It is considered normal for a breast-feeding mother to set a schedule of feedings that are a minimum of 3 hours apart.

**Is on-demand feeding an escape hatch?**   It is not just armchair psychology to suggest that a woman is avoiding something in her life by choosing on-demand feeding. Why else would a woman decide to devote her existence to nursing a constantly "hungry" baby, effectively leaving no time or room for anything or anyone else?

**Do not be coerced into "total breast-feeding."**   You might find yourself talked into on-demand feeding by another woman who chose this lifestyle. A new mother is vulnerable to being convinced by a persuasive friend or sister that this is the true and natural way to nourish a child. Stop and think what that woman's relationship with her husband was like before the baby. And what was their relationship like during the nursing period? What else does she have in her life besides this well-fed child? These are not value judgments, they are just food for thought.

**On-demand feeding isn't good for the baby, either.** For the baby's good, there are practical reasons not to allow total breast-feeding. If the baby is allowed around-the-clock snacking, she learns not to fill her stomach at one feeding. She also learns right from the beginning how to impose on your life, demanding your total attention instead of having to fit in with your routine and rhythms.

Regardless of what advocates of on-demand feeding may say, no healthy baby is hungry every 30 to 60 minutes. She may want to suckle, but a pacifier fills that need (you may not like the way it looks, but it doesn't do her any harm). Furthermore, if you are stressed or overtired from constant nursing, you may not develop the best possible relationship with the baby. Ironically, the end result may be that she may not get enough milk, either (see below).

*A diminishing milk supply can become a problem.* If a nursing mother is fatigued and not getting enough sleep, her milk may diminish. The obvious advice is that you have to make sure that you get some really good rest. You can also try changing your diet, drinking more fluids, taking brewer's yeast, or drinking wine or beer before nursing to relax.

You may want to talk to the pediatrician about the idea of a supplemental bottle of formula. Ideally the father or someone else should give this bottle so that you can rest while the baby receives extra nutrition. The doctor may also allow the baby a cereal supplement (if she's not too young) to satisfy her hunger and take the pressure off of you.

If you insist on giving the child nothing but breast milk, then you may be able to express some milk and refrigerate a bottle that the baby's father can give at night. This will give you those precious middle-of-the-night hours to sleep. With any luck this rest and break from the routine will restore a good milk supply.

*How should you make the decision to wean the baby?* The decision about weaning is ideally one that should be made by both parents. Only the two of you know the pressures and feelings you have about breast-feeding. You may reach a point where you feel pulled apart as a couple by the exclusive relationship the mother has had with the baby. A man may feel increasingly resentful of the demands that breast-feeding makes on his wife; maybe "relief bottles" don't give enough relief.

You may feel tied down, resentful, or irritated by leaking milk and sore breasts. You may want to go back to work or resume former activities that nursing doesn't permit. Your partner may want to have more of a life together, especially outside the house.

***Breast-feeding can become a chore rather than a pleasure.***   When nursing your baby turns into a duty rather than a freely given gift for your child, it may be time to wean the baby. Both parents should talk about whether they feel that switching to bottle-feeding will ease the pressures they are feeling. If you come to this conclusion, then have the courage of your convictions. Don't let outsiders' opinions interfere with what you think is best for your life. The feeding method that is the most satisfying for you will be the best for your whole family, the baby included.

## THE EFFECT OF BOTTLE-FEEDING ON YOUR MARRIAGE

Bottle-feeding presents its own set of problems for a couple. Whether you decide to feed formula right from the beginning or give up breast-feeding at any point, don't imagine that the bottle is going to leave you both free as larks. As has been said in quite another context, "There is no such thing as a free lunch."

***Bottles of formula don't grow on trees.***   There is a fair amount of tedious work and planning ahead to prepare the bottles. It takes teamwork. For some couples, that concept is even harder than fixing the bottles! Working as a team is something you probably haven't had to learn as a couple, unless you already run a small business together. Bottle-feeding means you have to negotiate who makes each night's ration of bottles. Then you have to decide who gets up to give the bottles to the baby, that adorable, wailing bundle. If you are like other normal, first-time parents, you'll find that your teamwork doesn't exactly mesh like an Olympic relay team.

You'll need several bottles to get the baby through the night. It also helps to plan ahead so that you have a bottle ready for the first morning feeding, too. Somehow it often works out that you're short that one critical bottle: at the desperate moment when the baby's screams of hunger are especially shrill, there's no friendly white bottle inside that refrigerator door.

*Who will make the formula?* And when? Which of you will get up for the 2 a.m. feeding? And what about the 6 a.m.? How much does the baby's father want to do? (And how much *less* does he want to do after the first week when the novelty wears off?) How much does the baby's mother expect her mate to help? (And how flexible is she in adjusting those expectations?) Bottle-feeding is sure to give you some memorable moments of crabbiness in your partnership.

There are short-cuts, of course. There are those expensive, disposable plastic liners that go inside the bottles so you don't have to sterilize the bottles. But even so, someone still has to prepare the formula, clean the nipples, and store the bottles.

*Ready-made formula can be a life-saver.* As a gift, you might ask someone for a case of ready-made formula, like the samples they give out at the hospital. These can be life-savers in the middle of the night when that aforementioned critical bottle isn't there. They can also be marriage-savers. It is a well-known fact of parenting life that the missing bottle is *always* your mate's fault. If you can reach for a bottle of ready-made formula in the middle of the night, you will have forgotten by morning how angry you were!

## CESAREAN BIRTH

If your baby was delivered by cesarean section, then you may be somewhat more depleted as new parents. You should be aware of the emotions and physical considerations following a cesarean birth: they can affect a couple differently than a vaginal delivery. You both have many feelings to sort out after the baby is safely delivered, especially because most cesareans are unexpected.

*You both are vulnerable emotionally.* The mother has increased emotional needs as she recovers from the surgery. A woman wants to be taken care of just when her husband and baby need her so much. The father needs reassurance that in all the confusion there's going to be time for him, that he's still important.

***You may be deeply disappointed.*** You may have had hopes and dreams about a shared birth experience and you may feel sadness or anger about missing that. One remedy for this is to hold and feed your baby as much as possible in the early days. Have the nurses bring him to you often in the hospital and spend as much time together with him as you can. You need the reassurance of seeing and feeling the baby: you need to be close to him as much as he needs you.

***Express your feelings and complaints.*** It is common for parents to have a lot of unresolved emotions, whether about their own relationship, the doctor, or attitudes at the hospital during the delivery. You may have a particular complaint if the father was not allowed to be there for the cesarean, which is becoming an option at more and more hospitals (but only in a nonemergency situation).

***A cesarean can alienate you from each other.*** Share your postpartum feelings with each other: a cesarean birth can disrupt an intimacy that you have to regain. You may be having feelings that your partner doesn't understand. A new mother often has mood swings after a cesarean, feeling fine one day and then angrily wondering "Why me?" the next. These feelings can be intensified because of normal postpartum hormonal changes or from any pain medication you've been taking that may have a depressant effect on you.

The baby's father may not be aware of your feelings because of fears and anxieties of his own. Your husband may be able to give you supportive understanding if he first has a chance to discuss the cesarean from his point of view. Once he is relieved of that burden, he may be better able to reach out to you.

***The hospital may have made problems for a new father.*** The difficulties a man may have with his wife's cesarean usually arise from the way he was treated in the hospital. If a man is with his wife early in labor and then suddenly cut off and excluded from the rest of the birth, he can feel frightened, isolated, and helpless. Sometimes fathers are left an hour or two without contact or information; every 30 minutes that passes without news can drive you up the wall.

It is the father's responsibility to keep informed about the progress of the cesarean. Hospital personnel have dozens of other demands on their time; often they simply forget the waiting father. If the hospital won't let you in the operating room, or you don't want to be there, or it's an emergency cesarean (which necessarily excludes you), then make it your business to **demand** information about how your wife and baby are doing.

*A man can have powerful feelings after a cesarean.* Many new fathers feel angry, powerless, guilty, disappointed, jealous, and more. As you can imagine, this combination of powerful emotions can have a negative effect on your relationship with your wife and baby unless you and your partner understand the reason for all these feelings.

A father is **angry** for being pushed aside in the birth process; **helpless** in trying to comfort or protect his wife; **guilty** for not being with her when she needed him. He is **disappointed** that he couldn't witness the birth; full of **self-pity** for having missed the thrill; **jealous** of other fathers who are high on having been there for their child's birth; **ashamed** of such selfish feelings when all he should be worried about is the health of the mother and baby.

Be aware of the possibility that you will experience some or all of these feelings. Have the feelings, then let them go and move on with your life. The bottom line is that you have a baby to discover and enjoy together. Participating in a vaginal delivery is something you may experience in the future; it may also turn out to be one of those things you're going to miss out on in life, like driving a race car at Le Mans or going up in a hot-air balloon. It would've been nice, but you shouldn't lose any sleep over it.

*Nursing can counteract some of the bad feelings.* Breast-feeding can be a wonderful way to capture the naturalness and intimacy that you may feel you missed in the baby's birth. It is highly recommended for cesarean mothers because the physical and emotional closeness of nursing can help overcome what may have been a difficult beginning. Also, nursing can make you feel that your body can do at least *something* right, since having a cesarean can make you feel your body has let you down.

***Parents often feel the cesarean was their fault.*** Although most cesareans are required because of fetal or maternal distress, it's common to feel you did something wrong. Outsiders may imply that the woman is to blame, that you weren't "strong enough" or didn't really want to become a mother. Prepared childbirth classes may also have encouraged you to think that any nonnatural birth is your fault. It is often implied that a couple will be assured of an unmedicated, natural birth if they are sufficiently dedicated. In fact, you have no control over the size of your pelvis, the baby's position, a stubborn cervix, the amount of oxygen reaching the baby, or even an unsupportive birthing environment.

It is not unusual to blame yourselves for the cesarean, to play the "if only" game: "if only" you had (1) practiced your breathing more, (2) held out longer and not taken drugs, (3) pushed better, (4) been more relaxed, (5) worked better as a team, (6) etc. This sense of failure can interfere with your self-confidence in parenting, because you're letting yourselves believe that you failed yourselves and your child right at the start.

***You may feel you're in competition with the baby.***
Feeling a conflict between herself and the baby is a natural reaction for a mother when she's recovering from a cesarean. You have a baby, but you've also had major surgery: you may feel torn between taking care of your own needs and the baby's. The simple act of getting up can be so difficult at first that you cringe when you hear the baby cry, dreading having to get out of bed. Then you feel like a heel for responding that way to your child's cries for help.

***Your scar can make you resent the baby.*** You may be angry at the baby for putting you through an operation. Some women feel that their baby "scarred them for life." It can make you feel guilty to have these feelings, but it's important to talk about them and work them through. That kind of resentment can affect your feelings toward the baby and interfere with your attachment.

*Household help is an absolute necessity for the first few weeks.* You can arrange for paid help, a relative, or your husband may be able to take time off from his job, but you cannot take care of the baby and house alone. No matter how cheerful you try to be, the fact is that you've had abdominal surgery and your body has healing to do. You need to use your strength wisely so that you make a quick, full recovery from the surgery.

*You might get depressed or impatient.* The fatigue and physical weakness that you'll undoubtedly experience can make you emotional. Physical limitations can increase your feelings of helplessness or guilt. Anyone who has surgery is going to get tired easily in the first weeks. You'll be dependent on others for baby care, household chores, and taking care of other children you may have. All of this can add up to frustration for you if you cannot just accept the fact that your abilities are limited right now. The best thing you can do is snuggle up with the baby and leave the worrying to someone else.

*Restricting visitors is important for a cesarean mother.* You need two full weeks to convalesce: if you exhaust yourself you'll recover more slowly or have a relapse. You may think of visitors as a pleasant distraction, but they require as much energy as running around a track. The same advice is true for mothers who had vaginal deliveries or adopted, so it's doubly true for you.

Do not let people pressure you into letting them come over to visit. They do *not* have to see your child right away, regardless of what they say! Don't let any potential visitor make you feel guilty about not letting them see the baby right away. You will be much better off if you postpone visits even from relatives; just say those are the doctor's orders. Everything in its own good time. If you take care of yourself in the beginning, your recovery will be faster and more complete. I'm sure your doctor will agree!

***There are physical limitations after a cesarean.*** Most rules are related to the healing of your abdominal incision. For the first two weeks you should not climb stairs (or as little as possible) and you shouldn't lift anything heavier than your baby for one month. Most doctors do permit a woman to carry her baby after a cesarean, but you should check with your own obstetrician about that and any other restrictions.

The physical discomforts you may feel are abdominal pain from the cut, pain in one or both shoulders (blood and gas collect under the diaphragm in your upper abdomen), and gas pains as your intestines resume functioning (usually on the third day). You can minimize many of these problems by turning over frequently in bed, walking as soon as possible after surgery, doing the breathing exercises the nurse will show you, drinking lots of liquids, and eating a diet high in fiber. If you have to sneeze, laugh, or cough, hold a pillow over your incision.

***There are two basic signs of serious problems: a fever or excessive vaginal bleeding. You should call your doctor if either of these occurs.***

***Resuming sex after a cesarean: the good news and the bad news.*** The bad news is that in the beginning, intercourse can be very painful for some women. To avoid pain, positions with the least amount of pressure on the incision are often best. The good news is that you'll probably experience fewer discomforts having sex again than a woman who's had a vaginal delivery. You don't have an episiotomy or any of the trauma to the vagina itself that has to heal.

***Try to look on the bright side.*** Instead of thinking of this recuperation as a frustrating time when you can't get things done, why not look at it as a time to hang out with the baby and your partner and get to know each other?

# 7
# Postpartum depression (PPD)

The technical definition of "postpartum" is when the uterus returns to its prepregnant condition, which is six to eight weeks after delivery. However, psychologically the definition of "postpartum" is more flexible: some experts consider a period as long as six years after birth, or when the child goes to school full time.

Postpartum depression is relevant to this book because if a woman suffers from it, it's obviously going to affect her marriage. Knowing about this disorder and what you can do about it will help prevent it from becoming a destructive event in your lives.

NOTE: *The baby's father may have to read this section and "translate" it for his wife. One symptom of PPD is an inability to read or concentrate—this is an effect of depression at any time in a person's life. So if a woman's depression is bad enough, she may need help in understanding and coping with it.*

## THE DEFINITION OF "POSTPARTUM DEPRESSION" (PPD)

The clinical definition of PPD (as I will refer to it in this chapter) is "the hormonally, biochemically induced reaction to the body's upheaval in giving birth." It is generally agreed by experts that after a woman gives birth there is a temporary breakdown in the normal flow of brain chemicals; this creates a natural, temporary state of mental imbalance.

*There is a disagreement about when PPD can occur.* Most doctors and books tell you that PPD will occur in the first days after the baby is born and will last only a few days. But some women don't suffer until the eighth week—and for some it can be the eighth *month!* There are PPD support groups that contend that up to a year after the birth is a relevant period. PPD is a condition about which not enough is known and not enough is being done.

*There is disagreement about a further definition of PPD.* Experts have a variety of theories about how to further define this syndrome. One medical school of thought divides PPD into three stages: the first 10 days after delivery; the next three months; and then the following three months ending with the baby's six-month birthday. There is another school of thought that divides PPD into two principal categories: "early syndrome" and "late onset" PPD, depending on when the symptoms begin after birth and how severe they are.

This second group of experts defines "early syndrome" as the first three weeks postpartum, with a range from mild or moderate "blues" to severe psychosis (hallucinations, mania, mood swings). They further define a woman with the early syndrome as experiencing no psychological disturbance in the first three days postpartum and then mild blues from the third to fifteenth days, with 25 to 50 percent of women having symptoms of restlessness, tearfulness, insomnia, and confusion. The specialists describe "late onset" as occurring from the 20th to 40th days postpartum, characterized by a depression with a slow but insidious onset. The woman may feel sad, futile, or lacking in energy, while in severe cases a mother may feel suicidal or fear that she'll harm her baby.

*Current studies often disagree with these theories.* There are many other experts who dismiss the previous two theories ("three stages" and "early and late onset"). They consider both these views of PPD to be conservative, old-fashioned, and incomplete, contending that the school of thought dividing PPD into three stages is incorrect because a woman's symptoms do not just disappear after the first 10 days. These people also take issue with the view of dividing PPD into two stages because they contend there is no significant difference between early or late depression.

It is thought by yet another group of experts that *any* reaction to birth should be considered as a postpartum *reaction,* not just depression. These experts have found that the physical and emotional pressure of giving birth can induce strange behavior: depression or euphoria, manic energy or listless moods. These experts say that we should be paying attention to any illogical or unexplainable emotional reaction postpartum.

**In America, PPD has not been seriously studied.** Although PPD has been recognized as a syndrome since the 18th century in England, so far it doesn't seem to have gotten the attention of the United States medical profession. PPD hasn't been looked at in an organized way—not much attention is paid to this problem either clinically or in research. PPD is not incorporated into the clinical practice of most obstetricians; it seems to be difficult for people to accept that this painful and debilitating syndrome can occur at a time when a woman is supposed to be happy.

In England, for example, there is the Marcé Society, an organization of doctors and other professionals concerned about PPD. The British also have hospitals with mother-baby units where women with PPD can be treated without being separated from their infants. There are no such specialized facilities in America.

The English have historically been aware of the devastating and tragic effects of severe PPD. In 1922, they passed the British Infanticide Act, which reduced penalties against women with PPD who kill their newborns. Although such a horrible possibility may seem unthinkable to you, British experts have determined that PPD is a condition to be taken seriously and treated accordingly.

# WHO GETS PPD?

*Almost every new mother experiences some PPD.*
Therefore, this syndrome can't properly be called a pathological condition, or even an abnormal one, since most women experience some form of it. Some studies show that 80 percent of mothers have some symptoms of what are called "baby blues," although for most women it passes quickly. Crying is most common from the fifth to the 10th day postpartum, with other symptoms of sleeplessness, anger or hostility, irritability and/or confusion.

*PPD can affect anyone.* Often it happens to women who appear not to be at risk. It happens to strong, well-adjusted women as well as to nervous, neurotic ones. It can be a result of your birth experience, your childhood, your hormones, or none of these. Women who are otherwise normal get PPD. New studies emphasize that PPD happens totally out of the blue, with no precipitating factors, to previously normal women. If you're affected by PPD, it is not a judgment on you as a mother or woman. It doesn't come from laziness or poor character. PPD is an illness that can be treated.

*PPD can happen after any pregnancy.* PPD can affect a woman after a first, second, or third birth. It can affect a woman in a later pregnancy even if she didn't have PPD after her first baby. The intensity of the PPD does not diminish, either.

*PPD is almost impossible to predict.* According to current research, there are only a few factors that are known to make a new mother vulnerable to PPD. A woman who previously had PPD is likely to get it again. Figures vary, but studies show that if you had PPD with your first pregnancy, there is a 20 to 80 percent chance it will recur. A woman who has had a severe depression at some point in her life is also at risk. Other research shows that if you previously had several symptoms of PMS (premenstrual syndrome), it is a signal that you should be on your guard against PPD.

**The following is a chart of stress factors.** These are elements that can predispose a woman to PPD before her baby is born. This list does not mean you will get PPD, it's simply a tool to help you identify elements in your life that may be stressful. If you have experienced several of these factors, then you and your mate can be sensitive to the emotional burden you've been carrying along with the baby.

---

### STRESS FACTORS CONNECTED TO PPD

- Childbirth delayed because of ambivalence
- More than one previous abortion or several miscarriages
- Family history of complications in pregnancy or delivery
- Unplanned pregnancy, parents ambivalent
- History of hormonal problems: early menses; irregular, painful periods; PMS symptoms
- First baby
- Marriage new, still in the erotic/romantic stage
- Recent move to a new home
- No relatives available for postpartum care
- Woman ill, because of the pregnancy or not
- Death of a parent (especially mother) in childhood or adolescence
- Recent death or severe illness of someone close to you
- Man or woman with education higher than their parents'
- Woman's career important to her, fearful of jeopardizing it with motherhood
- Man or woman taking on a new job or increased responsibilities at current job
- Man away from home a great deal
- Woman used to spending a lot of time outside the home, with her mate or not
- Marital tension, discord; feeling unloved or unsupported by your mate

***If you lost a parent, it has a lasting effect.*** If either you or your mate lost a parent in childhood, it will have a profound effect on you for your entire life. In general, losing the mother (or more specifically the "mothering" parent) is more significant for either a man or a woman. But as a child matures and begins to identify with the parent of the same sex, this can shift: the father becomes more important for a boy and the mother becomes more important for a girl.

It is believed that if a person loses a parent in childhood or adolescence, this can be an indication of the need for psychotherapy as an adult. Some experts believe that you would need professional help to give up the parent you lost and have unconsciously been seeking. If your parent died when you were a child or adolescent, that parent can become fixed in an ideal position in your subconscious. This can lead to a lifelong search for that person in a partner or in close, intimate relationships. This search takes place unconsciously and therefore would probably require the help of a psychotherapist.

***Multiple factors mean greater risk.*** If a pregnant woman has a lot of the stress factors on the previous chart, experts say she has a greater chance of PPD. Stressful events can lead to a temporary emotional imbalance. However, everyone has a different tolerance for stress and ability to cope with it: that individual resilience is as important as the stress itself. If you can be aware of the stress factor in major life adjustments, it may help you to prepare and cope with your feelings postpartum.

## THE SYMPTOMS OF PPD

*There are warning signs of PPD.* The charts of symptoms that follow on pages 172–73 sound mind-boggling—how could one poor person suffer so much!—but obviously you're not going to have *all* the signs. In fact, many of the symptoms are similar to the normal reactions of new parents in the stressful first weeks; this is why PPD is so difficult to identify.

*Early detection is the key to recovery.* If PPD is not diagnosed, it can progress and become much worse than it might have been if you'd gotten help early. Reporting symptoms as soon as possible may help prevent a snowballing effect. Unfortunately, many obstetricians are not sensitive to the problems of PPD; even if you describe a variety of symptoms, your doctor may dismiss your problems in an off-handed manner. A woman's problems coping with motherhood may just be too threatening or overwhelming for many doctors to deal with (husbands have a hard time, also). Just to complicate matters, PPD is very often not recognizable over the phone.

*Cancelling your OB-GYN checkup is a sign of trouble.* A common warning symptom of PPD is if you don't go to your six-week postpartum checkup. You may not be able to take a shower, get dressed, and organize the baby to go out. Unfortunately, the obstetrician or his nurse may not take note that you cancelled or just didn't show up. If you or your mate are reading this, please help yourselves by admitting that you have a problem on your hands.

*Your baby's adjustment is another clue to PPD.* Another serious sign of PPD is a "failure-to-thrive" baby. If your depression is severe enough and you haven't made a close attachment to your infant or have trouble caring for him physically or emotionally, he will probably be affected. Signs of a "failure-to-thrive" infant are that he is limp, nonresponsive, and doesn't make eye contact. If you leave your baby in this depressed state (which is a result of your depressed state), he won't bond, develop trust, etc. It is important for you to bring him to your six-week postpartum checkup for counselling. You should also contact the pediatrician or a children's hospital to get help for the infant and yourself as soon as possible.

***The charts that follow are only a guide.***   The following charts are a list of the many possible warning signs of PPD; their variety and complexity gives you an idea of why it's not easy to diagnose or treat. Some of these symptoms are experienced by many mothers and are mild reactions; other are an alarming indication of postpartum psychosis. If you are suffering from PPD, you will probably have several of these symptoms.

The symptoms are divided into two charts, physical and emotional, but of course there are physical complaints that can be psychosomatic, like severe headaches or backaches.

NOTE: If any of these symptoms become bizarre, exaggerated, or persist for any length of time, you may need professional help (see pages 185–87). If you experience these or other unusual signals you should seek a professional counselor.

---

**PHYSICAL SYMPTOMS OF PPD**

- Change in eating habits (overeating or poor appetite)
- Constipation or diarrhea
- Heart pounding; chest pains
- Feeling tense, unable to relax
- Dizziness, faintness
- Change in sleep patterns (difficulty falling or staying asleep, or oversleeping)
- Fatigue, lack of energy
- Itchiness
- Headaches
- Muscle soreness or stiffness
- Stomach aches or "butterflies" in the stomach
- Nausea
- Nervousness, shakiness, trembling
- Trouble concentrating; unable to sit still
- Hot or cold spells
- Inability to sleep for days at a time, even with a quiet or sleeping baby
- Spots before your eyes
- Pale complexion
- Back pains
- Loss of libido: no sex drive or orgasm

## EMOTIONAL SIGNS OF PPD

- Incessant crying or crying easily for no apparent reason
- Irritability, fussiness
- Crying for more than 15 minutes on several consecutive days
- Temper tantrums: extreme uncontrolled outbursts of hostility, screaming
- Withdrawal, loneliness; feeling no one understands your predicament
- Hypersensitivity to comments or criticism
- Hatred of husband or baby
- Impulse to injure baby
- Fear of being alone, need to be with people constantly
- Hatred of self; feeling inferior to others, feeling inadequate
- Impulse to leave family; feeling of being trapped
- Inability to touch or care for the baby
- Constant feeling of not wanting the baby
- Suicidal thoughts while handling the baby
- Feeling hopeless; extreme pessimism
- Religious preoccupations that are unusual for you
- Bizarre phobias (fear of common household items), fantasies of disaster
- General fear or anxiety
- Thoughts of death, suicide, abandonment
- Bad dreams
- No interest in previously pleasurable activities
- Increased desire for alcoholic beverages
- Excessive worrying, especially about child; unable to leave him/her
- Excessive guilt: over things that go wrong; because of angry feelings toward husband and baby; or because of lack of attachment to baby
- Forgetfulness; your mind goes blank
- Feeling confused; feeling you can't get anything accomplished
- Difficulty making decisions
- Having to do things slowly to be sure they're right; checking and rechecking things you do; asking advice or directions on simple tasks
- Failing to keep your appointment for the 6th-week postpartum checkup

## SOME REASONS FOR PPD

The most up-to-date research mentioned earlier may be correct that there aren't any reliable predictors of PPD. Nevertheless, I am including the following reasons for PPD because it may be useful (or comforting) to a woman or her mate to consider possible reasons for her condition. Studies done over the years have come up with various conclusions, some contradictory. Nevertheless, all theories are worth considering since every woman's situation is unique and PPD is still poorly understood.

*Your personality has nothing to do with it.* As stated earlier, personality is not a factor in PPD. There are strong, cheerful, optimistic, nurturant women who suffer from these symptoms, too. It is a myth that a well-adjusted woman with certain personality traits will have an easy adjustment and be a good mother. That woman is just as vulnerable to PPD as a gloomy, neurotic, insecure new mother.

*A "personality change" is not a normal reaction to childbearing.* Women who attend PPD groups often hear about other new mothers with PPD who didn't know they had it. Many of them passively accepted that "their personality changed" after the baby was born. These women were probably suffering from PPD without knowing it. Their depression deepened, was not treated, and finally the women incorporated those negative traits and attitudes into their personalities. Don't let this happen to you or someone you love.

*Your childbirth experience can cause PPD.* Insensitive handling of a woman in the hospital or a negative birth experience can cause depression.

*Medication given during delivery or afterwards can affect you.* Drugs used during labor and birth or postpartum can have a depressant effect on you.

*You may be extremely tired.* Exhaustion from labor and delivery and a lack of sleep afterwards can cause emotional disturbance.

***Previous depressions can put you at risk for PPD.***
A history of depression, particularly if it occurred during
your pregnancy, may mean a likelihood of PPD.

***There may be a genetic basis for PPD.*** Some experts
believe there is an inherited gene for depression. In some
women, manic-depressive illness has its onset in the postpartum period.

***You may have repressed problems.*** Unresolved emotional conflicts from before or during your pregnancy may
surface intensely after the baby is born. Your relationship
with your mate (feeling unloved or marital problems in general) and your feelings about the pregnancy (it was unplanned or you have ambivalent feelings) affect your
emotional state postpartum.

***You may have trouble with your new image.*** The inability to see yourself as a parent can lead to PPD. If you
can't identify with other parents, you may have a hard time
identifying with yourself as a parent. You may get positive
reinforcement by spending time with other new parents.

***A woman who feels insecure is at risk.*** If you feel
inadequate generally, if you often experience self-doubt as
you go through life, you may get PPD. You may be more
susceptible to PPD if: (1) you are a younger woman who
lacks confidence because you don't have much experience
in life; (2) you don't feel in control of your own life; (3) you
feel subordinate to your mate or other people.

***You may be having an identity crisis.*** A loss of your
self-image, a loss of your identity, can be the result of motherhood. Becoming a parent may mean that you've lost your
sexual self-image, your body shape and strength, perhaps
your job and economic independence, and the adult community you had. The PPD that may result is parallel to adolescent depression, when you had to contend with
hormonal changes and the emotional stress of a changing
self-image.

*Loneliness, isolation, or feeling trapped can lead to PPD.* A new mother may be cut off from family, friends, and other new mothers. Childless companions may not understand the changes you are going through (and you may not, either!). A lack of adult conversation and interaction can make you feel like you're trapped with an infant who is holding you hostage.

*Phobias can keep you housebound.* If you become a prisoner in your own home, it can lead to loneliness and depression. You may be afraid to navigate steps with the baby carriage, fearful about crossing the street, of weather conditions, of strangers approaching the baby, etc. You may have a colicky baby and be fearful and embarrassed that he'll scream in public, so you stay home. If you're phobic, you may feel disoriented in the outside world: these surreal feelings and fears can trap you in the house.

*Unrealistic expectations can lead to PPD.* The contradiction between what you're "supposed" to feel and what you actually experience as a new parent can be destructive. If you believe that parenthood is supposed to be all pleasure, for instance, then the dichotomy between that expectation and reality can cause inner conflict and then depression.

*Psychological resistance to parenthood can be a serious problem.* Maybe you don't actually like kids; you may not want to be a mother because it interrupts your career; you might not be able to make the attachment to the baby because he represents a younger sibling you hated. Any of these negative feelings can make you confused, guilty, resentful, and eventually depressed.

*Being a working mother can create psychic stress.* A career woman who is confused and guilt-ridden about her return to work can suffer PPD for multiple reasons. You may have expected to love motherhood—but find that you're miserable. To some women, full-time motherhood may seem so oppressive that they get symptoms of PPD from the moment the baby is born.

There is also social pressure not to put your needs

ahead of the baby's, so if you return to work you may feel paralyzed with conflict. Having a career may go against your deep desire to be a mother, or it may clash with values that you learned. You'll only feel good about yourself and your decision for a career when you realize and come to terms with the forces battling inside you.

***The constant demands of an infant can be a shock.***
Even if you're psychologically prepared for these demands, it may take you as much as a year to actually sort out how to organize your time and energy.

***Expecting to "know" the baby*** is a common assumption: many parents have an exact idea of what their baby will be like, physically and emotionally. But your baby is a stranger with her own personality. That unfamiliarity can be a shock if you're expecting the arrival of someone you already know; you may feel disoriented or disillusioned.

***Breast-feeding problems can lead to a depression.***
If you have problems nursing—for instance, your milk supply doesn't come in—it can make you feel inadequate. Or you may not be able to handle the emotional and physical demands of full-time nursing. You might want to consider having your mate or someone else give the baby a bottle at night or during the day so that you can get a break, sleep, etc. Using a breast pump to express milk for this bottle can make you feel less trapped and resentful if you have a few hours a day for yourself.

***Serious problems with the baby can cause PPD.*** An imperfect baby can be very hard for some parents to accept. Some people cannot stand imperfection, even a baby they consider ugly, or one with a birthmark. Perhaps they see the imperfection as a reflection on themselves. A birth defect or other handicap can be terribly hard for a couple to deal with, to the point that they can suffer from PPD. (There is more on PPD in fathers at the end of this chapter.)

***If your baby is the "wrong" sex, it can create problems.*** The Wrong-Gender-Baby-Blues can mean resentment (and then guilt for feeling it) if the parents are disappointed or feel they have failed in producing a baby of the "wrong" sex. If only one of you has this reaction, it can create additional conflict within your relationship.

***Your own mother may not have been a good motherhood model.*** Some women suffer from PPD, psychologists postulate, because they are trapped by their image of their mother. If you perceived your mother as unhappy, tied down, a slave to her children, then the very **idea** of "mother," the very sound of the word "Mommy" can be horrible to you.

You may admire and appreciate what your mother did but you may not want to wind up with a life like hers. Even though the women's movement brought some changes, you may perceive that your new role is not so very different from your mother's. This can be terrifying if her version of motherhood was something you'd always hoped to avoid.

Your perception of your mother's role, and maybe even your grandmother's, may be that when they became mothers they went from being girlish and carefree to being passive, burdened victims. If you put this onus on yourself when you become "mother," then you're loading yourself down with generations of baggage that can result in PPD.

You may want to talk to your mother about these feelings, but she may not give you much satisfaction. She might have had PPD herself which she repressed at the time: talking about your problems would disturb her buried feelings. She might be insulted by your misgivings about her mothering style or threatened by your experience of motherhood as an unhappy time. PPD can be passed on by generations of mothers who are afraid to acknowledge their own or their daughters' pain. Brushing it off as "Pull yourself together, be glad you have a healthy baby," leaves you no room to express your feelings and heal them.

## THE PHYSICAL/BIOCHEMICAL CAUSE OF PPD

***The postpartum hormonal changes are a central reason for PPD.*** The physical/biochemical aspect of the postpartum period is considered one of the primary reasons for PPD. Because of the hormonal changes that are reminiscent of adolescence, a new mother can have the mood swings of a teenager.

***The mind-body connection is powerful.*** A hormonal change alters your biochemistry, which in turn will affect your mental state. Your endocrine system is affected by hormones: the hypothalamus produces hormones which regulate sleep, body rhythms, appetite, etc. An overload on the system, meaning an imbalance of hormones, creates disequilibrium in the hypothalamus. This unbalances the neurotransmitters in the hypothalamus, which control moods and interact with all the other hormones to keep equilibrium.

***You have a hormonal "crash" after birth.*** Within hours of childbirth, there is a 50 percent drop in your hormone levels, the estrogen and progesterone. Also, thyroid levels fall to below the prepregnancy level and pituitary function decreases. There is a massive blood loss and drop in body fluids. Your plasma cortisol levels drop 50 percent in the first postpartum days. The body increases the production of prolactin for breast-feeding. Once you're aware of all these physiological changes it seems amazing if a woman does *not* have an emotional reaction.

***New research is studying thyroid levels and PPD.*** Thyroid disease and its relationship to postpartum problems is now being studied. Women are at a high risk after delivery for developing thyroid disease, which is characterized by psychiatric symptoms similar to PPD and psychosis. **All women suffering from PPD symptoms are urged to get a thorough physical exam with blood tests to rule out a thyroid deficiency or other imbalance.** There is no point suffering unnecessarily or looking for solutions to PPD when your problems may be easily solved by thyroid medication.

## WHAT TO DO ABOUT PPD

***Patience is a virtue.*** As a first resort you can just try to wait it out: PPD symptoms like headache, nausea, giddiness, overactivity, and depression may pass when your raging hormones regain their composure. The feelings are real although they are caused by physiological events. It may be that once your baby begins to sleep regularly, you will get some recuperative sleep and feel more in control of your life. You can try to just accept this barrage of feelings and give PPD a chance to blow over.

***Don't suffer needlessly.*** When I interviewed women who have suffered from PPD, they shared a recommendation. If your baby is two to four weeks old and you are still very down, **GET HELP!** There are women who struggle through PPD, barely able to keep themselves and their marriages together, and later they say, "But I thought that was what it was supposed to be like." There are options, outlets, and relief available to you.

***Use the following suggestions to suit your own needs.*** The advice in this chapter on what to do about PPD is a mixed bag of solutions, some of which may be helpful to you. Follow these recommendations depending on your personality, your instincts, and your particular problems.

## HELPFUL HINTS ABOUT PPD

***Take care of yourself physically.*** Depression is a physical illness as well as an emotional one. Your body lacks strength and energy; at the slightest stress it pumps out adrenaline, which makes your heart pound, your muscles stiffen, your stomach churn, and your mouth dry. In order to have a good recovery you're going to need extra rest, excellent nutrition, and gradually increasing activity.

***Get a perspective on how fast a baby grows up.*** You may have to keep reminding yourself: your child is only an infant for a short time. Your feelings won't last forever.

***Get temporary household help.*** If you cannot cope with chores, find someone who can assist you. Having help is especially important during the day so that you're not alone: companionship can combat feelings of depression and isolation. If you are breast-feeding, then household help will be more useful than child care. If you don't have a relative who can come, it is well worth the money it will cost to buy you some time and psychic space.

***Get out of the house every day.*** Go out daily, preferably in the morning to counteract any feeling of confinement. Also, fresh air will help the baby sleep, so you should take him with you.

***Go out alone for "nonessential" walks.*** Try to make a point of getting out of the house regularly without structuring your time: no chores, no doctor's appointment, etc. Try to enjoy the feeling of being light and unencumbered when you don't have to lug the baby with all her paraphernalia. Visit the library or book stores, window-shop, and so on. Even if you only go out for an hour once or twice a week it will do you good.

***Think of motherhood as a job.*** Try taking some time off from your work as a Mom, give yourself tea breaks and lunch breaks, just as an overwrought executive would if her job was getting the better of her. Dress up and go out to a special dinner with your husband: eat, drink, indulge yourself. It's important to get away from the baby and get some perspective, to think of other things, to be yourself again.

***Taking breaks away from the baby can help if you have trouble handling your baby.*** A mother's inability to touch or handle her own child is a frightening aspect of PPD but it's not abnormal. You are exhausted and may feel you are giving to others without being taken care of yourself. At this time you may feel nothing for the people closest to you or you may be afraid of emotional involvement. Turning yourself off emotionally is self-protective. Such withdrawal is a reaction to feeling as if you "feed" those around you but "who is feeding the feeder?"

Time away from the baby, even if it's only a half-hour break, is the best way to nurture yourself. A woman who feels unable to touch her baby needs time away; you must arrange for someone who can stay with the child while you go out. At first you may feel guilty leaving the baby, so leave for short periods of time and increase it to a point where you feel comfortable. Do whatever feels good to "feed" yourself: take walks, exercise, read, swim, go to a museum, a movie, see a friend, go shopping.

***There are remedies for the bottled-up rage you may feel.*** Anger is a common component of PPD. It is not the anger that's the problem, but how to get rid of it! It's important to get it out of your system, but not directed at your partner or the baby. It can be inhibiting to try and release anger with other people around. Find ways to express anger that are comfortable for you and don't hurt anyone else:

1. Try yelling in the car, shower, or in a closed room.
2. Scream into a pillow or punch a pillow.
3. Write down your feelings, maybe as a letter to someone (but don't mail it!).
4. A physical outlet for anger is helpful: run up and down stairs or run around the outside of your house or around the block.

***There are ways to deal with destructive thought patterns.*** Obsessive thinking and fantasies are a common part of PPD, yet they are frightening and can make you feel as though you're going out of your mind. These fantasies can make you feel guilty, ashamed or worthless. Such thoughts are usually about death, illness, or accidentally or purposefully harming your child. You may feel haunted by memories or experiences. You may have suicidal thoughts or hopes for something like a car accident to "end it all."

Do not try to control or deny these thoughts. Doing so will only make you more anxious and increase your destructive thinking (resistance creates persistence: if you fight the feelings they get stronger). If these feelings frighten you, get help by sharing your thoughts with a nonjudgmental person. Expressing the feelings will help you regain control. Remember that fantasy is not the same as action and you don't have to follow a fantasy with action. Just because you imagine something it doesn't mean you have done anything, or will.

The more tired you are, the worse these fantasies can become. Therefore, it is important to get rest and not allow yourself to become overtired. Also, exercise (see page 183) can help a lot. Even walking vigorously or doing deep breathing to relax can give you some relief.

***Exercise can be revitalizing.*** Doing any form of physical exercise can help you ventilate feelings you wouldn't otherwise express. It is also good because it gets you out of the house doing something positive for yourself, taking your mind off baby care. When a person is depressed she doesn't think she'll have the motivation or energy to exercise, but once you begin you may get immediate benefits. Using physical energy actually restores depleted energy. Exercise helps return your hormonal/biochemical system to normal. And strenuous exercise releases endorphins into your system. These are natural opiate/mood enhancers of the brain, affecting your neuroendocrine balance by releasing neurotransmitters that put you in a happy mood.

NOTE: **Do not do ballistic exercises** (jogging, jumping rope, etc.) for two months postpartum (this is also true during pregnancy). During pregnancy your body produced the hormone relaxin; it takes about two months for it to leave your body. Because relaxin makes joints and ligaments quite loose, you an sustain permanent injuries while it is in your system.

***Dietary adjustments may alleviate some PPD.*** There are several things you might try adding to your diet or eliminating from it, to see whether these help your PPD.

1. Avoid sugar, processed foods and drinks, and caffeine, which increases tension and irritability.
2. Eat small frequent meals and snacks to keep up your blood sugar levels and to avoid irritability and weakness.
3. Eat potassium-rich foods (bananas, oranges, tomatoes) to avoid a postpartum potassium deficiency.
4. Do not go on a diet immediately after the baby is born because it can trigger a depression. Especially if you are breast-feeding, take in the recommended extra calories or you won't have the necessary energy.

***Crying can be good for you.*** Tears can relieve stress and be healing. Don't fight or deny your sadness: *resistance* *creates persistence.* Accept your depression, deal with it, and eventually it will pass.

***Try to accept your feelings.***   You might want to write them down if you don't feel comfortable talking about them. Come to terms with the fact that you can't control these feelings so you might as well accept them. Then concentrate on what you can do to feel better. Don't ignore your emotional distress, don't deny your feelings; try to make peace with them.

***Give yourself credit for your efforts.***   Tell yourself as often as you possibly can, "I'm doing the best I can right now." Accept yourself with your flaws: tell yourself, "I am not perfect but I am a good—or a good enough—mother and mate." If you think you're alone with these terrible PPD feelings, you are not. Many other new mothers suffer from the same phenomenon. Don't "beat yourself up" emotionally because you think you should be handling things better. Every one of us has suffered or fallen on our faces in trying to cope with the challenges that life presents.

***Force yourself to take it easy when the baby sleeps.***   Use the baby's nap time as a chance for you to rest or pamper yourself. Listen to music, do some gardening, cook a pot of soup, anything that is pleasurable.

***Comradeship with other women can be a great comfort.***   You can plan a reunion with other new parents from your childbirth class, if you don't feel too depressed. Otherwise you may be able to find a group devoted solely to PPD. It's important to eliminate a feeling of isolation, that you are helpless, cut off, or misunderstood.

You may find solace and strength when you discover that you're not alone with your feelings. Other new mothers may not admit they're suffering, but PPD is common. It may give you some insight and relief to talk to other women who have had this syndrome.

***Don't expect other people to understand PPD.***   Family and friends who don't understand what you're going through can make you feel even more abnormal if they trivialize your pain by saying, "Things would be fine if you just had the right attitude." You may feel like hiding your feelings from your mate if he isn't able to cope with your intense emotions and needs. He may be scared by them, which can frighten you even further. This is why it can help to find a sympathetic woman or group of women in whom you can confide.

***You may feel a strong desire to be nurtured by your mother.*** A need for your mother's love and reassurance is a common feeling during PPD. If you feel you need more mothering now—because you didn't get enough as a child or because PPD makes you feel needy and vulnerable—then ask for it.

Be prepared, though, to find that your mother may not be able to give you the affection you crave; if she rejects you now (or did so previously), it is not a reflection on your worth. She might not have given you love when you were a child, or it may just be your perception that you lacked love. In all probability your mother was doing the best she could. For all you know, your mother might have had PPD herself (your current problems may help you understand her better).

If you recognize that you can't get maternal love from your mother, then seek it out from other people. And learn to give it to yourself. *If you nurture yourself as a kind, loving mother would do, you can grow from this, and perhaps become a better mother and partner.*

## PROFESSIONAL HELP FOR PPD

***How do you know if you need a doctor?*** Almost every new mother has some emotional discomfort—you are going to have to distinguish between a normal postpartum reaction and a severe depressive disorder that requires a professional's intervention. Some PPD can be treated chemically with progesterone, similar hormones, or other drugs (see the section on drugs later in this chapter). Other types of PPD may require professional counselling, perhaps together with chemical treatment.

*Professional help for PPD is not easy to find.* First of all, a good psychotherapist is hard to find at any time. To make things more complicated, there is no "specialist" in PPD; the best you can hope for is a doctor who has had experience in this area. Possibly your obstetrician knows of a psychiatrist who concentrates on PPD, perhaps through a university-affiliated clinic. Professional help may be very hard to find at a time when you don't have the strength or bravery to go looking for it. You may want to contact a self-help group in your area that can suggest counselors who are suitable.

*The longer you have PPD, the more you need a doctor.* The longer a depression goes on, the more important it becomes to get help. Untreated depression can be a stress on the mind and body, draining self-confidence and lowering self-esteem. If you misdirect your feelings to look for someone to blame, these unacknowledged feelings can lead to child abuse or an unnecessary divorce. If you turn your negative feelings inward, it can result in alcohol or drug abuse or attempted suicide.

*Obstetricians usually don't know much about PPD.* Don't expect your OB-GYN to be of great help. Many doctors have a hard time dealing with PPD. If your doctor is like many others, s/he may trivialize the problem by saying, "You just need more sleep, don't overreact."

*Experts agree that medication is needed as part of PPD treatment.* Drug therapy for PPD is controversial but many experts agree that it forms an important part of successful treatment. Psychiatric treatment alone is not usually considered sufficient. Top researchers have seen successful treatment of PPD with antidepressant and antipsychotic drugs. Traditionally the medication is combined with therapy, but the drugs are seen as the key to the treatment.

Recent studies have shown that it is not effective when professionals try to treat PPD solely by looking at a woman's past, her marriage, or how well she handles problems. The underlying physiological problems must also be treated, in the opinion of current researchers.

*It's vital that a doctor have experience using drugs for PPD.* Your doctor may prescribe antidepressants, tranquilizers, and anti-anxiety drugs. If these aren't given properly they can cover up the underlying cause of your PPD and/or interfere with your mothering abilities. Some psychiatrists also prescribe these drugs along with antipsychotics if you are having hallucinations or fantasies. If not handled properly, this can confirm your feeling that you're going crazy and can leave you unable to care for your baby.

## DRUGS CURRENTLY BEING USED FOR PPD

*Vitamin B6 has been used with some success.* However, B6 treatments must be administered only by a professional. *Do not attempt to self-diagnose or treat with this vitamin.* Because large doses of B6 also have side effects, this treatment must be attempted only under a doctor's supervision. The treatment is 400 to 500 mgs a day for one to two weeks. B6 is known to raise the serotonin levels in the brain. Many suicide victims have been found to have low serotonin levels, so research is being done to examine the relationship between these levels and severe depression. B6 makes the liver generate more tryptophan, which crosses the blood/brain barrier (a point in your neck) and raises the serotonin level. Serotonin does not act alone, but in tandem with another substance called norepinephrine (see below).

*Antidepressant drugs are often used.* Serotonin appears in the body in conjunction with another substance: norepinephrine. These are two biochemical substances at the neurotransmitter junction in the brain. If a combination of these substances is at a low level, then you are in a depression. The trade names of the two most commonly used drugs are Elavil and Tofranil: the former tends to raise the norepinephrine level, while the latter tends to raise the serotonin level. A doctor decides how to use these drugs not by blood tests but by his/her personal determination of your condition and the side effects of the drugs. Therefore you want to find a physician with experience in treating depression.

***Antidepressants are popular.*** They are being used by many doctors for moderate PPD. These drugs work on the brain chemistry—but some experts say there's no way to be sure they're working on the *right* brain chemistry. The drugs are used to reverse abnormal brain chemistry and increase the flow of neurotransmitters. It is recommended to use as little medication as possible, striking a balance between protecting the woman with the drug but not using so much that she becomes zombielike.

***Tricyclic antidepressants are preferable.*** This form of antidepressant doesn't give an artificial and immediate "high," which when it wears off can plunge you back down in depression. They are nonaddictive. Sometimes you'll have to take this kind of drug for three to four weeks before the effect becomes obvious. They act slowly and surely for most women (as vitamin or hormone therapy can) to restore your ability to cope. Even once you are feeling better your doctor will probably keep you on this medication for six to twelve months to avoid a relapse. These organic depressions take on a life of their own and can last as long as a year.

***Tranquilizers are controversial in PPD treatment.*** Tranquilizers, if used at all, should be administered cautiously, in small doses. Many doctors feel that tranquilizers are bad for PPD because they can increase fatigue and confusion. However, if a woman is a danger to herself or is extremely agitated, a small (25 mg) dose of thorazine can take the edge off her potential violence or severe anxiety. Sometimes mild doses of Valium are used, but this drug is a known depressant. The basic problem with tranquilizers is that they are a cover-up that can make a woman unreachable either to give her reassurance or to attempt psychotherapy.

***Anti-anxiety drugs are beneficial for some women.*** Certain anxiety or panic reactions are known to have an organic (physical) basis. For example, a patient with agoraphobia (fear of going outside) will experience a sudden panic reaction when s/he leaves the house. The person associates this panic with being outside, but it may have a physiological, inner organic basis. Medication can relieve this reaction.

Although many doctors will try to treat these problems from a psychological point of view, certain anti-anxiety drugs can alleviate panic reactions. The anxiety may have a physiological basis, yet it can persist until it becomes a psychological problem: at that point it interferes with a woman's ability to cope with her daily life. Anti-anxiety drugs like Xanax can reduce severe anxiety to a manageable level, allowing a new mother to talk about it in private or group therapy.

***Progesterone injections are a radical treatment.*** A small, egglike pellet is injected under your skin in the buttocks and dissolves slowly; it is reported to be very painful. PMS clinics have been using these injections for extreme cases of premenstrual syndrome. Obviously this treatment should only be used for PPD if hormone tests indicate that you have a serious shortage of progesterone.

***The following chart contains suggestions to help a woman with PPD.*** It was compiled by the Pacific Postpartum Support Society in Vancouver, B.C. (see *Appendix I*, page 533).

---

**PACIFIC POSTPARTUM SUPPORT SOCIETY SUGGESTIONS**

- Develop a *simple routine* for your day. Choose one or two manageable tasks. *Take one day at a time.*
- *Rest* whenever possible—it is much more important than doing chores or housework.
- *Eat* nutritious quick foods that are easily prepared, like fruit, cheese, yogurt.
- Take *breaks* the way people do on all jobs. Have a cup of tea when the baby is asleep. Take a bath. Have a friend over for lunch.
- Find a *baby-sitter*. This is important because it allows you to prove to yourself that you can cope with a problem by organizing and following through. Arranging for a baby-sitter is also a way to tell yourself that you deserve the help and the break.
- Do *good things* for yourself: have your hair done, get a massage, go to the gym, go shopping.
- Give yourself *credit* for the job you are doing. Mothering is hard, important work and society isn't going to give you any credit for it.
- Find support groups where you can go with or without the baby.

## SEVERE PPD

*How can you tell if you have severe PPD?*   How can you tell the difference between "the blues," moderate PPD, or the more severe, serious form of it? How can the new father tell whether his wife's condition is temporary or is serious enough to require a doctor or hospitalization? The answer lies in the *frequency* and *intensity* of a woman's feelings. Anyone can have the exaggerated feelings associated with the postpartum adjustment period, but you need help if they are frequent (or continuous) and very intense.

**WARNING: DO NOT ATTEMPT TO DEAL WITH SEVERE PPD BY YOURSELF.** PPD can be treated and cured like any disease. **But if you have the severe form of it, self-help measures are of no help.** The suggestions earlier in this chapter are only useful for mild to moderate PPD that develops slowly with no danger signals.

Extreme PPD usually occurs within the first two weeks and is intense and frightening. It is often characterized by suicidal fantasies and/or fears of harming the baby. You absolutely must get professional help if you find yourself in this position.

**Note to anyone other than the new mother who reads this: IF A NEW MOTHER THREATENS SUICIDE OR HARM TO HER BABY, TAKE HER SERIOUSLY. She needs help immediately.**

*PPD is not your fault.*   If you're suffering from extreme PPD, you have to know (or be told by someone) that your negative feelings are not your fault. In all probability you cannot stop these feelings or even help yourself. You have to depend on the people around you. If your mate refuses to recognize how profoundly you are suffering or he cannot acknowledge the danger you pose to yourself and the baby, you must find help elsewhere. I only hope you have an empathetic and alert doctor, friend, sibling, or mother who will step in.

*Treatment for severe PPD usually goes in stages.* The first thing you'll need is reassurances that you aren't going insane: your problems adjusting to motherhood will pass. PPD is an illness, not a reflection on your character.

The first step in treatment is usually for the doctor to try antidepressant medication and outpatient psychiatric care. However, if your suicidal feelings aren't alleviated in four to five days, many professionals would recommend that you be hospitalized at this point. One drawback of hospitalization is that these institutions can convince you that you really are going crazy.

***PPD can leave lasting scars in your family.*** Severe PPD is a debilitating condition that affects the couple and baby as well as the mother. Even once you have recovered you might want to consider some form of family therapy so that you can understand what effect PPD had on your lives as individuals, a couple, and a family.

---

#### SYMPTOMS OF SEVERE PPD

- Suicidal feelings
- Desire to harm or kill the baby
- Completely unable to cope, to care for yourself or the baby
- Cannot stand touching child; fear of harming him
- Unable to get out of bed
- Unable to eat or sleep
- High anxiety or panic attacks
- Constant crying

## THE EFFECT OF PPD
## ON YOUR RELATIONSHIP

*PPD has a profound effect on your marriage.* Because the new mother's predicament is almost always a surprise and disappointment to both partners, it can damage their relationship. PPD is one of those things that you think can't happen to you. Most couples never think they're going to be the ones to have a cesarean delivery; neither does a couple imagine that motherhood is going to cause such profound problems.

You may be disgusted or humiliated by your inescapable sadness and inability to cope with motherhood. Your husband may have similar feelings. Both men and women should realize that PPD is common—*it doesn't mean a woman is mentally ill*. It is an illness they have to deal with and overcome together.

*A new father may be devastated by his wife's PPD.* A woman's postpartum depression comes at a time when her mate counted on her to take care of the baby and house. The new father may feel that she has let him down; she may feel she has failed him and herself. It may be hard for him to relate to a totally dependent person. His wife's disability may make him angry, unless he can recognize that it is her total dependence on him that elicits his feelings. Then he may feel guilty for having felt angry!

*PPD gives a new father more things to worry about.* In addition to all the pressures a man already feels, PPD causes a great deal of stress for a new father. Often a couple and professionals around them can ignore the price that a man has to pay for his wife's PPD. He is worried about his wife's health and safety, the doctor bills, the baby's well-being, and his own ability to cope.

PPD often forces a man to become a strong, supportive partner in the house, taking an active role in child care and household chores. He was probably not prepared to do this and either feels unequal to the task or resents the imposition. All this adds up to a pretty messy emotional stew, when you stir the woman's own confused feelings into the pot.

***A new father may blame himself for his wife's misery.*** A man may feel responsible for his mate's unhappiness, even if he's aware that PPD is causing her problems. Her tears, moods, and irritability can cause feelings of self-doubt in him, perhaps subconsciously. A man may wonder what he has done wrong, how he has failed his mate, what he could have done differently. Then he may turn the blame back on his spouse and feel angry at her, without even realizing what he's doing.

***A man may turn his guilt into anger at his wife.*** By turning his guilt into anger, a new father can stop blaming himself for his wife's condition. Otherwise, his guilt can cause him to become depressed or overwhelmed by his emotions. This creates an unhealthy situation for a marriage: a man who is feeling this way will run hot and cold, alternating criticism and kindness. His attitude toward his wife may be one of hostility and withdrawal, which can then change to comfort and concern. His inconsistency will only aggravate his partner's depression and the confusion she's feeling in general.

***A man may have trouble relating to a woman's emotions during postpartum adjustment.*** For one thing, males tend not to suffer depression as women do, over issues like "loss of self" and identity problems. The male focus is usually on success and doing well; a man's sense of himself is usually measured by achievement, not in terms of relationships. Since many components of a woman's PPD have to do with her new identity and feelings about her changing self, you and your mate may not communicate well because of this difference in the male/female outlook.

***A woman may be disappointed if she wants comfort.*** A mother with PPD may turn to her mate for understanding and support with no success. If she tries to explain what she's experiencing emotionally with PPD, her partner may be frightened or confused by the information.

A man may not be able to give emotional support because he doesn't feel equal to the task. Just as he has to try to be gentle and kind about what his wife is going through, so must she attempt to show him the same thoughtfulness about his reactions during this time.

*Sex is usually nonexistent when a woman has PPD.* She is usually completely turned off sexually, although she may want cuddling and affection. She needs warmth and reassurance without sex. This can be confusing to a man who has a normal sex drive and can misread her desire for only holding or hugging. A man shouldn't mistake this for a sexual overture or she will withdraw and he'll be rejected. If the man misinterprets her signals and makes sexual demands, then neither of their needs will be met.

*Later-in-life parents have particular problems with PPD.* It doesn't seem to be acceptable to older parents to have a negative reaction to their baby's arrival. If you delayed parenting for a number of years, then you're probably facing parenthood with gratitude that you got pregnant and the determined enthusiasm and energy of people who are finally getting something they've always wanted.

How can you admit that becoming parents is not the fun-filled, inspiring event you anticipated? You may believe that as older parents you're supposed to be mature, prepared, and able to cope. If you have problems making the postpartum adjustment it creates a terrible conflict with this image you had.

Older parents often pressure themselves, perhaps without realizing it, to be impeccable at their new job. This leaves no room for reality. Their demands on themselves are a sure prescription for failure: how can you expect to juggle all the roles in your life, do everything very well, and above all *enjoy* yourself? PPD for later-in-life parents can often come from these unrealistic expectations of parenthood. Try to utilize your maturity and experience so you don't fall into this trap.

If you have PPD and are an older parent, give yourself a break. PPD is a common, normal, temporary reaction to parenthood. You've got the same vulnerabilities, Achilles' heels, and uncharted waters of your personality as newly-wed 19-year-olds. You are generally more mature and knowledgeable than younger parents, but it's this very combination that makes you harder on yourselves.

## FATHERS CAN GET PPD, TOO

***Everybody forgets the new father's emotions.*** The tendency to discount the man's needs when his wife has PPD is a common problem. You are expected to give emotional support and generosity to your wife while she's recovering—but who is there to give you encouragement? A man has the added burden of being expected to pick up the pieces if his wife cannot cope with household chores or child care. He needs positive feedback for making this adjustment.

***Today's father is expected to do it all . . . perfectly.*** There is social and media pressure on a new father that never used to exist. The joys of fatherhood are extolled; books are written about the modern, involved father who is as aware about orthodontic pacifiers as he is of a balance sheet at the office. For those men who have the energy and desire, this "new fatherhood" is wonderful; other men may suffer PPD in trying to achieve this (supposed) state of higher consciousness. There is always room for social evolution, but when social change takes on the aspect of *revolution* it takes a heavy toll.

***Today's new father is in a double bind.*** You are faced with increased financial responsibilities, as new fathers always have been, yet you're also expected to be an involved, nurturing father. You read magazine articles advising you that your dear little baby is going to cost from $50,000 to $150,000 to raise to age 18. Meanwhile, other articles suggest that your development as well as the child's will be impaired if you don't give your share of baths, bottles, and nighttime stories. If a new father suffers from PPD as a result of these pressures, it would seem like a logical reaction to an illogical, "no-win" situation.

*A new father experiences no less emotion than his wife does.*   Men have the same range of emotional reactions as women during pregnancy and the postpartum period. However, while women are encouraged to explore their feelings, men in our society are not permitted the complexity of emotion that can trigger PPD. The psychological and emotional upheavals of becoming a parent can lead to PPD, especially if a man has nowhere to go with his feelings. And most men do *not* have an emotional outlet. A woman can call her doctor with postpartum physical complaints as a way of seeking help and getting encouragement, which a man cannot do. A woman also has a community of other women to whom she can turn.

*If you are "acting out" feelings rather than dealing with them, this can be a sign of PPD.*   This should be a signal to you and your wife that you are having trouble making the postpartum adjustment. If you feel out of control or as though you can't really cope, you should seek counseling, or at least talk to your mate or to other parents in a group. Some signs of "acting out" are: drinking, running around, being irresponsible, taking risks.

## SOME FACTORS CAUSING PPD IN MEN

*Conflicts about becoming a father are a major cause of PPD.*   Your own childhood conflicts may reactivate when you become a parent. You may have unresolved problems with your parents—a bad relationship with your father in particular can cause problems adjusting to parenthood. If you have problems identifying with or feeling love from your father, it can make you afraid to confront yourself as a new father.

*Rivalry with the baby can lead to PPD.*   If you are jealous of your wife's attention to the child, this can lead to a common syndrome for fathers. You may go through a postpartum emotional cycle of anger/guilt/withdrawal. It is understandable if you are sad over the loss of closeness with your spouse because of this third person who has entered the picture. However, if your feelings of rivalry are really pronounced, it can lead to a confusion of other debilitating emotions.

***If you think your baby doesn't like you, it can cause PPD.*** If the baby cries when you hold him and seems to prefer his mother, this can cause PPD for some men. It can make you recall your childhood fears of not being loved or wanted, of being rebuffed in your attempts for attention or affection.

***Becoming less important in your own home can cause emotional problems.*** A man who is used to being the center of attention can have trouble making the postpartum adjustment. It is not just the loss of being the focus of your wife's attention, it is also the diminishment of your importance and power in the household. You may have been accustomed to making the decisions in your relationship, to being in charge. Suddenly you are incidental, a minor character.

Hospital staff, visitors, and even relatives can undermine a man's sense of importance in his marriage after his baby is born. Once you understand what is happening you'll feel less abused, but the person who can best reaffirm your importance is your wife. She needs to understand that your feelings of being displaced are justified: it seems that becoming a father can make a man a second-class citizen in his own home. Your mate is not the villain, but she can rescue you from feeling abandoned and diminished in importance.

***A new father with PPD needs plenty of TLC.*** You need tender loving care—explain this to your spouse. Your feelings cannot be dismissed as egotistical or selfish; don't allow anyone to trivialize the pain and confusion you are feeling. However, don't complain like an injured victim; don't criticize your spouse for being insensitive. Appeal to her loving, nurturant side and she is sure to respond. As with all postpartum predicaments, look for solutions, not blame.

*You may be at risk for PPD if you were very involved in the birth.* A man who took childbirth classes and was committed to participating may be more at risk for PPD than less involved fathers. You may have been gung-ho about functioning as a team before the birth and during it: you knew what your tasks and responsibilities were and felt good participating. The problem is that after the baby is born, you may feel you don't have a prescribed role; you get none of the attention and recognition that the mother does. You go from being an important central figure in the drama to feeling useless once the baby arrives.

*A bossy, authoritarian wife can cause PPD.* A woman can take control from a man once their baby is born and trigger all the negative emotions of PPD in him. Traditionally, child care has been the woman's domain, but in the semiliberated world in which we live, men are expected and/or demand to share in raising their children. This raises questions of power and control. Women's dominance in the home and raising children is a centuries-old tradition in almost every culture. For some women it is very hard to share decisions and actual infant care with the baby's father.

In the "olden days" (even as little as 10 years ago), a new father at least had the security of knowing his role was as provider and authority figure. Nowadays, many men are deprived of that traditional role, yet they are not truly welcome as an equal partner in parenting. A woman who cannot easily share "her baby" may push her mate aside.

*A domineering wife can cause more than PPD.* A man who is undermined in this way by his partner may very well take a hike. This pressure can break a marriage—don't take it lightly. Don't suffer in silence, withdraw, and then explode with rage. Make your feelings known and demand whatever level of involvement you want with your child. "Equal rights" means men, too!

*Feeling isolated from his wife and baby is another cause of PPD.* The less a new father is involved with his baby, the less connected he may feel. This can inhibit him from becoming an integral part of the baby's life and feeling comfortable with his new role in the home. Isolation is unhealthy: it leads not just to depression but to jealousy, resentment, and a lack of self-confidence in your parenting abilities.

The first weeks of the baby's life are the most important time to establish yourselves as a threesome in a united way and to make yourself part of your baby's routine care— even if all you have time for or want to do is one bottle or diaper a day.

**A *woman's PPD can trigger it in her mate*.** If your wife is suffering from PPD, you are required to be stronger, to take a more involved, supportive role than you might have expected. This can lead to doubts about who your wife really is: you may have to redefine or even discard your images and fantasies of her as the mother of your child. You may lose your dreams of the three of you as a happy family. If you feel as trapped as your wife does, if you worry that your life is out of control, you may suffer the same symptoms of PPD as she does.

**ated*Full-time fathering can cause PPD*.** A man who stays home full time with the baby has all the postpartum adjustment problems that a woman would, except that he doesn't have the support facilities she would. If you are home alone with a baby, you don't have a community of support the way a mother does at the park, with the obstetrician, or in a parents' group.

There aren't many men staying home with babies: your new, untraditional role may be treated with skepticism or outright suspicion. Although some people may think full-time fatherhood is wonderful, it can be threatening to other parents who have chosen or are stuck with a traditional division of parenting duties.

If one of the reasons you decided to stay home with your baby was to pursue a new career, or to take up an old interest, you may suffer frustration and depression because the demands of infant care may keep you from accomplishing your goal.

Full-time baby care may also cause you an identity

crisis, a gender crisis. You may begin to wonder about your masculinity, as seen by yourself and others. You may wonder what made you choose to sit home taking care of an infant. You may begin to ask yourself questions: "Who am I?", "Am I male or female?", "What kind of man would want to do this job?" You'll have to come to peace with these concerns in order to overcome whatever postpartum adjustment problems they are causing for you.

# 8
# Sex and romance

Is there sex and romance after birth? Some couples will laugh at that rhetorical question, others will want to cry. Of course there is—if you want it. Sex and romance aren't extinguished by parenthood, they sort of go into hibernation. It takes some coaxing to get them back.

*A man and woman are often out of sync post-partum.* Many couples have a sexual problem after childbirth because the man is hopelessly horny and the woman cringes at the very thought of intercourse! In simple terms, that is one scenario of the male-female sexual imbalance when you make the transition to parenthood. A woman may view sex as something strange that she did in another life; a man may lust desperately and unsuccessfully for sex as he did when he was an adolescent. Until things get back on track, a couple needs to understand the reasons for this temporary stalemate to avoid becoming hostile toward one another.

*There are physiological reasons for the problem.* A woman's lack of sex drive can be a problem during the entire pregnancy and postpartum period. If you were like many women you may not have had any sex drive in the final weeks of your pregnancy (or perhaps the entire time).

There are physical deterrents to sex after the delivery: there are hormonal changes and the painful healing of the episiotomy for most women. Or you may be so exhausted by the demands of motherhood that you couldn't stay awake to make love even if Robert Redford offered himself to you.

*Romance is as important as sex to a man and woman's relationship.* You may call it "intimacy" or "sharing" but whatever word you use, it is from these romantic, intimate feelings that sexual desire grows. However, romance and sexiness may seem pretty far-fetched to a new father who is bleary-eyed from sleepless nights with a crying baby and to a new mother with leaky breasts and 20 extra pounds of thighs.

*There are also psychological obstacles to sex.* A woman may lose interest in sex as she struggles with a new perception of herself as "mother" rather than "lover." If you are breast-feeding (or even if you aren't) you may find your sex drive is redirected to your new physical intimacy with the baby. Or you may resent your partner's sexual desire because it creates a conflict for you between the energy you want to devote to the baby (or think you are "supposed to") and your husband's sexual demands. Or you may be so exhausted that sleep is more desirable than sex.

*A new father can get a pretty rough deal.* Meanwhile, back at the ranch, a man's sex drive is usually normal through all the adjustments his wife is making. This can mean that he may be climbing the walls from sexual abstention by the time the baby has settled in. A new father often isn't "getting any," either sexually or emotionally, which makes the transition to parenthood even harder. His sex life with his wife was disrupted if not ended during the pregnancy; he may have waited patiently in the expectation that things would go back to normal once the baby was born. However, a new mother often views sex as an unimportant part of life in the newly emerging family. This chapter tackles these issues and many more about your sexual life as new parents.

# THE PHYSICAL ASPECT OF SEX

*Unrealistic expectations can be a big letdown.*   Although most doctors say, "Everything will return to normal in six weeks," many women still don't really feel 100 percent at that juncture. Part of a couple's sexual problems after a baby is born come from unrealistic expectations; they think something is wrong with them because six weeks has gone by and they aren't having a good time sexually. Maybe the solution is to **expect** a lousy sex life: you won't be upset if that's what you get and you'll be pleasantly surprised if things go well! Perhaps if you don't expect too much or try to rush things, you'll find that your sex life resumes more quickly and sweetly.

*How serious are the "doctor's orders"?*   Many obstetricians make rules about sex after childbirth that can seem arbitrary, but there are medical reasons for the rules. Some obstetricians advise that a couple abstain from sexual intercourse for six weeks after the baby's birth. They say this gives the vaginal canal and uterus time to heal, as well as the episiotomy stitches. If you had a torn cervix or other complications in the delivery, you may be advised to wait even longer.

If you add these six weeks to the abstention from sexual relations that many doctors recommend for six weeks *before* the baby's birth, your "celibacy" becomes at least three months. It is understandable that some couples disobey a doctor who demands an even longer wait postpartum.

*Some doctors take a less conservative view.*   There are other doctors who feel that six weeks is too long a mandatory abstention from sexual intercourse. They say that a couple's sexual timetable is an individual matter: you can resume sexual relations if you feel ready and comfortable (taking into account the healing process that must take place first). This less conservative approach allows sex as long as your episiotomy has healed, active bleeding has stopped (two to three weeks), and there is no sign of infection.

*Some couples resume sex quickly and easily after the baby is born.* If you didn't have an episiotomy, or perhaps even if you had a cesarean, you might want to start making love as soon as the flow of red blood stops. There are couples who have intercourse four to six weeks after birth and it's no big adjustment for them. There are doctors who claim there is no medical reason not to resume sex if there is no heavy bleeding or sign of infection. Call your doctor or go in for a checkup before six weeks has passed if you are concerned about making the decision without a consultation.

*It's helpful to understand the physical healing process after birth.* Before you make any decision about your own sex life, it's a good idea to know what takes place in your vagina and uterus after birth. It takes three to four weeks for the cervix to close after childbirth. While the cervix is open it is vulnerable to infection, therefore you cannot have intercourse or insert a tampon or vibrator during that time. Your vagina takes even longer to recover its shape and tone after the stretching and bruising of muscles and tissues during delivery. You will know when your uterus has returned to normal because after delivery it feels like a hard, round ball from the outside. Within a few weeks it shrinks back to its normal size and placement and you cannot feel it externally any more.

*Your vagina may be sore postpartum.* Vaginal discomfort after birth can be the result of the pressure of the baby's head and body that stretched and bruised your vagina during delivery. Her journey into the world can leave you with a swollen vagina and cervix. Lacerations of the vagina are uncommon but can be very painful as they heal. Your obstetrician may be able to give you something for the pain. Obviously do not use tampons during this time, as they can cause infection and further irritate the vaginal opening.

*Vaginismus is a sexual disorder that can affect a woman after childbirth (or any time in her life).* It consists of spasms and shooting pains in the vagina which make penetration impossible or intercourse painful. There is no physiological explanation for this problem. It has psychological causes. In the case of a new mother it could be the fear of getting pregnant again, the tension of new parenthood, or the pressure to perform sexually when you aren't physically or emotionally ready. This is a problem to discuss with a professional if it persists.

***You may both be worried about whether sex will hurt you.*** If either of you has fears about physical problems it can inhibit your sex life after childbirth. Most of the sexual concerns that a couple has after childbirth have no factual basis or are exaggerated. Discuss these issues together (or with your doctor) and they will become less distressing.

You may worry that your vagina will be bigger and your mate will be unable to fill it. He may have the same preoccupation. In fact, the opening to your vagina *will* be slightly larger and the tissues will be relaxed, but this can be minimized by doing Kegel exercises (see page 207).

Your husband may be worried if you complain about your episiotomy being sore, that you're having trouble urinating, or other vaginal problems. His discomfort about these issues can make him withdraw sexually. He may feel generally insecure, inhibited, and fearful about having intercourse with you after you've given birth. These concerns will pass when you start making love again and rediscover each other.

***A vaginal discharge can be bothersome sexually after birth.*** Some women bleed for six weeks and beyond. Some doctors forbid intercourse when a woman is still bleeding because of the possibility of infection. Other obstetricians say that intercourse is fine if the bleeding or staining doesn't bother you. Check with your own doctor about having sexual relations if you're bleeding.

***Absence of orgasm can be a problem for a new mother.*** There can be physical and psychological reasons for this problem. It can be several months before your body returns to prepregnancy hormone levels, which can eliminate orgasms or make it more difficult to achieve orgasm. At the same time, you and your partner are making conscious and unconscious adaptations to your new parenting roles that can interfere with your openness, relaxation, or sexual self-image.

Masters and Johnson did a study of postpartum sex and found that even at three months after birth women have a lower level of sexuality. Their study found that it can be more difficult to achieve orgasm after birth for a variety of reasons: breast tenderness, fatigue, tension, episiotomy soreness, fears that sexual organs have changed, and fear that vaginal muscles are tighter or looser.

*Sex can be improved after birth.* It should also be noted that some women—a minority—have better sex after childbirth. They find increased pleasure or even have their first orgasm. It is possible that a woman whose previous lovemaking experience was disappointing may have a stronger sexual response after delivery because in the initial postpartum period there is increased vascularity to the vaginal region. In other words, greater blood flow to your genitals can mean more sensitivity and pleasure.

*There are a few symptoms postpartum that require medical attention.* If you have any of these you should see your doctor and have a medical exam to make sure there are no complications in your healing after delivery.

---

### SYMPTOMS OF POSTPARTUM MEDICAL PROBLEMS

- Extreme sensitivity during intercourse
- Vaginal tissues seem unusually relaxed
- Difficulty controlling urine

---

## THE EPISIOTOMY AND SEX

*The episiotomy is a cut made in the perineum from your vagina to your anus.* The episiotomy is stitched up after the placenta is delivered. For some women it heals in a week or two, but for most it takes about six weeks for the scar to heal. Even after it has healed it can remain sensitive; especially if there is a little lump of scar tissue, it can be very tender. However, it may take several months for the wound to heal completely. The blood supply to the area has been altered, which creates disturbances in the nerve endings.

***There are various reasons for doing episiotomies.*** Some doctors explain that they cut an episiotomy to prevent tearing and to shorten the amount of time that the vaginal tissues are stretched. They claim that if the stretching is prolonged, the vagina won't return to normal (but Kegel exercises were designed to do just that).

In fact, the main reason for episiotomies is that American obstetricians are not trained in techniques of massage which help the vaginal opening to expand during delivery: the United States is the only country in the world with a 95 percent episiotomy rate.

***The episiotomy doesn't change your vagina.*** It is a myth, by the way, that the doctor controls how tight or loose your vagina is after birth. There are often comments made about how an obstetrician can make a woman's vagina smaller or tighter. In truth, an episiotomy repair consists of rejoining the skin at the edges. Nonetheless, you may find that your episiotomy feels too tight or too loose. Kegel exercises and sexual intercourse should return your vagina to a normal, comfortable shape.

***Kegel exercises are more important than you realize.*** All women should get in the habit of doing Kegels regularly. The exercise is especially important after delivery because of the episiotomy and the trauma and stretching that your vagina goes through during delivery. Kegel exercises consist of contracting your pelvic-floor muscles for a few seconds and then relaxing them. To get the feeling, practice stopping the flow of urine while you are on the toilet. Try a few Kegels at first and work your way to 100 or more a day while you are healing. (For more information, see the section on Postpartum Exercises, pages 144–46, in *Chapter 6: Practical Concerns in the Early Weeks.*

***There are remedies for pain after an episiotomy.*** It's a good idea, however, to check with your doctor before trying any of these suggestions. The healing process is more painful for some women than others. *Do not bandage the area under any circumstances.* If the incision feels tight and itchy, a sitz-bath (sitting in a tub of warm water) may be helpful. You can try cool alcohol or Witch Hazel compresses. For some women, using a heat lamp (on a low setting for a short time) gives relief. An anesthetic spray can also be helpful.

## VAGINAL DRYNESS AND SEX

*Vaginal dryness is a common problem after child-birth.* Your natural lubrication may disappear until your hormones return to previous levels. The sharp drop in your estrogen levels creates the problem: it is even worse if you're breast-feeding (more on that later in this section). A drop in the thyroid level, which occurs after childbirth, can also affect your lubrication. Your thyroid level drops below the prepregnancy level for many months postpartum. A loss of thyroid seems to directly affect a woman's sexual response.

*The first time you have sex can be a problem.* The first time your mate penetrates you may be quite painful: you might want to use a lubricant (see page 209). Do not be alarmed by the discomfort of intercourse when you aren't lubricated; don't worry that your vagina doesn't get wet even when you're aroused. These are normal hormonal changes that your body is going through, which will eventually balance out again.

*Dryness can make you fearful about sex.* An unfortunate side effect of severe pain during intercourse after childbirth can be that you become afraid of having sex. If you understand what is happening to your body it won't be so disturbing. A woman's natural lubrication is the equivalent of a man's erection, and can mean that she is physically ready for sex. However, although you may be physically ready for intercourse when you are naturally lubricated, you may not be emotionally ready. You may need more foreplay before you are sufficiently aroused to enjoy sex and/or have an orgasm.

***Don't ascribe any hidden meanings to the dryness.***
Your lack of natural lubrication can create communication
problems between you if you don't talk about it. Your mate
may interpret your dryness as a lack of interest and withdraw from you. You may avoid sex or lose interest because
you don't get wet. You may wonder whether you've fallen
out of love with your husband or whether you've become
frigid. Dryness is just a physical reaction after childbirth: it
doesn't "mean" anything else.

***Using a lubricant is a good solution to the problem.***
Petroleum jelly (Vaseline brand, for example) is **not** recommended because it isn't water-soluble. Use a water-
soluble surgical jelly like K-Y, or your doctor may prescribe
a vaginal estrogen cream. Either of you can also use your
saliva to lubricate the vaginal opening.

***What if one of you isn't comfortable about using a
lubricant?*** This will only increase anxiety between you
and you may wind up avoiding intimacy. Although it's hard
to talk about sex, it can really break the tension to talk
about the dryness issue. It will make a big difference if you
can overcome your misgivings that a lubricant isn't natural
or isn't necessary. Lubricants are commonly used and are
absolutely fine: using them can make your sexual life much
nicer while your body is returning to normal.

## SEX AND BREAST-FEEDING

***Breast-feeding may be incompatible with sex for
you.*** Sex and breast-feeding can be mutually exclusive,
depending on your personal reaction to nursing your child.
Before the baby was born, your breasts were part of your
sex life and uncovering them was sexual. Now, every time
they are uncovered it is for feeding. It may be too hard for
you to make the mental switch back and forth between
viewing your breasts as part of sexual foreplay and being
able to casually accept your naked breasts for a practical
use.

***A nursing mother may compartmentalize her
breasts.*** You may be one of those women who has to

consciously change her feelings about her breasts in order to nurse outside her bedroom. If you have to make such a conscious effort in your perception, it can be too big a mental adjustment to return to perceiving your breasts as part of your sex life. You may be uncomfortable letting your mate play with your breasts: you may feel like you are cheating. But on whom? To whom do your breasts ''belong''? Who has ''dibs'' on them?

*A nursing mother often forgets her own needs, especially her sexual ones.* Nursing may reduce your desire for intimacy with your mate. You may even forget that he has a need for physical closeness because you feel satisfied by the touching and closeness with the baby all day. More importantly, you may have already neglected, as a new mother, to clearly distinguish *your* own needs.

*Your mate may be turned on by your larger breasts.* At the same time, he too may have conflicted feelings about what is the proper place for your mammary glands. He may feel ambivalent about being sexually excited by his baby's food supply.

*Your mate may be turned off by large, leaky breasts.* Some men won't touch a woman's breasts the entire time she is nursing. Others avoid touching the breasts if they are leaking. These are normal reactions to the situation: you'll find your own way through it if you can be open about your feelings with each other.

*A new mother may withdraw from sex.* You may feel overwhelmed or resentful of the various demands on your body. You may be sick of ''servicing'' everybody, having your body constantly at the baby's beck and call. You may feel you have to reclaim your own body rather than answering to your husband's sexual desires. If you're worn out, you may feel it's asking too much to provide your body for your mate's pleasure.

*Some women feel more sexy when they are nursing.* The increased vascular supply to the pelvis can create stronger sexual desire. In a study of sexuality and breast-feeding, Masters and Johnson found that nursing women have more interest in sex sooner than bottle-feeding mothers. However, other studies claim that the hormones for lactation along with the mother's closeness to the baby suppress her sexual desire.

***You may experience an orgasm while nursing.*** Some women even have an orgasm while they are nursing the baby (and may then feel embarrassed or guilty about it). If this happens to you and you try to keep it a secret from your husband, it may increase your confusion and anxiety about this "misplaced sexuality." Your secretiveness and withdrawal can also make him uncomfortable. The best solution may be to make a leap of faith and tell your partner what you're experiencing, taking the risk that his reaction may be disappointing to you.

If you do have the courage to take that leap of faith, then don't be devastated if your partner's reaction is disappointing. You can be satisfied, knowing that you've been open and done the best you can. If your husband can't accept your directness, then the loss is his. It's important that you feel good about your courage, rather than having guilty or conflicted feelings ("If only I hadn't brought it up . . .").

***Hormone changes can once again be blamed for problems.*** There are physiological reasons why sex and breast-feeding may not mix well. Your breasts can also be sore or insensitive to stimulation, all of which interferes with your ability to feel sexy or enjoy sex. These postpartum hormonal changes can last from one month all the way to two years after delivery, or whenever your own body produces sufficient estrogens for a pleasant sex life.

***Your obstetrician may not know about sex and hormones during breast-feeding.*** Some doctors do not recognize the relationship between hormones and a nursing woman's sexual desire. There has been a distinct lack of research on the subject.

However, some facts are known. Nursing lowers your estrogen levels, which can make intercourse difficult if your breasts and genitals are oversensitive. On the other hand, your breasts and nipples can become *desensitized,* which reduces your desire for sexual intimacy. The decrease in estrogen levels can cause dryness in the vagina and a lack of lubrication even when you're aroused. Prolactin, the hormone that stimulates secretion of milk, has a diminishing effect on your sexual interest and sexual tension.

***Lubricating jelly will only help the symptoms of vaginal dryness.*** Although you can use lubricating jelly during the time you're breast-feeding, it won't increase your sexual desire or the quality of your orgasms (or ability to have them). Your body is occupied doing the important work of feeding your baby: you may just have to wait until she's weaned until you can enjoy sex again.

***Leaking breasts can be another sexual complication.*** For some women, the let-down reflex is automatic when they have sexual relations. You may find that when you're aroused or have an orgasm, you spout milk. This can be disturbing either to you or your mate, or you can view it as amusing or natural. Try to see it as part of the pleasure of lovemaking, accept it as part of this time in your life.

There are a couple of possible solutions if leaking milk bothers you. You can try to have sex immediately after nursing when your breasts are less likely to leak. You can also wear a bra to absorb the milk, unless the bra seems unsexy or unromantic to either of you.

## CONTRACEPTION AFTER CHILDBIRTH

***Don't make love even once without protection.*** You had better think about birth control the very first time you think about sex after childbirth. Just because you've become a mother doesn't mean it won't happen again! You can get pregnant even the first few times you make love postpartum.

***Use contraception as soon as you begin having intercourse.*** This is true whether you are breast-feeding or not and whether you've gotten your period or not. If you want to have sex before the six-week postpartum checkup, a condom plus foam is the best protection.

*Menstruation usually returns in six to eight weeks after you give birth if you're not nursing.*   Breast-feeding can delay your periods as much as one year **but that doesn't mean you won't get pregnant before that.** You menstruate when your body's production of estrogen stimulates ovulation and the progesterone builds up the uterine lining. However, it is possible to ovulate without having a period afterwards.

*Breast-feeding is not a contraceptive.*   Forget what you've heard or read: what you may not have heard is all the "oops" pregnancies of women with infants at the breast! Studies show that 15 percent of women can get pregnant at six weeks postpartum, and 40 percent are fertile at 20 weeks after birth. If a woman is nursing, she has a 25 percent chance of conceiving at 12 weeks postpartum and a 65 percent chance at 24 weeks. Nursing may suppress ovulation, but many women ovulate sporadically or regularly during breast-feeding.

*Your prepregnancy diaphragm will not fit during the postpartum period.*   Your vagina is temporarily enlarged after giving birth, so get fitted for a new diaphragm before you have sex. After your body has fully recovered from the effects of giving birth, you may need an entirely different size of diaphragm. *Do not wait for your obstetrician to bring this up.* S/he may forget what form of contraception you use or may not raise the issue out of sensitivity, expecting you to ask when you are ready to resume your sex life.

*Doctors have been known to forget to talk to their patients about birth control after birth.*   Don't expect your obstetrician to make sure you don't get pregnant again immediately. It is your body—*you* should assume responsibility for taking care of it. Doctors are people just like the rest of us—they are not superhuman, they are not infallible. Nonetheless, American doctors have to cope with the extraordinary pressure of practicing in a society that legally demands error-free medical care.

*A digression about how we're ruining our medical system.* You may not see what this has to do with postpartum contraception, but doctor/patient relations is a perfect example of our mistaken expectations. Unrealistic expectations are the root cause of many postpartum problems.

You may believe it is up to your doctor to raise the issue of birth control and take care of it, but the responsibility is yours. It's your body, your uterus, your life. Choose the best medical help you can but never relinquish control to anyone and then feel outraged about the outcome. You're a grown woman, you've become a mother, but you may still be making the mistake of expecting Big Daddy Doctor to take care of "little you." And if he *doesn't*, you'll sue him (or her) for his last dime!

I may sound harsh, but you may not be aware that we are losing thousands of fine obstetricians in America: they cannot continue to deliver babies because they cannot afford the malpractice insurance rates. Too many parents take a passive role in their health care and their baby's birth—then they become righteous and file lawsuits when everything doesn't go perfectly.

It is essential to your health and the practice of good obstetrics that you are a full partner in your own health care. As for birth control, you should assume responsibility for your own body and make sure that you protect yourself from an untimely pregnancy. Regardless of how many children you want, it is not a good idea to have one right on top of another. It is an unhealthy burden on your body if you get pregnant immediately and can also compromise the developing fetus. This is to say nothing of the additional pressure another pregnancy would put on your marital relationship, which is still adjusting to the first child.

## THE EFFECT OF PARENTHOOD ON SEXUALITY

*Becoming parents is going to affect your sexuality.* A couple's sex life is never static, anyway: parenthood can profoundly affect your sex life. Sex constantly changes in life, it's not something that you can resolve and then it remains constant. What's happening sexually in your life depends on who you both are and where you are emotionally at any point.

When most of your day is spent with a child, it's easy to lose touch with who you are besides being a parent. Many people are insecure about their sexuality and whether they are sexually attractive, and parenthood can magnify these doubts.

***Less frequent intercourse is normal.*** Studies show that when you become parents, you're going to have less sex. These studies indicate that marital satisfaction, and sex in particular, declines from the birth of your first child until the last one leaves home. If you had intercourse frequently before pregnancy (which is defined as several times a **week**), you may find that postpartum it becomes several times a **month**. Those who had sex less frequently before the baby was born will have even less now. Some couples who stop having sex during the pregnancy do not re-establish their sex life when the baby is born.

***It's actually possible to forget how to make love!*** Funnily enough, sex is not like riding a bicycle—you can't just pick it up any time and pedal away. Once you get out of the habit of having sex, it can be hard to start again. After a celibate period, it's not unusual for people to make rationalizations and excuses for not resuming an active sex life. A long abstinence can make you feel embarrassed or insecure about recommencing your sex life. It's like starting all over again: you'll need a courtship, exploration, and adjustment to each other.

***Losing touch with the sexual side of yourself is normal after you have a baby.*** The early parenting years sometimes cause sex to take a back seat. It can be frightening to lose touch with the passionate side of yourself. Don't panic, worrying that parenting has taken the place of passion in your life. Have faith: your desire for greater sexual intimacy *will* return. Knowing that it's on its way may make the waiting easier!

***Sex has a new meaning now.*** The profound meaning of having intercourse is obvious when you look at your baby. Even if you aren't conscious of it during lovemaking, it's plain to see that a baby is the result of sex. This can enhance your emotional experience of sex; it can become more intense and profound. However, it is still something different that you have to adjust to, and change can be stressful.

*It can be destructive to be nostalgic for the past.*   It can hinder your re-emerging sex life as parents if you are pining for the-way-we-were. You may think that sex was simple and satisfying before you had a child. It may just seem easier now to give all your attention to the child rather than going to the trouble of re-establishing sexual intimacy between you. You may give up your sex life without admitting or realizing it. The less effort you put into making love or solving sexual impasses, the farther you remain from having a good sex life.

Indulging in nostalgia for "how much better things were" is a destructive pattern that discourages growth and moving forward. Remember your sense of humor. Accept life as it is now, along with the changes that have occurred in your sex life. Intimacy doesn't always have to lead to intercourse. You can have sex that isn't goal-oriented, that isn't focused on the man penetrating the woman and having orgasms. (See *"Suggestions for Parents Who Want a Good Sex Life,"* later in this chapter.)

## THE MAN'S REACTION TO SEX AFTER BIRTH

*Your wife may not understand your sexual demands.*   It is common for a woman to misunderstand the sexual demands that her husband makes. You may not even understand your own demands! You may want sex or romance, but what you also want with your wife is time together, caring, and companionship. Often the way you express this is by wanting to go to bed. A woman may not know how to respond because she doesn't see a man's sexual demands as a sign of closeness and caring: she may interpret them simply as her mate wanting to satisfy his physical needs.

When a couple become parents, their sex life and even their intimacy may be seriously disrupted. It can be a lot less devastating if you know what to expect while you are both adjusting to your baby and new roles.

***Your wife may be your main source of nurturing.*** For some men, the only nurturing and real closeness they get is in their intimate relationship with their mate. Most men don't learn how to spontaneously give affection or know how to ask for it. Men often suffer from loneliness, unbeknownst to the women in their lives. They may not even know themselves how isolated they feel. The irony is that you may need the very intimacy that you don't know how to give.

***Women have more ways to get emotional feedback.*** A woman is usually able to get love and affection from many different people, primarily from her child(ren) but also friends and relatives. The ability to get her emotional needs met in a variety of ways is something she probably learned as a child with dolls and household pets.

***Your wife may reject you in bed.*** Sexual rejection by the new mother is a common problem that many men face after their babies are born. There is no problem in a relationship if both partners are uninterested in sex. The problem comes, obviously, when one wants it and the other doesn't. If you are being sexually ignored by your mate it can make you feel rejected, inadequate, and unattractive. You may also have fears of being abandoned by your uninterested partner, since the rejected person often feels (perhaps subconsciously) it must be his/her fault.

***Being rejected sexually can stir up insecurities.*** Sexual rejection has the nasty potential of feeding your existing insecurities or inferiority complex. Now you not only have the pain of being rejected but as a result you then feel worse about yourself generally! Few people are self-assured about their own sexuality. We all need to be reassured that we are attractive and desirable; sexual rejection is devastating to even the strongest egos.

***Rejection causes a standard range of emotions.*** If you are deprived sexually, some common feelings you might experience are: anger, frustration, bitterness, resentment, and guilt. You may have a depression, preoccupation, and/or obsession about the rejection. The rejection is so hard for some men to accept that they may develop paranoid fears that their wives are secretly lesbians.

***Impotence can affect some men in the postpartum period.***   If you feel rejected, left out, and jealous—and you are unable to communicate these feelings—your inner conflicts can make you impotent.

***The most common response to sexual rejection is to withdraw.***   Once you are spurned it is natural to retreat sexually to avoid further rejection. Another reaction to being rejected is to apply pressure to get a sexual response . . . which only worsens the situation. What can result is that both of you are "sitting it out," hoping the problem will just go away.

***A new father may feel deceived by his wife's sexual rejection.***   You may feel that your partner "used" you, that she was only interested in having sex with you in order to get pregnant. Your imagination may run rampant and convince you that she's turned off now because this is her "real" self. Your imagination may encourage your injured ego to assume that she's kept this side of herself hidden from you in order to have a baby. This may sound farfetched, but paranoid fantasies are one way to cope with the pain of sexual rejection. Your imagination can run wild in order to protect your ego.

***You may blame your wife or the baby.***   It's natural to look for someone to blame if you're not getting sexual or emotional satisfaction. Coping with your role change and adjusting to the concept of fatherhood is tough enough; it may already make you feel inadequate. Your mate may be so preoccupied with caring for the baby that you feel insignificant and abandoned. If she gives you the cold shoulder in bed it only makes things worse.

***Sex as an expression of intimacy is quite natural for many men but can seem alien to a woman.***   There are many men whose only way of expressing intimacy is by having sexual relations. A man can want to hold, be held, and make love. A woman, on the other hand, often wants to hold, be held, and *talk* as an expression of intimacy. Thus men and women may have very different ways of fulfilling their needs for intimacy and closeness. This difference between the sexes can be confusing for a couple and create serious conflict.

Closeness and intimacy are different, and in this context it is more likely that a man would want closeness while a woman wants intimacy. In simple psychological terms, closeness means the capacity to form a state of oneness with another person, to be able to tolerate the loss of self. Intimacy means the capacity to be empathetic, sensitive, and caring toward another person: to be aware of who that other person is apart from one's self, and to be concerned about what the other person thinks and feels.

### Sex may be a man's only way to express his feelings.

It is difficult for some men to admit that they have the emotional need to be nurtured or supported. It can be hard for other men to express their affection and appreciation for their wives, except by making love to them. Sex may be the only way they have to feel their needs are being met or to express their feelings.

If you find that this is true for you, then be aware how much more devastating it is for a man like you to be sexually rejected or be without sexual contact with your mate.

### You may have an affair to counteract your rejection.

Infidelity may be the reaction of a new father who is feeling sexually rejected. If your desire for sex is denied and on top of that you feel like a useless outsider in infant care, it can lead to an extramarital affair (more on infidelity in *Chapter 10: Bad Feelings*). You are suffering from a deep feeling of rejection at the same time that you're coping with a new self-image as a father. You crave positive feedback about yourself; your wife isn't giving it to you; having an affair may seem to be the solution. A man who feels rejected can be like a wounded lion in the jungle—suffering, dangerous, and unpredictable!

***Feeling shut out by your wife may induce you to be unfaithful.***    Sexual alienation can lead to emotional distancing between partners, which can lead to infidelity. If you feel alienated from your partner it may encourage you to contemplate or embark on an extramarital affair, seeking not only sexual fulfillment but emotional nourishment as well. Both partners suffer if a new father reacts to the situation by withdrawing from his wife or by seeking a replacement for her sexual or emotional attention.

***An affair can mix you both up emotionally.***    Your infidelity may make you feel confused or guilty. Even if your wife doesn't learn of your affair, your emotional withdrawal can make *her* feel the way *you* did before: deserted, lonely, and unattractive.

***New fathers are "in danger" of having affairs.***    Masters and Johnson report that marital infidelity increases during the postpartum period (as well as during pregnancy). You may be able to avoid this "nonsolution" to feeling rejected if you can find a quiet time to sit with your wife and discuss how you're both feeling about your sex life as new parents.

***Don't let the baby become your rival.***    If you aren't careful, a dynamic can be initiated in which the baby becomes the mother's new lover and you are the intruder. She may feel torn, her loyalties clashing between the baby and you . . . because she's feeling conflicted she may not welcome you sexually. Your reaction may be to feel hurt and withdraw.

***Be aware of signs that you are withdrawing.***    There are some common symptoms of a new father's withdrawal. Be alert if you have any of the following new habits: staying away from home more or avoiding going home; burying yourself in work as an escape; throwing yourself into a sport that takes a lot of time; drinking more than usual.

The most obvious sign of withdrawal and avoidance is if you contemplate or embark on an affair—which doesn't have to mean that you take another woman to bed. The intention is the same if you engage in serious flirtation (coming on to a woman, sharing intimate feelings). Taking a woman out to a long lunch with a bottle of wine can be even more intense and sexy than scurrying off to a motel. Don't kid yourself. Don't run away from your marriage or try to bury your head in the sand. The only person who can make you *really* feel better about yourself and your relationship is your wife: take it up with her, alone or with a counselor.

**A man may be turned off by his wife's mind and body in the postpartum period.**  A woman can be preoccupied with her healing body to the extent that it's a turn-off for you. Also, if she is overly concerned with baby chores it can drive you away. Rather than suffering silently and withdrawing (which is what men have done historically), you should speak up. Without attacking your mate you can try to explain how her self-absorption and intense focus on the baby is pushing you away.

**The Madonna/Prostitute Syndrome can be a problem for your sex life.**  This syndrome is one reason that a man may reject his wife after the baby is born. Some men feel that when a woman becomes a mother she enters a taboo category, specifically the incest taboo. This is a common syndrome that is related to a man's feelings about his mother, i.e., "mother" is not someone with whom you go to bed. If your wife becomes associated with your mother in your mind, how can you possibly have a sex life?

When a man feels (obviously unconsciously) that by becoming a mother his wife has been transformed into a Madonna figure, he can no longer make love to her. Some men cope with this dilemma by making love only in the dark. A man may need professional help to disentangle these confused feelings.

**You may be turned off if you think you have to perform.**  You may feel pressured to perform sexually although you have no interest in your wife: you may be generally lacking a sex drive. Although you may not be consciously aware of it, there is social pressure on a man to live up to certain standards of sexual performance. It is quite natural for a new father's sexual interest to wane temporarily, but many men are too tough on themselves. You have to consider the effect of outside pressures on your sex drive. Increased pressure to be a provider and other adjustments to parenthood can drain you.

***You may just feel too tired for sex or romance.*** There are many legitimate reasons for not wanting to make love. However, you can convince yourself that you're a failure for not desiring your wife or for not having intercourse with her. Try to understand that you are doing this is to yourself: don't project it onto your wife and imagine that she has created the problem. It's a monster you've created and only you can slay it.

***Father-infant closeness can promote sexuality between the parents.***   Babies are very sensual, there is a lot of touching and physical give and take. In our society this kind of sensuality is usually restricted to women, it is behavior that isn't encouraged in boys or most men. But hugging, kissing, stroking, bathing your baby can awaken you to the pleasure of physical contact and expression, which may be something that carries over into your sex life.

## REASONS FOR
## POSTPARTUM SEXUAL PROBLEMS

***The loss of sexual desire and drive is very common after you become parents.***   You may find that you not only don't want to have intercourse but that you have no desire to hold, touch, or kiss each other. Some couples find that they even lack affection and tenderness. During the first six postpartum months you may find that the frequency of your lovemaking is decidedly infrequent! You can do yourselves a favor if you gracefully accept your sexual inactivity. This temporary curtailment will be easier if you don't fight it.

***These feelings can begin right from the time of the baby's birth.***   You may feel self-conscious touching or kissing. You may deny that you have a need for privacy, sexual expression, or interest in nonbaby topics. You may decide that sex is something to be delayed until further notice, until "sometime in the future," now that the baby and parenthood are of primary importance. But how long can a marriage hibernate? How long can you go without sex before you don't even know how to make the first move? To stay alive and vital, a marriage has to be more than a child-rearing partnership.

***Perceiving yourselves as "Mommy" and "Daddy" can work against renewing your sex life.*** These new images of yourselves, along with household and baby chores, don't exactly conjure up sexy images for most people. It is guaranteed to put a damper on your sex life if you start calling each other "Mom" and "Dad"!

     If you see each other as "Mother" and "Father," you confuse your identities and your expectations of each other. You may be expecting your partner to behave as your own parents did. Unconsciously, this can trigger an incest taboo (i.e., you don't sleep with your mother or father) and can inhibit your sexual drive. The birth of a child can reawaken feelings about your own parents and can stir up unresolved sexual conflicts from your childhood.

***Being motherly can be antisexual.*** Motherliness appears to be incompatible with eroticism for many people. Motherhood can turn you (unconsciously) from a sensual, sexy woman into a Madonna figure (pure, untouchable, chaste). If you feel a conflict between motherhood and eroticism, be patient. Don't rush yourself. As you gain confidence in your mothering abilities you'll probably regain a sense of yourself as a sexual being, separate from your role as mother. This new nonsexual image of you can remind your mate of his own mother, or his feelings about her. Some men who take on a parental role may also find their eroticism lessening.

***Sexual problems are often viewed as the woman's fault.*** A woman often feels responsible for the sexual relationship, and therefore feels it is her fault if things aren't going well. Postpartum adjustments of all kinds are usually assumed to be the woman's responsibility and problem. You may blame yourself for not being able to entice or excite your mate. You may have sex even if you don't feel ready, just to avoid what you think of as the role of the sexless, boring housewife/mother.

*Not having sex can be an emotional strain.* A lack of sex life or sex drive can cause you extreme anxiety. You may believe you are damaged or weird for having an intense involvement with your baby that excludes wanting sex. This stirs up feelings of inadequacy and guilt, which can be increased by your husband's demands and frustrations. You feel like a failure. Some women are afraid that they've fallen out of love with their husbands or that they have a deep psychological problem. If your mate is a man who keeps nagging you about sex (in hopes that by trying again and again he can make you want it) it only makes you feel worse.

## A LACK OF SEXUAL DESIRE

---

### DETERRENTS TO SEX OR SEX DRIVE

- Disenchantment with each other as parents/partners
- Breakdown in communication since baby's arrival
- Inadequate amount and quality of time spent together
- Arguments over finances or child rearing
- Fear of being overheard (or intruded on)
- Sleep-in help, especially if mother or mother-in-law; especially if you're not used to others in your house
- Baby sleeping in bedroom can cause self-consciousness
- Sound of crying or even cooing and gurgling can interfere with the fantasies, mental images, etc., of good sex

---

*Becoming parents can play funny tricks on your sex drive.* Parenthood tends to dilute your sexuality, if not smother it, at least for a while. Some studies have shown that the first child has the greatest negative effect on the parents' sex life; in addition, the studies show that couples who have only one child have sex less frequently then parents with two or more children.

***Sex is a critical aspect of a man and woman's union.*** Some people would say that sex is the most critical part of a relationship. If you don't have sex together your relationship is diminished, it narrows the scope of your emotional connection.

***You can drop sex altogether.*** It is possible, although hardly advisable, to eliminate sex entirely from your lives. Many people have done it, often after their children are born. You may find that sex is not important to both of you, that other gratifications (children, work, affection, companionship) have become the priorities or minimize your sex drive. However, if you are in a harmonious marriage where you like each other, it isn't normal or healthy to feel no desire at all for your mate.

***A lack of sexual desire can make you feel like a failure.*** Either partner may feel inadequate, as though they've let the other partner down on a fundamental precept of marriage. You need to learn how to share your anxieties with each other and find a way back to sexual intimacy. You need help understanding the elements of new parenthood that can undermine your desire for each other.

***Don't lie and start having sex before you're really ready.*** Do not make the mistake of resuming sexual relations if you are too tired, preoccupied, or physically unprepared. Don't force yourself to have sex because you feel guilty, or feel you owe it to your mate, or out of fear that he'll stop loving you or have an affair.

Sex that you don't really want, or that you feel obligated to participate in, is probably going to be disappointing and cause resentment for both partners. Dishonesty about sex can become a hard-to-break habit that diminishes the quality of your sexual experience. Excuses, avoidance, or pretending pleasure can become a habit—and can turn you off even more.

*Being honest about your lack of sex drive removes the anxiety.*  Once you *admit* that you are not yet ready for a full sex life, you can both relax and accept it as a temporary situation. Both partners' needs for closeness, comfort, approval, etc., can be expressed in nonsexual ways. Also, oral or manual sex can relieve physical and emotional tension, allowing you time to resume intercourse when you both feel ready, without any rush or pressure.

*"When in doubt, make love."*  This might be a handy motto during the transition to parenthood. "Why not?" is another catch phrase to remember when your partner is eager for sex and you're ambivalent. This is not a contradiction of the previous advice not to force yourself to have intercourse if you really don't want to. What we're talking about here is feeling "iffy" about making love but going for it anyway. (Of course there's a difference between feeling iffy and feeling so little desire that you have to squeeze your eyes shut and think about something else to go through with it. *That* is not a great idea!)

You may not feel 100 percent gung-ho about making love for quite a while but it can be good for you and your relationship. If you're not totally in the mood for sex, *do it anyway.* If you have sex only to please your partner you'll probably be delightfully surprised at how pleasurable it is for you, too, once you let go. The unselfish act of making love to give pleasure to your mate can be satisfying just on its own.

*Fatigue can be a significant factor in a lowered sex drive.*  But it can also be used as a cop-out, an excuse not to have sex, for women who never had much sex drive or don't really enjoy sex. Try to be honest and ask yourself, "Is it *really* because I'm tired?" Don't take a cheap shot and rebuff your mate by saying, "Not tonight, I'm exhausted," if that's not truly the reason. This can make your husband feel guilty, or like a "bad" person.

*Any stress in a relationship may cause a loss of libido (sex drive).*  Obviously, the postpartum adjustment is extremely stressful. However, this lack of sexual desire can be directed specifically at your mate or can be a generalized reaction (you have no sexual fantasies, don't feel turned on by members of the opposite sex, don't masturbate, etc.). When the stress is reduced, your sexual desire should return on its own.

**Fear of intimacy is a cause of sexual withdrawal.** Shutting off your sexual feelings is a defense against the threat of having to be close. Pregnancy and birth can trigger these fears of closeness: people with problems being close often deny their sexuality.

The dread of being dependent on your mate can also undermine your sexuality if you feel trapped by a loving partner and baby—you may feel they've taken away your freedom. The loss of independence can mean the loss of power or autonomy to you. However, you may feel turned off only to your mate, not in general: you might be able to fantasize having sex with a stranger. In fact, either avoiding sex or having extramarital sex are common ways to avoid intimacy and escape your new life.

**A lack of spontaneity can undermine your sexual relations.** The fact that you can't make love any time, anywhere (which is a natural result of having a baby) can diminish your desire for sex and also the quality of your encounters. Sex can no longer take place any time in any room. It becomes something you can usually do only at night in your bedroom once the baby is asleep . . . and by then you're both too tired and too busy listening for the baby's cries!

It is not unusual for sex to become regimented for new parents: only in the bedroom, only at night. This makes sex predictable, uninspired, and boring because it robs you of any possible spontaneity in your sexual encounters. It probably also means that the sex is rushed—"Hurry up before the baby cries." It may also mean that your perception of sex becomes something you do in exhaustion at the end of the day, which is hardly a sexy image.

**Bonding with the baby can take the place of sex.** The emotional and sensual bond with the baby can replace adult sexuality, especially for the mother. You may be one of those new mothers who feels that the emotional attachment to your baby is so great that there's little, if anything, left over for sex or even intimacy. A baby can satisfy a lot of sexual needs aside from intercourse: with a child there's a great deal of body contact, physical embracing, and feeling that you are needed. The adult desire for hugs, kisses, and lovemaking decreases, especially for the parent who is deeply involved in feeding, bathing, and cuddling the infant.

Sometimes a mother's desire and capacity for physical contact is overloaded by the baby. You may find that your baby takes so much out of you that you resent the friendly sensual or sexual advances of your mate. Contact with the baby can be enough: anything more, even touching or kissing your husband, can seem repulsive to you. "Leave me alone, don't touch me," is a common reaction of new mothers.

*The pressures of parenting can also interfere with your sex life.*   Quarreling over chores and baby care is neither an erotic stimulant nor an encouragement for physical closeness between you! It's not easy for a woman to be giving toward her mate when she's been meeting a baby's needs all day. It's not easy for a man to be even-tempered or have a sense of humor when he's sexually and emotionally frustrated.

*Constant togetherness as new parents can also be a turn-off.*   You'll probably find that you're together more than you've ever been before: this can put you under a strain. You have to learn how to spend so much time under one roof without getting on each other's nerves. If you become aware that this enforced togetherness is an irritant, find ways to get some time out of the house or apart from each other.

*If the baby cries, it can interfere with sex.*   The baby's crying, or even the fear that he *might* cry, can be a deterrent to sex for some couples. Many new parents are convinced that their child knows telepathically when they are making love and lets them know of his superior powers by crying urgently at the absolutely worst moment!

If either of you *anticipates* this interruption it creates tension, which interferes with your lovemaking (or ability to make love, depending on how uptight and preoccupied you are about the crying). Your anticipation means that you don't feel free and relaxed, and that you can't really let go and make love because you're responding to the baby, not to each other. The best thing you can do is try to laugh at the absurdity of a baby that seems to cry right at the moment of orgasm!

## SEXUAL AVERSIVENESS (AVOIDING SEX)

---

### TACTICS TO AVOID SEX

- Avoiding initiating sexual encounters
- Avoiding showing any excitement during sex or foreplay
- Avoiding even nonsexual affection which might lead to sexual expectations
- Avoiding feeling turned on by thinking nonsexy, especially critical, thoughts about your mate
- Sabotaging possible sexual encounters by picking a fight or criticizing your mate before bedtime
- Discussing the child whenever the conversation turns intimate or there's a possibility of sex
- Concentrating on being sleepy, collapsing in an exhausted heap as soon as you get into bed
- Making no effort to look attractive; dressing and wearing your hair in styles your mate doesn't like

---

If neither one of you cares about having sex then you don't have a problem, but usually it is an issue. The problem is often more uncomfortable for the partner who would like to have sex, but it becomes a shared problem once it spills over and there is displaced anger, yelling, and criticism. At that point, it is time for outside help to untangle your feelings. This can happen at six months postpartum or three years down the road: it depends on how your sexual problems are affecting your relationship generally.

*Use the above chart as a guide.* This chart gives you an idea of some of the behavior patterns that people use when they are trying to avoid sex. You should be alert to these signs in yourself and your mate since new parenthood often entails a period during which your libido is out to lunch. You may feel confused or frightened by these avoidance tactics unless you understand that they are the result of the jumble of emotions that have assaulted you and your mate.

*Sexual aversiveness (avoiding sex) can develop in the postpartum period.* It can happen because of reduced sexual contact (fewer than a couple of times a month) along with anger, resentment, and guilt. This sexual aversion can be the result of a woman who is trying to do too much. Her fatigue, unexpressed anger, and ineffective communication are often at the root of the problem.

The first thing you have to do is discuss the source of your anger (with a counselor if necessary). Then you have to create time for lovemaking and start slowly and gently to rebuild your sex life.

One way to avoid sexual aversiveness is to make love even if you aren't gung-ho about it. There are experts who say that if only one of you really wants to make love and the other is neutral, you should go ahead and have sex. By the end, these experts contend, you'll feel closer, more loving and warm than you did before.

*A poor body image can make you avoid sex.* If the weight gain of pregnancy really upsets you after the baby is born, it can make you feel terrible about your body. Your body is still big but you're no longer pregnant: this can make you feel unattractive, unsexy, even unlovable. You may feel you don't want to look at yourself, much less be looked at or made love to.

The problem works in the following way: in our society, thinness equals perfection, thus the extra pounds from your pregnancy make you feel imperfect. Sexual contact is a reminder of the changes your body has gone through; you may mourn for your ''lost'' body. If you (or your mate) feel that sexual attractiveness means high breasts and no stretch marks, then you'll have a hard time desiring or enjoying lovemaking.

We've all heard disparaging comments about women who "let themselves go" after they had children. You may fear this and be too tough on yourself, expecting all the pregnancy fat to melt away immediately. You may be harsh and angry with yourself about your body, punishing yourself with strict diets and avoiding all sexual contact.

If you project your negative feelings to your partner (or overreact to a passing comment about your weight), you may imagine that *he* is the one who is critical of your appearance. Your mate may have a hard time understanding your obsession with your physical flaws since men aren't under the same social pressure as women are about their bodies. In fact, your partner will probably think there is something wrong with *him* if you avoid sex. You have to let him know what you're thinking so he doesn't feel personally rejected. If you don't express your feelings of despair about your physical changes and imperfections, your mate may feel sexually rebuffed because you avoid being naked or having anything to do with him sexually.

**Sex can be an indicator of other problems.**  What is happening to us sexually is likely to be a sign of changes in our own psyches and within our relationships. After the baby's birth there is a common problem of a new mother withdrawing sexually, especially in a relationship in which you mothered your husband before you had a baby. You may have enjoyed nurturing and caring for him; he undoubtedly thrived on being pampered, on being number one (perhaps his mother adored and catered to him).

After the baby is born, you may be surprised to find that you don't want to cater to your mate in a motherly way any more—you may even feel contemptuous of him for wanting it. You may take the baby in bed with you and not even mind if your mate sleeps on the sofa. Now that you have a real child, you may reject the person you used to love to nurture and pamper. However, your husband is the same man: he hasn't stopped loving you or needing your attention.

**The baby may be a scapegoat for underlying problems in your sex life.**  You may blame sexual problems for a more profound unhappiness in your marriage. When there is sexual rejection or withdrawal in a relationship, it can be about things other than sex itself: it can be an indicator of other changes in your life. You may be unwilling to look at deeper dissatisfactions within yourself or your mate (or be unaware of them). It's important for you to recognize and separate these issues from the problems of postpartum sex. There are common crises in adult development and a couple's sex life: restlessness, boredom, people growing apart. You have to be honest in identifying what may be going wrong between you.

*Sex is hard to talk about.* Feelings of self-esteem, adequacy, and acceptance are all wrapped up in sex. You will become discontented and unfulfilled if you don't make the effort to discuss what gives you satisfaction sexually and what makes you uncomfortable. You can alleviate some of the pressure by talking about sex at a neutral time, not during or after a disappointing sexual encounter. Try to choose a time when you are not tired or drained so that you can discuss your sexual concerns as two people who care about each other, who want their partner to be as happy and fulfilled as they hope to be themselves.

If you can talk to each other about what's going on sexually, what you're experiencing and feeling, it can make you feel closer and build intimacy. During this transition to parenthood you may feel freer to discuss sex and when, why, and how you engage in it. Try to use this adjustment period to open yourselves up to positive changes in your sexual life, to understanding what your mate needs and wants and how you can fit this in with your own desires. These revelations will enhance the rest of your relationship, just as hidden frustrations about sex can be poisonous.

## SUGGESTIONS FOR PARENTS
## WHO WANT A GOOD SEX LIFE

There are a few "ingredients" that are necessary in order for a couple to have a good sex life. You need to have mental well-being: feel healthy, energetic, and sure of your own self-worth. During the postpartum adjustment both partners are overloaded with emotional demands and tend to feel drained and inadequate.

***You have to seduce each other.*** In order to rediscover your own sexuality and encourage your mate's, you each have to nurture and stroke the other, both physically and emotionally. At least one of you has to make a concerted effort to "woo" the other, to reawaken the sensuality and sexuality between you. If you don't do this, you run the risk of losing your sexual connection to each other as you embark on parenthood.

***Your bedroom should be an oasis.*** Try to turn your bedroom into a hideaway from the clutter of baby equipment that may have overtaken your home. Make the bedroom an inviting, attractive room that is conducive to making love. Don't let it become a storeroom for extra diapers or laundry that needs ironing. Your bedroom should be a separate sanctuary.

***Sex doesn't "just happen" any more.*** Once there's a baby in your life there are too many distractions and demands on your time for sex to just happen spontaneously. You are certain to be disappointed if you try to leave sex to fate or to spontaneous combustion. And don't expect your partner to read your mind and "just know" when you're ready for sex, or what your need for affection and intimacy is, or what your anxieties are. Furthermore, most of the time you're not going to be able to have sex when the mood hits you.

It is counterproductive to maintain unrealistic romantic notions and expect that sex will happen spontaneously. You have to schedule sex. This may sound unromantic to you but it's the only way you'll probably "get any" in the chaos of new parenthood. Although planning for sexual contact may sound cold at first, it can be the opposite. Think of planning as something positive you're doing for yourselves, as something fun and exciting to anticipate and fantasize about.

***Make a time and place for sex.*** There is only a limited amount of time and energy that you have each day. You need to stop and think about your priorities. Make thought-ful decisions about how to protect and improve the quality of your relationship now that there's a baby in the picture.

Sharing baby care can be wonderful, but is it more important than having time out of the house as a couple? Or more important than having 45 minutes of intimate pri-vacy in your bedroom on a Saturday afternoon? Do not make the mistake of thinking that any kind of "together-ness" is what keeps a couple together. Doing things with your baby and around the house together may indeed en-rich your marriage, but if you don't also direct some of that time and energy to your sex life, this Ozzie & Harriet to-getherness can actually undermine your sexual bond.

***Learn to separate the two different parts of your life as a couple.***   Make a graceful transition between your inti-mate, sexual time together and the rest of your day. One of the obstacles to feeling sexy and having sex during early par-enthood is that baby care is unerotic. It's very hard to go to bed with your partner immediately after changing diapers.

Take the time to make an interlude and change gears between these two very different aspects of your life. Take a bubble bath alone or together to relax, to soak away the hassles of the day and get in touch with the sensual side of yourself. Play some music, have a glass of wine, or do what-ever relaxes you and helps you to make the transition from the nursery to your "boudoir."

***Change the time you make love.***   Now that your days are turned upside down by the baby's routine (or lack of it), you have to be more flexible about lovemaking. For ex-ample, you may find that you collapse after dinner and watch a bit of TV or do some reading. You're out cold by the time your mate finishes brushing his teeth. Try setting the alarm 30 minutes earlier in the morning and experiment with making love then.

***Different bedtimes can be a problem once you be-come parents.***   Let's say one of you is a day person and goes to bed early, the other is a night person and likes to stay up late. This may not have been a deterrent to your sex life before you became parents because you could make love at random times. Now, if you don't go to bed at the same time, it can become an unspoken source of disappointment.

Find the right time to discuss your different habits of going to bed, without making accusations. Do not suffer in silence, building up resentment and hurt because you assume that your partner's different bedtime is a form of sexual rejection. You need to talk about going to bed early or late, reading or watching television before falling asleep, otherwise this simple issue can become a problem that interferes with your sexual communication.

If you and your mate have different sleeping rhythms, you can take turns accommodating each other. For instance, the early-to-bed partner can stay up later by sometimes taking a nap in the afternoon. The night person can take turns by coming to bed earlier, even if he isn't tired. If you can make the effort to have a shared bedtime it can give you some sweet, quiet time together even if you don't make love.

***Try making love without having intercourse.*** Sex without intercourse is a gentle and pleasing way to rebuild your sexual bridge after the hiatus of pregnancy and the postpartum abstention. It is also a good solution for women who may not feel ready for intercourse yet. You may feel you are giving a lot to the baby and need holding and comforting now. You may prefer to give and/or receive oral or manual stimulation at this point and resume intercourse later. Remember that it's often harder for a new mother to become aroused so it will take a lot of stimulation and perhaps a lubricant to actually have intercourse.

There are many forms of sexual expression and enjoyment besides intercourse. You can deepen the bond between you if you explore the nonintercourse aspects of lovemaking now with a mutual understanding that you are rediscovering each other. Take a shower or bath together, soaping each other and enjoying the sensual, not sexual, aspect of your union. You can spend lots of time in gentle caressing and exploration of each other from head to toe, with manual and oral stimulation.

Many sex therapists recommend removing the ''goal orientation'' from lovemaking. They suggest creating an atmosphere where intercourse (or in some cases orgasm) is not the goal. Once you give yourselves permission not to have intercourse, you don't have to fake enjoyment or avoid sex altogether. Once you decide not to have intercourse you can lie together naked, caressing each other, discovering that tenderness and the enjoyment of each other's bodies does not have to wind up as intercourse.

***Don't forget foreplay!*** Foreplay is often forgotten in the rush to have intercourse once your body is ready. You have both abstained for so long that you may feel awkward about foreplay or just be too eager to get on with it. But don't just strip and hop in bed. Start with some wine and music, remember your teenage days and neck on the couch for a while, take an oil bath together, explore and pleasure each other. The more you draw it out, the hotter you'll get, and the better it will be.

***Masturbation can be satisfying at this time.*** During the transition back to sex, when a woman may not want sex or may want it less frequently than her mate, a man can get satisfaction by masturbating. Conversely, a woman may not have reached orgasm during lovemaking and may want to masturbate in order to have a climax while her mate is still in her or afterwards. She may also want to have an orgasm purely for herself. If you have never experimented with masturbation before, this may be a good time to start.

A vibrator is not only acceptable but can enhance your sex life: there is nothing dirty or perverse about a woman using a vibrator. If you haven't discovered this sexual aid until now, swallow your self-consciousness and go buy one. It is especially useful if you want to have an orgasm during the first six postpartum weeks when penetration is prohibited. You can't insert the vibrator in your vagina because it can cause an infection, but you'll probably find that using it externally can be very satisfying. You may find that you want to keep it in your sexual repertoire!

In our society with its Puritan ethic we've been made to feel guilty about masturbation. There is an unspoken belief that masturbation "shouldn't exist" in a good marriage or between partners who have a good sex life. But just the opposite is true. Masturbation can get you through transitions in your relationship when there's less sex than you'd like; it can also enhance your sexual experience together.

Solo sexuality is good for you and for your relationship. It puts you in touch with your own body and lets you discover what turns you on. An orgasm is a wonderful release, a pleasure you're entitled to, not something to be embarrassed about. One person cannot meet all your needs—sexual or otherwise. Learning how to meet your own needs, understanding the ways in which you can be good to yourself, is part of your personal growth.

*Take a weekend away together as soon as you can.* Try to get away, even if it's only overnight, after the baby is born and as often as you can afford. Even if you only go away overnight it will work wonders for your sex life not to have the baby around as a "chaperone" or "monitor." The point isn't to pick a location where you'll have a lot of activities. In fact, try to pick somewhere with no cultural offerings and lousy shopping: the best thing you can do for yourselves is to spend a whole day lounging around in bed together, maybe getting up every so often for a meal!

*Take a motel or hotel room for an afternoon.* Leave the baby with someone you trust (it's essential that you not be worried about the baby during this romantic tryst) and meet each other like clandestine lovers. Put some fun and humor into your lives, don't take everything so seriously. If this suggestion doesn't appeal to you, use your imagination. Do anything that encourages love, desire, fun, excitement, or adventure—the very things that can easily get lost when you make the transition to parenthood.

*Perceive yourselves as lovers.* Think of yourselves as lovers and make a conscious effort to treat yourselves specially. Every so often have a fancy dinner: put out candles and good dishes and a bottle of wine. Or, if your budget permits, dress up and go out to a nice dinner.

*Nonsexual affection is an important part of a relationship.* If it feels comfortable to you, make a point of hugging, kissing, and touching your mate without any specific connection to sex. Don't relinquish the physically affectionate aspect of your lives just because you've become parents. Affection which isn't directed toward sex (which has no intent other than to express love) can be a turn-on and can build closeness between you.

***Get a baby-sitter at least one evening a week.*** By doing this you can have a private time as a couple to discuss your feelings and the things that have been happening. You shouldn't view this evening as a regimented time for sex and romance (talk about a lack of spontaneity!) but rather as a way to keep in touch. This feeling of closeness is part of your sexual life together; it feeds the intimacy which encourages love and sex.

***Nonbaby conversation is an essential part of a good sexual relationship.*** This may seem petty to you, but it is essential: you both have to make an effort at nonbaby conversation right from the start. Good, interesting adult conversation fosters intimacy and closeness, which leads to good loving and sex.

You have to discipline yourselves to make time, even if it's only 15 minutes a day, to talk to each other. Remember: the forbidden subjects are the baby and household problems. No great passions were ever born out of heartfelt discussions about broken washing machines or how many diapers were used in a day. A baby is a fascinating subject, but in moderation. If you don't train yourselves to discuss other aspects of your lives, then the baby can become the only element uniting you. It's not enough to stimulate you intellectually and it's not the way to keep romance alive and well between you.

# 9

# The new importance of time

## ESTABLISH PRIORITIES

*Establishing priorities is a way to protect time.* You may have to eliminate certain activities, at least for a while. Some women with small babies give up cooking entirely; others minimize cleaning the house so that they only do what will keep the Health Department from investigating.

You have to decide as a couple what uses of time are important to you. How much time do you want to spend together, and in what activities? Do you want time alone as a couple, or to pursue separate friendships, sports, or hobbies? If you spend time with others, who will they be now that time is at a premium? What about childless friends— how will your parenthood affect those relationships? Which of those friendships do you want to sustain?

*Realize the value of your marriage.* Little by little, as the baby settles in, you can make time for your relationship. Both of you (and eventually the baby) have to recognize the importance of your marriage. Both of you are separate individuals from your child: he has to learn that from the beginning so that all of you can lead fulfilled lives.

***Parents are important, too.***  You need nurturing at the end of the day. You have a responsibility to your child *plus* an obligation to yourself and your spouse. You have to look after yourself with the same degree of tender loving care that you give your child. Recognizing this is the key to your personal well-being and that of your marriage. Taking care of your own needs, too, doesn't make you any less good as parents.

***Beware of your maternal instinct!***  If you don't keep a check on your desire to be the Greatest Mom, you'll expect yourself to do too much. Part of being a good mother is knowing when to rest, have a glass of wine, or go out for dinner with your husband. If you always put yourself second after meeting your child's needs, you won't be getting enough feedback to keep you vital and in touch with your adult self.

***Think about limits.***  There are times when you should take care of yourself or your spouse and ignore the baby. Don't just run on automatic pilot, programmed to making the baby your only concern. You have to know when to hold and rock him, and when to let the child cry it out. The concept of setting limits is one that you'll use later as a parent. For now, practice setting limits on yourself.

Each set of parents has to draw the line about what is appropriate adult vs. baby time—the issues will be different for every couple. For example, there are couples who eat dinner with the baby propped in an infant seat in the middle of the table. Some people say it's enjoyable for them because it keeps the baby quiet and allows them a relaxed dinner (of course this depends on the baby's temperament and mood). Other couples are horrified at the prospect of never having a normal meal again. There is no right or wrong, but you should certainly give thought to some of the choices you may be making which may not consider your needs as a couple.

Try to keep yourself from making your child the center of your universe. Once your child perceives that she is more important to you than you are, she'll eventually exert the right to control you. If you subordinate yourself to your child, you are creating a monster. Your total commitment to her whims will encourage her to develop into a controlling tyrant.

You cannot wait until the baby is a "certain age" before you give importance to your spouse's needs and your own. Learn to interweave the needs of all members of your family. Once you subjugate yourselves to a baby, you are teaching her that her every appetite and whim will be fed **immediately**. If someone prostrated herself like that in front of you, you would turn into a demanding little monster, too!

*"I'll make my child happy."* If you are even considering this as a life goal, as the reason for your existence, think again. You have to live your life alongside your child, not *for* your child. Otherwise you'll wind up a bitter, unhappy nobody, with no identity, no sense of herself. This is a futile life goal. You will have sacrificed your life for nothing. And consider this: if you are unhappy, your child is bound to be, too, so you will have failed doubly.

*Child-care books emphasize the baby's needs.* Many of these books actually do you and your child a disservice. The underlying message in such books—after they direct you to supply stimulating toys and games and prepare homemade food—can be that all *your* needs are secondary. Child-care books often suggest that by manipulating/controlling your child's environment, you can determine how your baby will turn out. These techniques can encourage you to teach your child that he is the center of the universe.

*Child-care books bully you into instantly gratifying the child.* Many of these books inform you that picking up a child when he cries is the way he learns to communicate and to develop trust. This point is so heavily emphasized that many vulnerable new parents are terrified of ruining their child's development if they don't respond to his every whimper immediately.

In real life, none of us gets our needs met instantly by pressing a magic button. Even if you were willing to give all your time to being on round-the-clock Baby Alert, you'd be telling your child a lie. Instant gratification of his needs isn't going to teach your baby anything about how the world really operates. Let him discover patience, and even disappointment, which will be much more useful to him.

***You don't have to love your kid every minute.*** There's no rule you even have to like her all the time! You and your baby both have to understand from the beginning that mothers have rights, too. It's unrealistic to the point of being cruel to let a baby think that the world revolves around her. There isn't always going to be someone there, just waiting to satisfy her needs. A good experience for learning to cope with life is the realization that everyone isn't totally trustworthy 100 percent of the time.

There's no denying that love and interaction between you and your child are what help develop an integrated personality and emotional wholeness. But there has to be equilibrium in how much you give your child. There should be a balance: your child should feel safe and secure without constant interaction or immediate gratification.

***You have choices.*** You may have to remind yourself of this dozens of times a day, but it's essential that you realize that *you* are running your life. You don't have to drop everything the minute the baby cries. If you've got bread in the oven, the phone is ringing, you're going to the bathroom or about to eat a sandwich, it is not necessary to run instantly to the child. It's not even a good idea.

Respect yourself, not just your child. Your baby's needs don't cancel out yours, or diminish them. In order to have the energy and patience it takes to be a mother, you need strength, calm, food, and so on. You are also half a couple that has needs which you have to fulfill if you're going to stay well married.

***Meet your own needs.*** Find a balance between yourself and the child. Separate your personal needs from your child's needs. Think about what your priorities are: what responsibilities do you have to your child and yourself? How can you find ways to satisfy both?

Do nice things for yourself and your partner. Go out for a drink or a drive. Stop nursing when you are ready to, not according to someone else's timetable for your child.

Recognize your need for adult times together away from the baby. You need to be selfish for yourselves and your marital relationship.

This is not a slice of self-serving philosophizing from the "Me generation"—it's common sense that a contented, self-fulfilled woman can take better care of her child and her mate. If you please other people without paying attention to your own needs, you'll be a frustrated, angry person.

**Meeting your own needs can reduce anger.**   All parents have times when they feel angry at their child for overtaking their life. For example, when your husband comes home at the end of the day he wants your attention, he needs your love. If the baby is fussing and you put her needs ahead of her father's, it can create a deep anger in him toward you and the baby.

**It's the two of you vs. the baby.**   That may sound harsh, but sometimes you have to look at it that way to protect your relationship. You are partners, allied against this adorable, lovable intruder.

It's okay to be mad at your baby sometimes. You can share your frustration and annoyance with your mate— you're in this together, you need each other's support. Having these feelings doesn't mean you're going to act on them, but holding them inside can magnify them. Venting feelings can help you through the situation, and probably will allow you to take better care of the baby as a result.

## THE LOSS OF FREE TIME

**Parenthood changes the nature of time.**   Being a parent devours time, especially personal time. Having a baby can be like falling in love: a passionate obsession that dominates everything else in your life.

It may not be possible at the beginning to balance the time among your own interests, your spouse's, and the needs of the baby. Don't expect that you can resolve this predicament. As new parents you may feel as though you've been up 36 hours without a minute to even go to the bathroom. There are still only 24 hours in the day; you just have to do the best you can. If you are realistic you'll be less frustrated and not expect miracles from yourselves.

***There doesn't seem to be "free" time any more.*** Many women feel the loss of being able to spontaneously take time for themselves. In a sense, you actually have lost your freedom. If it comes down to it and you have to make a choice, the baby's needs come before yours.

Motherhood is definitely a sacrifice, but the time you spend is for the baby's good. Having a baby is something you wanted to do. Keep a perspective. A baby doesn't stay an infant forever . . . not even for very long! So you'll eventually get back your time and the freedom to use it as you choose.

***A new mother can feel guilty about her husband.*** You may feel that you don't have enough time for your mate. It's a bad feeling when you have to decide that the baby comes first, which means neglecting your partner. You may have been brought up to believe (your mother's training or society's message) that your husband "should" come first.

This can put you into a double bind, feeling torn between husband and baby. However, the realities of mothering mean that you have less time, period. And unfortunately, a man who needs attention is a lower priority than a screaming baby with no clean clothes to wear. You can only do what you can do: don't have such high expectations of yourself that your spouse begins to think you're **right** to feel guilty!

***Full-time mothering means just that.*** A mother who decides to stay at home full time appears to have a "whole day" to herself, but the day belongs to the baby. There is feeding time (breast-feeding takes longer). There is bathing time. Diapering/changing time. Play time. Fresh air time. And for many women there are still errands to do and cleaning and/or cooking. By the end of the day a mother is so exhausted she hasn't got the energy, must less the time, to read the paper or fix her hair.

**Loss of control over your time can be a shock.** This can be particularly difficult for you if you've usually accomplished most of what you set out to do each day. You may expect this sense of being able to control your time to return once the baby is born. But even six weeks postpartum your life won't be working the way it used to—and that may not be comfortable.

**Don't hide your frustration and disappointment.** It may seem as though your day adds up to nothing for yourself, or doesn't add up to anything "productive." The house and baby take so much time—and all you can see is more of the same facing you tomorrow. It's important to air these feelings.

You may feel like a failure: motherhood isn't turning out the way you expected. You may have fantasized what life would be like, but the reality of parenting is that you never know how much free time you'll have. You pray for the baby to fall asleep, and then somehow you're standing around, waiting for him to wake up!

**You've had 25 to 40 years to do as you please.** Suddenly you can't seem to find 5 minutes for yourself, whether it's to read, make a phone call, take a bath, or go for a walk. Every minute is programmed with infant care or household tasks; if you're a working mother, there doesn't even seem to be enough time to do *those* things, let alone have time for yourself.

**A baby teaches you to use your time better.** This is one of the advantages of having a child, which eats up most of your time. You'll probably find that you don't waste much time any more. With so few hours to themselves, many parents find they are more thoughtful about how they use what little time they have.

Becoming a parent can have a stabilizing effect on you. You may find that you clarify what your goals are in life and use your time wisely to achieve them. You may feel repaid for the sacrifice of raising children because this is balanced by the help it gives you in reorienting your priorities.

***Think of time as money.***    You can manage time the same way you do your finances. Once you're able to see that time is something you have control over, you'll feel less stress about it. Look at time the same way you do money: talk about it, make priorities about it, budget it, allocate it, and even put some aside for a "rainy day," when something unexpected may crop up.

Think of your calendar as a bank statement. Get one of those all-in-one organizers if it will help you to get an overview of your time. Go over your calendar just as you do a bank statement. The essential thing to realize is that no one ever feels they have enough money—or time—for their personal, family, or marital needs.

***Your dependence on each other means no "free" time.***    Life has suddenly become your job plus child care and/or housework. If you don't have an extended family and/or paid help, you have to do it all yourselves. Now that you're parents, all your time is spoken for; it may seem as though you have to negotiate with your spouse for anything you want to do for yourself.

You have to clear it with your mate when you want to indulge basic personal needs like sleep, recreation, going for a run or workout, taking a nap, or being with friends. You've probably both been used to having independence: now you have to rely on your spouse's moods and schedule in order to plan your own time. You have to check in with your spouse for permission to use free time. This can make it seem as though your mate is "monitoring" you, and that you have to ask permission to do things, which can make you resentful.

The irony is that these new boundaries and restrictions can make you feel more like a child, at the very moment that you've become parents. It can make you feel like an adolescent to have to answer to your partner for how you've spent your time and let him/her know where you're going and for how long. You probably don't even want to know your mate's every move because it puts you in the position of being a domineering "parent."

# SUGGESTIONS ON HOW TO MAXIMIZE TIME

*Grab little chunks of time in the early months.* Don't expect to be able to utilize time the way you did in the past. Now it's harder to be flexible and it's almost impossible to predict when you'll have free time. You're "on call" all the time. Keep in mind that at about six months, most babies have settled into some kind of schedule. At that point you can begin to take charge of your own time.

*Some couples incorporate the baby into their rhythm.* Instead of completely rearranging their schedules and habits, some new parents are able to fit the baby into the rhythm of their life. If you want to do this, it can give you the sense that you are still the same people you were before, that becoming parents hasn't wiped out your previous lives or identities.

   If your baby sleeps a lot you may want to consider taking her along to the movies, out to dinner, or to sports or cultural events. However, incorporating a baby into social activities only works for some couples and also depends on the temperament of the individual child.

   The important thing is to recognize that you have needs, too, and a way of life that doesn't have to be tossed out just because you've had a child. You only need to change those parts of your lifestyle that you *have* to change for the baby's sake.

*Organize leisure time as seriously as business plans.* With free time at such a premium, you're going to have to schedule your leisure hours just as carefully as you do chores or other appointments. If you wait until there's a block of free time to do the things you want . . . you won't have much leisure time to enjoy!

*Some people divide their day into pieces.* You might want to try this method to see if it works for you. You set aside a certain chunk of time for household chores; set aside another piece for getting out with the baby (doing errands, or not); another parcel of time is for self-fulfillment (reading, being with adults, whatever feeds your needs). The usual infant care takes place in between this schedule.

***Some people make a list of things to do.*** In descending order, the list might have (1) cook dinner, (2) plant flowers, (3) clean the bathroom, (4) balance the checkbook, etc. Then you can give yourself a certain amount of time, perhaps 2 to 3 hours, in which to do these things.

This method means that you stop whatever you're doing when the time is up, regardless of whether you're finished. As a "reward" it's a nice idea to go out with the baby right afterwards or do something for yourself personally. This type of time planning is particularly good for compulsive women who drive themselves too hard: it puts a limit on how much you try to do in any one day.

***Do chores with the baby strapped on you.*** When your baby is small, there are various things you can manage around the house with the baby in a front or backpack. You can do sewing, laundry, ironing, chores at your desk, or work in the garden. Therefore you won't feel conflicted about using time you "should" be giving to the baby. When you cook or do similar tasks, you can put the baby near you in a basket or baby seat. Finding ways to get two birds with one stone is an important part of being an ingenious mother. When you have a baby, 24 hours just aren't enough in a day.

***Don't let the telephone eat up precious time.*** Try to develop the habit of *not* automatically picking up the phone when it rings. A phone machine is the best investment you can make to protect your time (and your sanity). It allows you to screen calls and only speak to people when it's absolutely necessary.

It also helps you to redefine a common automatic reaction to a ringing phone, which seems to have most of us trained like laboratory rats. You do **not** have to answer it: you have free choice in the matter!

If you wait until you have several calls to return, it allows you to take a 15-minute block of time in which to do so. Try to watch the clock and time yourself; you'll be amazed how much time we all waste gabbing on the phone, and how much time you save by controlling your phone time.

Get extra-long phone cords and a neck rest (although

it may give you a cramp in your neck!) for the phone extensions you use most often. This frees your hands and allows you to do cooking, cleaning, laundry, and baby care while using the telephone. Long cords can give you twice as much "value" for your phone time.

***Get a baby-sitter on a regular basis.*** If you don't have some kind of full-time or part-time help, then you have to make arrangements to have someone come in regularly. It is less important how often you have help (although once a week would seem a minimum); what matters is being able to plan ahead for free time. Also, if you have a relationship with a sitter whom you trust and the baby knows, then you won't be trapped when you need to go out at the last minute. You'll know someone to call.

***Time by yourself is a precious commodity.*** There are two kinds of time alone: inside the house and outside it. For the former, learn how to shut the door and teach others to respect it. That hour or more of privacy, to do with what you please, can be a life-saver. As for going out, you'd be amazed what an hour or two a day in the outside world can do for your outlook. You'll probably worry about the baby and may even miss him—which means you'll be that much happier to come home and be with him again.

***Set aside time every day to get out of the house.*** You should make this a permanent habit, **no matter what else comes up.** It can work magic to take a fussy baby out in a carrier or the car. Fresh air and contact with the outside world also works wonders on the mother!

***Cooking does not have to be so time-consuming.*** If you were a gourmet cook and made elaborate meals before you were a mother, change your style now. Dinners can be simple and quick to prepare—that doesn't mean they can't still be attractive and nutritious. This new approach to cooking is not a negative reflection on you as a homemaker, mother, or wife: your time is limited now and can be better spent on many other things, including a nap for yourself. You can return to gourmet cookery later on . . . say in 10 years!

Another way to save time in the kitchen is to set aside one day a week and cook ahead whenever possible. You can freeze meals and use them during the week, so that all you have to do is prepare fresh vegetables and salads. This requires some advance planning, but it makes shopping easier and uses your time more economically.

If you are not accustomed to using the freezer, start utilizing this wonderful modern invention! You can make meals for weeks to come, everything from hearty soups to pasta, meat, or chicken dishes. They are just as nutritious and delicious when you defrost or microwave them even months later. Cooking in quantity takes no more time than making the same dish for two people but it saves you many hours in the kitchen.

*Your schedule belongs to you.* A funny thing can happen to new parents: you imagine that the baby is in charge and has dictated the rhythm of every day. You may feel things aren't working out because you still can't accomplish what you'd like to and you're exhausted and feel harassed. Step back and get your bearings.

Your time is your own—you have free will to use it as you please. You control the schedule you've planned (or fallen into). If it isn't working and there isn't enough time for the things you want to do, don't get rattled. You are the captain of your ship: if your schedule isn't comfortable, **change it**.

## "QUALITY TIME"

*"Quality time" is a trendy catch phrase.* It is a concept that has grown out of the trend toward mothers continuing to work when their children are still young. Many mothers feel conflicted about not being full-time mothers. Since they only have limited time to spend with their children, the idea of "quality" time can be used to make everyone feel less guilty.

There **is** such a thing as quality time, but it's important to understand what it is, as well as what it is not. This section is intended to clarify the issue of how much (and what kind of) time you spend with your child so that you can be comfortable with your style of parenting.

***What if you can't get "quality" OR "quantity" time?***
It's possible in two-career families that neither parent can be with the baby for even a minimum amount of time, when he's awake in the morning or evening. Sometimes one of you may not see him for several days. This is not abnormal for the traditional image of a father, but it isn't the socially acceptable pattern for a new mother.

Guilt is the first thing you will probably feel, along with a fear that you may be depriving your child for life. **Don't succumb to those feelings**! If you must continue to work, either from emotional or economic need, feeling guilty about parenting isn't going to help you or your child. Accept the reality, do what you can to maximize the possibilities, and then get on with your life.

***Quality time means turning your attention totally to the child.***   For a working mother this usually means a specific time each day to spend with her child. Even with a preverbal infant it means focusing all your energy on the baby, without talking on the phone or doing any chores.

This concept of quality time is important for all babies, even those whose mothers are always around. A baby has physical needs, but he also has an emotional and social need to interact and communicate in a tactile, visual way. The caretaker must be constant and sincere: even the youngest babies can tell the difference! The first relationship that a baby forms is the model for the others in his life. Research has shown a direct relationship between a baby whose need for nurturance is satisfied early in life and his ability to make trusting, open connections with people later on.

***Love grows from spending lots of time together.***   But what you do with the time you have is also vitally important. All relationships are fed by the participants spending long periods of time together. For example, most couples' relationships will atrophy if they are separated too much. However, a child gets a great deal just from growing up in a secure, stimulating home with an atmosphere of loving concern. That environment is more valuable than just mere "time" around his parents.

***Don't use quality time as an excuse.*** A child's needs can't be fitted into the time you may have scheduled for her. A child needs you when she needs you—not just when you're available or it's convenient for you. Do not let the idea of quality time become a rationalization for not being around often enough for your child. A working mother or father can use the phrase to justify spending *too little* time with a kid. Some **quantity** of time is necessary if you're going to have **quality**.

Make a distinction between whether you are actually there and whether you can be reached. If you are **emotionally** available to your child (even if only by telephone as she gets older), this will make her feel secure even if you can't be there physically.

***Quality time cannot be controlled.*** All your interactions with the child are not going to be cozy, fascinating, or cheerful. It isn't as simple as just deciding to have quality time. A working parent imagines the end-of-the-day encounter with the child and fantasizes a fun, fulfilling, peaceful encounter. When the parent (or parents) comes home at the end of the day, there's going to be tension. Children often save up their emotions for their parents, and it can be an explosion!

All your interactions with your child are not going to be a ''10,'' no matter what plans you make. ''Quality time'' doesn't mean time free of conflict. The baby may be cranky, demanding, fussy, sleepy, or have a tantrum. You may feel exhausted, crabby, and impatient. But that's normal, it's real life. As part of his growth, a child also needs to experience time with his parents that isn't high quality: boredom, irritation, frustration, etc., are natural.

***All the baby's waking hours don't have to be devoted to him.*** The daytime hours when the baby is awake do not exist solely for interacting and playing creatively with him. It doesn't make you a better parent to structure your day around quality time for your child.

Make time for your personal and household chores and the child will learn to accept it. He may as well learn right from the start that you are an adult with many responsibilities and interests aside from him (*you* should keep that in mind from the start, too). Children who get love and attention, who receive quality time from their parents, learn that there are other things that demand the parents' attention.

***Parallel time can be quality time.*** A child can learn to play by herself while you're at your desk or on the phone. You have to teach a child not to interrupt you: most children will insist that you play with them or fix a boo-boo when you're on the phone. A child will test you—you have to set the limits. But being with your child while you do parallel tasks (she draws while you pay the bills) can also be quality time spent together.

## TIME ALONE AS A COUPLE

***You're really going to miss each other after the baby arrives!*** The biggest alteration you'll have in your life once you become parents is how little time you have for each other as a couple. For example, you won't really have weekends any more, in the sense of sleeping late and having unstructured time to do whatever you want. Because of your responsibility to the baby, weekends lose their specialness as a time for the two of you.

***The time for romance seems to have passed.*** It may seem that being carefree, unguarded, and spontaneous is no longer possible—and without those feelings you may also lose a sense of romance, sexiness, and excitement. In order to be alone together you may have to leave the house, which involves planning and expense. It is well worth it.

***A new father may feel like a third wheel.*** A man may feel he's sandwiched in between laundry and feedings. In the whirlwind of house and baby chores, romance can get lost. Even a man who is involved in baby care can feel he's not getting nurtured himself.

If you are working parents, you may have overscheduled yourselves into a corner so that you have to organize your parenting time in shifts. It can almost be like sharing custody of your baby, with separate but equal time with the child . . . and none for each other. If you have a colicky baby, the same problem can arise because you take turns eating, sleeping, and dealing with the crying.

If a new father isn't participating much in infant care, he can feel left out and unappreciated for the contributions he makes to the household. Even if a new father really wants a lot of involvement with his baby, it doesn't mean he doesn't also need time with his wife.

*A woman may not know how to ask for time as a couple.* Many of us have never been taught to talk about our feelings and needs, especially ones that are new or surprising to us. A new mother can feel just as unhappy and unloved as her partner from insufficient time together.

You may feel abandoned, unimportant, lonely, or sad about what you have lost together as a couple. This lack of connection can make you feel angry or hurt. Anger is often the knee-jerk reaction. You may withdraw to brood and sulk, but that's only going to increase the feeling of being out of sync with your mate. There are things you can both do to help yourselves.

*A good relationship doesn't just happen.* In order to have a meaningful relationship, it's necessary that you spend time together regularly. A relationship matures, and love grows, from spending hours together. You need to have one-on-one time as a couple to stay connected: to talk, have fun, develop intimacy, make love.

*If you want time together, it's up to you.* You're the one who makes it happen. You have to make plans, you have to work to preserve the quality of your time as a couple. You can meet for lunch, call each other during the day about petty or important things (as a way to touch base), or set aside special times of the day to jog together, watch TV, and so on. (See *Suggestions for "Making" Time* later in the chapter for more ideas.) You have to make and honor "dates" with your partner as respectfully as you would a doctor appointment or business meeting. You cannot leave it to chance or depend on your spouse to create this time.

*You have to protect that time together.*  Unless you make a point of doing this, weeks will slip by in which you barely communicate with each other. Spending time alone means you're protecting your identity and your future. It takes hard work to be parents who also remain individuals and maintain their identity as a couple. You'll be doing the best thing possible for your child at the same time. If you are fulfilled and nourished yourselves, you have more to give to a child.

*Set special time aside for your relationship.*  Regular, frequent time when you both have energy and can interact is essential to the health of your marriage. During that time, you two have to be the number one priority: your time together has to come before everything else. Both of you have to agree to this so that you can maintain or restore a real connection between you.

Get someone to sit with the baby, or better yet, send her out with the sitter (or to your neighbors or relatives). Shut off everything else—your work, financial issues, and especially the baby. You have to discipline yourselves to take yourselves and your marriage as seriously as you do your baby's crying. NOTE: Turning on the TV can be counterproductive during this special time, since one partner often wants to watch in silence.

*Time to talk is vital.*  If many days go by and you don't find the time to sit down together and talk, however briefly, resentment is going to build up. You'll begin to be crabby, to needle each other without really knowing why. You recognize that what's irritating you is the lack of communication: you may be taking your frustrations out on each other.

*Express your disappointment about the baby coming between you.*  Be sure to talk about the resentment and frustration you may feel when the baby interrupts you, either in general or specifically. Infants have been known to cry during your lovemaking or to wake up right as you sit down to dinner. (We all assume this is unintentional on an infant's part, although some parents would swear otherwise!)

If you hold onto your disappointment and annoyance it can get in your way as a couple. Getting rid of these feelings by admitting them will free your energy so you can stay close in touch with each other.

## TIME TOGETHER WITHOUT THE BABY

***Your baby can survive without you for a while.*** Whether you truly believe that depends on how attached and compulsive you are about your child. More importantly, do you believe that a marriage can survive if you don't have time alone together without the baby? Of course what we're talking about here is more than mere survival: time away from your child allows you to flourish in a special way.

***Taking a baby along limits you.*** Your life as couple is limited by having that little person between you all the time. The dynamic changes when it's just the two of you: giving your full attention to your spouse is quite different when it's really just the two of you without the baby around.

Being alone together gives you a chance to enjoy the pleasure of each other's company while reaffirming all the possibilities you have open to you. Walking hand in hand, listening to music, sharing a banana split, kissing, laughing, are some of the spontaneous experiences that just aren't the same when one of you is pushing the stroller while the other searches for the pacifier.

***Don't insist on leaving the baby.*** Don't push or force your mate to leave the baby before s/he's ready, but try to talk about it. Maybe you can agree on a time frame so the reluctant parent can prepare him/herself for the separation. But don't let too many months pass without taking some time for yourselves alone.

***Take short breaks in the beginning.*** When you first make plans to be without the baby, frequent small separations are better than an all-day outing. A new mother will think about the baby a lot while they're separated, but if it's only a short outing she'll be able to concentrate on her husband and on having a good time. Later on you can work your way up to a long dinner or taking a trip to get away.

Try a day's outing at first, then go away for a weekend or longer if you feel comfortable.

**Going out to dinner is very important.**   With all the intense demands of infant care you've probably forgotten how good it feels to dress up and go out together. It's important to indulge yourselves a little and stay in touch with those aspects of your relationship that nourish romance. Just the two hours of going out to dinner can really make a difference.

Some couples find that getting paid help is better for these evenings than asking a grandparent, friend, or neighbor to watch the baby. If you come home from a special evening, it's nice to continue the feeling of being focused on each other, at least until the baby wakes up. If someone you're close to is there, you have to shift your attention to that third person.

**Going out to dinner can be a disaster!**   Although it may look good on paper, you may go to the trouble and expense of going to a restaurant to get away from the baby—only to spend the whole time talking about the child! You may be eager to escape from the baby but your partner may not: the father who's been out of touch may want a "briefing" on the baby's progress; the mother may be focused so compulsively on the baby that she can't talk about anything else.

In order to avoid disappointing each other on these special evenings out, tell each other ahead of time whether baby talk is off limits. Since your child is the central issue in your life right now, you'll probably wind up talking about him anyway. It's important that you at least respect your partner's wishes so you can both try to focus on other things in your lives.

**Each outing has to be "perfect."**   It's hard not to expect your time alone to be extra-special, even though it's like stepping in quicksand to think this way. Before you had a baby it didn't matter that much if you went to a bad movie or a lousy restaurant. It wasn't even such a big deal if one of you was in a less-than-great mood. But now there's so little time and every evening is a big investment so it "has" to be great.

Without realizing it, you want every outing to be wonderful; this means you may wind up judging circumstances more severely. You may find you're angry at yourself or your partner if you don't have a good time. It's absurd to expect that all your time together will be a special treat you both **must** enjoy. Time is limited and you want to make it count—but remember that you can't control the outcome, only the intention.

***Staying home alone together can by very satisfying.*** Develop or continue mutual interests. If you gardened or cooked together before the baby, do it again now—or give it a try. Watch sports, share ideas about magazine articles or books, play cards while the baby sleeps. Try eating late breakfasts or dinners to get that time to yourselves while the baby is down. Maybe once a week you can turn off the phone, put on some music, and have some supper with wine.

***Have fun—without forcing it.*** Just because you've become parents doesn't mean you can't be silly or playful or "waste" time! It's so important to keep joy and spontaneity in your new life together as a couple.

## TRIPS AWAY FROM HOME

***WHAT trips?*** If that is your first reaction to the mention of taking a trip away from your child, then you need to read this section very carefully.

Every couple needs time away from home—and the baby—to re-establish their bond as husband and wife. It's irrelevant whether you **feel** the need or whether you **want** to go: take it on faith, it's good for you! As a new parent you are going to feel ambivalent about many things in your new life situation—but just because you feel conflicted about something doesn't mean that you shouldn't do it. You can't always trust your instincts during a stressful transition because you may be reacting out of fear or confusion.

***A trip can't turn back the clock.*** Don't expect a trip to give you back the life you had together before you became parents. Being alone together again can be thrilling, but it's not a good idea to indulge a fantasy that things between you can be as they once were. Don't raise false hopes because you may have a rude awakening the minute you walk back through your own door.

***You'll never take a trip if you don't start now.*** If you don't get into a frame of mind aimed at getting away every so often, then you'll always be able to find excuses not to leave. If you don't go away overnight (or for a few days) in the first year of the baby's life, then you'll probably never do it. Once you recognize the importance of these getaways, you have to incorporate trips into your lifestyle so you—and the baby—get used to it.

***Get the baby used to many different experiences.*** Take the baby out as much as possible, let her see new places and be held by new people. This will encourage her not to be shy or fearful. It will help her adapt more easily to new situations, which will make you feel more comfortable about having an independent life as a couple away from home.

***A suggestion for home care while you're away.*** If you have full-time household help, keep them on and invite a grandparent or other close relative or friend to also stay in the house. If you don't have help already, then hire outside help to do the housekeeping. This way you won't be imposing on your relative by asking her to do chores she may not be able to or may resent. Having a relative there can reassure you and give your child a sense of security, at the same time that he's building a relationship with the relative.

***You can prepare yourselves for longer trips.*** Once you're ready to go away for a weekend or longer, you can get yourselves and the baby accustomed to it by first going away overnight. You can have a grandparent or a sitter stay overnight, if you don't have full-time help.

***Stay overnight at a friend's house.*** If you have nearby friends or neighbors who are going away for a day or two, you can make a trial run for a trip by staying at their house. This is like using training wheels on a bicycle because you or the sitter have access to each other if you get cold feet. It also saves you the expense of actually travelling.

***Be careful of your attitude when you return from a trip.*** Be aware of the signals you give the baby after any time away, even if it's only for an afternoon. If you let the child know how badly you feel about your absence, you are cueing her to react also. Setting up this pattern means that you're undermining your ability to come and go with ease.

It's important to come home without showing the baby your own guilt and ambivalence about having been away. Even a tiny infant can pick up cues and vibrations from your body language and the sound of your voice. If you make a big emotional fuss about having been away, you are teaching your child to do the same.

***Feeling guilty about going away is common.*** Did you worry about the baby on the trip and feel guilty about going? If you return and find that your child was sad when you were away, or got sick or had other problems, it can give you an instant case of "the guilts." That's a natural reaction; the feeling should pass once you're all reunited and you realize that your baby hasn't been scarred for life by your absence.

The more often you go away, the sooner you'll realize how good the absences are for your family. By going away you aren't just nourishing your relationship, you're also giving your child a different kind of gift. Coping without you is a growth experience for your child. Each new life situation that he handles teaches him about the world around him and his own inner resources.

However, there are parents who feel so guilty about having gone away that they say it just wasn't worth it and vow never to do it again. If this happens to you or your mate, you'd better sit yourselves down and do some soul-searching. Do you **want** your child to miss you terribly? Does it make you feel like a better parent, or as though you're more loved, if you think your child can't manage without your constant presence?

Once a child learns to talk, he can whine and complain and make you feel **really** awful about taking trips. It can create real guilt and anguish for you. But look at it another way: your absence is a chance for him to manage without you, a life lesson that will serve him well.

***Leaving a child makes parents anxious.*** Even the most pragmatic and relaxed parents feel worried about going away without their child. As all of you get used to separations, the anxiety will lessen for everyone.

Leaving your child with a new person, or in a new place, or for a longer time than he is accustomed to can increase your anxiety. Try to keep as many familiar elements in the child's life as you can, and build up to longer trips as you all feel comfortable.

***Reunions may be disappointing.*** Your return home may not be what you expect or hope. Your child may not be as sweet and adorable as you've been imagining. She may be cranky or angry about the separation and will let you know it. You may be exhausted from travelling and don't have the patience to deal with her fussing. Don't worry about it: tomorrow's another day.

***You may feel lost without your child.*** Some mothers go away and feel lost without their identity as a parent. Instead of looking forward to the trip and being able to enjoy it, a woman can feel lost if the only sense she has of herself is as a mother. She may spend the whole time worrying obsessively about the baby.

If you feel this way and return home to find that your child was upset by your absence, this will only confirm and justify your worries. A trip away is a learning experience for your child. And for you.

***The age of your child affects the situation.*** An infant is the easiest to leave for short periods (if you're not breast-feeding). The baby may not even miss you. But one- to two-year-olds can be very hard on you because their emotions can be so raw and passionate. A two- or three-year-old with enough vocabulary can break your heart! This is another reason for taking trips right from the beginning so it becomes a natural part of life for all of you.

It is important that the mother/parents not be away from the child for extended periods of time. Although there are no absolute rules about trips, it is believed that you should not leave for more than two weeks, if you can, until the child is three to five years old. This does not mean that the world will come to an end if you have to go away for more than two weeks, but try to limit your absences. There is a theory about the stages of separation and individuation in a child's development which concludes that it's probably not a good idea for you to take extended trips, that is, for a month or more at a time. In general, in the earliest years it would be better to take shorter trips; as your child grows older, this is a less important issue.

## THE BENEFITS OF TRIPS

*One week a year away together isn't enough.*    Many experts feel that it's necessary for parents to have more than a yearly week-long trip. You need more time than that alone and away from home.

*Short business trips can be a good solution.*    You get some time together and the tag-along partner gets some quiet time alone while the business traveller attends to business. It also makes economic sense because the room is paid for, as well as at least half the travel expense and meals.

*A couple is reunited.*    After months of being a threesome, you get back together as a twosome and can get a feeling of where you are as a couple.

*You don't have to be super lovers.*    When you are able to arrange a weekend away, don't put pressure on yourselves to make it ideally romantic or sexy. You're both tired and you're going through a stressful time. It's okay just to hold each other and even not to make love. What matters just as much as sex is feeling close. A trip is a good way to feel united again—if only by the fact that you both miss the baby!

*You'll get insights about what you're thinking.*    The time alone together without distractions may give you the tranquility to be aware of what you've been thinking without realizing it. Time away can reveal how you're each feeling about parenthood and each other.

***You'll get in the habit of having private time.*** It will be easier for you and the baby if you get used to the idea of your absences right from the start. The child will accept it as natural and feels secure that you'll return. As babies get older they may rebel against your departures or even against your privacy as a couple; trips can teach your child that he doesn't have a monopoly on you and your time.

***Trips establish your child's independence.*** You'll see that your child can function very well without you. Your absence shows you that a familiar nanny, relative, or sitter can meet the baby's physical needs as well as give love and stimulation. Your ego may not like it, but it should give you some peace of mind to know your child's strengths.

## BUSINESS TRIPS FOR MOTHERS

***Should a new mother go away on business?*** Is a few days—or even two weeks—bad for you and your baby? Keep in mind the importance of limiting any trips you might make until about the time your child goes to school. It depends on how much guilt you already have as a working mother. It also depends on how much support you have from your husband and whether you have a nanny or other support system that can function in your absence.

***What effect does a business trip have on your career?*** Are you fearful of competition within your company? How ambitious are you about being promoted? Will taking trips away from your family advance your standing in the company?

***Can you take something entirely for yourself?*** Are you able to separate yourself enough from your baby (and perhaps husband) to really want to take a business trip for your own personal needs and benefit? If you can overcome the natural guilt many mothers feel, you may feel free to do something selfish, in the best sense of the word.

***What is your motivation for a trip?*** Are you trying to prove something to yourself, your spouse, or your boss? Or are you interested in the potential enrichment of such a trip? There are any number of good reasons for a new mother to take a business trip, if she feels comfortable about it. You can go away to enjoy your professional (nonmother) identity—to maintain balance and perspective between your two lives—to make new business relationships and increase your knowledge—and to collaborate with your peers and colleagues, to name a few.

***A business trip is an acid test.*** Having to decide whether you should leave your husband with the baby can be the ultimate test of whether you can balance the concerns of motherhood and the ambitions you have as a career woman. Is self-sacrifice necessary to be a good mother? Is a business trip going to enrich you sufficiently to compensate for the personal pressure it puts on you?

***The decision is yours, and yours alone.*** When push comes to shove, you're the only one who can honestly decide about taking a business trip. Your spouse and boss and friends and relatives all have their own reasons for whatever they might advise. There should be no doubt in anyone's mind that your needs are as important as those of your child (that is practically the theme of this book, after all). But only you can weigh how much any particular trip will mean to you in your personal and professional development.

## SUGGESTIONS FOR "MAKING" TIME

Every family has its own particular lifestyle and needs, but there are some specific ideas about how to manage time that may be useful to you. Everyone experiences the feeling that there just aren't enough hours in the day, or not enough quality time. What follows are some suggestions about ways to make the most of the time you have, and especially to make time for yourselves as individuals and as a couple.

***Once-a-week lunch with your spouse.***

**Turn down invitations.**   This is such an obvious way to protect your precious time, but many of us have trouble learning how to say, "No, thank you." Being very selective about the socializing you choose to do is a way to guard your time as a couple and preserve its value.

**Start a habit of early bedtime for children.**   If you train yourselves and your baby right from the start, you can preserve at least a portion of every evening as adult time. And don't fool yourselves that some children just naturally go to bed early—children don't arrive with Inborn Early Bedtime! Parents are the ones who socialize their children that way for their own convenience.

**Make mealtimes special.**   Before you had a baby, meals probably used to be a time when you and your partner would touch base at the end of the day. If you've got the baby when you're at the table it means that you've got to eat with one hand, often tending a crying baby and trying to chew at the same time. That doesn't leave much room for conversation with your partner.

Try to have an evening snack like cheese and crackers until the baby is down for the night. This may mean eating some late dinners, but at least you'll have each other to yourselves.

Along these lines, consider not inviting friends for dinner in the early months. Even if you have an angelic baby who never disturbs meals, and even if you have household help, you may want to save mealtimes as a special time for the two of you to connect with each other.

**Have Sunday dinner with friends who have children.**   Only friends with children will want to meet at 5 o'clock for dinner, but this is a great way to keep up friendships with your peers. And compare survival notes!

**Once-a-week private time for each parent.**   This doesn't have to be a predetermined hour, but the concept will do both of you good. Everybody needs a chunk of time when they can close the door and won't be disturbed unless the house is burning down. Use that time to take a long bath, do your nails, catch up on magazines, or make phone calls in peace.

***Arrange for deliveries and shop by mail.*** You can save a lot of time by having a regular dairy delivery and also using stores that offer free delivery (hardware, butcher, pharmacy). You can also shop through department store catalogues and arrange for various services over the phone by using the Yellow Pages. Mail-order catalogues can save time (and introduce you to strange and amazing products that you'll never see anywhere else).

***Make a "present closet."*** You can buy birthday, anniversary, and Christmas presents ahead of time for the people to whom you regularly give gifts. Make a list of those people and, if you can afford it, go on one shopping spree and get it done.

Unless the recipients are close friends, you can even get duplicate presents when you find a gift you really like. If you get them gift-wrapped when you buy, it can save you hours of time later. Be sure to attach a label with the intended recipient's name and a short description of the gift: three months from now you'll never remember what you bought!

You can do the same thing with wedding and baby presents when you know about the events ahead of time. Again, once you find a baby gift you really like, it's perfectly fine to get it for several different people. You can also set aside a space in the present closet for miscellaneous gifts. These can be good for unexpected occasions (a house-warming present when you're invited to a new house the first time) or when you forgot your niece's communion was coming up.

## IDEAS FOR COUPLES WITHOUT FULL-TIME BABY CARE

***Once-a-week sitter at night.*** This gives you one night a week to look forward to as a couple, whether you go out or stay home.

***Once-a-week sitter during the day.***   Think of this as a day (or half a day twice a week, if you prefer) when you are off-duty for the baby. This gives you the freedom to do pleasurable or practical tasks like shopping, running errands, tidying the house or your desk, etc.

***Once-a-week one parent is off-duty.***   (You can alternate weeks if having two nights a week apart seems like too much.) This means the on-duty parent stays home and the other goes out to play. This is a good time to see your male or female friends alone so that you can preserve those individual relationships that can get lost when people become parents.

***Share baby care with another mother.***   Make plans to regularly "baby-pool" one afternoon a week. If you know someone with a baby around your child's age, this is a good plan because you have a caretaker you can trust and it doesn't cost anything.

***Share shopping with a friend or neighbor.***   Take turns going to the market, which doesn't take that much longer for the mother who goes and saves hours for the one who doesn't.

***Take the baby to the grandparents every Sunday.***
Of course, you need willing and nearby in-laws for this plan. But if you are lucky enough to have a parent or other relative who will welcome the baby for a Sunday morning or afternoon, it gives you half a day for yourselves. You have time to go home and read the paper or watch a ballgame or make love or take a bath or do *nothing* for a change!

# 10
# Bad feelings

In this chapter I've tried to gather all the possible negative emotional reactions that new parents might have about parenting and their baby. This will prepare you for the possibility of having bad feelings (jealousy, resentment, etc.) that may surprise you, along with the reassurance that these feelings are normal.

As parents, you're going to have a full range of emotions. Love, hate, annoyance, fear, joy, sadness, despair, excitement, and frustration are just a few of the feelings you are certain to experience. You may have been looking forward to your positive reactions to parenthood, but you may be shocked by the bad feelings.

## SOME REASONS FOR BAD FEELINGS

*Nobody knows what they're getting into.* No one is prepared for what a baby and parenthood demand of them. Being a parent will not be what you expect—no matter who you are—and that is a shock. Being the parent of an infant requires a significant adjustment in how you live your life. It is also an enormous physical, emotional (and for the woman, hormonal) adjustment.

*The ease of your adjustment depends on many factors:* whether both of you wanted the baby . . . the physical and mental health of both partners . . . your ages . . . your financial circumstances . . . your supportiveness

268

toward each other . . . the reaction of your friends and extended family. Having second thoughts is normal even for couples who want a baby and plan for it. The adjustment is that much more stressful for people who have unresolved feelings or mitigating circumstances.

You can love your baby, be grateful you have it, and even feel tremendous identification with it—and still feel that life is impossible, at least temporarily. But that's normal. Has a new mother or father *honestly* ever said, "How great!" about the first three months?

**Our culture idealizes babies and parenthood.** Your preconceived mental images of "how it's going to be" can make it impossible for you to deal with the realities that confront you. The idealized images that many of us carry around about babies and parenting can be so powerful that you may even feel paralyzed by any negative feelings you may have. In order to feel successful in your transition to parenthood, you'll be better off giving up any false expectations about how easy and fun a baby will be.

Before you can genuinely experience the positive aspects of parenting, you have to feel free to express bad feelings that you probably didn't expect. You may feel a sense of loss for the lifestyle you had before the baby; you'll probably feel moments of anger, sadness, doubt, and disappointment about some aspects of parenting.

Since our society offers very little postpartum support or helpful services, both parents can wind up feeling vulnerable and alone. These unexpected negative emotions can be confusing and frightening, especially when you feel there's nowhere to turn for help. You have to care for a totally dependent infant just when you may be wishing someone would take care of you!

**Be a parent in the way most comfortable for you.** Be true to yourself. Every man and woman has different needs and has to guard against trying to conform to fantasized ideas of "mother" and "father." Studies have shown that the most important element in the growth of a child (and his mother's personal growth) is whether a woman approaches motherhood in the way that feels best for her. If you follow your heart (by staying home, going to work, or combining the two) you are going to be a happier, more effective mother. A mother's frustration at being forced or coerced into being a parent in a way that doesn't suit her can lead to emotional problems not only for the woman herself but also for her child and her marriage.

Obviously the same holds true for a man: you have to determine what kind of relationship you want with your child. A man who is denied a close fathering role—or is shoved into it—can become resentful and resistant to the point where he can't be the father he'd like to be.

## AMBIVALENCE, SECOND THOUGHTS

***Seesawing feelings are a normal part of becoming parents.*** It isn't unusual to adore your baby one minute and then a moment later find yourself daydreaming about "the good old days" of your pre-baby existence, wishing the baby would evaporate. You may feel embarrassed or guilty for having these emotions, but they are normal.

***Admitting ambivalence is the best way to come to terms with it.*** Don't lie to yourself or your mate and try to deny that you have doubts, that you feel "hot" and "cold" about your baby. It's okay to hate your child for crying and keeping you up all night and then to feel weak in the knees with love for the baby the next morning. There's nothing wrong with you: welcome to parenthood!

Having doubts about being a parent, doubting your mate's ability as a parent, or questioning whether you love your baby doesn't mean you love the child (or your partner) any less. You may feel inner conflict because although you've chosen to be a mother and are comfortable staying at home, you may not like feeling cut off from the outside world.

***A woman can feel torn between her husband and the child.*** You may feel you've being pulled in two directions by the emotional and physical demands on you. If you're like most women, you are the main caretaker for the baby. However, you're still expected—by your mate, yourself, and society—to also be a full-time partner to your husband. Feeling that there just isn't enough of you to go around is a common complaint of new mothers.

***Recognize and accept your negative feelings.*** They are part of "real" life. The emotions will seem less overwhelming if you don't try to ignore or deny them. But you and your partner have to guard against taking out your frustrations and fears on each other. The best safety valve you each have at this time is to turn to a trusted friend who will listen to your feelings without making a judgment about you as a person or a parent.

***Going out and leaving the baby can be a problem.*** It can stir up a lot of ambivalent, contradictory feelings. You may find that you can't wait to get out of the house together without the baby. But you may discover that it is a bittersweet experience. No sooner are you away from the house then you miss the baby or worry about her.

Here's a possible scenario: You arrange for a babysitter and rush out together to the movies, delighted by your freedom. But once you're away from the baby you find yourself thinking about her, wondering how she is, if everything is all right. In truth, there is no such thing as totally carefree "freedom" for you any more. This may be your first realization that from now on the baby and her well-being are your responsibility.

You may feel anxious to get home to see the child: if the sitter tells you how good she was, or how cute she is, you and your partner may wonder how you could have wanted to leave your little angel even for a minute! These are new, powerful feelings that will probably bring you closer to each other—and make your negative feelings about parenthood seem even more peculiar.

## ANGER, RESENTMENT

***Resentment, frustration, annoyance, and impatience are par for the course in the adjustment to parenthood.*** You're going to feel angry at each other and you're going to feel angry at the baby. The best way to handle anger is to acknowledge it and express it. Problems arise when you deny that these feelings exist. Holding it in and pretending that everything is hunky-dory can be destructive: negative emotions have a way of seeping out eventually. When you allow uncomfortable feelings to accumulate without expressing them, you'll find that they surface when you least expect them. Often the feelings are magnified from being held in.

Many new parents have looked back to the transition to parenthood and felt they would have been better prepared if someone had alerted them to how angry they would feel. Don't be victimized by the idealized notion that a "good" parent is someone who is only loving—never angry or resentful of demands that the baby makes, or the drastic change in their lifestyle. You will actually be a better parent if you can express your anger and come to terms with the negative emotions. By acknowledging your anger you'll be able to enjoy your child more and give more of yourself to him without resentment.

***Anger is a hard feeling to share.*** Most of us were taught from the time we were children that showing anger was potentially destructive and meant that we were out of control. If a woman does express her hostility, a man will often retreat from it. An unhappy, angry woman may drive a man away from her; he may look for excuses not to come home to have to deal with her. Her partner's lack of interest or compassion may only make her more resentful.

Most new parents will not admit their anger; they may feel it is an inappropriate emotion. They may worry they will be judged unfit parents for having these negative feelings. But how can you honestly say you're *NOT* angry at this little person who dominates your life and makes you feel trapped, confused, frustrated, and worried? It is absolutely essential that you face your feelings and find a way to let off steam before it builds up and you explode.

***The baby may change the way you get angry.*** New parents often find that once the baby is in their lives their fights are quieter and less nasty. You may feel you shouldn't raise your voice "for the baby's sake" when you have arguments. You may also find that you just don't feel like being loud and unpleasant. Some couples experience less anger once they have a baby, and/or find that their fights don't get as heated or last as long. You may have less energy for arguing, or you re-evaluate your priorities about what is really worth fighting over.

***Anger at the baby is a very different feeling.*** It can be a more intense anger than you've ever felt in your life. Then when the crisis has passed and the baby settles down, you feel terribly guilty for the fantasies you may have had about throwing the baby against the wall or getting rid of him. Feeling this anger toward your baby is frightening: it can make you feel out of control or as though you're going out of your mind.

Feeling angry doesn't mean you don't love your child or are an unfit parent. These feelings aren't abnormal and will come and go, but they'll probably last only a short time. What you're reacting to is your infant's helplessness and dependency: a baby's needs evoke strong emotions in adults. They tap into everyone's subconscious or hidden desire to be completely taken care of—the way an infant needs to be.

***A baby can awaken your desire to be taken care of.*** Depending on your personality, you may be uncomfortable with your own dependency needs. An adult who spends time around an infant will have a reaction to the baby's helplessness and dependence. If you are someone who prides him/herself on being strong, independent, or self-sufficient, you may feel angry at the baby for making you aware of your own vulnerability.

***The simplest thing can trigger your anger.*** Maybe you've had a long, exhausting day looking after the baby and the house. You finally sit down to relax: the baby screams just as you're about to take your first sip of tea. The same thing can happen when a man gets home after his long day, looking forward to spending some quiet time with his wife. No sooner do you sit down together than the baby wails. It doesn't take much more than this to make you feel like blowing your stack.

***Your baby's personality can make you angry.*** An irritable, fussy baby may not give you the kind of positive feedback that would be a reward for your devotion. However, your disappointment or anger will combine with feelings of love and protectiveness toward the baby.

***Mothers who were previously career women may feel even more anger and helplessness.*** A woman who is used to having control over her schedule and being organized may have an even tougher adjustment to the realities of everyday life as an infant's mother.

If a woman is breast-feeding there is no way to predict how long the feeding will take, or even the amount of time between feedings, especially in the early weeks. By the time you've finished one feeding you may find there won't be much time before the next one. If you're accustomed to being in control of your life and how your day is laid out, the unpredictability of infant care can make you angry.

***There is a difference between anger and abuse.*** The normal anger toward a baby, and the fear of hurting the child, is different in parents for whom that pressure builds until they actually do harm their child.

**IF YOU FEEL THAT YOU MIGHT ACTUALLY HURT YOUR BABY OR YOU HAVE ALREADY DONE SO, YOU ABSOLUTELY MUST SEEK PROFESSIONAL HELP.**

Do not try to deny your feelings or actions or rationalize them by telling yourself it won't happen again. The problem will not just go away: it will continue to haunt you and your family until you get help.

***Hospital and parent groups have "warm lines."*** You can call them at the moment of crisis. These warm lines and groups are often staffed by other parents who have been abusive themselves. They've been trained to do counselling and referral.

A parent who abuses a baby has serious psychological difficulties. You need to get help in order to work through these inner pressures so you can feel more comfortable as a parent, and more in control of yourself. If your partner is the one with the problem, you have to help him or her face it for the sake of your marriage as well as for the baby's safety.

## BOREDOM, FRUSTRATION

*Some women feel bored by their infant and baby care.* If you feel this way, you may have a hard time finding someone to whom you can admit it. You look around you and see other mothers who don't seem to mind staying home all day and coping with the time-consuming tasks of looking after a small baby.

You may wonder if something is wrong with you. You may feel angry at yourself or at the baby—and anger often leads to feeling guilty. Infant care may make you feel useless, that you're wasting your time tending to repetitive chores that seem to be endless. "How can I do nothing but this all day?" you may ask yourself. You may then ask yourself if having these negative feelings makes you an unfit mother.

Don't worry: if you don't like infant care you'll probably enjoy aspects of looking after your child when he gets older. Don't berate yourself for feeling bored, and remember that kids grow up very fast; just when you've gotten sick of one stage (or are crazy about it) it evolves into the next one!

*Don't take your frustrations out on your husband.* Often a woman who is bored at home with the baby will let those feelings come out in anger at her partner. You may feel resentful or enraged by your new life: it can seem you are homebound with no control over your time and energy.

During the early weeks of adjusting to your new life you may feel especially furious that the baby's father comes and goes as he wants while you feel trapped. If your husband wanted a baby more than you did, or your pregnancy was not planned, you may feel even more resentful.

It is okay to have these feelings—even though they may seem selfish, childish, or foolish. Recognize that these negative emotions are working on you; accept yourself, flaws and all. But don't blame your mate for whatever you are experiencing.

## CONFLICT, ARGUMENTS

*Conflict and fights are part of life.* Negotiating is the way that we resolve differences in our needs and wishes. Conflict is the healthy, necessary result of differing opinions—and as new parents, you're sure to have your share of disagreements!

It can be upsetting to have feelings of conflict in the postpartum period. Especially if you handled the baby's birth as a united team, it can be confusing to feel at odds with each other afterwards. It is quite common for both partners to feel isolated within the marriage, to feel abandoned, jealous, or divided.

*The longer you've been together, the less conflict you'll have.* Statistics show that relationships that have lasted longer tend to have a better system of communication. Also, the partners have learned ways to de-escalate conflict. Of course, it can also be true that a couple who've been together a long time are set in their ways and can have a harder time adjusting to the changes that parenthood demands in their lives. However, it usually holds true that the longer a couple is together before they have a baby, the less stress and conflict they have.

*You're more vulnerable to fighting now.* You undoubtedly had conflict before you had a child but now the stakes are higher. You also have to cope with physical exhaustion and the pressure of new responsibilities. Now that you've made the momentous commitment to raise a child together, you have more invested in each other. The consequences of your anger and arguments seem more frightening. Minor differences may now seem like major problems. Once you adapt to your new roles it will help put things in perspective.

*It's harder to ignore conflict once you have a child.* Some couples, before they have a baby, say they have a great marriage, a "perfect" relationship, they never fight. In truth, if you have no conflict in your relationship it means one or both of you is repressing your feelings. This may be because when you were growing up you saw too much fighting in your family of origin, or none at all.

The arrival of a baby usually strips away this facade of "perfection." It isn't possible any longer to pretend that there aren't any conflicts between you. These disagreements are a normal part of a healthy relationship and are part of being parents. But if you aren't accustomed to dealing with conflict, the sudden recognition of it can shake your marriage to the foundation.

If this sounds like you—if you claim that you "never had fights"—you might need professional help now. You might need a marriage counselor to learn new skills. You might need to learn how to identify your negative feelings (which you've denied until now), and then how to communicate them effectively to each other.

***Each marriage has a set of "rules."*** Whether you realize it or not, there are unwritten rules in your relationship: you have an "understanding" about each other that is a cornerstone of your marriage. Each of you has strengths and weaknesses, good points and bad. The way that people minimize friction in a relationship is by accommodating each other. The arrival of a baby doesn't mean you can make new rules. Becoming parents doesn't give you the right to change all those emotional balances.

***Trying to change your partner is utterly foolish.*** Parenting may bring out the desire to change your mate, but that's a sure formula for frustration and unhappiness. People do not change because someone wants them to: they grow, at their own pace. There are certain aspects of a person that will not alter; basic components of their personality and certain ingrained behavior are there for keeps.

This is something you'd better come to terms with right away, because it will also hold true for what you expect and demand from your child. Don't let parenthood turn you into a nag, trying to get your mate to conform to your ideas of how to behave. There's a catchy little saying to keep in mind at times when you feel you're banging your head against a wall. "You cannot teach a pig to sing: you will only frustrate yourself and irritate the pig."

***Total satisfaction and harmony in a relationship is impossible: expecting it is foolish.*** However, our society seems to say that it is possible to achieve an ideal marriage which is without friction. The cultural message appears to be that if a couple has conflict, then they have failed. People who believe that myth try to avoid confrontation because they don't want to admit "failure."

The marriages in real trouble are not necessarily those in which there are frequent arguments . . . a more serious problem is when there is too much silence between partners. You are paying too high a price if you're putting up a false front and fooling yourselves into believing you have nothing to disagree about.

It's okay and normal if things between you aren't peaches-and-cream all the time. Give yourselves permission to feel hurt and angry sometimes. Admitting that conflict exists is the first step. Once you can identify what's gone wrong you have a chance to correct it.

*Facing conflict is a sign of a healthy relationship.* If you're able to confront conflict, then you can maintain an honest partnership with good communication. Airing grievances is always healthy; dealing with a conflict is far better than swallowing your emotions and avoiding confrontation.

## LEARNING HOW TO SPEAK UP FOR YOURSELF

Before you can handle your conflicts, you need certain skills to express your ideas. It's not always easy to initiate a conversation or try to organize your feelings so that you can get them across clearly.

*Many people suffer in silence.*   Some of us are afraid to make a scene or hurt someone else's feelings. We may be afraid deep down that if we complain we won't be loved any more. Or we may be fearful about appearing vulnerable or inadequate. And frequently we're afraid of the anger we'll stir up in the other person.

*"Assertiveness" is not a dirty word.*   It doesn't mean that you're pushy or a troublemaker. It means that you know how to let other people know what matters to you. You can do this without becoming a villain (in your mind

or theirs) and without making the other person feel defensive. The goal is to communicate in order to avoid or defuse conflict, not to *cause* conflict as a result of expressing yourself.

**Believe in yourself.**   Corny as it may sound, unless you trust and respect your own feelings and opinions, you can't convince anyone else of what's important to you.

**Use positive phrasing.**   Often it's the ''packaging'' of how you present your point of view that will convince your partner. Be positive and constructive in getting your ideas across: emphasize what you want, not what you don't like or don't want. For instance, if you start a conversation with a positive phrase like ''I'd like to talk to you,'' it gives a different impression than if you say, ''I hate to say this but . . .''

The kind of reaction and results you'll get are related to how you approach a subject. If your partner criticizes your parenting you'll probably get a pretty good response if you respond to his/her interference by saying, ''I'd like to try it my way, even if I mess up. I want to learn how to be a parent from my own mistakes.'' But you're in for unpleasantness if you put your mate on the defensive. On the other hand, if your concern is your mate's lack of involvement, you're not going to resolve things by attacking him by saying, ''Why don't you ever do anything with the baby?''

**The way you start a sentence makes a big difference.**   Do not begin a sentence with ''You . . .'' or, ''Why . . .'' It will put the listener on the defensive because those words are almost always followed by an accusation or criticism.

Start sentences with ''I feel,'' not with ''I think,'' for the same reason. However, it's just as destructive to start a sentence with ''I feel'' followed immediately by the word ''you.'' These sentences usually wind up sounding something like ''I feel you don't . . .'' etc. Be aware of the power of words and make them work for you.

## How to Deal with Conflict

You can learn how to negotiate conflict with your partner. This is a skill you have to learn—there are rules and it takes practice to do it well. If you take the time to learn how, it will obviously help you not just to solve your conflicts as parents, but generally in your relationship.

***The ways in which you handle conflict are what count.***  This is what can make the difference between a strong, healthy, resilient relationship and family and one that is in trouble. Is power and decision-making flexible between you, or rigid? Do you communicate in a problem-solving style or in an accusatory way that increases anger and tension?

Do you have a positive self-image as a couple? Do you have high self-esteem or not think much of yourselves? If you have realistic expectations of yourselves and your child(ren) it will help you to solve the problems that every family faces. The ways you deal with the issues are what either help you to grow or slowly erode your lives.

***Choose the best possible time for a talk.***  You have to create a safe, calm environment for your interchange. It is stressful to deal with issues that are already highly charged—be thoughtful about when, where, and how you initiate a discussion.

---

### Bad Times to Start a Discussion

* When it's late and you're both exhausted
* At bedtime (you won't be able to sleep)
* During a meal (guaranteed indigestion)
* With children or others around
* On a special occasion (good way to ruin it)

---

***Wait until you're in the right frame of mind.***  Before starting a talk, make sure you are calm. Don't initiate a discussion when you are steaming mad: there's a good chance you'll have a conversation that will be hostile and unproductive because your partner won't have much chance to respond intelligently. A person who is bombarded with anger is usually deafened by it. Try to be pleasant. It doesn't cost you anything and it will gain you a receptive listener.

*Before you start talking, be clear about the issue.* Be specific and stay in the present, on the subject you have chosen. This is not a forum to air a "laundry list" of grievances that you've been saving up. It is infuriating to the other person if you jump around in the conversation; concentrate on one issue at a time. Otherwise you aren't trying to negotiate conflict, you're increasing it.

*Be clear about your feelings and needs.*   Once you know what you want, then you have to be certain that your partner understands clearly what that is. In return, you have the responsibility to understand his/her feelings and needs on the subject.

Explain the problem as you see it and ask for specific changes that you would like. (But remember: your partner's personality and habits are not going to change just because you've become parents. Accept him/her and only ask for realistic changes.)

*Deal with one thing at a time.*   Don't try to express all your feelings or solve everything at one time. Keep a perspective: this isn't your only chance to talk. You may feel there's hardly ever any time to sit down and talk, but keep in mind that there will be other opportunities.

*Communication has value regardless of the result.* The means are as important as the end: you both gain a great deal just by sitting down and making an effort to talk and listen to each other. You can have a talk session without intending to resolve a problem; it can be a way to share ideas, to let each other know your negative *and* positive observations about your new life and roles.

*Finding a solution is secondary.*   The most crucial thing is to get the problem out into the open; it is less important whether you can come up with an immediate solution.

***Acknowledge the other person's point of view.*** If your partner feels accepted and understood, s/he is more apt to listen to your perceptions. You're halfway home if you can just learn to tell each other your feelings and needs without being defensive.

***Be prepared for a negative reaction.*** If you want to bring up issues of conflict, you have to accept the fact that your partner may react unpleasantly to your views. If you have the courage to stand up for your beliefs, then you have to be mature enough to accept a negative reaction: anxiety, anger, tears, or whatever your partner dishes out.

***Give each other equal time.*** Just because you're the one who brought up the subject, it doesn't give you the right to be a bully or dominate the conversation.

***Approach talks as partners with a shared problem.*** Don't let yourself fall into the trap of thinking of it as a victim/villain situation. Do not attempt to negotiate conflict from an adversary position. Making accusations will get you nowhere: you have a better shot at resolution if you approach the issue as a problem between you for which you'd like to find a solution.

***Have realistic expectations for the outcome.*** Don't expect immediate results. In fact, don't build up hopes for any resolution, particularly a specific one that you have in mind. The intention of dealing with conflict isn't to totally eliminate it; it's to negotiate what you can, and find a way to live more comfortably with what won't change. It may take several talks before you see some improvement . . . or there may never be any. Every negotiation won't get resolved. It won't end with both of you in agreement; don't expect it and you won't be disappointed.

***Compromise is another kind of victory.*** Finding a middle road may be a more successful outcome of your talk than if one of you has to "be right," and get it "your way."

---

### RULES FOR NEGOTIATING CONFLICTS

- Sarcasm is prohibited—it is a below-the-belt way to express yourself
- Name-calling and stereotyping are forbidden
- Start sentences with "I feel" instead of with "You never"
- Don't try to be a mind reader: don't assume you know what your partner is thinking *or* try to anticipate his/her reactions
- Don't expect your partner to be a mind reader: explain yourself clearly
- Don't dictate what your mate "should" feel: accept what he/she says he feels

---

## PROBLEM AREAS THAT CREATE CONFLICT

There are certain issues which are often the cause of disagreements between new parents. If you know what these areas are ahead of time you can be prepared. The cause of the conflict usually comes from a difference between a husband and wife's **attitude** and **expectations** about certain key issues. If you were both raised with similar cultural backgrounds there may be fewer areas of misunderstanding. It can be enormously helpful to resolving your conflicts if you ask yourselves certain questions about your upbringing.

### SEX AND AFFECTION

Based on what your parents said or did, what are your attitudes about sex? How do you feel about displaying affection, either in private or public? Have your views changed now that you've become a parent? If you and your mate have different ideas about this subject, you can get caught in "should" and "should never" reactions to each other.

A man may become envious of a woman who puts too much into her bond with the baby. It can make him feel angry and/or rejected. If he doesn't understand his feelings, or feels guilty for feeling rivalry with his own child, or doesn't know how to discuss this with his wife—he may look outside his marriage for the sex and affection he isn't getting.

### MONEY

What were your parents' attitudes about spending money? Did they teach you it was something to enjoy and spend, or that it should be saved for the future? Was there conflict between your parents in their attitudes toward money? And is your mate's attitude different from yours? If so, the most fertile ground for conflict in a marriage is the issue of money.

### DEPENDENCE

A new mother may feel uncomfortable with the baby's total dependence on her, especially because it makes her feel completely dependent on her partner. Does dependence on your husband make you anxious or lower your self-esteem? Does your wife's lack of independence—which may be new—make you feel burdened or suffocated? Does it remind either of you of your parents' marriages?

### POWER AND ROLE PLAYING

What roles do you and your partner play in decision making together? Has parenthood changed the power balance? If motherhood means that the woman is no longer a money earner, does that effect whether power and decisions are shared or one-sided? How did it work in your families of origin? Do the words "mother" and "father" alter your sharing of control over your life together?

### WORK AND LEISURE TIME

What kind of work ethic was each of you taught as a child? You may not realize it, but your parents raised you with a belief system about work and play: from that teaching you've developed certain attitudes about how to use free time, and how people "should" handle their work.

A couple can have vastly different ideas based on how affluent their childhood was (and therefore how much pressure there was or wasn't about money) and also how much time was spent in "play time" as a family. Either of you may unconsciously mimic what you were raised with, or you may rebel against it in raising your own family.

However, if you have two ethics which clash, you'll have conflict. One of you might have been brought up with a strong work ethic, so that the emphasis is on working as much as possible for professional advancement. Yet your spouse may have been brought up to believe that the leisure time a couple and family spends is just as important as money and "getting ahead." You're going to have to be tolerant and nonjudgmental about each other's positions while you work out some compromises.

### VACATIONS

What you choose to do with your holidays may be totally different from what your mate might choose. Sometimes a couple feels compatible about vacations until they become parents: suddenly you may find differences in your preferences. The way you choose to spend time now can become a philosophical choice as well as a reaction to how your own family vacationed when you were growing up.

One of you may have been raised to think that three weeks in Hawaii or Europe is a good vacation. The other may believe that a family "should" spend holiday time at home together and only go away for one week, preferably camping. You definitely have the makings of a nice fight there!

### RELIGION

What was the importance of religion and religious training in your upbringing? Even if you are a nonpracticing member of your faith, now that you're a parent you may revert to what you were raised with. If one of you is deeply religious and the other is agnostic or an atheist, this can easily be a power issue between you about how the children will be raised.

### MORALS, ETHICS

Were you and your partner raised with different morals or ethics? What were you taught about lying, cheating, or stealing by your respective parents? The messages you got need not have been dramatic: did your mother teach you it was okay to eat fruit in the supermarket that you hadn't paid for yet? Did your father convey the message that if a big company made a billing mistake in his favor he would point it out to them? Or did your parents give conflicting messages? Did they contradict each other in their attitudes to finances, or were they inconsistent themselves, saying one thing and doing another? All these elements add up to the morality that you developed. There will be tension between you if yours is quite different from your mate's.

### CHILD REARING AND DISCIPLINE

If you are like most new parents, it's safe to say that you will inevitably have conflicts with your partner about this issue. The best way to deal with it is to agree to disagree. You are going to have some profound differences of opinion: if you can accept your partner's point of view without trying to change it, you will have many fewer battles.

If one of you is more protective than the other, you'll have constant arguments about what is "safe" for the child as she grows up. One of you may believe in being permissive; for example, that toilet training should be accomplished by the child on her own schedule. If the other believes in rules and teaching manners, you're headed for lots of conflict. This is such a loaded issue that it is covered more fully in the section on *Child Rearing* in *Chapter 14: Choices in Child Care*.

### CONFLICT CREATED BY A WOMAN'S CRITICAL ATTITUDE

If a woman is constantly criticizing her spouse it is a source of conflict and also creates more hassles between them. There are times during the postpartum period that many women feel angry and disappointed with their new life. The most convenient recipient of this distress is a woman's husband, who is usually an innocent bystander doing the best he can to cope with his new role and pressures.

***The husband's return home from work is pivotal.***
If your husband works, the moment when he comes home at the end of the day may be a "last straw" for you. You

may resent the fact that he can leave the house and have freedom from the baby; it may seem to you as though he has less responsibility than you do (in fact it isn't less, it's just different).

You've been home all day with the baby. You've spent the evening trying to settle her down. The baby may sense her father's return home and become noisier or more active. Or your partner may want to play with her and stirs her up, throwing off the schedule that you've tried to establish. You may resent your mate's intrusion. You want the baby quiet. So you criticize him as a father for upsetting things.

You may also feel competitive with the baby because you're desperate for some quiet time with an adult after a long day with an infant. But you probably don't speak directly of your needs, of your disappointment and frustration and desire to be with your husband. Instead, you let it out by criticizing him. Tension builds.

The irony is that your husband may also want some quiet time with you after *his* long day but he goes to the baby because he thinks it will please you. You may have criticized him at other times for not participating more, so he tries to satisfy you by playing with the baby as soon as he gets home. And then you read him the riot act!

**A woman may use the baby as a tool.** Some women don't feel comfortable stating their own needs, so they use the child as an excuse to make a veiled complaint. If you find yourself saying to your husband, "You should spend more time with the child . . . be a better father," what you may really be saying is, "Please spend more time with me." If you say the former, what you'll get is a growl from a man under attack; if you say the latter, there's a good chance you'll get what you want.

**A woman may use a two-against-one threat.** It is possible that if a woman feels angry and unappreciated enough, she'll go beyond criticizing and nagging and actually threaten her mate. If you've wanted things from your mate that he hasn't been able to give, you may feel so frustrated that you're tempted to say, "I'm going to take the baby and leave you if you don't . . . ."

It should go without saying that this is a truly terrible tactic. It builds up resentment, distrust, and rage in your husband, and will probably make you feel pretty awful, too. This is not a way to resolve conflict but a way to create more discord.

***Some men don't want involvement with an infant.*** This is not a feeling that you can change in your husband by criticizing him. There are many men who just aren't interested or don't feel comfortable with tiny babies. It may be because of his cultural background. He may feel inhibited by experiences of his own childhood or a lack of role models after which he can pattern himself as a new father. He may have other pressures that make it hard for him to focus on being actively involved with his baby. These aren't things he can change or fake just to satisfy your image of what an involved father "should" be like.

***Learn to voice resentment without accusation.*** Women have to learn to be as gentle with their mates as they are with their babies. Men are fragile, no matter how strong, macho, or tough they may seem. If you complain or criticize without some compassion, all you'll do is drive the man away and put up a brick wall between you.

Be patient. Be kind in your assessment of your husband as a father (a generosity he also has to extend to you). Each of you is being influenced by your own unique childhood experiences. If you come from two different worlds, the differences will be even greater. Each of us has had a unique upbringing, even if our backgrounds were similar. The more patience and compassion you can bring to the situation, the less conflict you'll experience.

## COMPETITION OVER WHO'S DOING THE MOST

Thinking competitively creates a seedbed for conflict. Couples argue over who is the most tired or who's done the most housework or infant care. They battle over who deserves to sleep late or which of them has earned the right *not* to get up for the night feeding. New parents have even been known to make lists of how many hours each of them has slept, which chores they've done, and how generally underappreciated they are.

***Nobody wins.***   You become competitors instead of being partners, in it together through good times and bad. If you fall into a trap of competing with each other, all it will do is make both of you feel angry, resentful, and selfish. If one of you "wins" and gets to go out and do something on your own, you've actually "lost." You can't enjoy yourself knowing that you've left a resentful, martyred partner at home.

***Whose needs are greatest?***   The mother who stays at home may begin to make resentful comparisons between herself and her partner. The woman feels deprived because she's home all day. But from the man's point of view, he's out all day in the cold, cruel world, trying to make a good living with the added responsibility of a new mouth to feed. He feels unappreciated and angry if he comes home to a wife who's complaining about being stuck at home with the baby.

　　If you've found yourselves caught in this vicious cycle, you know that the next step is to accuse each other of being selfish and self-centered. Then you both feel guilty because you realize that your own attitude isn't particularly generous or thoughtful, either!

***You'd both like someone to take care of you.***   You are more vulnerable now that you have to depend on one another to juggle housework, child care, and your job(s). This means that you may strike out at each other over minor issues. You stoop to making comparisons of who-has-spent-more-time-doing-what. However, if you argue over which of you has been more supportive, or whose needs are the greatest, then neither of you gets what you want. And you don't have much energy left to give anything to your mate.

***Acknowledge your partner's contributions.***   A real partnership will grow from being able to give each other credit for doing difficult and important work, although what you each do is different. Give each other acknowledgment for being tired and drained, although your exhaustion is caused by different tasks. If you compete with each other instead of being mutually supportive, it's going to put extra pressure on your relationship at a time when it's already stressed. It will also magnify any conflicts so that they seem more personally threatening.

*Take responsibility for your own life.* Once you do this, you're no longer a victim and your mate can no longer be the villain. Having a family means making choices. It means making sacrifices. The bottom line is this: it was **your** decision to become a parent. Nobody said it would be easy, so don't look for someone to blame (your spouse) when you feel overwhelmed. Handling it is your responsibility; don't look for a way to pass the hot potato by unloading all your gripes on your partner!

## ONE PARTNER'S MOODINESS CAN CREATE PROBLEMS

*Your moods can be threatening to your spouse.* If you are experiencing a lot of negative reactions during the postpartum adjustment period it can irritate or threaten your spouse, who is probably having many of the same feelings. If you constantly talk about being bored, frustrated, depressed, or unhappy, it can seem self-indulgent to your partner, who is thinking, "This is hard for me too, but I'm not complaining. So why should s/he?"

*Don't give your complaining spouse the brush-off.* Even though you may be angry for what seems to be self-indulgence by your partner, don't just dismiss the feelings or patronize him/her by saying, "Forget about it, you'll be fine." The unhappy partner will only feel more isolated, unloved, and misunderstood if you don't respond with some compassion.

Your spouse's moodiness may put a strain on you because you have to take on more responsibility and be more cheerful to compensate for his/her attitude. You may feel this is unfair because adjusting to parenthood is difficult for you, too, without this added burden. But who said life was going to be fair? Unpleasant feelings are part of life; so is feeling disappointed in someone close to you. Try to reach inside yourself for strength at times like this and live through the rough times as best you can.

## VALIDATING EACH OTHER REDUCES CONFLICT

There's a little voice inside the head of every new parent that says, "Help—this is too much for me! Tell me I'm doing okay!" If **you've** heard this little voice, you can be pretty sure your spouse has heard it too. But it can be difficult to recognize and admit to it, so people sometimes bicker and complain because they feel scared or inadequate.

*Try to develop a sympathetic ear.* Your partner may be groaning about parenthood as a way to get encouragement from you or to get the reassurance that you share some of the same doubts. You can defuse anxiety and potential conflict by soothing each other's fears. Be kind to yourself and your spouse: s/he isn't expecting solutions, just a shoulder to cry on.

Remember that it wasn't easy to decide to become parents, with all the life changes it entails. And just because you made the decision doesn't mean you won't have "buyer's remorse"! There will be times when you'll feel ambivalent; your partner probably has moments like that, too. If you're sensitive to each other instead of demanding or judgmental, you can avoid a lot of tension and conflict.

*Tell your mate what you need.* If you can relate to what you've read here, then spell it out for your spouse. "When I complain all I really want is for you to tell me what a great job I'm doing." Of course you'll get better results if you offer reciprocal cheerleading.

*Tell your mate if you can't provide the support.* You may feel that your spouse is too dependent on you for feedback or is leaning on you too much. S/he may need too much support, or his/her concerns and doubts may compound your own anxieties so that you can't cope with them. If you realize you can't meet his/her needs right now, you should lovingly say so and suggest s/he talk to someone else.

Conflict often comes from confusing mixed messages, which can cause hurt feelings or disappointment about unmet (unrealistic) expectations. Just as it was important for your partner to tell you what s/he needs from you, it's equally important that you gently but clearly let him/her know if you can't provide for them in the way they'd like. If you are open and honest about it, then neither of you should wind up resentful or disillusioned.

*Give each other pep talks.*   New parents often just need a pat on the back in order to get through the rough times. Your spouse is the best person to tell you that your sacrifices are appreciated. A woman may doubt her abilities as a mother or find it hard to stay home with the baby, even though emotionally it's something she wants to do. All she may need is to hear from her husband that it's worth her effort. A man who takes on extra work to provide for his new family needs the validation of hearing from his wife how much she appreciates him.

## EXTRAMARITAL AFFAIRS

Sometimes an extramarital affair can seem like a solution to the emotional difficulties of the postpartum period. It is usually the man who contemplates or embarks on an affair—a new mother doesn't really have the time, energy, or self-image to pursue sexual yearnings.

*Lust in the mind is still lust.*   Even if all a man does is *think* about having an affair, it can make him as confused or guilt-ridden as he might be if he had actually consummated the infidelity. Here you are, a proud new father, and you feel like a heel because you start thinking about having a stolen afternoon with your secretary!

Sometimes your sense of freedom (or your own feeling of being sexually attractive) is reinforced by being around someone who doesn't represent domesticity. Some men can feel overwhelmed by the way a new baby overtakes a household with infant paraphernalia and odors. Any woman who doesn't smell of baby powder may seem enticing, especially if a man is resistant or resentful of the new baby and its effect on his home life.

***Sexual fantasies are an escape.*** Fantasizing is a way to avoid your day-to-day life when you're frustrated, feeling confined and bored. People indulge in sexual fantasies because they dread falling into a rut; new parents may be afraid their lives will become dull, uneventful, and predictable.

If one or both of you is dissatisfied with the quality or quantity of lovemaking, an affair can seem more appealing than discussing your problem with your spouse and finding a compromise. Whenever a couple is having problems, it's common to think about having an extramarital affair: after you become parents, you may both crave reaffirmation of your previous personal/sexual identity. (See *Chapter 8: Sex and Romance* for a full discussion of this inner conflict.)

***An affair isn't going to make you feel any better.*** There may be a few exciting, sexy moments but they are outweighed by the negative feelings you will undoubtedly experience. Considering or embarking on an affair is no solution to your problems—actually, it can complicate or prolong them. However, it's certainly easy to see why it seems more tempting than doing the hard work of sitting down and confronting your dissatisfactions.

---

**SOME REASONS FOR HAVING AN AFFAIR**

- Sexual intercourse isn't physically comfortable for the new mother or father
- "Madonna image" psychologically affects either partner: they can't relate to "mother" as sexual
- Abstinence is just too much for some men, who cope by getting their needs met elsewhere
- A woman's figure postpartum may be disturbing or a turn-off to her or her mate
- Husband feels a loss of affection and attention
- Husband needs validation that he's attractive, important, and sexually potent: his self-worth may be diminished by new pressure and responsibilities
- As a release of pressure and tension, an affair can be a temporary outlet (the way drugs or alcohol might be for some people)
- A symptom of continuing problems in the relationship (especially if you had a baby to "save" your marriage)

---

***Having an affair is a reaction to a situation.***   Your husband isn't responding to you, he's reacting to the stresses of his redefined role and life. A new father usually contemplates or engages in an affair not as a response to his spouse, but as a way of coping with the adjustment to parenthood.

If you learn that your husband has had an affair, the best way to get a perspective on it is to see it as his reaction to a crisis he can't handle. I know that's asking a lot of mature detachment from you—but kicking him out and demanding a divorce isn't going to solve anything!

It's possible that all your husband wanted was to feel special, to get the caring and attention that he wasn't getting from you. It's possible that all he *really* wanted was to get close to another woman, but she interpreted this to mean he wanted to go to bed with her. Or perhaps he translated his own emotional/psychological needs into a physical expression that wasn't his primary intention.

As hurt, angry, and humiliated as you may feel, keep in mind that (unless he's an absolute boor) your spouse feels terrible about having betrayed you. He may also feel entitled to some anger of his own: he may rationalize that if you had been giving him the attention he needed (sexually, emotionally, or both) he wouldn't have been forced to go elsewhere to get it. Try not to view this as a villain/victim situation. Nothing happens in a vacuum; life is a series of actions and reactions. We all make mistakes and hurt each other—understanding and forgiveness are qualities you might want to practice now in anticipation of raising a child!

***An affair doesn't mean the end of a marriage.***  If a woman can view an affair as her husband's extreme reaction to a stressful transition, she can overcome her negative feelings about the breach of trust. Many new parents survive an affair.

Professional counselling is often necessary, however, so that you can constructively air your anger and resentment. It's very hard to do this by yourselves because you are hampered by so many emotions.

Unless you resolve the issue, the extramarital affair will remain an ongoing debate between you. You both have to deal honestly with your emotions and get on with your lives. Otherwise the woman can hold onto the affair as her "trump card" to pull out and use as a weapon during future disagreements.

## JEALOUSIES

***A triangle is the most complicated relationship.***
Sharing each other and the child is a hard balance to strike. Each of you wants the other one to love the baby, but you still have uncontrollable (sometimes unconscious) jealousies and needs. You may have noticed in adult relationships that triangular friendships are often complicated: in a threesome there is greater potential for misunderstanding, competition, and conflict.

***A baby is probably the first challenge your relationship has had.***  Now your partnership has to compete with another important and pleasurable relationship: the one you both have with your child. You'll probably discover a very different quality of attachment when you interact with a baby; children are dependent, responsive people with an enormous need and affection for us.

Your marital relationship may seem lacking when

you compare it to the closeness and intensity of your bond with the baby. You may not have realized it before, but now your partner may seem unsatisfying. An adult can be set in his/her ways, perhaps not particularly emotional or affectionate or demonstrative. In adult relationships one person may not feel a deep need or attachment, or may not be willing to show it. A baby is just the opposite.

***The father may make a beeline for the child.*** Some new fathers walk in the door and zoom right past their wives to the crib. A woman may be glad that her mate is an involved father, but she'd still like a "hello," a kiss, and maybe some verbal interaction before he descends on the baby with affection.

A new mother can be especially resentful of her spouse's show of affection to the child if her self-esteem is low (because she's still carrying extra weight from her pregnancy, or she's given up a job that gave her identity and independence, etc.).

***The opposite of jealousy can also occur.*** One of the pluses of parenting is that the love you give to your child can spill over back into your relationship. The depth of feelings you have for your child—even the discovery of untapped emotional resources within you—can rebound into your marital relationship and enrich your lives.

## PROFESSIONAL COUNSELLING

Sometimes a relationship in trouble needs a therapist to help sort things out. Going to a therapist isn't going to solve all your problems or make your decisions for you, but optimally it can help you to understand what's going on in your lives. Counselling is a tool that a couple can use to find alternative ways of reacting and coping.

***Don't view counselling as an admission of failure.*** Becoming parents is a stressful, overwhelming transition; seeking out a therapist's help doesn't mean that something is wrong with you or that you've failed. If anything, it's a sign that you have faced your situation honestly and have the self-esteem to believe that you deserve whatever preventive/corrective help is available.

***There are two cases where therapy is essential.*** Professional counselling will be especially important to you—and your baby—if you decided to have a child to "save" your troubled marriage. Even the strongest and healthiest relationships can buckle under the pressures of parenting; if your marriage was already weakened by problems, you may need a therapist to help you through this transition.

The second situation in which counselling is definitely advisable is if you have fears of neglecting or abusing your child, have already done so, or have those fears about your partner.

You or your spouse may have been abused yourselves as children—if so, I'm sure you know by now that with your background you are "at risk" for doing the same to your own baby. Instead of, or in addition to private therapy, you can contact groups like Parents Anonymous, which has a nationwide network of trained volunteers (often abusive parents themselves). Many hospitals and parent groups have "warm lines" you can call at times of crisis.

***There are critical issues at stake postpartum.*** You are seeing each other in a new light for the first time: sometimes your image of each other as parents can be negative. There is some form of struggle for power and control between all new parents. For instance, motherhood may give you a new feeling of power and importance as a woman. This can disturb the previous balance in the relationship which kept both of you "happy," in which the woman was powerless or passive.

Another example is that a woman's sexual withdrawal may be impossible for her spouse to accept or handle. It can make a man feel rejected, inadequate, enraged, or vengeful. Without help, these problems can develop into deep rifts between you that can snowball to the point where your marriage is threatened by unexpressed, unresolved feelings.

***Choosing a therapist is tricky.*** Titles and degrees don't mean very much. Often a psychiatric social worker (an

MSW) will have more training and experience in family therapy than an M.D. or Ph.D. One way to get recommendations is to ask friends if they've used a therapist, or ask your family doctor, obstetrician, or pediatrician.

There may be a problem asking some of these doctors for a referral because they may downplay your need for counselling: they may tell you not to worry, that the problems will pass. This is true for *some* people with postpartum problems—but if you've gotten to the point where you have the courage to admit the need for help, trust your own feelings and judgment. You have nothing to lose and everything to gain from therapy. Don't hesitate to get help if you or your mate feel that counselling could be useful.

*There are some things to decide about a therapist.* Before you look for a counselor, ask yourself and your spouse some basic questions. Would you prefer a male or female? Younger, older, or your contemporary? A professional who is also a parent? Someone of the same race or religion as you? None of these factors may matter, which is fine, but it's a good idea to discuss them beforehand to eliminate any possible obstacles to the selection of a counselor. Working with a therapist is intense, probing work; the less resistance either of you has to the therapist and the process, the more you'll get out of it.

*There are questions to ask up front.* In the first visit, or even on the phone, you may want to ask the therapist if s/he deals frequently with the concerns of a couple or individual parent in the postpartum period. Ask what the costs are. Ask what style of working the counselor prefers: listening, discussion, or suggestions? Or does s/he change method or style of therapy to accommodate different personalities?

*Is this the professional for you?* In order to decide, go on your gut feelings. There's no such thing as the one "right" person. However, there can be professionals who would *not* be appropriate for you. Will you be able to talk to this person? Do you feel more or less smart than the doctor? Do you think that either of you could "get away with" evasion or dishonesty?

Even though you're choosing to seek help, be aware

that there will be times when you'll want to avoid sensitive, painful issues—you may feel you can "duck out" emotionally if you choose a therapist who seems weaker, more passive, or less bright than you.

***Many professionals are not tuned in to PPD.*** If you are suffering from postpartum depression (see *Chapter* 7), you need a professional who is skilled in this area. You do not need a doctor who is going to delve far into your past and explore your childhood relationships and conflicts. A therapist who understands PPD will want to know your background and how you've handled previous crises (if any), but PPD is an immediate problem.

Short-term therapy and antidepressants have helped many women. You need a doctor who can help you to focus on what you're doing well, to teach you how to give yourself "strokes," or pats on the back. Often with PPD you cannot see for yourself what you've accomplished in the previous day or two. Therapy should offer specific suggestions on how to compromise in work or mothering so that you can lessen your stress level and self-criticism. A doctor should be able to give you concrete ideas about how to ease these burdens.

## STRESS

***Parenthood is a guarantee of stress and tension.*** You'll be able to cope much better if you're realistic about the pressure that this transition puts on new parents. There's an overwhelming change to your life and habits; there's the intense emotional involvement; there's the fatigue of infant care; and there's the pressure you create for yourselves about "doing it right."

***You may have additional stress factors.*** There may be issues weighing you down in addition to the obvious concerns and demands of baby care. You may not even realize that you have these concerns: if they remain unrecognized, there are various factors that can make your transition to parenthood even tougher. In order to find out whether you have any extra personal burdens, see the chart of *PPD Stress Factors* in *Chapter* 7. Many of these stress factors need to be discussed with your spouse, a close friend, or a therapist if necessary.

***You can feel disoriented.*** Disorientation can be upsetting unless you know that it's a normal by-product of the stress. It can be uncomfortable not to feel like yourself or to feel out of control, especially if you're usually an organized person.

You may hear nonexistent baby's crying (if you've gone outside for a moment or you're washing dishes or in the shower). You may find it difficult to do simple tasks. You may forget why you've gone into another room or taken a trip to the store. You may lock yourself out of your house or car. You may check on your baby's breathing all the time (which you'll stop doing: when your confidence increases, your anxiety decreases). All this will pass as you feel more at ease in your new role.

***You may think you're losing your mind.*** It's possible to reach a point of "overload" and feel overwhelmed by the endless small tasks and irritations of caring for an infant. It is not unusual for a new mother to feel that she just can't cope. Some reach a point where they feel they're about to have a nervous breakdown.

Don't panic. Take a look at the chapter on PPD. If you don't think you fit into that category, it means you're experiencing "normal" stress and the feelings will pass.

Nonetheless, you still need to take care of yourself. You have to rest and get time for yourself, away from the baby. If you cannot afford outside help you should consider letting your mother, mother-in-law, or other relative come in and give a hand. Even if this sounds like an unsavory idea, it is worth any potential personality conflict for you to get a break.

***Consider yourself.*** If only more new parents would do this, they could enjoy parenting **and** have a grown-up life, too. Self-sacrifice causes distress. It can also cause postpartum depression, alienation from your partner, etc. If you deny your needs and feelings—if you consider them less important than those of the baby—it can be dangerous to your mental health.

All mothers used to get help from their extended family. It is logical, natural, and healthy. Asking for help doesn't mean you are inadequate; it shows that you are looking out for your own well-being and the best possible care for your child. A stressed-out mother doesn't make a very good parent, role model, or spouse.

***Don't project your feelings onto the child.*** Don't imagine that your tension can cause your baby to have colic, for example. If you feel inept or inadequate as a mother, it will have no effect on how much the baby eats, cries, or sleeps. Recognize that being selfish, in moderation, can be healthy. Your own identity and self-esteem are on the line: you are nothing if you allow yourself to believe that you're only a handmaiden to an infant.

***Don't put up a front.*** Don't pretend that you're handling the stress if it's got you down. If you say, "I'm okay," when you aren't, you're asking for trouble. You may feel tense, angry, or resentful; if you try to act like a warm, loving mother, you are doing a disservice to yourself and the baby.

Tell someone how you really feel. It will reduce your stress level and release some of the tension. You have to grow into parenthood in your own way at your own pace. If you try to fake it, the pressure is going to mount until you can't take it any more. The following chart will help you recognize signs of tension so you can find ways to reduce the pressures on you.

---

### SIGNS OF TENSION

- Grinding your teeth (you have sore jaw muscles, especially after sleeping)
- Stiff neck
- Sore shoulders
- Stomachache or tightness
- Nervous tics (leg jiggling, playing with hair, fingernail biting)
- Lines in forehead (frowning, worrying)

## How to Deal with Tension and Stress

***Make an effort to slow down.*** Once you're aware that you have symptoms of stress, make a conscious effort to counteract it. Do everything more slowly: do even the simplest chores at a slower pace. Especially slow down when you're handling and responding to the baby. In the morning, when her crying wakes you up, **do not race out of bed.** Lie quietly for a moment, collect your thoughts, then go in calmly to the child.

***Become aware of the energy you're using.*** It's possible to get nervous and wound up just from making lists of chores and then dashing around, thinking you have to get everything done before the sun sets. Don't operate on "automatic": decide about each task whether the energy you're putting out is appropriate. Get any help you can; accept all offers of assistance. The less you have to do, the less pressure you'll feel.

***You can learn how to really relax.*** Relaxation means eliminating all physical and emotional tension. It's much easier than you think: you can do it by taking a few minutes (in the morning and evening and perhaps also during the day) to do a simple form of meditation.

You don't have to be religious or spiritual to do this; you just have to be tense enough to want some relief! Even if this sounds corny or you're skeptical, give it a try for a few days. If you give it a chance, it's sure to make you feel better, and may even allow you to be a better mate and parent.

***This kind of real relaxation is not "recreation."*** It is not talking on the telephone, visiting with a friend, watching TV, or writing a letter. Those activities use your body and mind, they don't relax them. Total relaxation doesn't mean a pleasurable activity like reading or playing a game, which demand your attention and use your eyes, back, face, and neck muscles.

Despite what you may think, relaxation also does not mean having a drink with your partner at the end of the day. Although it's nice to spend time together, and alcohol in moderation is fine, this activity isn't an example of total relaxation. Even though you may feel a drink relaxes you, alcohol doesn't actually release tension, it buries or numbs it.

*Remember the relaxation techniques for childbirth?*
The total relaxation I'm talking about here is simpler. Lie down and close your eyes. Take a cleansing breath, then breathe deeply, taking slow deep breaths. Tense all your muscles, scrunching them as hard as you can, then release them. Go completely limp. Tighten everything up again and release even more fully. As you let go of the tension in your body, let go of the mental stress, too. Imagine the tension flowing out of you, out the tips of your fingers and toes.

Turn your attention inward. Ask whatever higher powers you may believe in to guide your day. If you aren't comfortable with that suggestion, then clear your mind and ask yourself for serenity and patience. You may discover that achieving this true relaxation for a few minutes twice a day can really make a difference in the quality of your life.

## SUGGESTIONS FOR RELIEVING BAD FEELINGS

*Build a support system.*   It's important to have someone other than your partner with whom you can blow off steam. It may be another new mother with whom you can commiserate, or an old friend you can complain to without feeling judged. Both parents need help in raising a newborn. Because you need more than just each other, it helps to create a self-made extended family from relatives, friends, and neighbors.

*Encourage and praise each other.*   You'll be surprised what a little verbal reinforcement can do! Try not to focus on what *isn't* going well and how your partner may be disappointing you. Instead, try concentrating on what is positive and praising it. Make it a point to say "Thank you" and "Well done" for your mate's efforts. The more you're able to make your spouse feel good about him/herself, the more s/he'll be able to do the same for you.

***Practice being romantic.*** As a new parent it's easy to lose sight of romance, but it's worth the effort to stay in touch with it (you never know, it might come in handy again some day!). If you let romance get away from you it is hard to recapture. Try to remember the tangible niceties and the emotional generosity of courtship: flowers, little gifts, special dinners, listening compassionately, sometimes doing things just because the other person wants to (remember that one?). Simply deciding that you're going to be romantic can help you through the rough times.

***Set aside special "gripe time."*** You might want to try setting aside one evening a week to discuss problems. Each of you can air your grievances, or you can limit it to one complaint apiece. But complaining is then off-limits for the rest of the week.

This system won't work for all couples, but it's worth giving it a try. It will certainly teach you patience, and also by the time Friday rolls around you will have forgiven and forgotten Tuesday's transgression.

Remember that effective discussions begin with sentences starting with "I," like "I feel lonely staying home . . ." instead of, "Why don't you ever . . ."

***Keep small things small.*** Don't get bogged down in trivial stuff. If you have a perspective on your new life, you'll be able to see the humor in difficult situations. If you keep a perspective and a sense of what is truly important, the rough edges will smooth out because little things just won't matter. Save your energy for the quality of the new life you're growing into together.

***Laugh it off.*** The bad feelings of new parenthood are not the end of the world, they're going to pass. Laughter is a healing tonic. Instead of blowing your stack, laugh at it all. Sometimes you can't laugh until things get so bad that they reach the point of wonderful absurdity—only then can you have the perspective to laugh instead of developing an ulcer and frown lines.

Often the issues that get new parents crazy are the

silliest little things. A sinkful of dirty dishes can seem like valid grounds for divorce . . . unless you can laugh. When the dog trips you, spilling the full pail of dirty diapers so you fall in them . . . you'd better learn to laugh or your fury could land you in the loony-bin!

# 11

# Outside relationships

When you become parents you have new concerns and alliances and you make new bonds. When the two of you become a threesome it will alter your friendships and associations, as may have happened when you went from being single to being a couple.

Your interests will change because of this third tiny person you're identified with, who will interact differently in the community. Suddenly you may find yourselves involved in churches, schools, and play groups with other new parents. The common experience of being parents develops new friendships. It will also probably change, or in some cases end, your relationships with childless people.

*The baby's arrival impacts on all your relationships.* Every person who has an emotional stake in your baby needs a chance to adjust and find their way in your new life. Your expectations may be disappointed in some cases, but keep this in mind: some people in your life may feel disappointed in you, too!

*The birth is the first biological link between you.* The baby represents the first blood tie between his parents' families. There can be conflict and ambivalence about this amongst family members. If you have a strong loyalty and attachment to your own family it may be harder to accommodate the needs and feelings of your partner's relatives. (See more on this in the section in this chapter on Grandparents.)

***Do you expect help and support?*** Do not formulate too many preconceived notions about how people are going to interact with you after the baby is born. People's help is not going to come exactly the way you expect it; it may not come at all. You'll probably be hurt, angry, or disappointed by various people in your life: don't try to repress those feelings. Talk about your disappointment to someone who can understand. You have to be realistic about what outsiders can contribute to your new family unit.

***Ask for help and involvement.*** You'd be surprised how many people might want to be involved with you and the baby but they may be afraid to intrude or be pushy. There are people who would be delighted to be part of your new life if you asked them. Telling people how much you need or want them can benefit both of you. In this day and age of the isolated nuclear family, friends and relatives need encouragement.

***Friends see you differently now.*** You may feel abandoned, and as though friends have stopped caring, but they're really just viewing you in a new light. People treat you as though you've crossed over into another world— parenthood—where you don't count as an individual any more. It may seem that some friends ignore you as individuals now that you are parents. All the attention focuses on the baby.

Women seem to suffer especially from losing their social identity aside from motherhood. You may be looking forward to seeing a friend: you're exhausted, confused, and hungry for adult interaction. But the only question you're asked any more is "How's the baby?" Your closest friends and relatives seem to have forgotten that you have needs and feelings, too.

Male friends may be more apt to view a woman only as a mother now. You may feel as though you're considered no more than a caretaker and spokesperson for the infant.

A new father can feel just the opposite: he isn't perceived as having a fathering identity so no one asks about that part of his life. This may be particularly true if your friends haven't married or had children: they'll be less in tune with the life change you've gone through.

## ADVICE AND CRITICISM

*There's a difference between advice and criticism.* Advice is a suggestion which can be refused without any consequences. Criticism, on the other hand, can be negative or positive. Positive (or constructive) criticism is directed at helping another person to achieve his/her potential. Negative criticism implies that a person is bad or wrong and should change what s/he is doing. That change will often benefit the person who is criticizing.

You can often tell the difference between advice and criticism by the tone of the voice and choice of words that are used. For example, if your mother-in-law says, "You don't mean you're actually going to take that baby outdoors without a sweater?" this can be quite different than if she says, "How about taking a sweater along?"

*How to dress the baby is a big issue.* The baby's clothing is often a target for advice or criticism. People seem to have comments about whether the baby is going to be cold or hot. Even strangers on the street feel entitled to say that your child should be wearing a hat. A good rule of thumb is that if you are comfortable, the baby will be. Many pediatricians suggest that a child should have on as many layers as you do. Try not to get angry at meddlers in your child's sartorial choices: the people are usually trying to be nice.

*Don't listen to most advice.* The very act of giving advice operates on the assumption that all children are the same, or are consistent. When someone gives you an opinion, it's only based on their own experience. In fact, each baby has his own habits and preferences about how he's handled, when he's fed, how he plays, etc. You need to be open to his individual personality, and tuned in to his changing moods and needs.

Simultaneously, your baby is learning who you are

and how you function—the style of your care, your moods, your rhythm. A wonderful thing about parenting is that you can be yourself: you don't have to be perfect. Your baby will come to know you and accept you as you are. He's not going to care if his father mismatches his socks, forgets to powder his bottom, or his mother gives him three baths one day and none the next. Ignore what people tell you to do and break any "rules" that don't feel right to you; if something works for you, do it. Have fun and love your baby in your own way.

***Trust your instincts.*** There was a time, not so very long ago, when women raised their children without building a home library of books and taking classes and seminars in child rearing! Professional advice of all kinds (this book included) can undermine your common sense and your faith in yourself and your mate.

You can raise your child just fine, without anybody's interference. If you listen to advice and criticism it can breed confusion and insecurity. Outsiders may mean well but they can do you harm, if you let them. Listen to your gut instincts; develop trust in your own intuition.

***Trust your instincts about your marriage, too.*** Don't let other people interfere in your relationship. Their observations and advice are tainted by whatever they have experienced. Even well-meaning outsiders can stir you up or steer you wrong, intensifying the problem.

It's a question of not being mentally lazy. If you open your eyes and ears you can figure out your spouse's behavior; you can understand your own moods, fears, and doubts. In many cases, couples wouldn't need a counselor if they would pay attention, if they'd really listen to their partner and their own inner voice.

***Relatives may criticize your parenting.*** Your family (or your mate's) may not approve of your philosophies about child rearing or even the way you handle the baby. Remind yourself **and them** that no one style of child raising is "right." Your partner's family may have a different style and ideas but that doesn't make them wrong. Your child can benefit from experiencing and learning from many different people.

***Try not to react to advice by being defensive.***   There are various ways to handle criticism from each other and outsiders, but you should avoid defensiveness. You should also resist the impulse to put down the person who's made the comment. What if they turn out to be right? If you have a problem like a colicky or sleepless baby, people will be eager to help. But if you reject their advice and then (in desperation one night) try it and it works—well, laugh and admit it! It's a lot easier to do if you weren't defensive or haughty when the suggestion was made.

When grandparents or strangers on the street want to put in their 2 cents' worth, don't rebuff them. That will just create tension: they'll get in a huff and say, "You know what's best, I suppose!" Don't get drawn into a contest. They mean well and should be politely dismissed with a comment like "Thanks for your thoughts."

***You must stay united as parents.***   Don't allow yourselves to be divided by outside interference. Don't let other people bait you into disagreeing with each other; stay loyal to each other and discuss your differences privately. Your relationship as parents must always be protected from outsiders. There will be trouble ahead if you allow yourselves to turn against each other.

You can undermine yourselves without realizing it if one of you makes the primary bond with the child instead of with each other. The following issues are the areas to be careful about: when one parent joins against the other through the grandparents; or when one joins with the child against the other; or when the grandparents side with the child against the parents, or with one parent against the other.

## PROBLEMS WITH CHILDLESS FRIENDS

***You may lose touch with childless friends.***   You may find that there's a different quality to your friendship when you see friends who don't have children. You may find it hard to communicate because you're afraid of sounding like a stereotypical new parent who talks only about the baby: you may be self-conscious about boring them. It may seem to you as though this is a natural parting of the ways and that you have to move on in your life to other relationships. This isn't necessarily true.

***Try to maintain those nonparent friends.*** You share a history with your old friends and it's important to keep in touch with that sense of where you've come from and who you were before you were a parent. New friends with children see you as a blank slate before you had a child; it's important that you don't slide into viewing yourself that way. It's crucial for your identity and your marriage to keep a perspective on who you are besides being a parent.

***Take the risk of boring your childless friends.*** You'll have to make an effort to close the gap between parents and nonparents, but you may find that your friends will be interested in your problems or amused by your anecdotes. You aren't going to accomplish anything by avoiding the subject because you're afraid of being boring; if you don't talk about your baby you are cutting off a major portion of your life.

If you try not to say anything to childless friends about the baby, it can also make you feel detached from your experience as a parent. You are devaluing the importance of your new role if you try to deny it. Describing your personal experiences in adjusting to parenthood is a way to understand feelings and release tension. Sharing your experiences with friends is a way to feel close to them.

You may be afraid of being misunderstood or judged if you admit your complaints about parenthood to friends who haven't experienced parenting. It's one thing to bore someone with stories of your infant's brilliance and descriptions of your overpowering love for the baby. But it's quite another thing to discuss the boredom, fears, anxieties, and other negative reactions to parenthood. You can put up a front and deny your confusion and feelings of inadequacy. But in order for your friends to understand your true experience and remain genuinely close to you, you have to take the risk of being open and honest.

*These friends expect you to "get back to normal."*
They're waiting for you to get back to normal—meanwhile, you're looking for one free hour for yourself! The "normal" that they are referring to doesn't exist for you any more. You should talk about that.

*Some childless friends will enjoy your baby.* You may have friends who aren't ready for a child of their own or can't have one, but they are eager to interact with your baby. These friends can live vicariously through you, enjoying your pleasure at being parents and experiencing the delights of a newborn. Your new life may influence other friends to think about starting a family themselves.

*Jealous friends may cut you off.* Some childless friends may wish they were in a position to have a child and are so envious of you that it interferes with your relationship. Some friends who cannot have children of their own may find it's too painful to stay close to you. They may realize this consciously and be able to talk about it rationally, or they may be so caught up in their envy that they aren't aware of it. No matter how sad it may seem to lose certain friendships, it's often better to let them go than to try and force it.

*Nonparent friends are going to have to adjust.* There are accommodations friends have to make to your new life if you're going to maintain a friendship. Something that can be hard for childless people to understand is that they can't have your undivided attention any more. They're going to have to learn that with a child around, conversations are going to be stop-and-go, like rush-hour traffic—for a few years! Many conversations are going to be interrupted by the baby's crying or feeding; then the adult conversation can resume. You can explain this to friends, but you don't have to feel guilty and apologize for it. This is what real life is like with a baby and there's nothing anyone can do to change it.

*You may lose friends who don't want to adjust.* When you gain a baby you may lose some friends. There are people who won't be sympathetic toward babies or aren't interested in parents who are focused on their baby—namely, you. There may be smokers who are insulted by your request not to smoke around the baby—insulted enough to not want to be around you at all!

## MAKING NEW FRIENDS WITH OTHER PARENTS

You may find that you restructure some friendships in your life now that you're parents. You will probably gravitate toward expectant couples or those with little children.

*You need to share your experience.* At different points in our lives we seek out companions who are going through a similar stage, who have preoccupying interests in common with us. You don't want to just **tell** a friend what you're feeling, you'd like to **share** the experience. If you feel isolated or cut off from contact with sympathetic adults, it can lead to depression.

*Make friends with other new mothers.* It will take courage and effort to start conversations with strangers pushing prams at the playground or walking in your neighborhood. But you have an enormous need for contact with your peers, especially if you're a full-time mother at home. The need to commiserate, to share, to compare notes, is very important—and you don't have to worry about being boring! If you can't make contact in your neighborhood, then talk on the phone to friends and new mothers with whom you feel a bond.

You may be reluctant to reach out to other mothers if you have doubts about yourself as a mother—if you feel inadequate or incompetent. This can be a problem especially if you have a colicky baby that you cannot soothe. You may think that other mothers will judge you as harshly as you judge yourself—but you'll undoubtedly find that every parent has areas of self-doubt. You'll also discover that the best way to overcome these feelings is to "air them and compare them." It's always a delightful surprise to find that you're not the only one.

***New fathers need peer companionship, too.*** The isolation of new parenthood is a nightmare that women are cautioned about, and many new fathers also suffer from being cut off. Most men have nowhere to meet other men adjusting to fatherhood, yet they need a way to share their feelings and insights about their new life. Although a man may be critical of his wife's postpartum support group, he may actually be envious. He has a need to share ideas with other parents, too, but most of these groups don't seem to attract men.

Both parents need people to talk to and hang out with besides each other if they want to stay sane. It's too much to ask of a couple that they survive emotionally all alone, without other supportive relationships. A new father has to recognize his emotional needs and do whatever he can to seek out other men who can relate to his experience.

## ENTERTAINING

***Having friends over is not so simple any more.*** In the first months, when you're adjusting to the baby, entertaining can be an added burden on you and your relationship. Even the most informal entertaining takes time, energy, and money. Talk with your mate about your social life: think through why you want to have people over. Is it something you've done in the past and are continuing out of habit? Is it something you think you "should" do? Is the pleasure of entertaining worth the effort, at this point in your life?

***Choose your guests carefully.*** Think about your friends' personalities and attitudes before you include them in your early postpartum attempts at entertaining. You don't want to invite people you feel you have to impress or want to repay for a past invitation. You also want to avoid demanding guests, who are uptight or inflexible. There's a chance that one of you will be absent for the first hour of the evening (if the baby is hard to settle down). You don't need the additional pressure of guests tapping their feet impatiently.

If you're going to have people over, you need relaxed friends who can even bring part of the meal with them and will help clean up. You may have to learn to ask for their assistance, if you didn't previously accept kitchen helpers. This may mean a new style of entertaining for you, at least for a while.

**Have fair expectations for yourselves and guests.** Don't have unreasonably high expectations for yourself as a hostess now that you're a mother. It's okay if some of what you serve is prepared food, or if you have people over at nonmealtimes. And don't expect the evening to run smoothly: be flexible, because you can't dictate how the evening will progress. You are trying something new with the uncontrollable elements that the baby adds.

Don't expect *too* much from your guests, either. Don't expect them to want to spend the entire visit bouncing your baby on their knee! No matter how politely and sincerely they may praise your child, keep in mind that they have hectic lives, too, and are coming to your house for a social visit. They may have children of their own and were looking forward to a child-free evening.

**Don't underestimate the time entertaining takes.** It isn't just the food preparation, you also have to do the shopping and you'll probably feel you have to tidy up the house. Try to look ahead and decide whether you're going to resent doing those things. Ask yourself whether you'll be so tired from preparing for the guests that you won't be able to enjoy their company? One solution for this is to ask one of the people you've invited to come early and help you get ready.

**Your time is limited: consider entertaining options.** You may want to socialize with your friends at nonmealtimes because you have so little time as new parents. You may see less of people, at least temporarily, so that you can spend your free time together. But if you don't want to cut yourself off from your friends, you may want to limit how much time you do spend with them.

If you decide to see people for dinner, you might want to tell them ahead of time that you can't make it a late night and that you have to be in bed by 10 o'clock, for example. You also shouldn't feel embarrassed to "call it a night'' when you have people over. It's okay to say, ''We're bushed, so we're kicking you out.''

You can also invite people over for tea on the weekend, and specify 4 to 5:30 pm. Or you can invite them for dessert and coffee from 9 to 10:30 at night. At least you'll be able to stay in touch with friends and relatives without the strain of an entire evening or full meal.

***Entertaining is expensive.*** Even if you are a thrifty and inventive cook, having people over always costs more than you realize. There's liquor and wine, flowers, and if you don't already have household help you may want to hire a baby-sitter. In any case, don't spend money for entertaining right now if your finances are tight. Limit your goals and do the best you can within the framework of your bank balance. If Sunday afternoon pizza and beer is what's comfortable financially for you, then be content with that. True friends will be happy with cheese and crackers because what they really want is a chance to see you.

***Entertaining has an effect on the baby.*** Guests may excite the child, both the strangers handling her and the noise level in the house. The baby may have trouble falling asleep: play soft music in her room to blot out the noise of the guests. For your own sake and the baby's, do not keep her up past her usual bedtime. Guests can see her another time, but it's unfair to her to disrupt her schedule.

If you don't have household help and don't hire a baby-sitter, you and your spouse should decide ahead of time which of you will tend to the baby if she cries. It isn't particularly relaxing for your guests if they have to watch you negotiate over whose ''turn'' it is while the baby wails. You might decide that whichever parent isn't cooking and/ or serving will be on duty, and then after dinner the other parent can take over.

# THE PEDIATRICIAN

***A pediatrician should treat you as an equal.*** Your relationship with the pediatrician is important because it affects the way you feel about yourselves as parents. Ideally, you should be partners with the doctor in your baby's care. However, new parents are vulnerable and their egos are fragile. It's normal to feel confused, frightened, or unequal to the task of caring for your child. You have to overcome those feelings in order to become a full partner with your child's doctor.

It's the pediatrician who sets the tone for your interaction: s/he can either inform and support you or can be patronizing. Unfortunately, many doctors have low opinions of women and have no confidence in their natural mothering abilities (doctors with this attitude will not expect a father to know anything, either). The truth is that good parenting is a combination of common sense and good instincts, but you need encouragement. If you sense that a doctor is being scornful of your parenting (or has contempt for your doubts about yourself) it will increase your insecurities, which is the last thing you need at this time. Ask your friends for references to a more supportive pediatrician.

***Learn how to make effective calls to the doctor.*** If at all possible, both of you should have the experience of calling the doctor and also taking the baby in for checkups. When either of you does call the doctor, it's a good idea to take your child's temperature first and write down any symptoms the baby may have so that you won't forget or get rattled on the phone.

***You should choose a pediatrician together.*** Both parents should have a relationship with the doctor. That means that both of you have to agree on the choice of pediatrician and feel comfortable with his/her approach and style. Before you meet with doctors, you should agree as a couple on the issues that matter to you; only then should you make appointments to meet with potential doctors for your child.

Make a list of questions, using the chart that follows for ideas. Use your time wisely; if you pick a doctor carefully, it is a relationship that can sustain you and your child through his growing years. You don't have to feel apologetic about quizzing a doctor, nor do you have to be on the defensive or be aggressive, either. Doctors are used to these kind of interviews. You don't have to prove anything. You certainly don't have to feel self-conscious and worry what

---

### QUESTIONNAIRE FOR CHOOSING A PEDIATRICIAN

- Does the office appeal to you in the way it's organized, the cleanliness, play area? (If you interview a doctor after office hours, return to see it at full steam)
- Does the staff seem likable?
- Are appointments individual or "block" (a group of patients booked at the same time and seen on a "first-come" basis)
- Is there a long wait? (It's hard to judge promptness since each day is different depending on emergencies, etc.) An hour is the absolute maximum you should ever have to wait.
- Is there information available on parent and play groups, etc.?
- What telephone service is available? Are there set hours each day when you can call in?
- Does s/he have a partner? If so, you have to feel comfortable with that doctor, too.
- Does s/he make house calls in emergencies?
- What is the doctor's hospital affiliation? What are that hospital's rules about parents staying overnight, being present for all exams, etc.?
- Discuss financial arrangements up front (including asking on the phone whether s/he charges for the interview time).

---

he or she will think of you. Regardless of how intense/neurotic/anxious/compulsive you are, the doctor is sure to have gone through it before.


## THE BABY'S SIBLINGS

Other children at home are part of the stress you have to deal with when you have a new baby. In this section I will refer to the older child as though there is only one, although of course you may have more than one, with stepchildren, etc.

***There are general reactions that are common for most children of any age.*** An older child fears the possibility of having to give up his place in the family to the baby. He may also resent the little intruder and have fantasies of getting rid of her and be angry at you for producing her.

Put yourself in the older child's place for a moment and you'll realize that these concerns are realistic: you might have the same feelings. The sibling is no longer the center of attention, especially in the early months when the newborn demands so much of your time.

***You shouldn't feel sorry for the sibling.*** There is no reason to feel sorry for him; if you do, it can create more rivalry and anxiety for him. If you are on the defensive or feel guilty about the time you're spending with the new baby, that makes the older child think that something is wrong. This is especially true if your other child is young. A small child looks to his parents for reassurance that the new baby isn't going to affect his life or his parents' love for him.

***Your feelings toward the older child may change.*** You may expect jealousy from the baby's sibling, but you probably won't be prepared for your own unfavorable feelings toward the older child. You may be surprised that you feel angry at the older child for the way he acts out his feelings. This may be the first time that you have ambivalent feelings toward the older child, and that can be upsetting. You may have no patience or respect for the sibling's tactics.

If either of you has negative feelings toward the sibling it can create problems between you as a couple. If your mate is the one who's aggravated or impatient with the sibling, it can make you angry or disappointed in your partner. It has also happened that an older child has "teamed up" with his father, against his mother, because they feel left out of the mother's closeness with the baby. Their "ganging up" can make a woman feel unloving toward the older child and her husband.

***Traumatic rivalry between kids can be reduced.*** Sibling rivalry is not necessarily inherent to children; it can be a function of whether caring adults are available to them. Parents unknowingly turn away from the older child because the newborn is helpless and needs time and attention. Your other child still needs the same love and care he did before the baby was born. It's also common for parents to have unreasonable expectations of adult maturity from a sibling who is still a youngster.

Also, the number of years between children can mean less problems. Some experts suggest that you have a minimum of three years between children to reduce rivalry between them. Spacing children is less of a burden on you, too.

***The first child may regress.*** Older siblings often revert to babyish behavior: the newborn's crying and screaming "works" to get attention from you, so the older one tries it. Some children, who gave up the bottle long ago, may suddenly demand a "baba" or blanket. Some child development experts say that these regressions are an attempt to control you as parents. They suggest that if you don't respond, the older child will drop his babyish behavior.

Other experts say that a sibling acts like a baby to get your attention from fear that the infant is going to usurp his role in your life. Although you may find his regressive behavior obnoxious or annoying, you should not say things like "Act your age, there's only one baby in this house." That can increase the sibling's fears that he is being replaced.

The sibling is testing your love, says another group of experts. They theorize that what the child wants from you is what the baby is getting. If you sing lullabies to the older sibling or allow him to have a bottle or to get into the crib, that may be the support he needs to work it through. You know your own child well enough to decide what approach you should take with him.

## SUGGESTIONS FOR HELPING SIBLINGS ADJUST

***Make an effort to show your affection.***    Special loving attention from you is going to make the transition much easier for the older child. Also, if he is regressing to babyish tactics, your attention will probably mean he will return to behavior that's appropriate for his age.

***Give the sibling special tasks.***    You can make the older child feel involved in the new family group if you give him special assigned responsibilities. It's good for her to feel she is important in the daily working of the family. Give her every opportunity to do as much as possible with infant care, even if it's only picking out the baby's clothes or choosing toys.

***Set aside special times for the sibling.***    You need intimate, exclusive time with the older child, even if that means getting a sitter for the baby every so often. In order to find out how the other child is feeling and what's going on in her mind, you have to spend the time and ask her, if she's old enough to articulate. If she's still too young to communicate verbally, then use the special time to make her the center of your attention.

***Explain your moods to the older child.***    Being the parent of a newborn is an exhausting, demanding task. It means there will be times when you are exhausted, burned out, or just plain crabby. It is so important to explain this to the older child: tell her that you are tired and cranky but that your moods **are not her fault**. Repeat this so that the sibling doesn't feel at fault.

***Give the sibling the right to express his feelings.***
Just as you should feel comfortable saying what's in your heart, so should your child have the same right to say what's on his mind. There are difficult topics and negative feelings that are part of the adjustment the whole family has to make to the newcomer. If you censor your older child and don't allow him to be open and honest, it shuts down communication. Once you've done that, misunderstandings and bad feelings are bound to occur.

# GRANDPARENTS

***The baby changes everything.***   With the arrival of your baby there is suddenly a blood tie between you and your in-laws: you go from being the "outsider" who married in, to being a blood relation through the baby. In most cases this brings the baby's parents and grandparents closer together, which can be joyous or stressful, depending on your circumstances. It is a complicated transition because there are several adults involved; it's important for each of you to understand what the others are experiencing in this momentous change of roles.

***"All is forgiven" is a common reaction.***   If you have had a bad relationship with your parents or in-laws, this is the time to heal the rift. It's common that grandparents who were previously opposed to your marriage, lifestyle, etc., may suddenly become more accepting. The baby means a continuation of the family line and that overcomes a lot of petty disagreements.

A baby's birth or imminent arrival is a natural time to mend your relationship with the grandparents. Don't make a big deal of it: just make peace and move forward. You and your spouse may have to make the first move, or be more tolerant and forgiving about the past.

***How much power do the grandparents have now?***
You may not be aware of it, but one set of grandparents or the other may have substantial control or power over you that will come to the surface when the baby joins the family.

Not all power is financial, of course, but ask yourselves some basic questions to determine how much power the grandparents do have in your lives. Do you accept gifts or loans of money? Are both of you comfortable with the arrangement? Your financial dependence may give them some control over you—even if it's only in **your** minds.

***The expectant grandmother can be overpowering.***
Your mother or mother-in-law may try to take control of events and decisions in the evolving family. She may try to

side with the new mother, unconsciously gaining control
by turning her away from her husband.

A domineering grandmother may have a field day if
her son or son-in-law turns to her during this stressful time!
The new father may turn to his mother for extra attention
because of the pressures on him to be a strong, responsible
adult. Be aware of your own frailties during this transition
to parenthood so that neither of you plays into the hands
of an overpowering grandmother.

***Don't let the grandparents divide you.***   There are already many forces pulling you apart as you become parents,
at a time when you most need each other. You have to
decide together what role you want the grandparents to
play in your life and what approach you will take to let
them know your feelings and needs as a couple. Then stand
firmly together: decisions about your family are yours to
make. In order to keep the grandparents at arm's length
you'll need a united front against any disruptive input.

***There will probably be more contact between the
families.***   There will be more telephone calls and visits
with the grandparents than before. They'll probably want
to tell you and your spouse stories about you as infants,
which can be an enjoyable way to see how everything
comes full circle in life.

You and your mate are going to have to cope with
these interfamily changes together. Make sure that the increased contact is comfortable for both of you; if it is not,
try to be tactful about it. You can't just tell your spouse
that his/her well-meaning parents are driving you crazy! If
the grandparents try to interfere in your new life, you have
to control the situation together. But keep in mind that you
are dealing with deep, complicated relationships.

***You have to set limits on grandparent involvement.***
You two have to determine together how much you want
the grandparents to participate in the child's upbringing.
You also have to decide how much time you want to spend
with the grandparents. If you feel your privacy is not being
respected—the grandparents just drop in or call to "an-

nounce'' they are coming over—then you'll need to have a family discussion to set some polite limits.

## THE PARENTS' FEELINGS ABOUT THE GRANDPARENTS

***You may understand your parents better now.*** By becoming a parent you are more able to sympathize with your parents and what they went through to raise you. There may be one parent you've always blamed for what is "wrong" with you, or an in-law you've blamed for your spouse's problems. Parenthood teaches you that it's not possible (or even desirable) to meet all of a child's needs. Now that you've been a child **and** a parent you gain a different perspective.

This new understanding may help to heal real or imagined wounds from your childhood that you've been carrying around all these years. Empathy with a parent you've had resentment toward can free your positive feelings, not just toward that person but by relieving you of the burden of that hostility. A baby can be a chance for you and the grandparent to rediscover each other, or an opportunity to discover your in-law(s) for the first time.

***Grandparents are only human.*** They have faults and weaknesses just like you do. You can come to terms with your parents and in-laws once you accept them as fellow human beings. If you put them on a pedestal they don't have a chance to be themselves.

***Have realistic expectations of the grandmother(s).*** Just because she raised you (or your mate) doesn't mean she is going to be Mary Poppins with your baby! Your mother (or mother-in-law) probably hasn't been around an infant for 25 or 35 years. How can you expect her to know how to diaper the baby? She can't even find the sticky tab because they used pins in the "olden days"! And don't imagine that just because she was once the mother of a baby, she has some kind of magical touch. Your baby's colic, sleeplessness, or incessant crying cannot be "cured" by anyone.

***Evaluating your parents is a part of parenthood.*** Looking at your parents in a new way is a normal reaction to first-time parenthood. This evaluation can change your feelings and the relationship itself; it can rekindle old feuds or rebuild old bonds between you. Looking objectively at your parents, perhaps for the first time, is part of the process of differentiating yourself from the baby's grandparents and becoming a parent yourself.

***Your perception of your mother will change.*** You may have spent your life making assumptions about your mother, judging her or holding grudges against her. (This holds true for your father, too, in some cases.) You may have thought she was weak or selfish or cold or passive or harsh. Now that you can see pressures of child care for yourself, your vision of your mother will change.

***Beware of trying to be perfect for your parents.*** It is not unusual for new parents to try to put on a perfect show for the baby's grandparents. You may find yourself trying to clean the house compulsively and have everything flawless . . . only to find that your mother or in-law still finds something to criticize! The point is, it's a losing battle anyway. If you expect yourself, your spouse, or your child to conform to the grandparents' standards of behavior or way of life, you're in a no-win position.

Some new parents revert to old childlike patterns for the grandparents—and the spouse pays the price for this futile attempt to please "Mommy." For example, if you find that a grandparent is interfering, you may suggest that s/he back off. But your mate, who will do anything to protect his/her parent at this point, will come to the grandparent's defense. If your spouse feels this way, s/he won't join you in feeling intruded upon or bossed around by the grandparent.

Try to be patient, with the hope that your spouse will calm down and stop trying so hard. When s/he is in a listening mood (definitely *not* when the grandparents are around), try to point out that s/he is trying to be perfect in order to get parental love and affirmation. Your mate will probably relax once s/he realizes what is motivating this drive for "perfection."

***Your parents may not treat you as adults.*** Even though you've become parents yourselves, your own parents may still treat you as children. Visiting them at their house can magnify this problem. Don't be angry at the grandparents for this, try to be compassionate. They are trying to find their way in this new set-up, just as you are. Try to rise above your hurt feelings and give the grandparents time to adjust. If you are treated like a child and then respond like one, you are feeding the situation.

There is a potential problem for a couple around this issue. If your spouse's parents are the ones treating you both like children, you may find it so irritating that you think your mate is weak or foolish for putting up with it. Somehow in your frustration you may even blame your spouse for his or her parent's behavior.

***Separation from the grandparents is essential.*** It's vital to making this new transition in your lives that you both are separated emotionally from your own parents. Studies have shown that if either partner is too attached to his or her parents, it can undermine the marriage. If you haven't fully made the separation from your family of origin, it means you'll be unable to commit to your spouse as the most important person in your life. The birth of a baby can make you aware of these issues for the first time.

***You may want your parents to take care of you.*** It's not unusual to feel torn between wanting to be responsible adults and hoping your parents will "make it all better." Some grandparents will treat you as though you're still children, while others see your parenthood as an initiation into adulthood. If you expect your parents (or in-laws) to give you more attention and time than they have in the past, you may be in for a disappointment.

***If your parent(s) are dead, the baby can rekindle your grief.*** If either (or both) of your parents is dead, you should be aware that the birth of your baby can be a sad time for you. You'll be imagining how much pleasure the child would have given them. You may also fantasize how nice it would be for you if your parent(s) was alive.

***A woman's desire to be mothered increases after childbirth.*** You may find that in the period immediately following your baby's birth you have a strong need for your mother, or to be mothered. This can be an especially strong feeling if your mother is dead, or if you feel you were not sufficiently mothered as a child.

There's no reason to be afraid of this feeling, or to be embarrassed by it. Needing your Mom doesn't mean that you are regressing or giving up your independence or your separate identity. There is no reason not to indulge your impulse to ask your mother for her help and advice.

***A baby can propel you toward your mother.*** This can be either a pleasant or uncomfortable propulsion! You may find that one aspect of gaining self-confidence as a mother is that you yearn for closeness with your own mother. If you haven't had an easy relationship with your mother, this may mean a reconciliation or even an **unpleasant** intimacy. Your closeness may come through arguments and conflicts, if that happens to be how you interact. The baby can give both of you a whole new arena for having disagreements or feeling angry, rejected, competitive, or deprived.

However, there is often a new bond of understanding that develops between you and your mother now that you've shared the common experience of motherhood. You may have felt an emotional distance from your parents that started in adolescence or early adulthood and was never really repaired. Often the baby can wipe out that distance because you realize that your mother and father are not that different from you and your spouse. Your parents were two people who did their best to handle the pressures and demands of a totally dependent infant.

***You may want to be closer to your mother.*** Most new mothers are eager for their Mom to love the new baby, but for some women this comes from a craving to make peace (if there has been friction in the past) and be connected. You may want your mother to be enthusiastic about the baby because you identify with the infant. You may not realize this consciously, but you feel that if your mother shows love to the baby, she is loving you, too. If the grandparents are lukewarm toward the baby, this lack of effusiveness can feel like a rejection of you.

***Some women withdraw from their mothers.*** There are a variety of reasons why you might pull away from your mother when the baby arrives. You may feel too much rivalry with her, about issues like who is the "best mother." It isn't that unusual for a new mother to want to prove that she can be a better parent than her mother was.

You may have dreadful memories of your childhood and the way you were mothered so that you want to keep your child away from her grandparents. Your image of yourself as a mother is influenced by these powerful ties to your past and your parents. Once you're able to recognize and resolve these conflicts, you will be free to be the best mother that you can possibly be.

***You want your mother's (and father's) benediction.*** You may hope that the grandparents will be ecstatic about the baby and share your joy. A baby can create a bond between the older generations that never existed before. There is no one who can love and admire your child—and compliment you on how wonderfully you are raising her—the way a grandparent can. You may feel as though your baby is an achievement that your parents are applauding.

But it's useful to remember that parent/child relationships remain complicated right through adulthood. Some new parents may feel jealous, for instance, if the grandparents show a great deal of love to the infant. The new parents may crave this parental love for themselves. Other parents may feel they've been the center of attention for too long and are only too glad to have the grandparents riveted on the baby for a change.

***Reach out to the grandparents.*** Let them know you need them and want them in the baby's life and your own. If grandparents feel that they matter, that they're needed, they'll probably also lighten up on criticism and disapproval. Although becoming grandparents is joyous, it is also a sign that they are aging, so you have to make them feel special.

All of you lose out if you don't welcome the grandparents' insight and experience. You may be surprised to find that they have talents and skills you didn't know about or took for granted until now. By drawing the grandparents into your family circle you make a warm bond among you, the people who love your baby the most.

## THE GRANDPARENTS' FEELINGS

***What else is going on in their lives?*** It might help your attitude to the grandparents if you stop to consider where they are in their lives when the baby arrives. Are they retired or considering it? Do they have financial problems? Have the grandmothers already gone through menopause? Have they recently had a friend or relative who died? Do they still have any children at home? All of these issues, and more, will influence how they treat you as new parents and the interest they'll show the baby.

***Grandparents have needs, too.*** They have to grow into their new role, and they are going to have growing pains just as you will becoming a parent. It's easy to get wrapped up in your own feelings and forget that the grandparents have their own accounts to settle. You may be angry or disappointed if they're aloof. You may even feel jealous if they are intensely wrapped up in the baby (did they love *you* that much as a child?). Keep in mind that you aren't the only ones with feelings and needs. Your parents and in-laws have complex needs now, too.

***Grandparents can feel an "empty nest" syndrome.*** It can be hard for the grandparents to accept that you are adults with your own child now. They may try to reassert parental control over you through the baby by criticizing, being bossy, and so on. They aren't acting from malice, but because of fear and anxiety. Grandparents often feel isolated and lonely. Try to make them feel important in the baby's life, while maintaining the level of control over your life that you want as a couple.

***Grandparents may resent losing their child.*** When a grandparent gains a grandchild, he or she may get angry because they "lose" their son or daughter in the process. Your parenthood may mean to them that you are no longer a child . . . and thus no longer theirs. A grandmother can be angry or jealous of her daughter-in-law for making her son into a father, which takes him out from under his "mother-hen's" wing.

A grandfather might want to "take back" his daughter from his son-in-law and "protect" Daddy's little girl. As part of the confusing, deep-seated feelings that grandparents experience, they may perceive that their son-in-law has "knocked up" their daughter (his wife, that is!). On a subconscious level, the pregnancy and baby's birth may be the first time that a woman's parents accept the fact that their son-in-law is having intercourse with their daughter.

*A baby can make grandparents feel old.* The beginning of a new life is beautiful, but it is also a reminder to them that they are heading for the downhill side of their lives. If your child is the first grandchild, then this is the moment when most grandparents realize that they may have already lived more years than they have left ahead of them. These are sobering realizations: be sensitive to these possibilities.

*Some grandparents aren't interested in the baby.* Don't take this as an insult. Even grandparents who live nearby may not spend much time with the baby because they have busy lives of their own. Or they may feel uncomfortable around an infant. Try to respect their lifestyle and feelings. Don't be put off by their disinterest; continue to make them feel welcome and some day they may start to come around more.

Your baby may not be the first grandchild, which means they've been through this before and the novelty has worn off. Or the grandparents may be disappointed because they have previous grandchildren and yours isn't the sex they had hoped for.

*How involved will the grandparents be?* You may have to change your expectations of the grandparents' involvement after the baby arrives. Are you expecting advice, support, baby-sitting, and/or infant-care lessons? You probably haven't given any thought to what the **grandparents** are expecting! You'd better **ask** them how involved they'd like to be, or there can be misunderstandings. They may not know how to say, "No thanks," so make it comfortable for them.

*Grandparents need private time with the baby.* Your wishes as parents have to be respected, but the grandparents also need room to develop their own relationship with the baby. They can't always have you breathing down their necks. Their private time can take place at your house or theirs, as long as you don't intrude. But if you can't keep yourself from meddling, it might be best to let the grandparents take the baby off on their own.

### CONFLICTS WITH THE GRANDPARENTS

*Grandparents can have unexpected emotional reactions.* Especially if your baby is their first grandchild, the grandparents are sure to have emotional conflicts and some unpredictable responses to the new situation. Some parent-child patterns may change for the better between you after the birth, and others may worsen. Your best protection is to be aware that there's a potential for problems.

*Do the grandparents live nearby?* This can be a treat for all of you, but it can also be a problem if you feel hurt that they don't visit enough, or angry that they're around too much. If grandparents develop the habit of just dropping in, it robs you of your privacy, which is essential to any couple. But if they avoid you in deference to your privacy, then you also have a problem.

Grandparents usually just want to please, but they can't read your mind or understand your rhythms. Discuss your feelings with the grandparents and tell them what plans you have and how you'd like them to fit into your life. Ask them to call before coming, or invite them for specific times, and everyone will feel easier.

*Are you going to have a grandparent stay with you?* If one or more of the grandparents is planning to come stay with you in the immediate postpartum period, there are several things you might consider to minimize conflict. On paper, it may sound so cozy—Grandma coming to help with the new baby. But in real life there can be serious problems.

A grandparent moving in can create conflict unless you're used to spending a great deal of time together. Both of you need to sit down with the grandparent who's coming to stay and have an open discussion before the baby is born. What are your hopes and fears? How do you imagine the division of work, the rhythm of nights and days?

**Be specific** about the help you think you're going to need from the grandparent. Otherwise a grandparent may become another burden on you: a sort of house guest who's come to enjoy the baby. A new mother needs a lot of help with mundane tasks around the house, especially if you've had a cesarean birth. There is cooking, cleaning, and taking charge of telephone calls and visits so that you can protect your energy and privacy in the early days. A grandmother may only be thinking in terms of help or advice about baby care, so you'd better talk this out ahead of time.

*Asking the grandparents to baby-sit can be problematic.* First of all, realize that there will always be some conflicts between parents and their grown children. When you throw the children's children into the equation, the stakes are raised. Then there are issues you'll have to decide for yourselves: Whether to pay or not? How often to ask without taking advantage?

If you are going to have a grandparent baby-sit, both parents must have no misgivings about leaving the child, especially if you have any doubts about the grandparent's attitudes.

*If the arrangement doesn't work out, forget it.* Whether it's not working out with a live-in grandparent or one who is baby-sitting, you should all face it. If the plan you made isn't meeting your expectations, there is no reason to tough it out. Sometimes old emotional injuries or personality conflicts are too strong to have the grandparent intimately involved in your child's care. Or there may not be enough room in your house for another person. Or the baby's father may feel excluded from his new family by a strong mother or mother-in-law. Whatever the reason, find a gracious way out of the original agreement you made with the grandparents.

***Be careful not to "favor" one set of grandparents.*** If you spend more time with one set than the other, or ask for more help of any kind, it can create rivalry. If one grandmother comes to stay when the baby is born, the grandmother who didn't come to stay may be miffed. If one set of grandparents lives nearer they will probably develop a closer bond with the baby, which can make the other grandparents envious.

***Friction with grandparents over choices.*** There can be bitter arguments between a mother and grandmother over the smallest aspects of how to take care of the baby. Remind yourself that this isn't a proving ground. You can't prove to your parents that you're an adult by standing up to them and explaining why your way is "right," or trying to debunk their old wives' tales. When the baby's grandmother insists that you do it "her way," sometimes it's easier to just give it a try. You might learn something, and you'll eliminate unnecessary conflict.

***Your lives are very different from your parent's.*** It's difficult to raise children when you're deviating from a pattern set by your parents. (It can be even harder if you don't think there was any set pattern for you to deviate from.) For example, your parents may react to these differences not with direct criticism but by saying (if you're a working mother), "Don't you think you're pushing yourself too much?" or, "Don't you think the child needs you more?"

One enormous difference is the involvement of today's fathers in their children's lives. Your parents may have lived in distant spheres from each other when you were growing up. If you are an involved new father it can seem strange to your father (or father-in-law), who may feel your lifestyle is a rebuke or a rejection of the kind of fathering he gave you. A grandmother may envy a working mother, if she has a close relationship with her husband. If he is also an actively involved father, it can make the grandmother even more jealous.

***By doing things differently, you "challenge" the grandparents.***   It can be hard for the older generation to be open-minded when you want to do something differently: your mother may take that as a criticism of how she did things with you. If you decide to raise your child in a radically different way than you were raised, the grandparents can feel rejected by your decision. If you breast-feed and extol its virtues, that can make your mother wonder if she made a mistake or was a bad mother because she bottle-fed you. If you maintain a career while raising your child, that can make her question whether she wasted 18 years at home raising you.

***Child-rearing conflicts are the main source of friction with the grandparents.***   The main topics of disagreements seem to center around feeding (the grandparents usually want the child fed as you were), followed by the use of pacifiers and spoiling the child. Before you blow your stack because the grandmother insists on feeding cereal to your two-week-old, keep in mind that the grandparents love your baby and want what's best for him.

***You have to make decisions as a couple.***   If there are conflicts with the grandparents over dressing the baby, using a pacifier, taking her outdoors, or other controversial subjects, you have to remain united. Decide with your spouse what your positions are about these issues and make it clear: don't allow these areas to become a battlefield over "right and wrong" with the grandparents. If the two of you are determined to find your own way to be parents, there won't be any room for debate with the grandparents.

***Child-care theories change every generation.***   This evolution can make it difficult for you and the grandparents to understand each other's ideas. Once you can relax and see that beliefs about child rearing seem to change as quickly as women's fashion, it isn't so important to prove a point or be "right"! Also, once you begin to feel confident about your parenting abilities, you won't feel as much need to argue or prove your point with the grandparents (or anyone else).

When the grandparents disagree with you, your first

inclination may be to blurt out your opinion or swallow it in anger. The best thing would be to try to listen to their point of view and then explain your feelings. If you can hold some kind of discussion, all of you will feel less threatened. It's so important that all of you feel that your ideas are at least being taken seriously rather than summarily dismissed.

***Learn to change the subject.*** There's no harm in trying to change the subject if you see a conflict brewing. Instead of frustration and anger, you can also learn not to get hooked in. Try saying, "Maybe you have a point," and then turning the conversation elsewhere. This can be done graciously and subtly without offending the grandparents. This tactic isn't meant to "put them in their place" or shut them up, but rather to avoid an unpleasant and useless disagreement.

***Invite the grandparents into the modern world.*** One way to help grandparents understand today's thinking about child rearing is to educate them about it. You can show them the child development books that you admire, or articles that you read. You can bring them along to a parent group, or invite them over when your friends with children visit, so the grandparents can see other couples your age.

You might want to consider inviting them along to a visit with the pediatrician. This will give them an opportunity to ask questions or air their ideas in a professional setting (but perhaps you should forewarn the doctor that Grandma is going to descend!).

# 12
# Adoptive parenting

## HOW ADOPTIVE PARENTING IS DIFFERENT

*It helps if you acknowledge the differences.* The strain in adjusting to adoptive parenting as individuals and as a couple can be more burdensome if you try to deny the problems. If you try to sail along as though there's no difference between your family and the Joneses next door, you are lying to yourself and your partner. Eventually this lack of honesty can create rifts between you, to say nothing of the effect it can have on your adopted child.

    This does not mean that adoption is less good than biological parenting, just that it is different. Being able to admit those differences and to recognize what they are is part of the special sensitivity and parenting skills that are so important for adoptive parents.

*You'll vacillate between acceptance and denial.* If you're like most adoptive parents, you'll admit to the differences between your family and a biological one, but then there will be times that you'll want to convince yourselves otherwise. One sign of denial can be if you refuse to join an adoptive parents' group.

    Having a foreign-born child, or a child of a race different from yours, forces you to acknowledge the difference in your family because it is always visible. You can't pretend, the way other adoptive parents may sometimes want to. Interestingly, parents of foreign-born children can be more at ease in the long run because they may not experience the anxiety of being tempted to keep a secret.

***Feeling comfortable doesn't happen overnight.*** Don't expect yourselves to feel immediately at ease in the role of adoptive parents. Of course many biological parents don't feel instantly at home in their new roles, either, but you have additional issues to confront. Understanding the many levels on which adoption can affect you and your child, and learning to be comfortable with them, requires time and effort. It's a process that will be ongoing throughout your lifetime. If you and your partner can be open and honest about what this means in your lives, being an adoptive parent can enrich your lives and enhance your relationship.

***There are no guarantees in life.*** Nobody owns their children. Biological parents don't have any greater hold on their children, although as adoptive parents you may fear that you are just "baby-sitting": that the birth mother may reappear or your child may abandon you eventually. How your children will turn out and what your relationship with them will be like is a gamble—for all parents.

Will your child like you as adults when she grows up? Will she have 100% loyalty to your family? Do you feel that if she seeks out her birth parents, it means a rejection of you? These are all imponderables that remain to be seen. The two sets of parents that your child has can create an overlapping loyalty—but so do biological children who have stepparents. The important thing is to be straight with yourselves from the beginning about the differences and difficulties in being an adoptive family: from that fundamental honesty, love and trust can grow.

## ADOPTIVE PARENTING IS MORE DIFFICULT

***Recognize the difficulties.*** Building a family by adoption is not only different from biological parenting, in many ways it is more difficult. All of the issues involved in adoption mean more pressure on you as parents. In addition to all the adjustments that any parent has to make, you have added burdens. You have to prepare for a child that exists only in your imagination and that you may have trouble believing is yours when he finally arrives. You have to develop confidence in yourselves and a belief in your entitlement (see below).

***Your fantasies of parenthood will rarely match the reality.*** This is true for you more so than for biological parents, because they didn't have to jump through so many hoops in order to have a child. You have probably suffered years of infertility, then years of waiting for your baby while being scrutinized as potential parents. All these factors weigh on you, whether you recognize them or not.

***Do you lack a sense of entitlement to your baby?*** Sometimes adoptive parents have a hard time feeling that they are entitled to their baby. They may have difficulty claiming their baby and bonding with her.

Adoptive parents are not prepared culturally for the way they've become parents. Without a role model of other adoptive parents, you may feel unsure as to whether you can fulfill the role of parent adequately. This can make you question whether you "deserve" to have a baby.

***Feeling guilty can interfere with feeling entitled.*** Your sense of entitlement may also be hampered if you had outside help or advantages in finding your child. You may have guilt feelings if you have an above-average income, connections to an influential lawyer or doctor, or had other special assistance in finding a baby. Your feeling of entitlement may be impaired if you have guilt feelings and aren't acknowledging them.

***How can you tell if you lack a sense of entitlement?*** If you have doubts about whether or not you are successfully accepting your baby as your own, the following chart may help you to identify signs of problems in this area.

---

**SIGNS OF PROBLEMS IN FEELING
ENTITLED TO ADOPT**

- Trying to keep the adoption a secret, to the extent of refusing to discuss the adoption with nonfamily members
- Obsessively discussing the adoption, frequently and at inappropriate times
- Prolonged denial of sadness about your inability to be a biological parent
- Obsessively worrying that the child won't share physical similarities with you or measure up to your standards
- Prolonged fears about the birth parents' intelligence and the baby's I.Q.
- Prolonged fantasies about what your biological child might have been like
- Ongoing discomfort about the birth parents, especially a fear of a search
- Prolonged anxiety (that doesn't diminish after preliminary conversations) about discussing adoption later with the child
- Inability to deny the child anything (or to discipline later) for fear s/he won't love you

---

## THE PREPARATION FOR PARENTHOOD

***You may be fearful.*** The impending reality of becoming a parent can be frightening for you. As adoptive parents you may experience an uncomfortable range of emotions (the same as many biological parents do). You may have second thoughts, fears, and self-doubt as a parent. Once he arrives, you may feel yourself retreating emotionally from the baby at the same time that you embrace him. These feelings are normal and will pass as you become more at ease in your new role.

***You may be afraid the adoption won't happen.*** A fear of noncompletion can be counterproductive in preparing for adoption and in making your adjustment to parenthood. There is always the possibility that you won't receive your child, especially in independent adoptions (through lawyers, doctors, or personal advertising). This may mean that you are secretive about your plans and don't want to celebrate when the baby arrives. However, if you indulge your fears rather than trying to overcome them, you are robbing yourself of the preparation and validation process.

***Try to arrange for a parenting class.*** Learning about infant care can be difficult for adoptive parents. Although you may have read some books about child care, you may have postponed learning about it for fear that the baby might not come. If you have not felt support from your families or others close to you, your enthusiasm to familiarize yourself with baby care may have been dampened. There is the danger that if you feel personally inadequate, you may feel inadequate as a parent: the more you know about infant care, the more confident you may feel.

However, you may feel awkward attending Red Cross classes where all the other women have bulging bellies and are discussing their fears of labor. Local adoptive parents' groups (see *Appendix III*) or the infertility organization RESOLVE has nationwide chapters that may offer parenting classes. It's important that you develop as much self-confidence as possible before your baby comes. Otherwise you may be at a disadvantage because you haven't had the opportunity to feel comfortable taking care of an infant.

## GRIEVING FOR YOUR UNBORN BIOLOGICAL CHILD

***You may have unresolved feelings about infertility.*** You probably have feelings to work through about your inability to get pregnant and give birth. Being able to accept your infertility is another aspect of feeling good about yourselves as parents and partners. It's important to go through your own personal grieving process for the loss of your ability (or your spouse's) to procreate. Grief has recognizable stages: denial, depression, anger, and acceptance. Both of you will probably go through this process, but understanding your feelings can make it easier.

*Accepting your infertility can make you a better parent.*   Couples who are able to accept their infertility as bad luck and then get on with their lives often find that this acceptance increases their self-confidence and pleasure as parents. You may find that once you've worked through your feelings, you can then make a full commitment to your baby. Otherwise, your child can be a painful reminder of your infertility rather than a source of joy.

*Expressing your sadness prepares you for parenthood.*   Grieving for the unborn biological child that you cannot have is part of the psychological preparation for adoptive parenthood. Letting go of the child you'll never have biologically, and grieving for it, is an essential part of building a family by adoption. Only then can you make room in your hearts for the child who is coming to you. Recognizing your sorrow during the decision and waiting process in adoption allows you the freedom to bond to your new child; you can feel free to completely love and accept your baby.

*Admit your sadness about not being pregnant.*   Once you realize and admit that it is painful for you to miss the experience of pregnancy and birth, you can go forward with your lives. Sometimes you'll see a pair of baby shoes in a shop window and start to cry—until you can recognize that your sorrow is for the pregnancy you'll never have. But dwelling on this subject is not going to make things any better. Actually, if you dwell on the subject of how much pregnancy would have meant to you, your relationship with an adopted child can hurt your spouse, relatives, etc. Be aware of your feelings and then go forward.

*You may feel guilt about your infertility.*   If one of the partners is the one with the infertility problem, s/he may feel a terrible responsibility. It's common to think, "If only my partner had married someone else, s/he would have a family by now," or, "If it weren't for me, my partner could have a natural child." Carrying guilt feelings can only be harmful: if you cannot talk through your guilt with your partner so that you feel relieved of it, you might want to consider an adoptive parents' group or professional therapy.

***Resentful feelings can be destructive.*** The partner who would otherwise be able to conceive may harbor angry feelings toward the infertile spouse. The fertile partner then probably feels like a heel for having that resentment—which initiates a nasty cycle of emotions. You have to make every effort to encourage each other to be honest and open about feelings so that you can come to terms with them.

This anger can have particular impact if the woman's infertility comes from PID (pelvic inflammatory disease) that she contracted from sexual promiscuity with multiple partners earlier in her life. (Of course, PID can come from IUDs and other causes, so be sure you are well informed about the reasons for your PID.) If this is the cause of a woman's infertility, her husband may have anger that causes overpowering guilt in his wife. You will probably need help from a professional counselor if you find yourselves in this position.

The grief and sadness you feel over being infertile will never leave you completely, but anger and resentment over your failure to conceive can be damaging, particularly after you have adopted. Persistent resentful feelings can affect your relationship with the child and each other. If you have not come to terms with these negative feelings, you may have trouble telling your child that she is adopted. And if a parent cannot admit the facts, then how can anyone expect the child to accept the truth?

## SOME PRACTICAL CONCERNS

***Pack the baby's bag so it's ready.*** As part of your preparation for parenthood, there are practical aspects of adoptive parenting that you might want to address. One of these is to pack a bag for the baby with diapers, clothes, a receiving blanket, and a bottle and formula, just as a pregnant woman packs a bag in anticipation of going to the hospital. This will allow you to have everything ready when the big day comes and you get the call to bring your baby home.

***Plan for help at home ahead of time.*** There are various conveniences you can plan in advance to make your life easier when the baby arrives. You can find a laundry service, interview temporary cleaning services, and seek out whatever child care you think you'll want. Because new mothers have so little time or energy for cooking, you can investigate take-out food possibilities in your neighborhood. You can also cook and freeze meals ahead of time. You will probably have too little notice and be too excited to make practical preparations when your baby arrives.

***There are preparations you can make for a child from abroad.*** It can help you to learn about the culture of your child's birth country. Other adoptive parents who have a child of the same nationality can be helpful. You might want to find out about family relationships in that country and child-care practices that may differ from ours, especially if the child is not a newborn. For example, in some Asian cultures babies sleep with other children or adults, or spend a lot of time in a backpack. Your child may be used to certain habits: if you can duplicate these at first it can soothe the child and ease the transition.

***There are financial concerns to consider.*** You might want to review your finances and start budgeting for the baby as early as possible. You should change your will to include your child—it is terribly important for you to make or remake a will as soon as your baby enters your life. Don't procrastinate or talk yourselves out of it because you are young and healthy, superstitious, or any other excuse.

In many states an adopted child does not have the same rights of inheritance under the law. To protect an adopted child, it is often necessary to insert a clause in a will saying that biological and adopted children are to be considered equally as beneficiaries. If you don't protect your child, who will?

***Choose a legal guardian for the child.*** You also need to arrange for a guardian in case anything should happen to you. This person should be named in your will. Once again, if you don't make plans for the worst possible scenario then you aren't being responsible parents. Obviously, you'll have to discuss the adopted child with whomever you choose. People whom you would never suspect may have personal problems with the idea of an adopted child.

*Life insurance may not cover your child.*   Some policies refer only to biological children. You need to write a letter stating that you have adopted a child, whom you would like to be specifically named in your life insurance policy. Do not assume anything: state that you want written confirmation that your policy will cover your child. Do not leave something this important to chance or fate.

*Health insurance is vital and can be a problem.* First and foremost, remember to get all clarifications and promises in writing. That is the only proof you will have that your child is covered. Be sure to get insurance on the child before she arrives in your home, not when the adoption papers are finalized. Some insurance will cover an adopted child only once the adoption is legal, others when the legal proceedings have begun. It may be necessary for you to get additional coverage from your insurance carrier or another company to cover your baby until the adoption becomes final.

It cannot be stressed enough that, especially with an adopted baby, your policy should cover **pre-existing conditions.** Furthermore, be sure that it covers pre-existing conditions **whether they were diagnosed or not**. Do not be so arrogant as to assume that nothing will happen to your child, or that because she looks all right or you were told the birth mother was healthy, everything is fine. There is no need to regale you with anecdotes of medical and financial nightmares when adoptive parents did not take these precautions. Health problems are a tragedy . . . but the financial ruin they can visit are a nightmare from which you may never wake up.

*Choose a pediatrician ahead of time.*   It is worth the time and money to have consultations to pick a pediatrician beforehand. Many pediatricians have no special training about adopted children. Doctors and nurses have the same prejudices and misconceptions about adoption as anyone else. Don't expect sensitivity, although you can hope for it.

Ask the doctor what his/her attitude is toward adoption and what experience s/he has had with adoptive families. If it is relevant to your situation, ask the doctor whether s/he has treated children from Asia, Latin America, etc. Ask whether incomplete medical records are a problem. If you cannot find a doctor you like who has experience with adoption, then try to find one who is open to being educated.

## PAID MATERNITY LEAVE

*Paid maternity leave is rare for adoptive mothers.* Although biological mothers usually get six weeks off from their jobs, you are treated differently if you adopt a child. In one survey, less than 25 percent of employers considered adoption a "physical disability," as they do pregnancy and childbirth. An obvious reason for this is the lack of power in numbers: only 4 percent of women adopt, so there is little pressure on employers to provide benefits to these mothers.

*There is a double standard.* An adoptive mother has the same rights to a career as a biological mother, but society seems to think otherwise. A mother who builds her family by adoption is no less committed to being a parent just because she needs or wants to work. Yet the social message seems to be: If you adopt a child, then prove how devoted you are by giving up everything else.

Just because you waited years for a child doesn't necessarily mean you want your life to be dedicated exclusively to motherhood. Maternity leave should not be about recuperating from childbirth, but rather about giving people time to make the transition to parenthood and build a healthy foundation for a family. This is the major reason that some fathers are now getting paternity leave: not because they have been "disabled" by pregnancy but because they want to spend time with their spouse and newborn.

*Find out your company's policy ahead of time.* When you make the decision to adopt, that is a good time to find out whether your employer will give you maternity leave. It can be harder to plan for adoptive maternity leave because the "due date" is usually so vague (unless you've arranged for private adoption through a lawyer).

Ask how the leave would be arranged and what it includes. How many weeks—paid or not—are you allowed? Do you have to give advance notice and by how much time? Is your job guaranteed on your return? Will your health and welfare benefits still apply?

***What can you do if no leave is offered?*** If your company does not officially offer adoption maternity leave, try approaching your boss or the department of human resources (or its equivalent) in your company. No employer wants to lose a valuable employee. Make your request on a person-to-person basis rather than as a point of social justice. However, if you encounter resistance you might get your labor union behind you, assuming that you belong to one. You can also write to the National Adoption Exchange (1218 Chestnut St., Philadelphia, PA 19107) for their booklet on the different corporate adoption benefits plans that exist. Based on one of those plans you might then make a proposal to your employer.

## THE WAITING PERIOD

***All adoptive parents have to suffer the wait.*** Waiting is often the hardest part of adopting a baby. You might want to use this time to discuss your dreams and fears with your partner and plan for the future. You can also make good use of the time by talking to your relatives and friends about the adoption. You will probably have very little advance notice of your baby's arrival: it can ease the sudden transition for your family if you talk to them ahead of time. However, there are instances where an adoption does not go through and having many people know about it can intensify your disappointment (see pages 362-63).

***The home study can be a miserable experience.*** Most adoptive parents say that waiting is horrible, but the home study is the nadir of the nightmare. Being checked over by a social worker who will subjectively determine whether you are acceptable people, fit to be parents, is a humiliating, intimidating, and invasive process. Many women become so paranoid about the social worker's preliminary visit to their home that they spend weeks scrubbing the walls, reorganizing cabinets, and trying to cover stains on their couch. One adoptive mother tells of getting so crazed about throwing out old clothes and cleaning her closets that she gave most of her clothes to charity and had nothing left to wear!

***Supplying references can be uncomfortable.*** The references that are required as part of a home study can destroy any privacy you might have wanted to maintain about the adoption. It also puts you in the awkward position of having to ask your friends or associates for their validation of you. You are forced to go down on one knee for approval to do something that fertile people do without anyone raising a question. This is one more strain in the string of emotional assaults that you have to handle as adoptive parents.

In some adoptions there is also a "supervision period" that can last from a few weeks to a year. There is rarely much contact between you and the adoption agency during this time, but the very fact that it exists can be an irritant.

***Join an adoptive parents' group.*** It can help you through the difficulties of waiting if you can share your feelings with other parents who are experiencing the same thing or have already been there. Once you've made this contact, you can always call someone from the group for moral support when you're low. Almost all adoptive parents go through periods of thinking they are going to go nuts from waiting—then they may feel foolish for feeling so obsessive. Having other parents with whom you share this experience can help you to be more self-accepting and see that your intense reactions are normal.

***Don't stop living your normal life.*** It's important to carry on with your normal life, even though you may be tempted to put everything on hold. You have to try to continue with plans that you may already have had, like taking a vacation or starting a new project. It can help to keep busy. Keep working if you have a job and do not quit until your child actually arrives. This may help to keep your perspective so that you don't become obsessive during the wait.

***Avoid unpleasant situations while you're waiting.***
It can be painful for you to be around people with children while you're waiting. It is okay to protect your feelings and avoid social situations that can make you uncomfortable. Don't accept invitations to gatherings where everyone but you will be bringing kids if that makes you uncomfortable. Children's birthday parties or family outings to the beach can be torture during the waiting period.

Good friends should be able to understand your needs. Avoiding social situations like these is better than putting yourself in a position that you know can upset you. Visiting a friend who has just had a baby can be painful, especially if she's still in the hospital. If seeing one little baby is painful, a nurseryful of them can be torture! Unless you have a masochistic streak, stay away from maternity wards. If you have a friend who has just become a mother, wait until she brings her baby home to see her.

***Fixing the nursery can make the wait harder.*** Getting the baby's room ready and telling all your friends can wind up being mental agony for you. The completed nursery is a constant reminder of the baby you so desperately want and do not yet have. For some adoptive parents, just having to walk past the nursery door can increase their anxiety.

However, other people want to prepare the room, choose baby names, and learn about child care and child rearing. These tasks can constitute an adoptive couple's "pregnancy," the time during which they prepare mentally for the baby and begin the bonding process. You'll have to choose the style of waiting that suits you best.

## SEX AND ADOPTION

***It may be time for a break from sex.*** If you've been trying to conceive for years, then sex has probably become work for you without much enjoyment or privacy: you may have been living under the impression that the infertility specialist was peeking through the keyhole! Sex by thermometer and chart removes all spontaneity—and most of the passion.

Deciding to adopt may be a natural time to take a vacation from sexual relations. It may be a relief for both of you not to have sex, at least for a while. Simply giving yourselves permission *not* to have sex may rekindle your libido. However, it may take some time to reorient your bodies to the concept of sex for the sake of pleasure.

***Birth control is recommended during the wait for your baby.***   Birth control may sound ludicrous to you after years of trying to get pregnant, but many infertile couples do conceive when they least expect it. There is even a mistaken belief that couples who try and try to get pregnant finally conceive when they decide to adopt. This is no psychological trick—there is a spontaneous "cure rate" for infertile couples of about 5 percent regardless of whether they adopt. Pregnancy is never totally out of the question for most couples, but the adoption period is considered a bad time to tempt fate.

***Birth control is required by many adoption agencies.***   Many adoption agencies will demand that a couple protect themselves from a possible pregnancy even after the baby arrives. This may seem like an unreasonable request from the agency or an invasion of your privacy, but it's probably best for you and the baby you're waiting for. Many experts do not consider it a good idea to run the risk of getting pregnant; it could upset your adjustment to parenting and your bond with the new baby.

***You need time to prepare psychologically for your baby's arrival.***   You can't prepare for parenthood if you're still trying to get pregnant, focused on the charts and drugs of infertility treatment, the two-week cycles of hope and despair. Use your time instead to learn about adoption from books, adoption groups, or other adoptive parents. Prepare yourself for parenthood with parenting classes; take time to prepare your extended family for the new baby by talking about adoption and educating and enlightening them when necessary.

*Getting back in touch sexually can take a long time.*
After you have brought your baby home, it is surprising
how long it may be before you reestablish enjoyable sexual
relations with your partner. It can take six months to two
years after the baby arrives to really enjoy each other in
bed again. You may both need to take a break from sex,
and then resume slowly and gently. Try to be patient with
each other and don't assume anything. Communicate your
needs and feelings so that you can rebuild your physical
pleasure and intimacy.

*Try to recapture the spirit of lovemaking you once
had.* Sex on demand and making love by the calendar for
months or even years is not much of an aphrodisiac. Passion and romance may seem like only faint memories from
a distant past. You probably enjoyed sex before your infertility . . . but who can remember? You may have a hard
time recalling what your sex life was like before you had
infertility problems and sex became a chore and challenge.

## LOSING AN ADOPTED CHILD

*Losing an adopted child is like a death.* If you are
assigned a baby who never arrives, it can cause you grief
and an emotional trauma similar to the death of a baby.
Fertile friends who have miscarried can relate to what you
have to suffer through. Your pain is equal to that of biological parents who lose a baby before she is born.

*There are several ways to lose an adopted child.*
There are a number of situations that can cause your baby
not to come home to you. An assigned baby may not arrive
for health reasons, including being stillborn, dying soon
after birth, or being severely malformed. A relative of the
birth parents may come forward to take the child, either
before he reaches you or afterwards. If you have adopted
an older child, she may run away. Or the birth mother may
change her mind (a possibility dreaded by many adoptive
parents).

*No other child can eliminate your pain.* No new baby
can compensate for the baby you anticipated and had al-

ready begun to love. You had already included that baby in your hearts and plans. Your loss is as intense as that of any parents who lose a child. Another child will probably be assigned to you in time, but she can never replace the baby you have lost.

## THE INITIAL ADJUSTMENT

***What can you expect from the moment of the call?*** How will you feel when you get the call: "Your baby has been born"? One phone call catapults you into parenthood: it is natural to have confusing and contradictory feelings. Many adoptive parents have doubts and want to back out— don't worry if you feel this way. Second thoughts are normal; biological parents often feel the same way.

***Your feelings may flip-flop.*** You and your partner may seesaw between elation and confidence and the feeling that you've made a terrible mistake. You may have "stage fright" about meeting your child, which can increase your doubts. It is common for parents to feel excitement and want to reach out with love, yet feel an involuntary withdrawal at the same time. Things will settle down as you adjust to the idea and reality of parenthood.

***Complex feelings are par for the course.*** From the earliest days of parenthood you'll probably experience a wide range of feelings. It can help if you, your friends, and family can understand the emotional process of becoming adoptive parents. While biological parents have nine months to prepare emotionally for their child, the idea of a baby's actual existence in your house is purely theoretical—and may take years. Suddenly the baby arrives, often with only a day's notice. You may have little time to prepare a room and the baby's supplies, and even less time to organize yourself emotionally.

***There are a series of predictable emotions.*** Some of the feelings common to adoptive parents are defensiveness, anxiety, and insecurity. Unconsciously, you may feel a sense of responsibility to the birth mother. You may worry about how well you will perform as a parent. You and your partner can help dispel these debilitating thoughts by reminding each other that you have only two responsibilities: one is to the baby you've been given, the other to yourselves.

## YOUR INITIAL REACTION TO YOUR CHILD

***You may have an "involuntary withdrawal" from the child.*** Although you may be shocked if you feel this way, it is common for adoptive parents to retreat from the baby at first. It's possible that when you see the baby, you can withdraw at the same time that you feel desire, love, and gratitude. This feeling of withdrawal will pass as you adjust to the image of yourselves as parents.

***You may have a negative reaction to your child.*** Biological parents often are turned off to their baby when they first see him, particularly if he isn't the prototypical chubby-faced, smiling cherub they imagined. The baby can destroy their expectations if she's an "FLK," Funny-Looking Kid (see *Chapter 16: Problems with the Baby*) or screams a lot. Biological parents can be confused and embarrassed by their reaction, but adoptive parents are even more unprepared for negative feelings about the child they've waited so long to embrace. If you feel this way it can cause you doubt, guilt, and confusion.

***The issue of genetics vs. environment is critical.*** Your attitude toward your child may be easier if you can accept your baby as she is: many of her characteristics are genetically coded. The baby's genetic code influences her hair, eyes, and height, but researchers are also finding that a person's genes influence their intelligence, personality, and even outside interests.

There is a complex and subtle interplay between nature and nurture: what any of us is born with and then what we do with it. If you accept the role of heredity in your baby's make-up, you can accept her innate personality; then you can take responsibility for providing a good environment. Just as with a biological child, the motivation, challenge, stimulation, and love you give her can bring out your child's inherited tendencies and potential.

**The new father may have an especially hard time.**
If infertility was an emotional issue for a man before the
adoption, then the baby's arrival may stir up negative feelings. A new father may feel inadequate if he was unable to
conceive, or he may feel angry about his wife's infertility.
A man who feels he is inadequate may withdraw from parenting at the start.

**Seeing your adopted family as "real."**  It can take a
while for some couples to accept their baby and their new
family unit. The first step you have to take is to resolve any
infertility issues that may still bother you. Then you have
to deal with negative reactions to adoptive families from
the world around you. The next step is to accept the significant difference that exists between adoptive and biological parenting (see the beginning of this chapter). After all
that is done, you have to "claim" your child. This is a process that all parents go through: by kissing, holding, and
loving their child, they make him their own.

**Stay in a parents' group.**  If you've been fortunate
enough to participate in an adoptive parents' group while
waiting for your baby, it can still be of great help to you.
The baby's arrival doesn't end your need to share experiences and information, and to get support. A group can
help you through simple but sticky times like how to deal
with outsiders' comments about your child. Those questions about how long your labor was, or the remarks about
the baby's "real" parents can hurt a lot less if you can share
them with people who have been through similar predicaments.

**You may not think you're entitled to emotions.**  As
adoptive parents you may not feel you have the same li-
cense or reasons for postpartum depression or confusion as
biological parents. You may not have sore breasts or an
episiotomy, but your feelings in adjusting to parenthood are
every bit as valid.

Fatigue, self-doubt, resentment, confusion, anger,
and disillusionment will affect you just as they do biological
parents (who also have difficulty admitting their negative
emotions). Unlike biological parents, you may be afraid to

admit your difficulties because finalization of adoption can take time and you may be afraid they'll "take back" your baby. Holding these emotions inside can be destructive, however. Find someone to whom you can express them: a professional counselor, an adoptive parents' group, a clergyman, your doctor, or the pediatrician.

***You may not give yourself a chance to be human.***
You may expect saintly behavior from yourself, not permitting yourself the "indulgence" of self-pity, fear, or the myriad other postpartum feelings. Yet an adoptive parent is no more or less prepared for parenthood than those who give birth. You share the same sense that your life is in a crisis during the postpartum transition. In the early days it's just as exhausting for you to entertain company or fix bottles of formula as it is for couples who went through labor and delivery.

## THE CHILD'S ADJUSTMENT PROCESS

***What about the lack of bonding with your baby at birth?*** It is in vogue to stress immediate parent/infant bonding at birth: the implication is that those who don't experience this have lost something essential in their relationship with their child. Biological and adoptive relationships begin differently—perhaps the "coming together" is more complicated—but these beginnings are only different, not better or worse.

***Bonding is not a magic cure-all.*** The social value assigned to immediate bonding is terribly misleading. Even biological parents have to discover that there is no perfect birth experience that will guarantee a great kid or great parenting. Bonding with your baby at birth is nice—but it is not essential.

***Biological parents don't always have a chance to bond.*** Maternal-infant bonding doesn't take place at birth in adoption, but it is also absent in cases where babies are delivered by emergency cesarean, cases of maternal complications during delivery or infant distress afterwards. Couples hear so much about the importance of this bonding that those who miss it are led to believe that they and their child have been cheated.

***Bonding is a process, not a one-shot thing.*** Bonding is a reciprocal process between you and your child; it is not one event occurring at birth, although it can begin then. Maternal-infant bonding at birth is not automatic, nor is it instinctive. The idea has become popular (just as Leboyer's "nonviolent birth" theory did) because it has sentimental appeal (and also because the theory has been well promoted by Klaus and Kennell, the two research doctors who developed it).

Bonding actually takes place over the first three to four months of the baby's life. There are even studies which show that infants do not respond in particular to people caring for them until about the fourth month of life—until then they can attach to anyone who meets their needs. So bonding is actually the result of going through the process of caring for your child: holding, feeding, loving, and responding to her.

***The baby has an adjustment to make, too.*** Some experienced foster mothers, who have taken in many babies, say that a baby who has been placed in a foster or adoptive home knows that everything has changed. These foster mothers claim that even the tiniest baby knows she has been moved, that things are different. In fact, studies have shown that an infant does notice a change in her environment: diet, colors, odors, and sounds. Even if she doesn't notice a difference in the individual caring for her, she's aware of a change in her surroundings.

A baby needs time to settle down. She'll need extra warmth and affection from the two of you during this transition. Spending quiet time alone with the baby in the beginning can give your child a feeling of stability and security. This is one reason to postpone guests as much as possible in the early days.

***The baby's age can determine how he will react.*** If your baby is placed with you immediately after birth, he isn't yet accustomed to certain smells/sounds/routines or being cared for by one specific person. It is usually thought that from four to twelve weeks of age an infant is vulnerable to feeling stress about a change in his environment. Before that age, an infant is not as acutely aware of his surroundings.

*A baby may have problems eating and sleeping.* If your baby does have an emotional reaction to the change in his life, experts say that infant grief is usually expressed with eating or sleeping problems. A baby can refuse to eat, may spit up, have chronic diarrhea, lose hair or weight, be irritable, or have prolonged crying. Of course any baby can have these problems, but you should have a pediatrician check your child for ongoing sleeping or eating problems, as well as any possible physiological reason for irritability or indigestion.

*Avoid pity in your attitude toward your child.* Treating your child as you would a biological child will make him feel like one. If you pity him and see him as unfortunate, he will develop that image of himself. A child treated differently from others will feel insecure and abnormal, the opposite of what you would hope to give him.

*You may be afraid to discipline your child.* Some parents feel they have to make it up to their child that she—and they—missed out on sharing the experience of pregnancy and birth. Some adoptive parents are afraid to discipline their child because they think she's already had a tough time—or because they fear she won't love them. Discipline and rules are an expression of parental love and caring. You are asking for trouble if you think a child should not be disciplined, or must not be denied anything because of her "unfair" start in life. Life is not "fair" to anyone (in case you hadn't noticed). You are doing your child a disservice if you try to make it up to her or attempt to protect her from frustration or disappointment. By doing so there's a good chance that the result will be a maladjusted child.

## ADOPTING AN OLDER CHILD

***An older child may rebuff your affection.*** An older child may not accept your love right away, but there are even infants who may reject physical closeness with you. Your physical expression of affection is part of the bonding process, which is delayed if the child rejects you. The child may be going through grieving and depression for the loss of previous caretakers, but it can shatter you emotionally to be rebuffed as new parents. Give the child time, respect his feelings as he adjusts, but you must not withdraw in reaction to the child's rejection of you.

***An older infant can have a harder time.*** If your baby is older when she comes to you, she may need more time to adjust. She may need time to grieve over the loss of the previous adults in her life. She'll need time to get to know you. If you are thinking of getting a professional baby nurse, it may not be a good idea if your baby is not a newborn. Baby nurses specialize only in newborns and actually may not handle an older infant well.

***An older child is more likely to be upset by adoption.*** If a child isn't placed with you soon after birth, he's likely to have difficulty eating and sleeping when he comes home to you. This is called infant grief. It has been documented even in children as young as one month of age. Infant grief is caused by the loss of familiar voices, sounds, smells, and handling. It will often happen whenever an infant's primary caretaker or familiar secure environment changes.

***Let the infant determine his own schedule.*** Unless your pediatrician tells you otherwise, allow your older child a chance to let you know what his rhythms and habits are. Try to get a list of the baby's likes and dislikes if you can. Ask the foster parents, or whoever provided for the child before he came to you, for an idea of what the baby's schedule was so that you can recreate it to make him feel at home.

## PPD AND ADOPTIVE MOTHERS

*Adoptive mothers do suffer from PPD.* You don't have the hormonal shifts that can throw a biological mother into PPD but you have many other factors that can cause postpartum (or postplacement) depression. Self-imposed silence can be a problem for some biological mothers who have PPD but don't admit it. Yet silence appears to be mandatory for an adoptive mother, whom society expects to be overjoyed in her new role.

*Many of your problems are the same as a biological mother's.* As an adoptive mother you have most of the same emotional strains as a natural mother—with a few more thrown in for good measure! You have the same frustrations and emotional turmoil in making the transition to parenthood. The shock of reality compared to your fantasies is just as jarring. You can suffer the same sense of imprisonment, loss of identity, and the fear that you've made a mistake.

*PPD can be worse for you than for a natural mother.* An adoptive mother may feel stronger guilt, shame, and confusion about her postpartum depression. A biological mother has the freedom before, during, and after pregnancy to question whether she wants to be a mother, whether she wants to delay childbearing, and so on. Society doesn't give an adoptive mother that freedom. You have to prove that motherhood was the primary dream and need in your life. PPD can make you feel like a liar.

*PPD can be a "dirtier" secret for you.* A biological mother often has trouble admitting to her emotional suffering—it's even more problematic for an adoptive mother. After the long struggle you've gone through to have a child, how can you admit to your deep unhappiness?

*Your self-image as an ideal mother can cause PPD.* You may feel you're expected to be a perfect mother; any self-doubts you may have can trigger psychological distress. An adoptive mother who has had to go through years of infertility testing can have a negative self-image. If this is true for you, you may have feelings of low self-worth as a woman and mother. Actually becoming a mother and experiencing this low self-esteem can set PPD in motion.

***You may be afraid of losing your baby.*** You may be afraid that if anyone knows you are suffering from PPD, your baby will be taken away. You have spent months, even years, waiting for a baby, often feeling that you have to prove how "normal," balanced, and fit you will be as a mother. PPD may make you feel that you will be considered a fraud, undeserving of a child.

***Grief for your unborn child can cause PPD.*** You may find that your baby's arrival makes you grieve for your unborn biological child, the one you tried so hard to have and gave up hope for. On some unconscious level you may also be grieving for the image of yourself as a child, which can no longer be reincarnated in a biological child. You may also have expected to adopt an idealized child and you may have grief that leads to PPD over that unrealized fantasy.

***The suddenness of adoptive motherhood can trigger PPD.*** A telephone call can transform your life and turn you into a mother. This overnight transition gives you almost no time for the actual preparation for the baby or the emotional rehearsal for parenthood.

## THE SUPER PARENT SYNDROME

***The adoption process can make you expect perfection of yourselves.*** Adoptive parents often undergo strenuous personal procedures to be judged as potential parents. Letters of recommendation can come back to haunt you now. If you found your baby through an adoption agency that required reference letters from friends and associates, you may feel you have to live up to people's high opinion and expectations of you. Thus you have to contend with your own personal expectations of being a "good" parent as well as what you imagine the adoption agency, lawyer, or others may think.

***You may think a good mother is a slave.*** When your long-awaited child finally arrives home, you may feel tempted to dedicate yourself to answering his every whimper. You may feel that a Super Parent is one whose existence is devoted to a child, especially a child you've wanted so much for so long.

Feeling obligated to constantly please your child can damage your child and your marriage. A child who has a parent enslaved to him has a good chance of becoming a self-centered child who believes he should try to control adults. Your constant catering doesn't give him a chance to be rewarded for good behavior or penalized for misbehaving. This can also undermine a child's natural personality and deny him the comfort of being treated normally, like any other member of a family.

***You may expect a child to solve all your problems.*** All couples idealize their child and what it will be like to be a family, but infertile couples wait so long to be parents that they may expect all problems to be solved by the child. This idealized vision of yourself as a parent and what your child will be like can bring you down. You're likely to be disappointed if you expect such a high level of satisfaction from parenting, or demand too much of your child.

## OUTSIDERS' REACTIONS TO THE ADOPTION
### GRANDPARENTS AND OTHER RELATIVES

***Introduce the idea of adoption gradually.*** Don't present adoption to your family as a decision you have made that they have to endorse wholeheartedly or risk alienating you forever. Remember: an adopted child may satisfy your needs, but not those of the grandparents who may care about their genetic line being carried forward.

***There are ways to inform your family about adoption.*** You can encourage your family to learn about adoption through books. You can invite them to attend an adoptive parents' group with you. You can introduce them to any adoptive families you may know. It can help dispel misconceptions and aid in overcoming any prejudices they may have when they see how "normal" a family is that's built by adoption. If they are still resistant, then encourage an open discussion, no holds barred, in which all feelings can be aired and resolved.

***Don't be angry at remarks they may make.*** You are going to have to learn not to get angry or judgmental about people's thoughtless, callous remarks about adoption. You can begin to practice your attitude by forgiving your family for any insensitive remarks they may make as they adjust to the concept of an adoption inside their family.

Taking a high-and-mighty stand is not only counter-productive, it's probably hypocritical on your part. None of us is blameless in the area of being intolerant or judgmental toward others. Perhaps you, too, once had thoughts or made comments, racist or otherwise, about adopted children? In any case, your family is just the front line of people who will ask questions and make comments that are unintentionally hurtful.

***Encourage early contact with your family and child.*** The sooner you invite the grandparents and other relatives to get close to your child, the sooner an extended family will begin to flourish.

***Grandparents may need time to adjust.*** Your decision to adopt may come as a shock or surprise to your parents and in-laws. You have had months or years of infertility, with all its frustrations, before you made the decision to adopt. But the grandparents are often presented with adoption as a fact, without the time you've had to adjust.

***Adoption means the loss of a biological grandchild.*** You probably haven't given much thought to what adoption means to the grandparents, but many may feel a tremendous sense of loss about the biological grandchild they've been expecting. The older generation needs a chance to think out and talk about their feelings without feeling defensive. They may have to grieve and resolve resentments, just as you have to. They are going to need time and encouragement from you to help them understand and support your decision.

***The grandparents' anxious phone calls can unnerve you.***   The grandparents—and others close to you—may mean well by their daily phone calls to know what news you have of the baby you're waiting for, but their eagerness can drive you crazy. Their anxiety can add to the stress you're already feeling. As nicely as possible, let them know that the constant phone calls are too much for you to handle right now—as it is, adoptive parents' nerves jangle every time the phone rings. Tell the grandparents that their passive support is most helpful now, rather than being actively involved in the progress of the adoptive process.

***You may not get support from friends and family.***
Unfortunately, adoptive parents often find that there is a lack of festive support from the people closest to them. Your friends and relatives may not be as happy for you as if you were expecting a biological child. They may have ambivalent feelings about adoption.

***You may feel alone and abandoned.***   Biological mothers get a lot of attention, they're given baby showers and strangers often smile as they walk by. As adoptive parents you may find yourselves waiting anxiously alone. This is one of the differences and added burdens in the way that you are building your family: you'll have to depend on each other a great deal and accept these pressures. Try not to place judgment on the people who let you down or disappoint you.

## GUIDELINES FOR TALKING ABOUT THE ADOPTION

***Tell very few people about the adoption.***   Although you may be enthusiastic about the impending adoption, don't make things harder on yourselves by telling a lot of people about the baby you are expecting. All the attention you may get, some part of which will be negative and disturbing, can increase your nervousness. Also, once the news is out, you will have to answer a lot of questions that can make you uncomfortable. Many adoptive parents suggest that you give information about the pending adoption to as few people as possible, and tell others when your baby actually arrives.

***Say nothing about the child's birth parents.*** It is a good rule of thumb not to divulge even the smallest detail that you may know about your child's birth parents. People are certain to ask you questions about the baby's background. However, even to your closest friends and family it is most prudent to say that you have no knowledge about the birth parents.

***Birth information should be confidential.*** Everyone will be curious about where your baby came from, but you should protect his privacy and your own. Giving information about the biological parents can do no good (except to satsify people's curiosity) and may very well cause your child irreparable harm later on.

People can become insistent about wanting information and may swear up, down, and sideways that they'll never repeat a word you tell them. They may become angry and huffy if you withhold information. You might relent and decide to tell them something which is a seemingly benign piece of information. However, that comment can easily be distorted and get back to your child in a hurtful way later in life. In addition, giving this information can influence people's reactions to your child now.

***Say nothing negative about the birth parents.*** Anything that you say about your child's natural parents has a good chance of getting back to her when she is older. Anything negative that you say is not only certain to cause her emotional suffering but can also complicate her identity crisis as she grows up.

Don't imagine that people you talk to won't tell anyone else: they will. There is nothing to gain and so much to lose from speaking without thinking. You run the risk of causing your child pain with negative comments about her birth parents' education, occupation (or lack of same), or motivation for giving up their child.

***Be aware of the way that you define and introduce
your child.*** Words have a lot of power. The terminology
you use about your child can influence the way that people
react. Also, the tone of voice that you use when talking
about your child can telegraph your attitude toward adoption: it will make a big difference if you can use a positive
tone and choice of words when replying to any questions.

***Do you refer to your child as "adopted"?*** Adoption
is a process by which a child joins a family, it is not a way
to describe a child. It can be confusing and demeaning to a
child to be referred to that way. No one refers to a child as
our "C-section baby" or "our contraceptive-failure kid,"
so why pigeon-hole a child as adopted? Labelling your child
as "our adopted child" gives the listener permission to
judge a child—some will think that makes him special, others will think he's inferior to a "biological" or "real" child.

***Do you also have biological children?*** If you have
children you gave birth to, do you or others refer to them
as your "real" children or your "own" children vs. your
"adopted" child? All children are natural—they are all con-
ceived and born.

***"Our child" is a good phrase to use.*** If you refer to
your child as "adopted," you are promoting prejudiced attitudes toward adopted children. This is especially true if
you have children that were born to you and you refer to
them as "our own." You are giving your children and other
people a signal that you are confused yourselves about
which children are really yours and what their status is.
Your definition gives others permission to view adoptive
families as second best, or to look upon an adopted child
as inferior.

## OUTSIDERS' MISUNDERSTANDINGS ABOUT ADOPTION

***People may not understand your motives to adopt.***
People can mean well but say the most horrible things to
you. Some people don't truly understand that adoption is a
way to build a family; they mistake adoption for an act of
charity. They may treat you as though you have done some-

thing saintly or noble—which is not a motivation for adoption. You are going to have to educate people about your decision to adopt and let them know how insensitive remarks can be hurtful to an adoptive family.

*There is a general attitude that adoption is second best.*   Outsiders may think that adoption is second best for the parents because the child is "not their own." They may pity an adopted child who is separated from her "real" family. They may look down on birth parents as inferior human beings because they gave away "their flesh and blood" to strangers. It helps to cope with people's small-minded attitudes if you realize it is social conditioning. Just as these outsiders should not judge you or your child, neither should you judge anyone for his/her ignorance about building a family through adoption.

*Prejudices come out when others learn of the adoption or meet your child.*   It can really help if you two are united as parents in your approach to other people. When you encounter people with strong negative attitudes to adoption, it can be stressful to be the parent of an adopted child. You need your partner's support.

There are people who have prejudices against Jews or blacks, because they've never met one. The prejudiced person is so wrapped up in rumors and myths that it can take a while once they've met the object of their prejudice to discover that s/he's not so different. Although outsiders would never question a couple's decision to conceive a child, they can be prying and negative about your decision to adopt. You may find that there are people who will meet your child and realize for the first time that not all children are born to the parents who raise them.

*People may question your parenting abilities.*   Nobody would think to doubt that a biological mother is doing the best possible job with her baby, but people have warped ideas about adoptive parents. For example, if a biological mother has a baby who cries a lot, she'll probably get sympathetic smiles and advice. If your baby cries a lot, you may be told that the baby is crying because he is adopted and misses his "real" mother. Or it may be insinuated that you don't really understand the baby's needs.

These attitudes can make you hostile or defensive toward others in the postpartum (or postplacement) period. You may even feel so angry at people's misunderstanding that you want to withdraw from people entirely.

***You may hear comments about how much easier adoption is than childbirth.*** Although people may be well meaning when they make casual comments, it can be painful or frustrating for you. You may get statements like "Take it from me, childbirth is no picnic. Adoption is the easy way to have a kid."

Someone making a comment like that is probably just trying to make you feel better by saying that you didn't miss anything by not being pregnant. **But both of you know that isn't true.** This attitude may fill you with rage, but if you blast the person with your anger you may damage your friendship. On the other hand, it's in your best interests to straighten this out by sensitizing your friend to how painful her comment was. You might say, "Please don't say things like that. We struggled for years to have a baby—twenty-four hours of labor would have been a picnic compared to that."

***Discussions about labor and delivery may bother you.*** If you find yourself in a group of women who have recently given birth, you may be uncomfortable hearing stories of their labor and deliveries. If the subject really bothers you and they are close friends, you can let them know that the discussions make you unhappy. An even better solution would be to talk about your experience of seeing your adopted baby for the first time.

Take comfort in knowing that these discussions won't last for long. If you are a younger mother, your peers will probably have given birth recently and want to discuss the labor and delivery in detail. But this will be less true as the children grow. The focus will turn to child development, schools, and other subjects.

***You may encounter some tacky questions.*** Outsiders can repeat clichés they've heard without even thinking how they'll make you feel. If people do say insensitive things, **tell them so.** Most people are not aware of the implications of their comments, they are just repeating conventional social thought. Outsiders do not mean to be hurtful on purpose, but nonetheless their comments can sting. What follows is a chart of comments you'll probably hear at some time. The constructive way to handle such comments is to swallow your anger and discomfort and try to explain to people how they have offended you and why their attitudes are misguided.

---

**THOUGHTLESS QUESTIONS ABOUT ADOPTION**

- Do you love him as if he was your own?
- Why would anyone want to give her away?
- How kind of you to give the poor kid a home.
- He's so lucky to have you for parents.
- The baby looks so much like you she could be your own.
- Do you know anything about his background, about his "real" parents?
- Why take on someone else's problems?

---

**An adoptive parent support group may help you adjust.** For an excellent and thorough list of support groups nationwide, you might want to pick up a copy of a fine book by Charlene Canape, *Adoption: Parenthood Without Pregnancy* (see the *Bibliography*).

# 13

# Career vs. full-time motherhood

It seems difficult, nowadays, for people to feel comfortable with their choice about how they will be parents. Our society gives double messages about motherhood and what a woman is expected to do with her life. The role of a full-time mother seems to have low value in our society, yet at the same time career mothers are frowned upon because they "neglect" their children.

A working woman may be afraid to set aside her professional life for a while and to allow herself to feel good about devoting herself to motherhood. At the same time, a woman who had a career and decides to take a break for motherhood may find herself apologizing—"Yes, I'm a Mom"—and adding, "But I'll be going back to work soon." It is traditionally thought that a woman who spends long hours at a job is a bad mother—yet one who dedicates herself entirely to her child is obsessive or deficient. Each woman will have to find her own way through this maze of contradictions in order to make a life that is satisfying and fulfilling for herself, her spouse, and her child.

***Statistics about mothers are surprising.*** More than half of all women in America have a job. The U.S. Labor

368

Department released a study in April 1986 which showed that 49.5 percent of married women with infants under one year of age worked outside the home. Other studies show that nearly half of all career women return to their jobs before the baby is one year old.

***There are several options about mothering and working.*** For most women, the minimum six-week leave is usually not enough time for them. You may find that having to return to work after such a short time with your newborn is sudden and disruptive of your bond. At the same time, quitting your job forever may seem too severe a move, unless you hate the job. The following are your options about returning to work (or not) after having a baby:

---

### OPTIONS ABOUT RETURNING TO WORK

- Take a maternity leave for the minimum time (2 to 8 weeks), then return to work full time
- Take a leave of absence for 1 to 12 months
- Return to work part time after a minimum leave
- Find part-time work once the child is old enough for preschool
- Start your own business or get a new job part time while the child is still an infant
- Never go back to work

---

## MATERNITY LEAVE

***Plan maternity leave in advance.*** First of all, tell your employer that you are pregnant before he sees you in a maternity dress or hears rumors around the office. Then leave the door open about your future plans. If you declare a definite date when you will leave your job, you don't give yourself room to change your mind because your employer may already reorganize or hire a replacement.

***Can you get your job back?*** Get a clear statement from your employer about your right to resume your same job with seniority and pay scale intact after your maternity leave. Ask for confirmation in writing.

***What if your employer is hard-nosed?*** If you don't like your employer's attitude toward your leave, or you don't like what s/he's offering, try to put yourself in his/her position. Above all, stay calm. Point out your value to the company, in years or special abilities or potential. Mention your legal rights (no one wants a lawsuit or complaint filed against them). If your employer cites company policy, then suggest that the policy be changed.

***What can you do if you don't get satisfaction?*** If your employer is rigid or difficult about your maternity leave, you have several options open to you. You can go to a higher department in the company or to the personnel department. You can go to your labor union, if you belong to one. You can file a complaint with your city or state human rights commission, usually through the local office of the Federal Equal Employment Opportunity Commission. You can contact an organization like the National Organization for Women (NOW) or a lawyer for help in filing complaints.

***Don't take "No" for an answer.*** Laws regarding maternity leave are changed frequently—you may have to be aggressive in determining your rights. Take nothing for granted and get everything **in writing**, including medical insurance, paid leave, or bonuses from your professional organization or union. Pregnancy-related job benefits are a murky social and legal issue, so you have to stand up for yourself.

***State disability insurance varies widely.*** There are enormous variations between what states offer in pregnancy benefits, and these benefits are changing all the time. Most states give six weeks paid maternity leave, but there is no hard and fast rule. For example, employees of the federal government get no maternity leave—women have to take sick leave and vacation days. In addition, very small companies may not subscribe to their state's disability plan.

**How can you determine what you're entitled to?**
The first thing you should do is check with your employer about maternity benefits. If they don't offer formal maternity leave, you can suggest a creative compromise. For instance, if you have sick leave saved up you might get it as maternity leave from your employer, who might be willing to add supplementary benefits.

Also check with the unemployment insurance office in your state, which is usually listed in the phone book under "State Offices: Employment Development, Disability Insurance." Find out if you are eligible for state disability insurance and in what amount.

**Be patient and thorough in your research.** Government programs are a mass of red tape, so check and recheck the rules to be certain. You may get different answers depending on whom you talk to on the phone. Rules about waiting periods and different rules on what day of the week to apply for benefits can make a big difference in how much you receive.

## THE CONFLICT BETWEEN CAREER
## AND FULL-TIME MOTHERING

**There are two entirely different ways to be a mother.** The fundamental difference between being a full-time mother or one who has a job is that the first mode of mothering is child-oriented and the second has a dual career/child orientation. This chapter explores the benefits and problems in both styles of mothering.

**A woman's attitude toward her choice of lifestyle is what counts.** Some studies have found that it doesn't matter as much whether a woman works as it does how she feels about the way she's decided to live and raise her child. Experts have found that if a woman feels satisfied with her life, she'll probably be a more effective parent, which means her children will probably be better adjusted.

**Don't allow other people's judgments to influence you.** Society is going to pigeon-hole and discredit a new mother for any choice she makes: a career mother is "selfish and irresponsible,'' a full-time mother is ''boring and unmotivated.'' Since you cannot win anybody else's approval for the choice you make, what counts is how you feel about your own decision about how to live your life. If you have positive feelings about yourself and your decision, things generally work out.

***Your adjustment as a couple depends on your expectations of "a mother."*** The image and expectations that you and your spouse have are essential to your adjustment to whichever style of mothering you choose. Things will be fine if both you and your husband want and expect you to have a job—and if you make arrangements for child care that satisfy you. However, if either of you expects a woman to be a full-time mother, yet the mother has to work out of need or desire, it can lead to defensiveness, rationalization, and denial. This is a conflict that can be very hard to resolve and can leave a couple in a stalemate.

## THE INNER CONFLICTS OF CAREER MOTHERS

***Mothering can be a difficult adjustment for a professional woman.*** If you've had a career that gave you a sense of accomplishment and prestige, you may feel ambivalent about liking your baby or feel awkward being a mother. Some professional women have difficulty being loose and unself-conscious: being silly, making funny noises, singing silly songs, etc. Your feelings of ambivalence may increase if you make a deep connection to your baby and enjoy her: you might then find it more difficult to return to your professional life.

***Most of our mothers were full-time parents.*** If your mother was a housewife, then you have no role model if you want to have a job while raising your child. Because you didn't learn how to be a career mother at your mother's knee, it can mean that you will feel insecure, confused, and guilty in your attempt to manage dual roles.

***A career mother can be riddled with doubts.*** You may want to continue your career while raising your child but still doubt whether it is the right decision. You may find your work interesting and fulfilling; you may feel a sense of commitment to your employer or co-workers; you may enjoy the money and independence of working. Regardless how deep your attachment is to your job, you may wonder whether this is justification enough. You may worry that people will condemn you as a cold, self-indulgent mother—and you yourself may wonder whether you are.

**You may have fears about the future.** Some women worry so much about whether their career will affect their relationship with their child that they begin having regrets about working from the first day. You can twist yourself into a pretzel worrying how your child will resent you later in life.

It is possible to become obsessed with thinking that you can't have the relationship with your child that you want to (or fantasized). You may have anxieties that you'll look back on aspects of motherhood which you missed and feel like kicking yourself. Think of it this way: for every fork in the road when you turn left, there is a path to the right that you didn't take. Some people try to avoid feeling regret about making "a mistake" in life by not taking any fork at all, staying rooted in one spot and letting life pass them by. However, not doing anything is a choice, too, which can leave you open to the deepest regrets. Every decision creates its own benefits and disadvantages. Try to determine what is best for you and your child and remember that a decision is not irreversible.

**Both parents can be conflicted about career motherhood.** You and your husband may share similar emotions when you return to work. Powerful guilt is a predominant reaction, and then all the questions follow: Are you making the wrong decision? Will your child suffer from not having her mother at home all the time? Will you be able to find safe and loving care for her?

There is no proof that a child is harmed because her mother pursues a career. A baby needs affection, consistency, and a secure environment, but these things don't have to come only from her mother. For many women, their relationship with their child is improved because they have fewer boring hours and less frustration with infant care than they would if they were with her full time.

***Guilt can be a career mother's middle name.*** Some women experience years of guilt and depression if they have a job while their child is growing up. A career mother can feel guilty and inadequate because neither her baby, her husband, nor her work seems to get enough of her. You may feel guilt and frustration because there never seems to be enough time for your husband or managing your home: on top of that, you're exhausted from trying to do it all yet feeling you keep coming up short.

You may not be able to overcome a constant nagging feeling that you should be with your child; this can lead to feeling you're failing your child, husband, and yourself. On the other hand, when you're with the baby you may be concerned that your career is suffering from your shortened hours or attention span. Guilt can become a way of life unless you get a hold on it and force yourself not to indulge in self-recrimination. There is no easy answer to resolving these feelings of guilt, but refusing to give in to them is a beginning.

***A mother who works can feel pulled apart by her loyalties to her family and job.*** The conflict between work and mothering can be so strong in some women that they are physically and emotionally drained by trying to do both jobs well. While you're working you may worry about your child and whether you've made the right decision by continuing to work. Some career mothers may prefer their jobs to the task of full-time mothering and feel guilty because of it. Other mothers may not want to have a job but must work out of economic necessity; this can make them resentful toward their job, their husbands, or even other mothers who don't have to work outside the home.

***You may become irrational about leaving your child.*** A career mother who cannot cope effectively with her inner conflict may become phobic about leaving her child. Some women become paranoid about leaving their baby, even with their own mother. If this happens to you, it can be confusing and upsetting because you can become hostile toward your husband and/or resentful of people at your job whom you perceive as trying to keep you and your child apart. Obviously, you could benefit from professional help if you find yourself being irrational or paranoid about leaving your child.

***You may feel envious of your child's closeness to your husband or other caretaker.*** If you go back to work, be prepared to feel guilty toward your child and envious of your husband, baby-sitter, mother-in-law, or whoever takes care of the baby. For example, your child may get used to spending time with her father—you may even think that she prefers him to you. When someone else is caring for the baby, you are no longer the central, all-important person in your child's life, which can feel threatening. You may have given up primary responsibility for your child but you haven't given up her love, even though you may worry about it.

***Your time away can be good for the baby's father.*** A career mother's absence can encourage a positive experience for the father and child. A mother who stays home and retains total control of the child can make it impossible for her husband to share in the full range of emotional and physical aspects of child rearing. The husband of a career mother has a greater chance to interact with his child.

***The barrage of problems and doubts can overwhelm you.*** In addition to your conflicted feelings about being away from your child, surrogate child care is often inadequate. Child care is hard-to-find, expensive, and difficult to evaluate. The problems of finding good day care can increase your qualms about being a career mother. This deluge of negative feelings can lead to postpartum depression or at least an identity crisis as you try to figure out your self-image as a woman, mother, and worker—and how they all come together.

***The motivation for working can affect your feelings about your decision.*** Leaving your child with a caretaker because you have to work for the money can cause you less guilt than if you decide to continue your career for reasons like personal satisfaction. It is perfectly valid for a woman to choose to work because of a personal need for achievement and self-expression: that decision can be as important for her as another person's economic need. However, if you are a career mother out of choice, you should be prepared for criticism from outsiders who may disapprove of your reasons for working. Keep in mind that family and others may criticize you not out of concern for your child's well-being but because these people are frustrated and dissatisfied themselves.

## THE FINANCIAL ASPECT OF
## YOUR DECISION ABOUT MOTHERING

***You may feel that having an income is a protection against "becoming" your mother.*** Some women are afraid to give up their jobs because they perceive having money as a way to escape their mother's lot in life. You may perceive your mother as powerless and perhaps downtrodden; you may think that her weakness was a result of having no money she could call her own.

You may want to be a full-time mother but feel compelled to work so that you can avoid what you feel was your mother's unhappiness. Your perception may have been wrong, however, and your mother may not have felt the unhappiness you imagined (alternately she may have been unhappy but economics might have had nothing to do with her discontent). If your mother is alive and you can find a way to talk with her about her lack of economic independence, it may help you to make a decision about the kind of mother you really want to be.

***Are you working solely because you need the money?*** Many new mothers return to work because their income is essential to their family. But it may be pennywise and pound-foolish to make the decision to work based on money alone. You may need the income, but what about child-care costs? Some studies show that nearly one half of a mother's income goes toward child care. You also need to factor in the taxes you have to pay on your salary, along with the other costs of working (transportation, meals, clothing). You may find that the amount of money that can actually go into your bank account is negligible, and becomes insignificant compared to your desire to be a full-time mother.

***You may be uncomfortable giving up your income.*** If you had a job before and decide to give it up to raise your child, losing your financial base can make you anxious. You may feel you are giving up part of your image or identity.

***You may not like being dependent on your husband.*** If a woman gives up her career to raise her baby, she may feel awkward that she is no longer able to "pay her own way." If you previously had your own income to contribute to the household or use for yourself, the transition to being dependent on your husband for money can be difficult. Using your "husband's money" may be psychologically uncomfortable for you, or your spouse may consider his income to be "his" money.

***Make a list of how much you save as a full-time mother.*** If you aren't comfortable with your loss of income, it can be enlightening to make a list of how much money full-time motherhood is saving you. Figure how out much you would be spending on transportation, clothes, lunches out, and in some cases business dinners. In addition, make a list of the money you would have to spend on child care and household help if you had continued your career. The grand total should make you feel okay that you're not bringing in any income and also allow you to feel at ease about spending "your husband's" money.

***Discuss your finances with your husband.*** Sit down with your partner and determine whether it would be financially possible for you to take a leave of absence from your job. Would you be able to live on one salary? Even if you do continue to work, will you be able to afford acceptable child care?

# THE DECISION TO RETURN TO WORK SOON AFTER THE BIRTH

*What is the right time to return to work?*   Each mother who decides to return to her career will have to make an individual assessment of when she is ready. The timing of when you've had your child in relation to your professional life is fundemental to deciding when you'll resume your work. First off, do you have any desire to stay home and be a mother for a while? Are you at a point in your profession where you are able to stay home for six months or a year? Will your savings account permit you to take time off?

There is no "correct" time to go back to work, any more than there is a correct time to have a baby; it all depends on where you are at that point in your life. Of course there are child development experts like Burton White, Selma Fraiberg, et al, who stress the importance of the first two or three years of mothering, but this section of the book is directed at women who return to work relatively soon.

*What do child development experts say about a mother who returns to work?*   Some experts say that if you're going back to your job, three months after the birth is ideal; others say that closer to five months is best. Certainly by the fifth month your baby will probably be sleeping longer and settled into a routine. Also, at five months a baby is starting to show signs of independence so that leaving may not be so devastating for him or you. However, all parents and children are different in their growth and reactions, so it's pointless to generalize.

*Don't expect to suddenly wake up and feel ready to leave your child.*   For most women there is no such thing as a "right time" to go back to work because you will always have ambivalent feelings. If you try to wait until you don't feel any guilt, you'll probably be waiting until your child is captain of the basketball team before you resume your career! Do not wait for your feelings of guilt to go away—leaving the baby is going to make you feel conflicted whenever you do it. You have to try to make the decision without letting the guilt overwhelm you.

*Forget any plans you made about your career when you were pregnant.* Many women find that the decision they made about working when they were expecting does not hold up once they become a mother. You may have thought that you'd need the money, that you'd miss your job, or you'd be unhappy staying home with an infant. Everything will look different when you're holding that baby in your arms. The very thought of leaving your child to go back to work can make you feel panic, guilt, anxiety, and depression. Don't lock yourself into plans you made before your baby was born.

*You may find that you don't want to go back to work.* You may have anticipated that after six weeks or six months of full-time mothering you would want to return to your job. Yet you may discover that parenthood is fun and fulfilling and that you don't want to continue your career. This change of heart can make you feel guilty because you are not meeting the expectations you had for yourself; it can also make you feel apologetic toward your husband if you think you have let him down. You may wonder whether he will consider you less of a person for giving up your profession. As always, it is important to discuss these fears rather than let your imagination run wild.

*Your husband may pressure you to go back to work.* It is possible that your spouse may expect you to go back to your previous job after the first few months of motherhood. He may fear that you won't be satisfied without an outside career, or he may feel uncomfortable having to be the sole provider.

*You may find that motherhood isn't enough for you.* You may have decided ahead of time that you were going to be a full-time mother, but the reality may be different from what you expected. After six months (or weeks) of baby care you may realize that you want to do more in life than be a mother. You may want to go back to your job but you may feel conflicted about leaving your baby in someone else's care. For some mothers, rejoining the outside world when they had decided to be a full-time mother can be a source of continuing guilt and stress.

*Many women return to work and then quit.*    You may be one of the mothers who thinks she wants to resume her career but then you leave your job two or three months after returning to it. Women decide not to be career mothers for a variety of reasons. You may find that you miss the baby and you also may not trust the infant care you've been able to arrange. Another reason for quitting may be that you aren't able to devote your full energy to your job—many women find that once they've had a child, their careers just don't have the same meaning as before.

*Returning to work and then quitting is the least good solution.*    If you return to your job and then decide not to continue your career after all, this can have painful psychological repercussions. If you decide to return to work it means that you have to suffer being separated from your baby in the critical early months; if you then decide that working was a bad idea, you have the additional burden of feeling like a fool or failure for leaving the job you returned to. Try not to set yourself up for failure by putting yourself in a situation in which you beat yourself up emotionally.

*You can prevent the problem of quitting your job.* If you return to your career for all the right reasons (for you, that is), then it's unlikely that you'll do an about-face and rush back to full-time motherhood. You can prevent this error by knowing your goals, priorities, and the options open to you before you take action. If you are honest and clear-sighted, then you can return to your job with a reasonable certainty that your career is vital to you. By planning your return in a calm, orderly way you can avoid the embarrassment and discomfort of rushing back to work, only to leave again just as abruptly.

## KEEP YOUR OPTIONS OPEN

*Don't announce your plans to everyone.*    Whether you decide to stay home with your baby or want to return to your job, you need to leave yourself room to change your mind. If you broadcast your intentions ahead of time you may feel constrained to follow your initial plan. However, you cannot know beforehand what you will feel like being a full-time or career mother, therefore don't lock yourself in by making pronouncements before the fact.

*A full-time mother shouldn't burn bridges.* You may plan not to return to your job, but you have no way of knowing what being a full-time Mom will feel like until you try it. One way to leave yourself some options is to maintain contact with your workplace. You may find that you want to go back to work, perhaps only part time, and if you've stayed in touch, possibilities may be open to you.

*A career mother should leave her options open.* Once you've become a mother, make an honest assessment of what it means to you to have a career, a salary, coworkers, and the personal satisfaction of working. Try not to be influenced by your expectations of career motherhood or what you imagine your husband or other people's expectations to be.

*Giving up your career doesn't mean giving up your dreams.* If you had a profession and decide to become a full-time mother, you should not feel that this means an end to your dreams or plans for your own future. Just because you've decided to dedicate this part of your life to raising a family, you should not lose sight of your own needs and how to fill them. Keep sight of your own future and what can await you down the road when your child is older.

## FULL-TIME MOTHERHOOD

*Parenting is not viewed as a valuable profession.* Being a parent is perhaps the biggest challenge that any of us faces, yet society isn't passing out Brownie points for a job well done. There's so little positive social feedback for couples who accomplish the difficult task of raising well-adjusted, happy children who have confidence, self-esteem, and are secure in their parents' love.

*Motherhood doesn't receive much stature or social respect.* Most people look upon mothering as something "any teenager" can do. In our society, money and a person's value as a human being are often tied together. A person's status is often measured in dollars earned. This translates to mean that a woman who stays at home without pay, doing tasks that are often menial, has little social value—even though raising children well is obviously a great social contribution.

*Is something wrong with you for wanting full-time motherhood?* Social attitudes may cause you to wonder whether you are deficient because you choose to devote yourself to raising your child. If you hear that a woman lacks ambition if she decides to be a full-time mother, you may wonder whether there is any truth to that statement. You may worry that you'll smother your child, or your child will become too dependent if you are with him all the time. Perhaps your spouse thinks there is something wrong with a woman who stops pursuing her career and gives up that image and identity?

*Raising a child is an honorable job.* Being a mother is a job: it is a commitment that requires a greater devotion and effort than any other profession. Don't belittle your task, or let other people run you down for being "only" a mother.

*How do you answer "What do you do?"* You may find a negative response if people ask what you do and you tell them you're a full-time mother. There is no quick solution to this situation. There are no "good answers" since that question is based on the assumption that "doing" something means having a job title and receiving a salary. If it is any comfort, you are not the only one in the awkward and annoying position of being put on the defensive by this social stigma against full-time motherhood. Many full-time mothers have to deal with the social problem of people's judgmental attitudes.

*Your attitude to motherhood makes the difference in your experience.* If you make the choice for a lifestyle as a full-time mother, you can feel content rather than defensive about having to organize your life around your child. However, there is no denying that while child rearing is important, it is often a frustrating job. It would be immature to expect motherhood to be fun and rewarding all the time. Many of a mother's tasks are repetitive and unchallenging: feeding, washing clothes, changing diapers, keeping the child out of danger and later teaching manners, etc. Yet someone has to do those things for a child. It can help to realize that in every job in the world there is a measure of boredom and drudgery.

***It's okay to hate the boring part of mothering.*** It's fine to hate the drudgery of caring for your child but try to see it as part of an important job: just because it can be boring does not make it any less significant. But if people tell you, "It's worth it, the rewards are greater than the hassles," you're entitled to tell them they're full of it! There are many days in motherhood (just like in any other intimate relationship) when you are in a negative balance—you are putting out and putting up with a lot more than you are getting back. However, it has been found that in the long run, few people regret parenthood.

***Full-time motherhood can make you financially insecure.*** For some women, motherhood is the first time that they are not financially independent. Having to rely totally on your husband for money can diminish your self-assurance if you don't like feeling dependent or being unable to provide for yourself.

***You may feel anxious that you don't have money of your own.*** You may panic when you first realize that you don't have money over which you have control. What are the unwritten rules in your marriage: does the spouse with the higher (or sole) income have a greater say or control? Losing your earning power may make you fear that you will lose your position in the relationship. However, your discomfort about finances is not necessarily linked to your mate's attitude toward money or his feelings about you as a full-time mother. Your confused feelings about money may be your own hang-up or the habit of years of having an income of your own.

***You may become neurotic about spending money.*** You may agonize over whether to buy things for yourself, worrying whether you "deserve" or are entitled to spend "your husband's" money on yourself. Yet you may be comfortable buying things for your husband or child as a way of indulging yourself. You may find yourself tied up in knots trying to decide whether it's okay to splurge on a Christian Dior nail polish: buy it and then remind yourself of your value as a person, how much you're working, and how much you'd have to pay someone else to raise your child. Buy two bottles while you're at it!

## LOOKING OUT FOR NUMBER ONE

***Being a mother can take over your whole life.*** If you allow yourself to be consumed by motherhood it can mean that you will lose self-esteem, lose a sense of your own identity, and feel trapped. You have to find a balance between yourself and your child. Where do your child's needs end and yours begin? How can you be true to yourself despite the enormous responsibility you feel for your child? The way to avoid these problems, as well as to cure them, is to carve out time for yourself right from the beginning.

***Take time for yourself.*** Part of your day should be just for you—a little selfish indulgence. A mother does not have to be a drab, practical person. Social conventions may lead you to believe that a true mother is focused only on her child, not on her own needs. However, if you are fulfilled you won't be angry, frustrated, or a resentful martyr toward your child or partner. Making time for yourself each day is an important aspect of full-time mothering.

***What about personal fulfillment?*** A woman who expects total contentment from motherhood may be shocked to find that she is not fulfilled. You may find that child rearing and house tending are just not enough for you. You may need to go back to school or back to work in order to find personal satisfaction. This can also make you a better mother because you feel better about yourself.

***You may not know what to do with yourself!*** If you have already lost a sense of yourself, you may also have lost a sense of knowing what to do when you do have time on your own. Remember, time for yourself is essential to your emotional well-being. You need to take time out for yourself, making sure that it isn't just one rushed half hour between other tasks. In addition you need to use your individual time without guilt.

If you aren't sure how to use this personal time, recall what you used to do in your pre-baby life: reading, sports, exercise classes, dance or yoga classes, adult education courses, going to the movies alone or with a friend, volunteer work, lunch or dinner at a friend's house or a restaurant, shopping, etc. You'll see that you'll find lots of things to do once you get it into your head that you deserve and need time for yourself.

***Develop outside interests.*** Your personal growth and education do not stop when you become a mother. You can continue to take classes, read, go to the library, get involved in charity work, and so on. If you make the effort to thrive and remain active intellectually, you won't become a bored or unfulfilled housewife.

***You may be reluctant to develop outside interests.*** Some new mothers are hesitant to create outside involvements for themselves, other than having a job. You may feel uncertain about leaving the baby and arranging for a sitter; you may lack confidence or not know what kind of involvement would be satisfying for you. As a new mother, you may have to make an effort not to lose your identity: one way to do this is to remain involved with the outside world. You are not going to be a new mother, nor a full-time mother, forever. If you try to live your life through your child's life it can only bring unhappiness to both of you, so make the effort to maintain a separate identity and interests.

***Take your time deciding what you'd like to do.*** It's important that you think through how you'd really like to use your free time. You don't want to just rush off half-cocked in order to get away from home, only to find that you've wasted energy or money or felt foolish. Consider the alternatives; perhaps you can use your family or friends as sounding boards to think out what you want to do with your time. However, don't let anyone pressure you into a decision or a commitment that you're not ready to make. Respect your own instincts about when you are ready to explore possible activities outside the house.

*Start small and see how you feel about outside involvements.*   In the beginning you might like to start in a small way, taking a class for a few hours a week and seeing how you feel after a month or two. How do you feel about yourself? What effect is getting out regularly having on you? How are the arrangements for a sitter working out? How do you feel about leaving the baby? If you aren't pleased or comfortable with your choice of outside involvement, don't worry about it. Don't feel pressured or desperate—you will find activities that are meaningful to you by experimenting.

## YOUR RELATIONSHIP WITH YOUR HUSBAND

*The man's return home after work can be a rough transition.*   By the end of the day a full-time mother is often bored and cranky, craving relief from her spouse—not just physical relief but that of having someone to talk to who actually talks back. The only problem is that your husband has probably been talking all day and is dying for some peace and quiet. You're standing there with the baby in your arms, waiting for your "saviour" to arrive, and in walks a tired, hungry man who needs to unwind.

*You are in two different worlds all day.*   A working man and full-time mother have such diverse lifestyles that their needs and expectations are out of sync. He wants relaxation and you want stimulation. This can happen in a relationship even when there isn't a child involved, but as parents you become more dependent on each other to get your needs met. This is something to discuss and negotiate: the father can come home and take the baby for half an hour to give the mother breathing room. Another option is for the man to reserve the first half hour at home as private time for himself before he joins his wife and child, at which point she can take some time for herself.

***Motherhood can give a woman new power.*** If a woman was a housewife before she got pregnant and didn't have much self-esteem, full-time motherhood can legitimize her role. She may begin to gain power in the marriage, since child care is considered a woman's domain. Motherhood can increase a woman's relative competence and control in her home, which can upset a previous balance of power with her husband.

***A woman may not allow her husband to participate.*** A full-time mother may be afraid to let her husband share in baby care because that is her one and only domain. If you are a woman whose husband's career was more prestigious and respected than what you did before motherhood, having a baby can balance the scales. Women who feel this way may always be trying to be a better housekeeper and better parent to reinforce their self-esteem.

***A new mother needs praise from her husband.*** A full-time mother needs encouragement and feedback from people around her, and especially from her partner. A woman who is home alone all day with the baby runs the risk of feeling taken for granted. She needs to know that her husband appreciates her for raising their child, running the household, being a hostess, growing a garden, etc. The more support and affirmation a woman gets for her efforts, the less stress and resentment she is likely to feel.

***A man may resent that his wife doesn't have a job.*** Your husband may feel angry that you aren't "working," that you're just staying home with the baby (a role reversal for a day will probably cure him of the misperception that you are on easy street). He may also be jealous of all the time that you have with the baby, tuned in to the child (and not to him). A new father may feel that he's got all the financial responsibility and that his wife is avoiding carrying her share of the burden. He may think you are stalling about resuming your career. You'll need to sit down and air your feelings.

***A man may pressure his wife to have a career.*** Your husband may lobby for you to continue your career or even begin one once you become a mother. A man may have a distorted understanding of the women's movement, which can mean that he belittles full-time motherhood as a life's work. Some men also feel social pressure when they are asked, "What does your wife do?" Your partner may share society's low opinion of women who are "just" house-wives and mothers.

*A man can find a full-time mother dull or boring.* Many full-time mothers worry that they will become bored or boring, and sometimes their fears are realized with their own partners. A man can feel this way whether his wife gave up a career for motherhood or never had one. He may feel—and perhaps accurately—that you are not sharing his interests in the outside world any more, and that you have stopped growing at the same pace.

*Your husband may withdraw from you.* If your part-ner does not show you tenderness or express emotions to you, it can be devastating, especially since he may be the only adult with whom you interact when you are caring for a newborn. If your husband is critical of you it may be because he doesn't "approve" of full-time motherhood, be-cause he feels inadequate as a parent himself, or for more complicated reasons.

*A man's criticism of your mothering style can lead to serious marital problems.* If your partner maintains an aloof distance it can make you afraid that he will leave you (many women have those fears during pregnancy). You may feel deprived, lonely, unnurtured, and even par-anoid that your mate has chosen his work (or another woman?) over you and the family. As you adjust to full-time mothering you'll probably be feeling overburdened; this can make you resentful and insecure about the pressure from your husband to do "something more" than mother-ing. You may feel misunderstood, unfairly judged, and un-appreciated.

*Your husband may turn to another woman.* Your husband can feel that you are failing him or coming up short of his expectations for you. His reaction may be based on plans you had for your own professional life before you became a mother, that you have since abandoned. Your partner's disappointment and perhaps boredom with you, added to your insecurities about yourself and your femininity, can lead to a breakdown in communications.

All these pressures can lead to less sex and less good sex. The stress may even lead to an extramarital affair. These tensions can push people to test themselves with a new partner, and the feeling of carefree days before parenthood. Will someone else be a better lover, a better mate? It is normal to have these doubts at times of stress in any relationship—whether you or your mate act on these questions is quite another matter.

## CAREER MOTHERHOOD

***Unrealistic expectations are once again a root problem.*** Before your baby was born, you may have thought you were going to work until the last minute of your pregnancy and then go back to work a week or two after the birth. There are a few women who can do this, and seem to manage without catastrophic wear and tear to themselves or their marriage, but these tigers are few and far between.

***Don't expect the impossible and then feel inadequate.*** Don't hold such impossibly high hopes for yourself that you set yourself up for disappointment and even a feeling of failure. Most new mothers are not going to be able physically or emotionally to handle a return to their jobs when their babies are only a few weeks old. Many experts would say that it is not good for the emerging family if the new mother returns at a gallop to her career. At any rate, as a new mother don't set such formidable goals for yourself that you feel you're deficient if you cannot meet them.

***Don't harbor fantasies about taking your baby to work.*** Although you might have a job where you can comfortably take your infant once in a while, it is a fantasy to think that you'll be able to take him with you every day. It is absurd to think that you can just plunk a baby down beside you and get to work. A child is not a pet that you can stick under the desk while you concentrate on your work. Allowing yourself to have this kind of unrealistic fantasy can make your adjustment to career motherhood even tougher.

***Child-care books are written for full-time mothers.*** Read whatever books you want, but don't take them to heart: the attitude of these books can be distressing because they are written with full-time mothers in mind. Many child development experts do not seem to acknowledge that half of all American mothers have jobs. Many books about child rearing are written with the assumption that a mother is someone who spends the majority of her time with her child.

***The timetables described by books can be misleading.*** Many books describe a baby's development month by month, often with the premise that every day is crucial—which can be devastating to the working mother. If a career mother has to work late nights it can break her heart to read a child-care book that declares, "This is the point at which your baby recognizes you and becomes totally attached to you—this is the month in which you become the central love object in his universe." If you can't be there, you may worry that he'll love the nanny (or baby-sitter, day-care staff) instead of you.

***Society's attitude toward career mothers is usually negative.*** A new mother who continues to work is often seen as neglectful by society, or it is assumed that the woman did not marry "well enough" (otherwise her husband would be able to provide for her). Most women work because they need the money—with today's inflation, one salary is usually insufficient to raise a family and live well.

***A career mother is in a no-win situation.*** It's important to know up front that it's unlikely anyone will give you credit for juggling career and motherhood; there's even less chance that you'll be praised if your child does well! In fact, if your child thrives, then it will be thought that he did so *despite* your "neglect." On the other hand, if your child has problems, people will blame it on the fact that his mother works.

***A career mother is swimming against the tide.*** Although many mothers in America have jobs, you are still going against a societal norm by choosing to work. It is as though you have to **ask** for a privilege that men have always had: to have children and also to work outside the home. Once you accept the fact that you're going against the norm, you can be prepared for resistance from other people. A working mother soon realizes that it's up to her to change people's attitudes toward her.

***Motherhood is not a new career.*** If you are a professional woman who decides to become a full-time mother, beware the trap of viewing motherhood as a new job to conquer, in which you will be tested and "promoted." If you were obsessive or compulsive in your career, you may feel driven to be the same way as a full-time mother in order to prove something to yourself or others.

Trading motherhood for a career is not a good idea; being a mother requires a different approach and skills from the workplace. If you bring an executive's style to mothering, you may feel self-conscious and eventually guilty about being too protective or controlling or domineering. Try to strike a balance by bringing your organizational and other skills to mothering without letting these aspects dominate.

***You may have anxiety about your job performance as a mother.*** On your job, success can be measured by your salary, the results of your labor, job "perks," promotions and/or bonuses. There is no way to measure whether you are getting "high marks" in motherhood, especially in the beginning with a tiny baby who doesn't interact with you and may even cry a lot of the time.

For some women, the only way they can measure their own effectiveness is from the outside, from the encouragement and praise they get from their husband. A career mother often has an exceptional need for feedback from her mate. You may be accustomed to external validation of your worth, to getting "strokes" from your job situation. It can be devastating for a woman in this position if her husband comes home and goes right past her to pick up the baby (which may be what he thinks she'd like him to do). If you've been waiting all day to talk to your spouse and have him pat you on the back for a job well done, you may be crushed if he doesn't pay attention to you.

*A career mother can be hit hard by the Superwoman Syndrome.* A woman who is a professional or executive can be self-critical, conscientious, hard-driving, and compulsive—these are some of the qualities that may have helped her achieve success. However, you cannot demand that level of excellence from yourself if you're going to be a mother and continue your profession. It is not humanly possible to attempt to do everything perfectly, and you'll undoubtedly feel like a failure in the end because of your unrealistic demands on yourself. You may have a romanticized vision of what a mother should ideally be like, but you can wind up in trouble if you allow this to collide with a supercritical view of how you don't measure up to the ideal. Being too tough on yourself can lower your self-esteem and erode your self-confidence as a mother—if you let it go far enough it can deteriorate into depression.

*Accept your limitations as a working mother.* If you are going to raise a family and continue your career, there are some facts that you'd be well off to accept. You're not going to be available to your child the way you might like to be. You're going to have to hire help, probably full-time help unless your husband wants to have a major involvement in child care and/or he has a job that's flexible enough to allow him to devote a substantial amount of time to the child. Also, you'd better prepare yourself for the possibility that you will lose some ground in your career when the child is small.

## YOUR HUSBAND'S ATTITUDE TOWARD YOUR CAREER

*A man may have great resistance to a working mother.* Don't be surprised if your spouse is vehemently against you resuming your career once the baby is born,

even though when you were pregnant he accepted the idea
that you'd continue to work and he'd share responsibility
for the baby. There can be even more of a problem if you
expected to stay home and be a full-time mother and then
you need or want to work while the child is still small.

***Your partner's old-fashioned attitudes may shock
you.*** You may not want your partner to view your ability
to work as a privilege, but it may turn out that way. Many
men were taught from childhood that a mother should be
at home. Sometimes this can create an impasse for a couple.
A man may suddenly begin proclamations against your career with phrases like "No wife of mine will ever . . ." or,
"I won't allow the mother of my children to . . ."

***A man may feel threatened as a provider.*** Even if
your mate knows that your salary is needed, it can still be
hard for him to accept your job. If you didn't work before
the baby was born, or if your salary is less than his, you
may have to correct your spouse's old-fashioned assumption: he provides support and you do the nurturing. He may
have always assumed that a mother cooks meals, cares for
children, and fills a home with the smell of baking cookies.

***A career mother may seem too independent to her
husband.*** Once he becomes a father, your spouse may
worry that if you are financially independent, you won't
need him as much . . . that he can't keep you happy as his
wife . . . that other people will think he can't provide a
decent living . . . that other people will think he's not in
charge and doesn't wear the pants in the family . . . and on
and on. A man may have these feelings even if he's the one
who suggests that you continue or start working.

***You need your husband's support and involvement.***
It's hard enough being a career mother, don't imagine that
you can manage without your husband's support. Your husband's involvement is essential if you are going to balance
your two roles. His attitude may be that he'll go along with
your working but he doesn't have to like it—so don't expect any encouragement from him.

***Dividing child-care responsibility is necessary for a working mother.*** It is important that you divide some part of the responsibility for your child with your husband. You need to sit down and calmly discuss which of your jobs is more flexible if the child has to be taken somewhere, especially on short notice. If your husband can take time off postpartum, or an afternoon or two during the week, it can enrich him and his relationship with the baby while liberating you from total responsibility. However, if your husband is resistant to your work, you will probably have to be the one who organizes and pushes for shared care and responsibility.

***Your mother or other relatives may pressure you not to work.*** Your mother may try to talk you into quitting your job in favor of being a full-time mother. Your mother may unconsciously want you to be "loyal" to her by being the kind of mother she was—she may be threatened or envious of your independence. If you continue to work despite her advice, it will probably turn you into a super homemaker! You may try to prove to your mother that she's wrong and that you **can** do it all.

## IS YOUR WORKPLACE FLEXIBLE AND SUPPORTIVE ABOUT YOUR CHILD?

***Certain jobs can be very unsympathetic to mothers.*** There are some occupations that are particularly negative in their attitude toward motherhood: clerical, secretarial, nursing, teaching, and service industries are often mentioned as unsupportive of a working mother. Employers in some of these professions may be worried that career mothers may take advantage: your boss may be suspicious of women who take their sick days for their child's sake, for example. Jobs like these may force a woman to return sooner after the baby's birth by making her fear that she will lose her pay—or her job.

***Some high-powered professions frown on motherhood.*** A woman executive functioning in Big Business may have a hard time blending her role as a mother into her professional life. Hours are long and inflexible, there is often travel required, and most employers have no interest in the need for good parenting, either within families or for society at large. American business almost seems to be against parenting—at least by high-level employees. The attitude often seems to be "It's your kid or the job; pick one. We can always find a qualified replacement who will not hesitate to make this job their number one priority."

***What is the attitude to your absences?*** The boss may be able to accept your absence for dental work, but women who are successful in business rarely have the liberty to take time off when their child is ill or in a school play. Discuss hypothetical possibilities ahead of time with your boss: what will happen if your child is sick with a fever or has a piano recital? Are you going to be able to tell the truth or will you be forced to lie to your employer in order to be with your child? Will an inflexible workplace put you in the position of often feeling conflicted and/or being forced to lie in order to be a more involved mother?

***Flexibility in the workplace is a consideration.*** If you are going to continue your professional life once you become a mother, or if you are going to start working, there are issues to consider. The most important aspect of a job for a mother is whether her hours are flexible. "Flextime" can be a good solution if it allows you to work less hours and/or take home extra work. Although most jobs do not offer day-care facilities, it is worth considering whether child care is provided by your workplace.

## SUGGESTIONS ON MODIFYING YOUR CAREER FOR MOTHERHOOD

***The only way to adjust your job to motherhood is to ask.*** Don't expect your employer to offer solutions to career motherhood. You are never going to get what you don't ask for: what have you got to lose by asking? All your employer can say is "No." If you are an older, long-time, and/or valued employee, you have more in your favor than you may realize.

*See if you can arrange flextime and shorten your days or work week.* You might be able to arrange for a four-day work week or to put in less hours per day. Shortened hours are not going to eliminate the exhaustion or conflict of having two roles, but they can give you more time with your child. Juggling your child's needs and perhaps bringing work home can take its toll on you but reduce guilt. You may have to put your career on hold for a while since career advancement isn't likely when you are "down-shifting."

*Look for a less pressured atmosphere in your field.* If you put your mind to it you can probably come up with ways to get a looser working environment. If you have a boss who is a dictator or a workaholic, how about looking for a new job? Another way to take the pressure off is to look for a teaching position in your field—instead of continuing your practice as a lawyer or CPA, you could try teaching the subject.

*Try to find part-time or free-lance work in your field.* If you aren't sure how to go about working reduced hours or on your own, ask freelancers in your field how they started and how they maintain their careers. See *Appendix VI* for the organizations "New Ways to Work" and CATALYST, which may be able to help you arrange professional part-time work.

*Learn to compartmentalize your life.* It is often said that one way in which men differ from women is that a man has the ability to shut out certain aspects of his life (say personal problems) while he is concentrating on other areas (his work). As a career mother you can learn to compartmentalize your life: you can discipline yourself not to be obsessed about your child's welfare or your own conflicted feelings while you are on the job. Make sure that your child's caregiver can reach you at work and then put your full concentration on your business, not on your home life.

*Use your time with great care.* Time is the most precious commodity you have as a career mother: use it wisely so that you aren't tyrannized by the multiple demands on you. When you are at work, see if it's possible to take your breaks and/or lunch at your desk. This will give you more work time, and also ease the guilt you might otherwise feel when you need to take an hour or two from work for family business.

***Be judicious when asking for time off.*** Be parsimonious in making special requests for time off from your job for maternal responsibilities. As a working mother you simply aren't going to be available for everything that crops up in your child's life—either the good times or the bad. Once you recognize that you cannot do everything or be everywhere at once, you can weigh the importance of each circumstance and wait for times when it really matters to leave work for your family's sake.

## CHILD CARE FOR CAREER MOTHERS

***A live-in housekeeper can save your life.*** If you work more than 40 hours per week, having full-time household help can make the difference between being able to cope or being buried beneath the weight of your multiple responsibilities. If you are a victim of the Superwoman Syndrome (see that section in *Chapter 5: Your Identity as a Mother*), then you may have to face yourself in the mirror several times a day and say, "I cannot do it all—and of all the things I could be doing, 'ring around the collar' is at the bottom of the list!"

***A housekeeper/nanny buys you time.*** If your child and spouse are the most important priorities in your life, the best way to demonstrate that is by devoting the majority of your nonworking hours to them. For example, it usually isn't hard for career mothers to learn to protect their family time by turning down other people's requests and invitations. However, unless you have help at home, your housekeeping chores may wind up dominating your time at home: how can you say "No" to the myriad demands of the house, laundry room, and kitchen?

***Invest your nonworking time in your family.*** Protect your relationship with your partner and child by turning household tasks over to someone else and making those chores the lowest priority in your life. If you were a perfectionist about housekeeping or cooking before you became a mother, it may be necessary to retrain your eye about wayward dustballs under the sofa and meals that are functional rather than spectacular. Do not devote too much energy to cooking, cleaning, or grocery shopping; compromise on the quality of all aspects of homemaking in order to concentrate on the quality of your personal life.

***Cut your budget if you can't afford household help.*** If you can't afford a live-in housekeeper, arrange for as much help with the house as you can manage. If necessary, cut all incidental costs out of your budget: cut back on transportation costs, don't shop for makeup and clothes (you probably don't need them anyway), don't go out for lunch or drinks, etc. You won't feel deprived of luxuries and indulgences if the money is going toward relieving you of household duties.

***You can justify the cost of child care.*** If you are uncomfortable with the high cost of a nanny or full-time housekeeper, think of it as an investment in the future. The money you spend for child care is a benefit to your child as well as helping you do your job well. Knowing that you've got top-quality help at home can give you the confidence to concentrate on your work. Your salary may only just cover this care, but the expense can be worth it. Your child won't need this level of care forever, and also the household help can allow you to advance in your profession, perhaps to a higher pay level.

***You can get tax credit for child care.*** You are eligible for a tax credit if you have children under 15 years of age, or a spouse, older child, or other dependent who requires care. Even single working parents are eligible, as is a married parent who works full or part time, is actively seeking work, or is a full-time student with an employed spouse. You are eligible if you pay for care in your home, a day-care center or nursery school, a camp, or another person's home. You can even get credit if the caregiver is a relative living with you, as long as you don't also claim that person as a dependent.

***A tax credit can be better than a tax deduction.*** Do not confuse an income tax **deduction** with a tax **credit:** the definition of the former is an amount subtracted from your gross income before your taxes are computed. On the other hand, a tax credit is subtracted directly from the taxes you owe, which can be even more valuable if you're not in a very high tax bracket.

***How do you calculate a tax credit?*** Add up what you spent for child care during the entire year. You can also include any taxes you paid as the employer of a household worker, which is another reason to pay a nanny "on the books." Transportation is not considered a child-care expense, nor is private school tuition from first grade and above. Save all proofs of payment (cancelled checks, receipts from day care) for three years in case you are audited.

## A CAREER MOTHER'S NEGATIVE FEELINGS

***Motherhood may give you bad feelings about your job.*** Once you are a mother you may feel guilt about not doing your job as well as you did before—or you may feel guilty that you don't enjoy infant care. In either case, your working life is still being compromised. If you are working in a job environment that is not supportive to motherhood, or if you have to stay at a job that was never compatible for you anyway, it can lower your self-esteem. Harboring resentments is not healthy for you or for your emerging family.

***You may not like mothering an infant.*** It can be hard to admit that you do not enjoy being the mother of an infant. Not all women enjoy playing with babies or caring for them, even if the baby is their own. There is a set of skills that not all women have—and it doesn't make you any less of a woman or a mother. Staying home and being bored and resentful is not going to promote a loving relationship with your child. It is better to work and learn to put your guilt to rest than it is to force yourself to be the kind of mother you don't want to be.

**Admit you'd hate being a full-time mother.** If you know that you would hate being stuck at home all the time—if you feel sure that you lack the patience, creativity, and selflessness to entertain a small child, then you are probably better off at your job. If you can come to terms with your real feelings about motherhood, it can release you from unnecessary guilt. Admitting your feelings can also release you from the pressure of being torn between career and motherhood. When you are actually doing what feels best for you, you shouldn't have to apologize to anyone for it.

**The isolation of the suburbs can be tough.** If your family has recently moved to the suburbs "for the child's sake" it can create problems for a woman with a career. If you continue to work where you previously lived (a city, presumably), you may not have in common with women in your new community. Local women may be full-time mothers, so you will have no one with whom to share your experience of career motherhood. This can be lonely and alienating.

**PPD and the successful career mother.** Postpartum depression can be a surprise when it hits any new mother, but it can seem even more incongruous when it affects a woman with a thriving career. A career mother isn't expected to suffer from PPD because she appears to be organized and accustomed to handling pressure, people, and new situations. People assume that a successful career woman can get a higher salary and more flextime than a less successful woman. Presumably a woman who can afford a high quality of child care will suffer less guilt and other emotions that lead to postpartum depression—but it does not necessarily work that way.

**A successful career woman's self-image can lead to PPD.** Motherhood can be more of a shock than you anticipated if you are a professional woman. A woman with a career has often discarded the traditional female role and has an image of herself as being different from other women; having a baby can destroy that perception of herself. Pregnancy, childbirth, breast-feeding, and diaper changing can shock you into the realization that you are, in fact, just like other women when it comes to being a mother. Career mothers frequently feel a loss of identity and a sense of inadequacy, which can become postpartum depression.

**The contradiction of mothering and working can cause PPD.**  As a working woman you were used to having control of your time, to being capable of meeting pressures and demands, to being praised for your efforts and accomplishments. Your work was probably a major source of gratification that you may feel you lose as a mother, since babies don't give compliments or raises and don't even smile at you in the early months!

### THE TRANSITION FROM WORK TO HOME

**There is an intense personality shift from your working self to motherhood.**  Some working mothers feel they are living two lives, one at work and the other at home with their child. For some women, the different demands on different aspects of their personalities can be a shock to their system. You may feel you are straddling a constantly shifting canyon, one foot on each side, without being totally committed to either one.

**Your return home at the end of the day can be difficult.**  It can be especially tricky to make the shift in tempo from the pace of the adult workplace to the rhythm of child and home. This transition comes at the end of the day when all of you are tired and the baby can be particularly demanding. Even with years of practice, this end-of-the-day transition can be the hardest part of being a mother with a career.

**The first half hour at home is crucial in easing the homecoming transition.**  Use the first 30 minutes at home wisely, and you may have the beginning of a pleasant evening rather than a chaotic melodrama. If it seems im-

### WAYS TO EASE YOUR RETURN HOME

- Turn on the phone machine and do not pick up any calls that are less than extremely urgent.
- Take a shower and/or change into comfortable clothes and shoes as soon as you get home.
- Some parents find that getting into a bathtub with their partner and/or baby can be a relaxing bridge between work and home.
- A mother who is breast-feeding will want to nurse the baby right away.
- You might want to close the bedroom door for 15 minutes to read the mail or the newspaper—some fathers find this helps them make the transition from job to home.
- You might allocate 30 minutes to watching the TV news, either alone with your spouse or with the child(ren) if s/he can remain tranquil.
- Plan half an hour that is sacred and inviolable to be alone with your partner, to have a drink before dinner (or coffee afterwards).
- Plan late dinners—have cheese and crackers, raw vegetables, or other snacks to take the edge off your hunger so dinner is not an immediate problem.

possible to do this once you get home, then try taking time for yourself before leaving work or on your way home.

***Weekends can be hard for a working mother.*** After five days away from your child and partner, you may want to immerse yourself in home and family but feel overwhelmed by everything else there is to do. You may need to catch up on household chores, run errands, go shopping for food and/or cook for the week ahead, see friends or relatives, exercise, or do a sport. You have an awful lot to juggle, so you're going to have to learn the fine art of compromise: try to grab some time as a couple, keep your child happy, and find some "down time" to nurture yourself.

# BREAST-FEEDING AND THE CAREER MOTHER

*Wait until you have the baby to find a way to combine nursing and working.*　Don't try to decide ahead of time how you'll combine breast-feeding and working because you'll probably just be frustrated and disappointed when your well-laid plans don't work. You have a better chance of finding your own way to combine nursing and a career if you view it as a series of decisions that you have to make at various points in your life as mother. The decision to breast-feed and work should be one that you make freely, without feeling you are locked into any choice that you make.

*Make your decision looking at all sides of the situation.*　In order to decide whether to breast-feed, or for how long you want to nurse your baby, it can help to evaluate your situation at intervals: during the pregnancy, in the early postpartum weeks, around two months of age, etc. At each point you should look at your feelings and needs, as well as those of your partner and child. There are too many variables that you can't fully consider ahead of time. There will be ups and downs, benefits and pleasures, exhaustion and frustration when you combine nursing and a profession. Be careful not to make any decision at those moments when you are on a pressured schedule and are dead tired, since you'll be robbing your child and yourself of a thoughtful decision.

## WHEN SHOULD YOU GIVE A BOTTLE?

*Begin giving your baby a bottle before she's two months old.*　There are experts who say that some babies will absolutely refuse a bottle if it is introduced after they are two months old. They recommend that even when you are still at home full time, you give your child one bottle a day so that she will accept it as part of her normal routine. It will also help if you can have someone else give this relief bottle, to accustom the child to being fed by other people.

*Other experts say it's best to wait three months before returning to work.*　If you can afford to stay away from your job that long, there are experts who say that after three months of age the baby is more likely to learn two styles of sucking, breast and bottle. They point out that after four months of age the baby can take solids when you are away.

## DRAWBACKS IN GOING RIGHT BACK TO YOUR JOB

*There are drawbacks in going back to work at six weeks postpartum.* If you decide to return to work within six weeks, you are effectively making a decision to partially wean your baby. Expressing milk is fine for the occasional bottle but it is impractical for full-time nourishment. If you go back to work full time you can realistically breast-feed in the morning and evening and perhaps express enough so the baby has a bottle of breast milk as well as formula during your absence.

*The baby is vulnerable to disease at this point.* The antibodies in breast milk give your child a good deal of protection from infection, but if the baby is no longer nursing she becomes vulnerable to illness. If you decide to go back to work and effectively wean a six-week-old baby, then you have to consider the child's susceptibility to disease when you make child-care arrangements.

*A tiny baby should not be weaned and placed in day care.* Many experts say that day care increases the chance of illness, and the bigger the center the greater the danger. Therefore if you must put your child in a center, you should avoid weaning her from breast milk. It is a bad idea to increase her exposure to disease at the same time that you stop nursing. If she is taken off the breast and put in a day-care situation with many children coming and going, your child is probably going to get sick. If possible, choose home care or family day care where there are preferably just the woman's own child(ren) and yours.

*There are certain illnesses that abound in group-care situations.* Ear infections and diarrhea are common ailments for infants in day care. Diarrhea can be dangerous for a baby or toddler—it is easy for them to rapidly lose a high percentage of their body fluids. Infectious hepatitis can also be picked up in large centers—and passed from the baby to adults at home.

***What nursing schedule should you have once you're back at work?*** Mothers who have successfully nursed and worked find that it's good to nurse first thing in the morning, at lunchtime (if you can get to the baby or vice versa), as soon as you get home (which is a good way to relax and make the transition from professional to mother), and late at night.

## HAND-EXPRESSING BREAST MILK

***A nursing mother with a career has to express her milk.*** You have to be highly motivated to express your milk and leave it at home to be given in a bottle while you are on the job. Expressing breast milk by hand or pump can be disturbing to some women (or their partners)—it can remind them of milking a cow. But if you want to nurse and continue your career, you'll probably have to express your milk.

***Express milk during the day at work.*** Even if your baby is given a bottle of formula at home during the day, you'll probably want to express your milk for your own comfort. If you don't do so, you will become engorged and uncomfortable and your milk supply will eventually diminish. You can express the milk for 15 or 20 minutes during a coffee or lunch break.

***You can bring the milk home to the baby.*** If you want to keep your milk for the baby, you can express it directly into a sterile container and refrigerate it immediately; breast milk can stay 24 hours in the refrigerator and up to several weeks in the freezer.

***Switch your baby to a bottle gradually.*** Prepare your baby for your return to work by giving him a bottle (whether formula or expressed breast milk) one feeding at a time. A gradual transition will be easier on both of you.

*Maintain the same feeding schedule on the weekends.* Continue to express your milk and give a bottle just as you do during the week at work. If you try to switch back to full-time breast-feeding on the weekends, it can be difficult for the baby to keep readjusting.

## THE DECISION TO WEAN THE BABY

*Talk to other mothers about their decisions.* Find a supportive full-time mother or preferably another career mother who breast-fed so that you don't feel insecure or isolated in your decision. Knowing that others have survived the bad days—the days when you and the baby are feeling tense and irritable and put upon—can help you get through the hard times.

*Make the decision but don't act on it right away.* Give yourself some time after you make the decision to wean the baby. Take a few days to decide and during that time simplify your life as best you can. During the decision period reduce outside stress and influence as much as possible. Of course, discuss weaning with your partner and get his advice as well as his personal feelings about it. You want to be objective and rational when you make this decision, since it is one that you cannot reverse and that you may regret if you wean your child before you are both ready.

*Have faith in yourself.* Once you make the decision to wean the baby, have confidence that your decision is the best choice for your family. You and your partner may have to support each other in this decision since other people may have different criteria for what makes a "successful" mother or nursing experience.

## A CAREER AT HOME

*Working at home can give you the best of both worlds.* If you can arrange to conduct your work out of the house, you can avoid the pitfalls of being a full-time mother or of having a job outside the home. A career at home protects you from the hazards of full-time motherhood such as feeling trapped, mentally unoccupied, and financially dependent. You can also avoid some problems of the career mother such as role confusion, exhaustion, guilt, and a lack of time for all the demands on her.

**There are disadvantages to working at home.** When you have a career at home the pay usually isn't great and there's often little status or prestige. If you are very ambitious this may be too much of a compromise. A person working at home also doesn't get job benefits, days off, or paid sick leave. If you are a woman who doesn't want—or doesn't know if she wants—a working life outside of mothering, then there's no point in going to the trouble of setting up a career at home.

**You'll probably need child-care assistance.** If you're going to get any serious work done at home, you'll need blocks of time that you know are yours. Whether you have a live-in housekeeper or nanny, or plan for regular babysitting, it's essential that someone is there to take over when you are working, otherwise you'll accomplish very little despite a great deal of effort.

**Your relationship with the caregiver should be clear.** The nanny must know that your work is important; it is from your attitude toward yourself and your work that she will understand this. Be clear about what her tasks are: whether she answers the door or telephone and under what circumstances you can be disturbed to deal with these interruptions. Don't interfere with her or look over her shoulder while she's doing her job—and she'll show you the same respect.

**Find a nanny you respect and trust.** In order for your working situation to be successful, you should have faith in the caregiver you choose. The woman should also be someone to whom you can delegate responsibility. She's not going to interrupt you with questions and problems if you have confidence in her abilities with your child and in handling household matters that may arise.

**Demonstrate your seriousness to everyone around you.** If you don't want to be disturbed while you are working, then prove it. Being firm about your work hours and work space is important for you, your child, and others in the house. Inform friends and relatives of your "Don't Disturb" hours, and let business associates know that this is your working time.

***Don't let the telephone control your life.*** The telephone has a remarkable way of ringing just as you're concentrating or finally getting down to work. It may be someone trying to sell you the newspaper, a dentist confirming an appointment, or a friend calling to chat, but in any event you can't afford these interruptions if you're going to work effectively at home. Let someone else in the house answer the phone and take a message. You might prefer an answering machine so that you can screen calls and pick up the ones that might be important for business.

***Make time work for you.*** In order to use your time efficiently, you should learn what is the best time of day for you to work at home. You can determine this by finding out what your own rhythms are and what kind of schedule your baby and household have. There is no point in trying to force yourself to work in the morning, for instance, if you have trouble concentrating at that time or you see that those are the most pleasurable hours to be with your child.

***Become efficient about household demands.*** Being at home means that you are prey to the inherent interruptions and chores—"a woman's work is never done," etc. If you're going to work at home, then you have to protect yourself from the myriad demands on your time. You can organize things so that you return all phone calls at one time. You can plan to do all your errands at once and devote half a day to them. Having a career at home requires more self-discipline and organizational skills than you might need for a high-powered job "on the outside."

# 14

# Choices in child care

This chapter takes a look at your options in raising your child, with a view toward the impact those choices may have on your marriage. You need to examine the possibilities available to you in caring for your child. There isn't any perfect or "best" solution: any choice you make will involve some trade-off or compromise. My intention here is to help you be protective of your relationship with your partner when deciding how to care for your child.

## PHILOSOPHICAL DIFFERENCES ABOUT CHILD REARING AFFECT YOUR RELATIONSHIP

*Differences of opinion are a crucial factor in marital conflicts.* Perhaps two of the most prevalent topics for arguments between husband and wife are finances and child rearing. One way to head off problems at the pass is to find out exactly what your attitudes are and where you got your ideas. Once you understand what has influenced your philosophies about child rearing (and your partner's), you may be more open and flexible to other ideas.

*Your upbringing influences you.* Look back at your own childhood and try to recall how you were treated by your parents: at the dinner table, about schoolwork, about sports and activities, about showing affection or expressing anger. Your experience influences the ideas you have about raising your own child. If you and your partner take time to explore each other's attitudes toward all aspects of child rearing, it may turn out to be a good investment in future harmony and understanding in your family.

***Don't be upset if you have arguments.*** You may have unrealistic dreams of marital harmony and togetherness while raising a child. In reality, it will probably be rare that the two of you are in perfect, peaceful agreement. Parents feel passionately about raising their children: where there is that depth of feeling, there are bound to be fights. It's normal for parents to have conflicts about their different expectations. Do not blow things out of proportion and worry that every difference and conflict between you is an indictment of you and your relationship. Arguments are a normal and natural part of child rearing.

***It's okay to disagree.*** Once you agree to disagree, you're on the right track. There is no right way to raise a child. There are no absolutes, no "facts." A child can benefit from a variety of child-rearing techniques, which is another reason that neither of your styles should monopolize your child's upbringing.

***A child can respond to two different parenting styles.*** Studies have shown that a child develops a separate relationship with each parent; he does not make a relationship with his parents as a pair. A child learns to respond to your different styles and he'll adapt accordingly. For example, if the child has an authoritarian mother and a permissive father, he might accept a strict rule from Mommy while he would discuss or argue about the same rule from his Dad. A child soon learns that there are things he can do with his father, and others with his mother.

***Different parenting styles are not a problem.*** Just because you have differences it doesn't mean there has to be stress or tension between you two or your child. Your recognition that complementary styles of child rearing are healthy means you won't feel the need to impose your own style of parenting. This can also eliminate the stress of mistakenly believing something is wrong with your partnership because you don't have the same style or attitudes.

*Consistency between parents is overemphasized.* Many child-rearing books and experts suggest that it is important for parents to present a united front. Although consistency between his parents may be easier for a child to live with, it can be dishonest and burdensome for his parents. It is an unnecessary strain on the two of you to try to disguise your disagreements.

Harmonious consistency between you also doesn't paint an accurate picture for your child of how the world works. Differences of opinion are a natural part of human existence—it would be impossible for you as parents to be completely consistent about everything even if you chose to try.

*Both parents need to have a strong voice.* It can be beneficial if both parents are actively involved in decisions about the child. Arguments between you may often be about the child's rights and what is best for the child—but they are also about the fact that both of you would like to have control. The issues at stake may be insignificant, but which parent has the final say is important for the balance of power in the marriage and parental roles. Ideally, neither of you should monopolize.

*Both parents need independence in their parental role.* Each of you needs room to develop your own style and relationship with your child without your partner breathing down your neck. Attacking each other's style won't prove anything, nor will it resolve your differences. Ugly disagreements only alienate you from each other. It is common for one parent to grind his/her teeth over something about the child's behavior that the other parent doesn't even notice. Better to walk out of the room rather than create an issue that can only end as an argument or power play between you and your partner.

***Don't get in each other's ways as parents.*** Neither parent should interfere with the other's relationship with the child. Neither of you should feel responsible for what takes place between your spouse and child in technique, rules, attitudes, or even something as minor as a tone of voice. Each parent has to have the space for an autonomous relationship with the child, and be free to make his/her own mistakes and triumphs.

## LEARN TO COMPROMISE YOUR BELIEFS

***Consult a third party if you can't find a compromise.*** Sometimes it's necessary to talk out—or even fight out—your different attitudes toward child rearing. It may clear the air if you go together to discuss your differences with your pediatrician or a couple's therapist. If you feel your child's physical or psychological well-being is actually at stake, you may need an objective third eye on the situation.

However, it will be helpful if you're careful to distinguish between child-rearing practices of your mate's that are really dangerous . . . or those that simply get on your nerves. You may think your partner is overprotective, s/he may think you are too relaxed, even to the point of being neglectful. You simply have different outlooks on life, which you may not have known before.

***You have to learn to function together as parents.*** Raising a child means becoming an authority figure, but not one who functions independently. Each parent has to learn to function with the other—child rearing may be the first time that a couple experiences a true partnership with each other. You may feel absolutely positive that your way is the best; but sometimes you have to bite your tongue when your spouse is doing things his/her way.

***You have to try to find a middle ground.*** It is unusual for both parents to adopt the same personal style as authority figures or to have identical attitudes about child rearing. This means that you have to accept the differences between yourselves and find compromises. Otherwise, one parent will take over and the other will retreat and eventually remove him/herself from child rearing. This kind of adversary situation means that the partner who withdraws will give no support to the dominant parent; the withdrawing partner may actually hope that the dominant mate's style does not work.

***Avoid below-the-belt tactics.*** If you are seeking a peaceful compromise to child-rearing disagreements, there are certain cheap shots to be avoided: contradicting, undermining, belittling, or criticizing each other. (This style of discussion should optimally never take place in front of a child who is old enough to understand.) Mutual respect is a good foundation: try to see things from your spouse's point of view and then explain your viewpoint in hopes of finding a middle ground.

***Rational compromise isn't always possible.*** Many arguments between husband and wife come from different perceptions of their child's needs. This has nothing to do with right and wrong; you simply have different expectations of how children (and parents) should behave. There are times when you are not going to be able to reach an agreement.

***An inability to compromise can divide your loyalties.*** If you cannot reach a settlement with your spouse over some child-rearing issue, you may be in the position of having to make a difficult decision. You have to choose between honoring your mate's strong opinion or your own heartfelt perception of your child's needs. If you have the presence of mind, try to take a deep breath and step outside the situation for a moment. Ask yourself which is more important and will have a greater effect on your life: whether the baby goes out without a hat, or whether the two of you have such a nasty fight about it that it takes days for the air to clear?

## EXPECTATIONS AND IMAGES
## OF EACH OTHER AS PARENTS

***Each parent has images of what a parent is.***   You
have ideas about what your own role and your mate's
should be as parents. These images are bound to be different from the ones your spouse has envisioned; such differences can create conflict and competition between you.
Unless you're able to understand and revise these images,
they can put you in a position where the child is a pawn
that you fight over to "win" or "lose" in each situation.

***You have to revise your images of parenting.***   One
of the tasks of early parenthood, and one of the possible
difficulties in the transition to parenthood, is the revision
of images that you may have had your entire life. Now that
you are confronted with the reality of being a parent, you
have to adapt your expectations.

You have to adjust your image to include your imperfections and limitations, along with those of your spouse
and child. This is especially true if you and your partner
have different values. For example, what does "fatherhood" mean to you? How involved do you think a man
should be with his child? How do your spouse's expectations of parenthood differ from yours, and how does that
affect your imagery? What can you realistically expect?

***You need to adjust your images of perfection.***   Most
of us have a fairy-tale image in the back of our hearts and
minds of what a wonderful family we'll have. You may have
been nurturing a fantasy of a cozy nest with perfect children and parents. The moment that you become parents,
this fantasy is going to be shattered! You'll need to discard
those images and replace them with new, more realistic
ideas that leave room for human frailty and flaws.

***Your images are powerful.***   You may not realize what
a potent effect your expectations can have on your relationship, especially if your partner's images are in opposition to yours. Whether you're conscious of it or not, there
is a lot of power in the images you have about the way that

you expect a family to function, and a child to be raised and behave. One way to defuse potential friction before it starts is to talk with your spouse about your expectations. If you can do this before the birth, or when the baby is still very young, the differences between you are less likely to cause conflict.

***Your mate's attitudes may surprise you.*** You may have known each other for years but find that you are shocked and upset by your partner's attitudes toward child rearing. Many couples never really sit down to discuss each other's theories and styles of child care. The most relaxed, unemotional time to do this would be before the baby is born, although most couples who talk about the future do so in a romanticized, unrealistic way.

When you suddenly find that you've become parents one fine day, you may be amazed to learn that your partner is too serious (or not serious enough) about the child's safety, cleanliness, feeding, and so on. Stylistic differences and disagreements about child rearing are often based on your own childhood experience: each of you wants to raise your child as you were raised (or in opposition to it), but in either case these are not logical decisions. You are usually not deciding what seems objectively good or bad, but reacting to your own past.

***Raising children can bring out emotional extremes.*** You may find yourself feeling a confusion of emotions toward each other, from hatred to adoration, despair to euphoria. You may feel closer, more connected to each other than ever before—and then hate each other's guts because of a fight over whose turn it is to wash the dishes! During the transition to parenthood the issues can be trivial but your reactions can make you feel as though the future of your relationship is at stake.

***Child care is the first time that a couple works closely together.*** Unless you and your spouse have flown an airplane in tandem or run your own company together, raising your baby will be your first experience working at something together with so much invested. Because the stakes are so high, and your interdependence is an unfamiliar feeling, the potential for emotional fireworks exists. As new parents, both of you are insecure and vulnerable to criticism. In addition, you may be convinced that anything you do "wrong" as parents is going to damage your child for life. The fear that your errors may turn your child into a social misfit can cause passionate battles with your spouse over even trivial issues.

***You may be supercritical of each other.*** Sometimes parents nag and criticize each other's parenting as a shorthand for other complaints. If your partner reacts to your parenting by saying, "Don't hold the baby so much," what s/he really may be saying is, "What about me? Aren't you going to hold me any more?"

You can save yourselves a lot of aggravation if you sit down together to discuss your feelings about each other's responses to the baby. In many cases, the criticism will be more about your relationship than about child-rearing attitudes. Sometimes the real issue won't be how your partner responds to the baby's crying, for instance, but rather how your mate's reaction feels to you. One reason that you may hear new parents criticize each other's parenting in a nasty or impatient tone is because their reaction is to more than just the surface behavior.

***You may dislike your spouse's style of parenting.*** There are going to be certain things that drive each of us nuts about the way that our mate is a parent. Both of you will probably also have pet peeves about certain behavior in a child that annoys, offends, or embarrasses you. In most cases, each of you may not even notice things that are terribly irritating to the other.

Certain aspects of how to treat a child—and how a child should behave—may be especially annoying because you were instructed not to do them when you were a child. Seemingly unimportant aspects of child rearing can hit a nerve in you or your spouse. If your partner is the one having this reaction, try to be sympathetic, don't be critical or try to impose your logic on the situation. His/her reaction may not be rational, but your partner needs your understanding and help to understand and modify it.

*One parent may take the role of the baby's advocate.* There is a prescription for misery when one parent sides with the baby against his/her spouse. By aligning him/herself with the child, your mate becomes a self-righteous nag who has put you in an adversary position. Your partner may pick fights, arguing with you over the baby's rights and putting the baby's needs first. Various psychological explanations cover this behavior, but the end result is to drive you away. Professional counselling may be needed to help you out of this situation.

*Too strict/too permissive.* The issue of being strict vs. permissive doesn't have a practical application until the child is old enough to understand rules, but right from the beginning discipline can be an irritant between you. If you think your mate is too strict, you may compensate by overlooking as much as possible in your child's behavior. If you think your mate is too permissive, you may try to offset what you see as laxness by increasing the control you exert over your child. A vicious cycle that creates tension between you may be the result.

Parents often label each other without having a rational discussion about the difference in their discipline philosophies. It's a good idea to talk about what bothers you in your mate's behavior as a parent, and explain why.

*One parent may try to overprotect the child emotionally.* One of you may want to cushion your child entirely, to protect him from feeling fear, anxiety, stress, sadness, frustration, etc. You may want to fulfill the child's every whim, anticipate his needs so that he can have a stress-free childhood. It is rumored that there are parents who strive to have a child who is so completely catered to that he never has to cry.

There is a philosophical point here. It is okay to say "No," or to allow a baby to cry: in fact, it is considered important to a child's healthy development. A child must experience difficulty. Frustration, fear, and anxiety are emotions that a child needs to learn to live with; a realistic, loving parent will not "lie" to a child by giving him the impression that he will be able to live in the real world without experiencing these emotions.

## THE DANGER OF CHILD-CARE
## EXPERTS AND BOOKS

***Books talk about the "typical" baby.*** Most books and experts refer to the "typical" baby without taking into account the actual full range of normal behavior. These experts can make you wonder what you're doing wrong that makes your baby behave so differently from the infants described. Individual differences among babies are often overlooked: these books are of limited value or can make you feel inadequate.

***You may expect your baby to fit the "norm."*** Many books on child rearing give a timetable for an infant's development. These books can create a competitive atmosphere between you and other parents: whose baby sleeps through the night, drinks on her own, crawls, is toilet-trained, and so on.

If you try to apply the "normal" yardstick to your child, she's sure not to fit the graph in all areas. Although you may be aware that each baby has an individual development timetable, you can still be influenced by the competitive atmosphere. You may still want your baby to be "fast" or "above average." You may feel superior if you have a child who is bigger, or quicker to perform certain developmental tasks. Conversely, you may feel inferior, or fear your child is inadequate, if she is slower to develop.

***Each baby is an individual.*** From birth, each infant has a unique way of responding to hunger, noise, sleep, temperature changes, being wet, and new experiences. Research shows that a newborn infant is not a blank slate, as once was thought. Each baby is an individual, born with his own personality and characteristics. He has specialized behaviors and reactions to the world around him. A baby is not a passive blob to be formed according to your wishes.

***Concentrate on getting to know your baby.*** Each baby is an individual. Even if you've had other children, what worked with them won't necessarily work with this child. For this reason, pay attention to your baby's facial expressions and movements. These are signals, the first form of communication between you and the infant. Discovering and accepting your baby's unique characteristics is the foundation for raising this child—not just a generalized "typical" child referred to in books, but this unique individual.

*A baby's personality is affected by you.* It is thought that a baby's personality is pretty much formed by the time he is two years old. The way that you relate to the child has a considerable impact on how he develops: your way of handling him influences his growth and development. Your baby's individual way of responding to you also contributes to the relationship that will gradually emerge between you. Studies have shown that a child will react and cope differently with both of his parents, even if they handle him in a similar fashion. This means that who you are, and how you treat the baby, makes a difference.

*Your baby's behavior affects you.* Your baby's individual characteristics and personality affect your responses. There is a give-and-take communication from the very first meeting. Your baby's responsiveness to you influences how you feel about parenthood and about yourself as a parent.

*You and the baby will have to learn to adapt to each other.* Mutual accommodation is the key to a parent/child (or any other) relationship. Fitting your rhythms and personalities to your child's may not happen quickly or easily, but it's essential to a harmonious family life. It takes time to develop synchronized behavior and nonverbal communication. After the first few weeks you will probably have already adapted to each other's personalities and routines.

Your baby is probably not going to mold easily to your fantasies or your lifestyle. This is especially true if you have a temperamentally difficult child. It is going to be a process of give and take: you'll have to be flexible and adapt to your infant, too. Once you accept that your child has her own set of needs and responses, you may be able to let go and stop trying to control the situation. This is the beginning of learning to accommodate each other.

***There are no clear-cut answers in child rearing.***
Books can give you the impression that there are "right"
and "wrong" ways for you and your child to behave, when
in fact just the opposite is true. Parents who can accept the
fact that life is full of uncertainty are often the ones who
get the most pleasure out of parenting. Once you're able to
accept that there are no absolutes, you'll probably relax in
your parental role. Nondependence on authorities should
free you to lighten up and get more enjoyment out of being
a parent.

***Make the best decisions you can.*** Your ideas on what
is appropriate for you and your child are as good or better
than those of people who know your child less intimately.
Learn to trust your instincts and intelligence instead of trying to find the "right answer" from books, or from "experts" like your older sister, mother, your pediatrician, or
nurse. If you want to consult experts, gather their conflicting advice, look at the situation yourselves, and then make
your own decision.

***Never forget that a child is a child.*** A child is an
emerging human being who is able to love but has a limited
ability to rationalize. Don't make the mistake of thinking
that the baby is your equal, and don't ascribe thoughts and
motives to an infant which he isn't yet mature enough to
have. Especially as the infant grows, don't lose sight of the
fact that you are the adult, you are in charge. You have to
make decisions and make the child do what you want. Of
course you have to gear your expectations to the child's
age, making sure that your command makes sense, and that
the child can comprehend it.

***You don't have full responsibility for how your child
turns out.*** No parents are entirely responsible for how
their baby responds and behaves. Each child reacts to her
environment depending on her unique temperament and
abilities. You can do everything "right" with an unhappy,
colicky baby and not change her one bit. You can also do
lots of things "wrong" with a child who has an easy temperament and she won't take any notice.

An innate danger exists in believing that you are totally to blame (or praise) for your child's personality—if the child is unhappy, uncomfortable, or troublesome, it automatically becomes a reflection on your adequacy as parents. And then you are stuck. Both of you need to let go of the idea that you can control your infant. Once you recognize that he is a separate person from you, your expectations of yourselves and the baby will become more realistic and relaxed, and you're sure to feel more capable and comfortable as parents.

***Bad consequences are unlikely if you make mistakes.*** So many new parents worry about damaging their child for life if they make "mistakes" in child rearing, but it's hard to imagine real problems arising from something you've done with love. It's highly unlikely that there will be a bad result for your child from any reasonable, well-meaning decision that you make with good intentions. Don't allow yourself to be influenced by the proclamations of one child-care expert or another. Each individual decision about baby care is not that important; the overall picture is what counts.

***There are no guarantees.*** No matter what you do as a parent, there is no guarantee that your child will have the personality you desire. You do the best you can and hope for the best. If nothing else, child rearing is sure to teach you humility, patience, and forbearance.

## OBSERVATIONS ABOUT HAVING SOMEONE ELSE CARE FOR YOUR CHILD

***No society expects 100 percent parenting.*** I know of no culture in which mothers provide 100 percent of the care for their babies, but segments of our society are returning to earlier beliefs that full-time mothering should be the ideal. This attitude in America may be a swing of the pendulum away from women's liberation, but there is a trend to frown on parents who aren't willing to devote themselves entirely to child rearing. Such social pressure can make you feel guilty or confused about not taking total responsibility for your child's upbringing. You have to avoid these feelings if you're going to have self-esteem as a parent and harmony in your marriage.

***Child care is not "bad" while parenting is "good."***
The way that you perceive the child care you are providing—whether you see it as "good" or "bad"—has an influence on the success of your choice. What counts in your decision on how to raise your child is the **quality** of care—whether by a parent or someone else.

For parents who cannot provide full-time parenting, a number of options are available for child care. Some of the research on day care does not show any long-term ill-effects on the children's development or on their attachment to their mothers. However, these studies stressed that an optimal child-care center should have a stimulating staff and small group size, with a low staff/child ratio (see the section on *Licensed Day-Care Centers* later in this chapter).

***There are tax consequences to child care.***   By law, you are supposed to pay Social Security and other benefits even for a part-time employee. You may think it's an advantage to find a child-care provider who wants to be paid in cash and doesn't want these contributions paid. However, if she is not reporting her income to the IRS, then you probably cannot deduct your child-care costs from your income taxes. Losing child-care deductions is a direct loss to your pocketbook. Also, there can be legal problems if you are caught.

***Plan ahead for sickness.***   If you are a career mother, you have to protect yourself by having a contingency plan for what you will do if your nanny or day-care provider is sick. Don't wait until seven-thirty in the morning on the day of the problem to figure out what to do. Staying home from work or fighting with your partner over which of you will do so is the least good solution. You'll be better off if you can line up a friend, relative, or neighbor ahead of time who can pinch-hit on short notice.

You have the same problem if you use day care and

your baby gets sick: you aren't supposed to send a sick child into a group situation. Make plans for what you'll do in the event that the baby does get sick. Perhaps one of you will be able to take time off from work on short notice. If not, you should be able to find a friend or neighbor who can step in at the last minute.

## SUGGESTIONS FOR A CHILD HAVING DIFFICULTY ADJUSTING TO CHILD CARE

*There are things you can do to help the baby adjust.* A child may need your help in adjusting to being separated from you and to being around unfamiliar people in a new place. The more you can do to ease the transition, the more pleasant the child-care situation will be for everyone.

*Don't be angry with your child if she has separation anxiety.* Don't be judgmental about a child who has a problem separating from you. It is a normal sign of a strong attachment. Be patient and reassuring: you are both going to survive this!

*Accustom your child to new experiences.* Take the child to places with other people around. Take him to the park, the market, other people's homes. If he's uncomfortable at first, comfort and reassure him.

*Introduce the child gradually to the caregiver.* If you're going to use a baby-sitter or nanny, have her come play with your child while you're still at home. *However, you should stay in another room, not hovering over them.*

*Give the child a familiar security object.* If you are leaving the child at a day-care facility, bring a familiar toy, blanket, or bottle. If the child uses it in a particular way, explain that to the staff.

*Stay in touch by phone.* In the first week, be available by telephone to a nanny or day-care facility if they need to reach you. You should be prepared to go to the child if necessary during the transition period.

## SIGNS OF PROBLEMS WITH CHILD CARE

***Beware telltale symptoms of problems.*** You may have to make a change in the provisions you've arranged for child care if your child gives you signals of being unhappy.

***A child may get bored.*** By the time a child is a year and a half to two years old, if you've kept her at home with a nanny or relative she may be getting bored. She may not be getting enough stimulation from the outside world, even if she sees other children at a playground. A play group or nursery school at age two to three can cure a child's boredom and break the monotony of always being at home.

***"Stranger anxiety" is not a sign of a problem.*** Stranger anxiety often occurs in the second half of the baby's first year of life, and often again around the beginning of the second year. So if you have a 10-month-old who is crying and grabbing for you when you try to leave him with someone else, don't worry about it. It means your child can now distinguish himself from other people, and one caretaker from another.

***Crying may be a sign of boredom.*** A child in a child-care facility who is crying a great deal may not be getting enough individual attention. Crying may be the baby's way of expressing feelings of loneliness or rejection. If the staff/child ratio is not low enough (no more than three children for each adult, especially with very young children), you may find that you have to change the child-care arrangement so that your child gets more personal attention.

***You know your own child.*** Has her personality changed in any noticeable ways since she's been in child care? For example, was she friendly and outgoing and now seems to be picking fights with other children in the play group? Keep in touch with your child, stay tuned in to her moods and reactions. Even if a child is too young to talk, you should be able to tell what's going on.

***When in doubt, drop in.*** If you have any doubts or fears about the child care that you've arranged for your child, the best way to check it out is for you to drop in unexpectedly. If you have a sitter or nanny, come home during the day and see what's going on: are they playing with blocks or is the child plunked in front of the television? The same is true for a day-care center: stop by and see what the dynamic is like. Dropping in will help prevent major problems like sexual abuse of children, as well as less dramatic problems like burnt-out, disinterested staff members or an uninvolved nanny.

*If you're not satisfied, don't "settle."* In order to feel comfortable with the arrangements you make for your child's care, you shouldn't settle for less than what you really want. You may have to check and double-check the arrangements that you've made for child care until you feel certain everything is all right. You may even have to spend more than you anticipated; in the long run it may mean less guilt and stress for you, and a happier experience for your child. As it is, child care probably costs at least half of your salary—you might as well pay a little more if that means you'll get real satisfaction.

## EXPERTS DISAGREE ABOUT THE EFFECTS OF CHILD CARE

*Many experts agree that infants need personal attention.* Although they disagree on related issues, many child development specialists share the opinion that a tiny infant requires close personal attention. Some experts say that a newborn is so demanding that it requires the full attention of one person (although that need not be a parent). There is wide agreement that under two years of age a child does best in the smallest group possible. It has been found that if a group with infants has more than 10 children, it can mean that the children may be socially, intellectually, and/or emotionally deficient.

*Some studies show that infants in centers suffer emotionally.* Some experts feel that a baby under the age of one suffers when he does not have his mother's care. A large number of babies in certain studies have been described as "insecurely attached" to their mothers because they were separated from her before their first birthday. This research also showed that such babies then become aggressive or uncooperative in their preschool and elementary years.

These experts recommend that if a mother can afford to stay home without terrible consequences, she try to do so for the first year of her baby's life.

***Other experts have found that infants are emotionally flexible.*** There are specialists who say that although infants require the devoted attention of an adult, it doesn't necessarily have to be their mother. They say that tiny infants can develop sustaining attachments to several adults, not just to their mothers.

***A child's own disposition can affect her reaction to child care.*** Some specialists say that there is no hard and fast rule about how day care will affect a child, but rather that the child's personality can affect her adjustment to a sitter or to day care. A cranky, uncomfortable baby can be overwhelmed by too much stimulation, so she may have a harder time in a group. A group situation can be difficult for a shy child who may have a hard time making his needs known.

***Stability is considered a key element in a child's life.*** Finding a sitter, nanny, or child-care facility that fits your child is important; then it's equally important to maintain consistency and stability. Some specialists feel that infants and toddlers can fall apart at the seams if there is abrupt change in their lives. New adjustments can cause turmoil in the family, with more stress for the child and your marriage.

## USING A RELATIVE FOR CHILD CARE

***You should know and like the relative.*** If you are going to use a relative for child care it should optimally be someone you know quite well. It also helps if you genuinely like her! Ask yourself whether you'd go on a vacation with this person—if the answer is "No," then you probably wouldn't want her around your house during the postpartum period.

**You should share similar opinions about child rearing.** It helps if you've discussed attitudes and theories about child raising with the relative. A serious difference of opinion can be the cutting edge of whether the arrangement will work: issues like sexist attitudes or reactions to a child's masturbation can create conflict between you.

**There are several advantages to using a relative for child care.** First of all, your child will be cared for by someone who has a stable place in her life and who loves her unequivocally. Secondly, your child can remain in a familiar environment. Also, the amount of money that this will cost you is modest or none at all.

**You can't really complain to a relative.** It's difficult to tell a relative that you don't approve of her style of child rearing. Only you can make a decision if the area(s) of conflict is more important than what might otherwise be an ideal child-care situation. If you have a paid baby nurse, you can criticize or even fire her. If your relative is doing you a favor and baby-sitting for free, there's no comfortable way for you to complain.

**A grandparent can be physically limited.** Before you enter into an agreement with your mother or mother-in-law, take into consideration her age and physical health. Even infant care requires a fair amount of physical exertion, whether it's lifting the baby, doing household chores, or whatever. A grandmother may want to be involved with her grandchild's care but may underestimate the amount of work involved.

**Be precise and clear about arrangements.** If you are going to have a relative "working" for you, it's important to have a clear understanding of what her duties will be and what compensation she will get. Conflicts over issues like hours, duties, and payment can cause bad feelings in the family.

*You need a relative who is flexible and nonjudgmental.* If a relative is going to help you during the transition to parenthood, she should be someone who can give you the room to grow into parenting. You don't want someone around who will make judgments about you, criticize, or ridicule your parenting. It's equally important that your baby's caretaker be someone around whom you can change your mind and experiment with techniques of baby care, as you put your theories about child care into actual practice for the first time.

*What if you have to end an arrangement with a relative?* Sometimes you just can't co-exist with a relative as a caretaker for your child. The best way to handle this is to face it honestly yet diplomatically. Your relative has done the best that she is able to for your child and loved him well—perhaps just not the way you would do it. It's important for your future relationship that you don't blame her for the failure or perceive her as being "wrong." You are simply different people with different attitudes toward child rearing.

## BABY-SITTING COOPERATIVES

*An informal co-op consists of a few parents who exchange services for free.* Baby-sitting cooperatives are organized so parents can regularly plan for social excursions without their child, leaving him with dependable caretakers and no actual expenses. An informal arrangement would consist of two or three couples who are easygoing—the attitude is usually "I'll do it this week, it's your turn next time." To avoid misunderstandings it can help to keep a calendar with the hours each couple has baby-sat. Otherwise you may hear, "We sat for more hours than you," or, "We're always stuck with Saturday."

*A larger baby-sitting co-op needs structure.* If a co-op consists of more than three couples, it's usually a good idea to make a list of the members and take turns functioning as secretary each month. With a larger group, there is no way to assure that you will sit for the same couple who sat for you.

*There are various advantages to a co-op.*   Depending on where you live, a baby-sitting cooperative can give you a wide selection and availability of people to call upon. You can trust other new parents to be caring and responsible. You can make new friends and can meet other children, which can give you a perspective on your own child. Best of all, it's free!

*There are also drawbacks to a baby-sitting co-op.* In order to get free hours, you obviously have to sit for other couples. This can be hard for dual-career couples who are already overworked. There are also probably going to be some organizational and social problems in a cooperative that can make it more trouble than it's worth.

*A parent cooperative center is another option.*   In this case you have a center operated and administered by the parents, but staffed by trained teachers whom they hire. What this option has going for it is that it will probably cost less than outside day care, the parents can have direct input, and it allows you to make adult friends with small children. The potential problem in an arrangement like this is that it is a large responsibility and working parents may not be able to give sufficient time to the center.

## INFORMAL FAMILY DAY CARE

*Informal family day care is not licensed.*   An informal family care home is run by a woman out of her home and is not licensed, which can make it hard to know the quality of care you will be getting for your child. This means that you will have to make extra efforts to examine the facility being offered and assure yourself of the safety and personal attention you want for your child. It is vitally important that you *check and recheck periodically* to be sure of the quality of care provided.

*There are a number of practical reasons to recommend informal family day care.*   The cost of informal day care is usually reasonable, even inexpensive (from $50 to $100 a week with meals). Because you will undoubtedly pick a facility near your home, you have the convenience and familiarity of your neighborhood. You get the added convenience of flexible hours, which is so important to working parents (licensed day care usually has fixed hours). And because it is not a formalized situation, you can have a more personal and direct relationship with your child's caregiver.

*There are several benefits to your child from this type of child care.* Participating in family/day care is considered a good experience for a healthy, well-adjusted child. The presence of other children is thought to be stimulating, and family day care gives your child a chance to interact with children of various ages. She will be able to get personal attention because there won't be too many other children around. And it can teach your child independence; she can learn to trust that others can love and care for her outside of her immediate family.

*How can you evaluate the woman running the home?* A woman running family day care may not be highly educated but she may have a nice temperament and be good with children (otherwise she probably wouldn't have chosen to do this work). A caregiver's personality and competence are the primary consideration in choosing family day care. Evaluate if she is friendly to you and your child. Does she seem mature and sensible? Would you trust her to handle unexpected changes or emergencies?

*Don't necessarily look for a woman who has been doing day care a long time.* You may feel reassured if you find a woman who's been doing family day care a long time, but many experts say that this is *not* a recommendation. Burn-out can be a real problem for people looking after children. After a few years, all children may begin to look the same to her: she may even view them as difficult and ungrateful. How would you feel, being trapped all day for years with other people's small children? Therefore, try to find a woman with energy and enthusiasm for her job.

*There are questions you should ask a family day-care mother.* Besides the personality of the woman herself, you also want to find out what the physical environment

---

### QUESTIONS TO ASK A FAMILY DAY-CARE MOTHER

- How long have you been doing this and why did you decide to do this work?
- May I see the areas of your house used by the children?
- Is there someone to substitute if you get sick?
- Have you ever had an emergency with a child? What did you do?
- What is your daily routine? What interesting plans do you have for the children's day?
- Do you have safety features like caps on electric outlets, child-proofed cabinets, a protected, fenced-in outdoor play area, etc.?

---

will be like. In addition, you should ask how many children she is looking after. Some experts say that there should be no more than three children under the age of two to ensure proper care.

***There are potential problems with family care.*** Unlicensed programs can be closed suddenly if there are any legal problems, and then you're stuck without any child care. The mother usually has no training in child development, so you just have to rely on her intelligence and imagination to stimulate your child. There may be inadequate facilities or overcrowding, and/or the age mix may too wide. Finally, if the day-care provider is sick, you are stuck unless she has made provisions for a back-up caregiver.

## LICENSED DAY-CARE CENTERS

### THE AVAILABLE OPTIONS IN LICENSED DAY CARE

***Licensing is required for more than six children.*** A child-care facility has to be licensed when there are more than six or seven children. Licensing usually means that child/adult ratios and safety and space considerations are observed. Caregivers pass health tests and some are professionally trained in early childhood education. However, even though they are licensed there are no set standards of care, so once again you have to investigate the facilities on your child's behalf.

***Profit-making day care is financed by tuition and investors.*** Some parents complain that profit-making facilities can seem commercial and impersonal. There are experts who contend that for-profit centers cannot work for children under the age of three, but of course one cannot generalize about individual facilities that might be good.

***Private, nonprofit centers are run by universities, unions, hospitals, or corporations.*** The same experts who doubt the value of profit-making centers for very young children say that nonprofit centers run by corporations or universities may be preferable. They cite the usually low child/teacher ratio and the fact that there is usually a lot of parent involvement in the center. Nonprofit community-organized centers funded by the government, a church, or charitable organizations are available, but most centers of this kind do not accept children before they are two years of age.

## How to Choose a Licensed Center

***Visit several centers if possible.*** In order to evaluate a center, you'll want to visit while it is operating and stay for a while to get the flavor of the place. Spend at least one hour at each center and observe what is going on. How do the children behave? Do they seem happy or teary and whiny? If there is a lot of crying and fighting, this can be a sign of an understaffed facility. Do the children seem comfortable?

***Check prices of the centers near you.*** Although there are no set standards, these facilities can be expensive, running from $100 to $200 a week. Even at these prices, good centers have waiting lists, so many couples apply when they are pregnant.

***The child/staff ratio is an important consideration.*** A high staff-to-child ratio is considered a crucial element in choosing a center. Ideally, there should be no more than 10 children per play group. The federal requirement for these centers is that the group be headed by a trained professional with four adult assistants. However, it's not just a matter of how many adult bodies are there, but **who** those people are. Beware of untrained, unsupervised young staff. Child development experts suggest that the best ratio is one adult for every four children, but a ratio of one adult for every three children if they are infants.

**What is the training and personality of the staff?** The director of the center should have a graduate-level education in early childhood development. When you make your visit to the center, what is your impression of the people caring for the children? How do staff members handle little everyday "crises"? Are they patient and cheerful or strung-out and stressed in their reactions to the kids? Do they hold babies in their arms when feeding them or leave them with propped-up bottles?

**What is the attitude toward parents?**   Does the place encourage parent visits and involvement in the center itself? Is there a parent association and does it have meetings? Do parents have a say in how the center is run? Talk to other parents about how satisfied they are with the facility.

**Trust your gut reaction to the facility.**   Your instinctive reaction to a center can mean a lot. Do you feel welcome, or does something not feel right to you? Finding good day care for your child is important, but in addition **you** must feel comfortable with the arrangement. If you have doubts and worries, these emotions will eventually plague you with guilt and conflict, which in turn can interfere with your job performance.

**What is the physical environment like?**   Is the space large, clean, and brightly decorated? Are there individual cribs and cots for naps? Is it well heated and ventilated? Are there separate areas for different activities? Is there an outdoor play area that is protected and fenced in?

***What safety precautions are there?***    Are the floors smooth? Are there safety guards on doors, stairways, and windows? Is the furniture sturdy and does it have round edges? Are there dangerous pieces like glass shelves or tables? Are all cleaning and other supplies safely out of reach? Are heaters and radiators covered and electric outlets capped? Is there a smoke alarm and fire extinguishers? What is the procedure in case of a medical emergency?

***What equipment and amenities are available?***    Is there a good selection of toys, like large blocks and balls, puzzles with large pieces, dolls, books, plastic toys, musical instruments, and so on? Are there enough cribs and play-pens for infants and cots and blankets for toddlers? Often these centers supply miscellaneous items like diapers, milk, or formula, hot meals, and snacks (be sure these are nutritious and not candy or chips).

***How is the program organized?***    Find out what the daily routine is for child and caregiver—how do the children spend the day? Do the children get affection and information? Does someone read stories to them? Is there structured activity? Are there rest and snack periods? Outdoor activities? What are the rules on the use of a television, if there is one?

## THE BENEFITS OF LICENSED DAY CARE

***Licensed day-care centers are always open.***    Even if one caregiver gets sick, a licensed center can remain open with the other staff. With informal home care, if the child-care provider gets sick, you can't leave your child.

***A good center has good staff.***    If you're lucky enough to find a well-run facility, the staff will usually have child development training of some kind. This can mean a more stimulating, responsive environment for your child.

***Your child learns to trust someone other than you.***
Some parents may feel uncomfortable not being the sole adult provider in their child's life, but it can help the baby develop healthy, well-adjusted attitudes to other people.

Parents with these doubts may have to suppress their jealousy and ego and allow someone else to be important in their child's life, too.

*A child is exposed to stimulating experiences.* A child has playmates and activities in a day-care setting that she wouldn't have at home.

*Your child may develop more quickly.* Children in day-care programs often develop speaking and motor skills sooner than those raised in an isolated environment.

*Your child may learn to socialize better.* Children in group care often learn to interact better socially with other kids than they would if they didn't have a group experience. Your child may learn to get along better both with other children and adults.

## POSSIBLE PROBLEMS WITH LICENSED CENTERS

*The hours may be inconvenient.* Most day-care centers are open only from 8 to 6, presumably to service working parents with 9 to 5 jobs. This may not always be enough time for you, and may mean the additional cost and problem of finding an interim sitter in the morning or evening.

*The location may not be convenient.* Unlike family home care, which is in your neighborhood, a licensed facility may be far enough away to necessitate an expensive and/or time-consuming trip out of your way.

*There can be an inadequate staff with high turnover.* Often a center will pay low wages for very demanding work, which can mean frequent staff turnover. If your child loses people who are comfortable and familiar to her, it can create instability and anxiety in her life. Staff turnover can be more upsetting to a young child who had a consistent interaction with the caregiver. An older child will probably focus more on her playmates, and infants up to six months old have not yet differentiated one caregiver from another.

***There can be overcrowding.*** There can be too many children for the space and number of staff, which can put a strain on all the participants in the center. The adult/child ratio may also not be small enough for good care.

***Disease can spread.*** Find out what the center's policy is on bringing in a sick baby. Even if they have a rule, there may be selfish parents who try to bring an ill child anyway. With a large group of young children there is always the possibility of spread of disease.

***A lack of hygiene can be dangerous.*** It is possible for infants to develop severe diaper rash because of a lack of hygiene at their day-care facility. If diapers are not changed frequently enough, and if babies' bottoms and caregivers' hands are not properly cleaned, diaper rash will be the result.

***Some children can't handle a group situation.*** Some children just don't do well in a group: they need both solitude and concentrated personal attention. A very young baby, or a shy preschooler, may not do well at a center. They may need the positive reinforcement and interaction of a one-to-one relationship.

## A NANNY/GOVERNESS?

There is a wide variation in what couples consider when they want full-time, live-in care for their baby. A "nanny" can be anything from a professionally trained governess all the way to a non-English-speaking illegal immigrant—and everything in between. No matter what you consider acceptable as a nanny, this option in child care is not a fiscal possibility for most new parents. However, this section may interest you even if you can't afford full-time child care (who knows, after you read what's involved you may feel glad that you can't!).

*Live-In Child Care* is a good book for an in-depth examination of all aspects of having a nanny (see the *Bibliography*).

## A BABY NURSE IS DIFFERENT FROM A NANNY

*A baby nurse is different from a nanny.* Many couples are shocked and disillusioned by a baby nurse. A baby nurse is usually someone who specializes only in short-term, newborn care. You may be dismayed to learn not only how astronomically high her price may be (often $100 for a 24-hour day) but also what it does *not* include. Most baby nurses will not do anything but direct baby care: they won't cook or clean house or tend to you. In fact, often they expect their meals to be prepared for them.

*A baby nurse is supposed to teach you things.* She is someone you hire for the first few weeks of the baby's life. Her job is to look after the baby while you rest and recuperate from the birth. She's also there to give you confidence as you learn the basics of infant care.

*A baby nurse can be intimidating.* Some baby nurses are bossy which can undermine your confidence and take the fun out of getting to know your baby. For example, a nurse who has the wrong attitude toward breast-feeding can make nursing more difficult for you by undermining your attempts. If she weakens your confidence sufficiently in the early vulnerable stage of breast-feeding, she may cause you to have a nursing failure.

*There are things that a nurse should never do.* A baby nurse **should not** tell you that her procedures are the only "right" ones; you should not be put in the position of going against your own instincts about picking up the baby or anything else. A baby nurse **should not** undermine a new father's involvement with his child by criticizing him, nor cause a mother to withdraw by criticizing her parenting style.

*There are alternatives to a baby nurse.* If you have a mother or mother-in-law who is still competent with infants and willing to spend a week or two with you, you might want to weigh the possible problems of having her rather than a stranger at $100 a day. You might want to consider spending the money you would have paid to a baby nurse by getting a cleaning service, laundry pick-up, and food delivered instead. This will give you time to be with your baby and learn about him without interference.

## THE POSITIVE ASPECTS OF HAVING A NANNY

*Your child is in a familiar environment.* Being able to stay in his own home can be an asset, especially if you have a baby who reacts poorly to change in his surroundings. Other children can come over to play, at your convenience.

*The child forms a close attachment.* If you are lucky, the nanny can become like a member of your family. The baby's bond with his caregiver can be an important aspect of your child's development, for your peace of mind as well as the baby's happiness.

*The hours are flexible to your needs.* If you have a nanny, her hours can accommodate you and your spouse if you have to work late, have to go out to dinner, or if you have to travel (she can stay at home with the baby or they can even travel with you).

*If the baby is sick, she is still cared for.* If your baby is sick she won't be allowed in a day-care group, which means that you would have to stay home or make emergency arrangements for her care. With a nanny you don't have this problem.

## THE PROBLEMS WITH HAVING A NANNY

*Nannies cost a lot of money.* Nannies are expensive beyond most people's means. No matter what level of live-in caregiver you consider a "governess" (from fully trained to non-English-speaking), full-time child care is an expensive proposition. You can expect to pay a large part of your combined salaries (so that you can go out and earn a salary to pay for the privilege of leaving your baby in safe hands!). You have to pay not only the nanny's salary, which usually starts at around $150 weekly and can be two or three times that high, but also room and board, perhaps Social Security payments, and even an extra car.

***It's very hard to find a competent nanny.*** No matter how many references or even diplomas a nanny may have, it's difficult to find a woman whose personality and skills suit both you and your child. Most women applying for these jobs don't have training in child development, so you can't be assured of educational stimulation for your child.

***It's hard to judge the quality of care.*** Everything may seem fine to you, but it's not easy to ascertain whether the nanny is performing her job to suit your desires. If you have serious doubts about the caregiver, try coming home unexpectedly during the day. If you are not able to get home to do that, then ask a friend, relative, or neighbor to drop in. If, for example, you find the nanny and kid watching soap operas, that might be a clue that your doubts about the quality of her care are well founded!

***You sacrifice family privacy.*** Having live-in help, particularly someone intimately involved with your child, means that you give up a certain amount of privacy.

***The baby may suffer if the nanny does housework.*** Although you may think it's a bonus to have a nanny who might cook or do chores around the house, that can mean that your child is deprived of ample quality time with the caregiver. The child's needs may come last if the nanny has to do housework as well.

***The sudden departure of a nanny can be a trauma.*** The down side risk of having a nanny to whom the child gets very attached is that if she leaves suddenly, it can be a shock to the child.

### PARENTS' ATTITUDES TOWARD A NANNY

***Don't search for the ideal caretaker.*** Nobody is perfect, including you. However, some new parents think that if they search long and hard enough they will find Mary Poppins. If you can't find the "perfect" governess (or baby-sitter) you may be avoiding the issue of trusting someone else. There are people who are qualified to take care of your child, although they may not do it the same way you do. I wish you lots of luck in your search for perfection, but in all likelihood you'll have to lower your sights.

***Hire someone only for baby care.*** Child development experts suggest that if you are going to hire a full-time caretaker for your child, her job should be primarily to look after the baby. Your baby needs to have that person's full attention, yet priorities can get confused if the woman is also expected to clean, cook, iron, and so on. This confusion of priorities can be especially true with an infant, who needs a great deal of interaction and yet could just as easily be ignored except for feeding and changing. If at all possible, hire someone else to do your house cleaning— otherwise dusting the bric-a-brac may become more important than playing with and loving your baby.

***Don't compromise on the quality of the nanny.*** Full-time help has to give emotional and intellectual stimulation to your child. Initially, your infant needs warmth and cuddling, a loving, responsive person. But the child's mind is also developing, and you don't want to sell him short by consigning him to a nanny who won't be able to give him the optimum feedback. And later on, it will make a great difference in your child's life and yours if you have been able to find a nanny who is really gifted with children, who has the imagination and energy equal to the task.

If you hire a non-English-speaking servant from a culture with different values (especially about intellectual stimulation), then the nanny may consider that her job is done if the child is fed, diapered, and quiet. There isn't much you can do to substantially alter her attitude toward child rearing.

***Even with a nanny, you are on call.*** There will be times when one of the parents will have to put aside work for the baby, even with the world's greatest nanny. There can be childhood emergencies (and later school plays and baseball games) when only a parent will do.

***What will you do when the nanny is ill?*** If you and
your spouse work, you can't just take it for granted that a
nanny will always be available. Make a contingency plan so
that you have a sitter or relative with whom you can leave
the baby on short notice, unless you can take time off yourself.

***Live-in help is uncomfortable for many couples.***
Some parents take it for granted that they will have help in
child care, while others are conflicted or uneasy with the
idea. Your ability to adapt to having a nurse depends at
least in part on what you are accustomed to. The presence
of someone in the house may be easier if you've had a maid,
cook, or laundress before. If the nanny is the first "servant"
you have hired, you may have trouble adjusting.

***You have to give up privacy.*** One price of having live-
in help is that you may feel you can no longer traipse around
the house with the freedom you had before. You no longer
have total privacy to make love or have fights or walk
around naked. Some couples find that giving up their privacy is too high a price to pay for a nanny.

***You may feel self-conscious or formal.*** Having a
nanny can make you feel out of place in your own home.
Her presence can make you feel distant from the baby and
each other. You may feel that you are being judged: this
can make you concerned about the appearance of your
house or other superficial aspects of your life.

***You may have guilt about hired help.*** If your parents
had household help when you were growing up, you may
have felt uncomfortable or guilty about those servants. Or
you may feel badly about a nanny having to do all the dirty
work with the baby while you get to have all the fun. Even
though she is being paid, you may feel uncomfortable. Some
parents also feel guilty about their baby, imagining that she
knows they are "neglecting" her by having a nanny look
after her.

***You may feel jealous of your child's closeness to the
nanny.*** If you're feeling uncomfortable about how much

intimate time the nanny and child have together, one solution is have her take the child to a mother-infant play
group (often called "Mommy and Me") so that their time
together is not exclusive. However, optimally you should
overcome your jealousy since a close relationship with her
nanny can be wonderful for your baby. Be glad that your
child has this interaction with another person: a baby's experience of intimacy can help develop a capacity for intimacy later in life. Try not to lose track of the fact that the
nanny's closeness to the baby frees you and your spouse to
have exclusive, intimate time together.

***The nanny's personality has to fit yours.*** Every
mother has different insecurities; the nanny you choose
should not be someone who threatens you. Only you can
make this decision about what kind of nanny will fit your
personality. For instance, you might feel no threat from a
"grandmotherly type" because she dotes on the baby in a
different way than you do. A "motherly type" might be
good for you because she might give support and mothering
to **you**, especially if you're a working mother who could
use the stroking. Or you might feel best with a young girl
for a nanny, which may give you more sense of control
over the situation.

***To make the decision, ask yourself some questions.***
Do you want someone living in your house, taking care of
your baby? How will it affect your marital relationship, your
relationship with the child, and your self-image as parents?
Only you two can answer these questions. This decision
can impact your life on so many levels that other people's
advice and experience are irrelevant.

***A maid can be an alternative to a full-time nanny.***
Some couples find that they can have a more satisfying relationship with their child if they hire a person to do housework while they do the baby care themselves. This
obviously won't work for dual-career parents. In any case,
it will mean that you'll also need someone to look after the
baby during the hours you'll both be out, so that you can
still have an outside life.

## How to Find a Nanny

***Agencies are not considered a great source.*** Agencies are not always reliable sources for nannies because they will often hire just about anyone who seems sober. Of course there are also agencies that have been in the business for years and have a reputation to protect. They claim to screen nannies and demand references, but these procedures can often be superficial and not carefully checked. You can have more confidence if you know a friend, or preferably more than one, who has been well served by an agency.

***Agencies are also very costly.*** An agency is a business: their goal is to place a nanny in a home and hope that she stays for at least one month so that they can get their commission. Some agencies charge 18 percent of a month's salary, but the rule is to charge a full month's salary. Some agencies keep commission only if the employee remains a full month, others promise to replace the nanny within three months.

***Word of mouth is a good source for nannies.*** Talk to other mothers you may know or meet; even women who don't have a nanny may know sources for finding one. Your pediatrician may also have some suggestions.

***Take out an ad in the newspaper.*** You will probably be inundated with replies if you use a large urban newspaper to advertise for a nanny. Using a local community or ethnic newspaper may prove more manageable. In the ad state your needs precisely: the age range for the nanny, the baby's age, and the hours you want. Then you can screen applicants on the telephone. Use a legal pad and write down each woman's name and telephone number. If she sounds as though you'd like to meet her, take notes beside her name to remind you about her.

***There are questions to ask on the phone.*** Before you take the time to meet a potential nanny, there are several key questions to ask over the phone that can give you a good idea of the person. You can judge how good her English is, but **do not judge** her personality by her voice on the telephone. Many people are shy on the phone or sound slow or distant. However, trust your own instincts even over the phone. Either you'll communicate and get good vibes, you won't get any clear sense of the woman, or you'll feel something isn't right.

1. "What experience do you have?"
2. "Do you have any references?"
3. "Do you have children of your own?"
4. Tell her the basic requirements of the job and the child's age (as you did in the ad) and ask whether she is available for those hours, etc.
5. "Why does this work interest you?"

*What are your first impressions on meeting her?* Is she well groomed—acceptably neat and clean? Is she on time? If she is late, ask her why she is; if she got lost, how did she handle it? Can you imagine her living in your home, being with your child?

*See her with your child.* A woman might be shy with you but great with your baby—she also might be charming with you and not relate to your child well. If your child is asleep when you interview her, no matter how much you might like a candidate you should ask her to return so that you can see her with your baby. Is she warm and talkative? Does she make eye contact with the baby? How does the child respond to her?

*Encourage her to talk about herself.* "Tell me about yourself" might be a good way to get a candidate to open up. Rather than bombarding a possible nanny with questions, let her talk. You can probably learn more about her that way, especially after she overcomes any initial shyness, than by giving her the third degree.

*She should be clear about what the job entails.* Be specific about what the job entails. Don't wait to spring it on her later, or she may quit or take out her resentment on the child. It's a good idea to encourage her to ask questions, too. If she wants to know specifics about what you expect and how your household functions, it's better for her to find out now rather than taking the job and waiting for weeks to find out she's not comfortable with it.

***Don't make unreasonable demands on her.*** Some people feel that because they are paying a nanny a lot, she should be some kind of Superwoman machine who can do it all. She can't "do it all" any more than you can! You should be sure that you and your partner aren't operating on the principle that you want your "money's worth," which is unfortunately more common an attitude than it should be.

***Check the references of anyone who interests you.*** If the voice of the person you call sounds as though they may be a phony reference—a friend or relative of the woman—ask very specific questions. "What were her duties and was she able to perform all of them well?" "How old was your child and what was she like with him? How did the child feel when she left?" "When and why did she leave you?" Only a genuine previous employer could answer these questions easily and quickly. Then you have to decide if the person giving the reference seems like someone whose opinion you can trust.

### SUGGESTIONS ON YOUR RELATIONSHIP WITH A NANNY

***Treat her with respect.*** You should never undermine the nanny's authority with your child. If you do not agree with her decisions and attitudes most of the time, then she's not the right person for the job.

***Physical discipline should be forbidden.*** A cardinal rule with a nanny in any household is that spanking should be forbidden. This is one area in which you can override your nanny's point of view about discipline. The reason for this is that your child is defenseless—what you might consider a smack on the bottom, someone else might consider a great big wallop. A nanny may hit your child either too hard or too often if spanking is considered permissible.

Suggest other disciplinary tactics to the nanny if she doesn't already know them. She can distract the child from whatever behavior she doesn't like. When the child is older, she can be sent to her room or have privileges withdrawn (bedtime story, dessert, television).

**Be clear and concise about her duties and hours.** There is the tendency, when someone is being well paid and lives in your home, to take advantage of her time. Being a nanny is not a 24-hour-a-day job. Besides her day(s) off, a nanny's daily free time should be precise and sacrosanct except in emergencies. Usually a nanny gets a couple of hours off during the day and is generally off-duty when the child is asleep at night.

Discuss any additional duties that she might have, like housework, shopping, meal preparation, or running errands. Will she be paid for these services, or will you "barter" extra hours or days off?

**Be generous with time for the nanny.** Don't think in terms of getting every last drop of energy and time from your nanny. Be flexible with her hours. Try to think of her needs, of the time she needs to recharge emotionally after the exhausting work of child rearing. On top of simply being the decent and considerate thing to do, your thoughtfulness and generosity toward the nanny will make her a better companion for your child.

**Be generous with money for the nanny.** If your nanny is getting a large salary, don't imagine that she does not also deserve or need a bonus from time to time. If she is a caregiver with fewer skills who is working for lower wages, then a bonus will mean a great deal to her, too. Don't make the mistake of thinking that if you give her pass-me-down clothes, or take her on a lovely trip with you and the baby, those things take the place of cash bonuses or a raise. In any job a person feels worthy and appreciated if they get praise, good wages, decent treatment, and incentive bonuses.

**Be clear about payment for overtime, sick days, etc.** You should discuss what kind of payment you will make if the nanny has to work additional time, like weekends, off-hours, etc. You don't want to impose or take advantage of a nanny, who may then become resentful and thus less effective in her work. Rather than paying, you might want to give her extra days or hours off at a later date.

Don't lose sight of the fact that you are an employer, with all the legal and ethical obligations that entails. For example, as a minimum a nanny should be entitled to one week's paid vacation and five paid sick days a year, as well as some holidays. You should spell all this out clearly before she takes the job so that neither of you is resentful later.

***Have regular talks with the nanny.*** If you are a career mother who is constantly on the run, there may be times when you only see the nanny fleetingly as she's leaving and you take over. If this happens, you should make a point of sitting down to talk to each other. This gives you both a chance to exchange notes on how the baby is doing and whether there is anything that either of you would like to change.

## CHANGING NANNIES

***If a nanny is going to leave, don't let it drag on.*** If you decide that you have to let a nanny go—or if she tells you that she isn't happy and wants to leave—have her do so immediately. It can only be uncomfortable for everyone if she sticks around after the decision is made. You don't want an angry or resentful person around your child, even if it means inconvenience and sacrifice for you until you find a replacement. Of course this would not be the case if the nanny's departure is because of some personal problem of her own, like homesickness for a foreign country or illness in her family.

***Discuss the possibility of her leaving when you hire her.*** It can really make a nanny's departure smoother if you've already worked out the mechanics of her leaving. It is usual to give two weeks' severance pay, unless she's been with you for years. In most cases, severance is linked to how long you employed the person.

***Changing nannies doesn't have to be a trauma.*** Losing a nanny doesn't have to be the end of the world for you or the baby. Kids are more adaptable than you might think, even if they are deeply attached to someone. If you and your spouse are primary, dependable caregivers in your child's life—if your love and the time you're able to spend with your child is consistent and of good quality—then the coming and going of other people in his life should not be a problem. It can make the transition easier if you're both around as much as possible and you keep the rest of household life calm and stable during the changeover to a new nanny.

## BABY-SITTERS

### HOW TO FIND BABY-SITTERS

*Most couples use a mixture of sources for sitters.* Many parents use a combination of teenagers, college kids, other mothers, and occasionally a relative. If you don't have a steady sitter with fixed hours, this catch-as-catch-can arrangement will probably work best if one or both parents have only part-time work, or have overlapping hours so that one parent is often available.

*An experienced, mature woman may be better for an infant.* With a newborn baby, he may get more precise care and you may have more peace of mind if you choose a mature, experienced sitter.

*Be selective with teenagers.* Teenagers under 16 may be too immature, but you have to judge by the individual. Those over 16 may want higher wages, since they can get jobs in fast-food restaurants, etc. You may have to offer the older teenagers the minimum wage, which they could get in other jobs.

*Tell everyone you know or meet that you want a sitter.* Word of mouth is always effective in finding household help.

*Check bulletin boards or put up a notice of your own.* Some logical places for checking offerings or placing an ad are: the pediatrician's office, high school or college placement centers, churches, senior citizen centers, nursing schools, the supermarket bulletin board, or the local newspaper.

***Don't forget to always have a back-up sitter.*** Even if you are lucky enough to find a sitter whom you can use regularly, there will come a time when she is sick, has a school prom, doctor's appointment, etc. At the very least you should be informed about any local day-care center where you might be able to leave the child on short notice.

***Don't tie yourself to one sitter.*** If you become too attached to one sitter, then you become a hostage to her schedule and the time she is available. Also, the child may get too attached to someone who is basically a temporary caregiver. It's best to develop a network of sitters that you can rotate.

***Make a regular weekly or monthly commitment to someone.*** If you discover that it is a hassle to make last-minute arrangements for sitters, it might be a good investment to fix a regular time and day with someone. Planning ahead gives you the freedom to make personal plans for that specific time, knowing that your child will be well looked after.

***What about paying for a sitter if you cancel?*** Child care is an important job and should be treated seriously. If you show respect and commitment to a sitter, she will return it to you. You should be clear ahead of time about whether you pay (or what amount you pay, depending on how much notice you give) in the event that you have to cancel. If baby-sitting is the main income for the person you hire, and she declares the income, then you should also discuss paying Social Security taxes on her behalf.

## SUGGESTIONS FOR MANAGING BABY-SITTERS

***Don't wait too long to use a sitter.*** Some couples make a mistake in waiting too long to introduce the concept of a sitter in their child's life. If your child is always with you and never left in anyone else's care, he may not understand or accept a sitter later on.

***The first time you leave the child is the hardest.***   The initial separation is usually harder for the parent than the child. You may have feelings of conflict, loss, and preoccupation once you've gone out. You may be upset by jealous fantasies that your child could like another woman more than you. You may find that you're plagued by worries until you come home and see with your own eyes that your baby is fine. Some women have fits of crying the first time they leave the baby and make continual calls to the house to reassure themselves that none of their nightmares have come true!

***Give youself extra time to leave the first day.***   If the first time that you leave the child with a sitter is in the morning, then get up half an hour earlier than you imagine is necessary in order to be able to spend as much time as you need with the baby that morning.

***If possible, have the sitter visit beforehand.***   Whether you pay her or not, it can be easier on all of you if the sitter has a chance to meet your child before you go out— preferably even days beforehand. This way her presence is not too foreign to the baby and the sitter already knows her way around your house.

***The baby will react to your attitude about going out.***   A child can pick up your feelings about leaving her with a sitter. Be calm and definite in your departure, don't linger or make a big emotional scene. A child's crying usually stops very soon after a parent leaves. If you're concerned, you can always call in after you leave.

***Leave the number where you'll be.***   Leaving a referral number should be a rule of thumb no matter who you leave the child with or for how long. It gives everyone involved a certain peace of mind. If you don't know the telephone number before you go out, then call in and give it to the sitter when you reach your destination.

***Do not put the child to bed.*** Do not let your child go
to sleep before the sitter arrives. Unless your child knows
a particular sitter very well, it can be traumatic to wake up
and see a stranger. Waking up to an unfamiliar face when
your parents disappear can undermine a child's trust. Some
children can be deeply disturbed by this shock, especially
children who are shy or have problems adapting to new
experiences. The trauma of the "betrayal" can be such that
leaving the child with a sitter in the future becomes a major
problem. If he does fall asleep, experts recommend waking
him to say goodbye so that there are no surprises, even if
it means a tearful parting scene.

***Explain light switches, etc., and leave emergency
numbers.*** Show the sitter how lights, stove, front-door
lock, and so on, function in your house. Then leave a number where you can be reached. If you can't be easily reached
or won't be able to get home if needed, include a relative's
or neighbor's number. Be sure that you always have on display the numbers for the pediatrician, police, fire, poison
control, and other emergency services.

***Make clear, concise rules about the house.*** Unless
you have two phone lines (or "call waiting"), you'll probably want to forbid the sitter from using your phone so that
you can call in. The other areas of rules to consider are:
whether the sitter can smoke (or in what restricted areas),
have friends over, use the kitchen, and so forth. You should
leave some snack or beverage for a sitter, unless you just
want to let her help herself from the refrigerator.

***Be clear about payment and transportation.*** Discuss the sitter's fees ahead of time, and whether there are
extra charges if she stays past a certain hour. It is your responsibility to get a sitter home, especially if she is young.
If you do not take her home yourself then you should pay
for a cab, which you assist her in getting.

# 15

# Shared care

Is it possible for a couple to share baby care, house care, and other responsibilities? Is it good for the baby? Is it good for your relationship? The answers to these questions depend on your personalities, the division of labor that already existed in your relationship before the baby's arrival, and also what you define as "shared" care.

## THE DEFINITION OF "SHARED" CARE

*Fair sharing doesn't have to mean 50-50.* In order to share in your baby's care you don't have to draw up a tally sheet and assign each other parallel tasks in a tit-for-tat way. Shared care is a state of mind as much as it is a practical division of labor. Sharing roles as parents doesn't mean that task equality is your goal. Equality means a parity of activities; equity means a fair arrangement. Be realistic in what your expect.

*You are sharing a new goal, not just tasks.* Having a baby means that you have to restructure your lives—careers, finances, lifestyle, etc.—because both of you want the same things from your new life as a family. You want a quality of environment for yourself and your child, in terms of housing, schooling, safety, and economics, that may require you to make sacrifices and adjustments in the short run. You may have to be patient with your present conditions because they lead to a future goal.

*Once again, patience is a job prerequisite for parenting.* Change is slow and difficult when people are learning new tasks and new roles. Take things one step at a time. Is your wife a woman who, before she became a mother, never enjoyed cooking? Then don't expect her to suddenly put on a gingham apron and bake bread! Nor does fatherhood compel a man to rush out and get himself fitted for rubber gloves. Changes in personal expectations and orientations are slow. Take things one step at a time.

*You have to be willing to make trade-offs.* Both of you should be aware of the compromises and trade-offs that are necessary when you decide to raise a child. These trade-offs may temporarily be greater for one partner—usually the woman—but they are for a mutual goal. Therefore it's imperative that child rearing not become a contest between the two of you over who is doing more tasks or more adjusting.

*Forget what you promised each other during pregnancy.* Often when a couple is waiting for their baby they discuss sharing care. Sometimes a couple will discuss shared care even before they decide to have a child: a woman may have made her decision to have a baby based on the belief that her mate would truly shoulder half the burden. If her husband then doesn't hold to his word once the baby arrives, she may feel betrayed, angry, and put upon.

Perhaps a woman should look upon her partner's pre-baby declarations as she would promises made in the heat of passion! A man may agree ahead of time to a 50-50 split of tasks and responsibilities, but these are only theoretical discussions. Most men don't actually think that their wives literally expect them to change every other diaper. Many men just assume (perhaps unconsciously) that once they have a child, they will become "normal," that they will be like their own parents. If a woman sticks to her guns and tries to hold her spouse to his vow of total sharing, she's going to be one unhappy cowgirl!

*Don't expect saintliness from your partner.* Don't ask your mate to change his or her behavior and also be gracious about it! Don't expect a man to learn to chip in with baby care or tasks around the house and whistle while he works! He's entitled to feel put upon and irritable while he adjusts, as is a woman with a career whose life is turned upside down by motherhood. Give each other the space to be cranky and resentful: those are honest, legitimate responses to the transition to parenthood.

## NEGOTIATING THE DIVISION OF LABOR

*Negotiations are antiromantic and tiresome*   Negotiating with your partner is not a pleasant task but it's a realistic necessity. Part of growing up is accepting responsibility for organizing a life together that meets everyone's needs.

*Beware of forgetting your private life.*   Don't make the mistake of negotiating your private relationship right out of the picture. Some couples try to be so precise and organized that they plan tasks to be done in shifts. The problem with that is you may wind up never being together. Even sex and other "extracurricular" activities have to be planned and agreed upon now that you are parents—spontaneous sex or other pleasures will probably become distant memories during your adjustment period. Almost everything you do together has to be planned and traded off. Don't shortchange your precious time together because "the baby has to have a trip to the park right now" or the washing machine is crying out for attention.

*Assess the situation and your partner realistically before negotiating.*   If a woman wants more participation from her husband (which is often the case in negotiations), then she should first evaluate what is the most she can hope to get. What kind of man is your spouse? Is he old-fashioned and traditional? Is he open to the idea of sharing care? Forget what you may have read about shared care in a women's magazine. Some men are not going to pitch in: period, full stop. A successful 44-year-old businessman is going to have a different outlook on fatherhood than a 23-year-old painter.

On the other hand, a man may want to be more involved in caring for his child but meets resistance from his wife. A father in this position should dispassionately try to understand his spouse's orientation to marriage and motherhood. What kind of woman is she? What was her parents' relationship like? What has the balance and division of labor been in your relationship before? Is either of you expecting too much of an about-face from a spouse who is set in his/her ways?

*Be thoughtful about the way that you approach negotiations.* The form that you use in approaching your mate is as important as the content of what you have to say. When you sit down to work things out, make an effort to talk as calmly as possible. Becoming parents and learning new ways of interacting with each other requires that you be kind and empathetic. Try to be as gentle with your mate as you would be with a child.

A person will resist change when it is demanded or pushed for. Do not get hostile, indignant, or place blame. Those attitudes are bound to lead you to arguments, not solutions. Instead, discuss what needs doing and **ask your partner** what solutions s/he recommends.

*Confrontation is difficult for many people.* Although negotiating (especially with someone you love) may be hard for you, the only way to solve a problem is by confronting it. If you reach an impasse and find that there are areas where you just can't negotiate an equitable distribution of responsibilities, then you may be able to solve your problems by digging into your bank account. Get as much outside help as you can afford; some of these problems are the rare kind that can actually be solved by throwing money at them! Your tranquility is worth more than money in the bank. If you cannot reach an agreement, then use whatever resources you have to alleviate the pressures between you.

*Negotiating can put a woman in a double bind.* A woman can feel that she's in a no-win position as a wife trying to encourage her husband to share in household responsibilities. If you stand up for your rights you may be labelled as a "nagging wife." If you are willing to maintain the pre-baby status quo, that means you are a "nice person" who keeps her mouth shut and demands nothing. Just keep in mind that if you're willing to open discussions, expect some ruffled feathers.

*Your priorities must change.* Even though there's a new baby in the house, if a woman previously had total responsibility for the household her husband may still expect a tidy house, nice food, the laundry done, errands run, and the checkbook balanced. He may feel resentful if she cannot continue to accomplish these tasks, in addition to looking after their baby.

We're not talking about a problem of male chauvinism here: the problem can as easily be a woman's attitude toward her role. If a woman expects a certain level of energy and competence from herself, then she may feel like a failure and recriminate herself for not managing everything at once. If you find this happening to you, stop what you're doing and take a good look at your priorities. Baby care and baby love are more important than well-folded towels. Self-love and thoughtfulness toward yourself and your spouse are more important than asparagus with perfect hollandaise sauce.

*One parent cannot have full responsibility.* Parenting in our culture is already a job that can be very isolating. If one of you (usually the mother) has to shoulder the full burden of child rearing and house running, it can make you feel alone and depressed, as well as lowering your self-esteem. The parent who does most of these tasks deserves what should be looked upon as "job benefits." The parent who has the most responsibilities needs time off and other considerations as in any other job.

*Try to be aware if your partner is burning out.* If one parent gets to the point of feeling overwhelmed and is losing patience with the baby, the other parent can learn to be tuned in to those signals. Your relationship need not reach a crisis point about shared care if you are sensitive to each other's needs. You can develop an unspoken communication so that the less stressed parent takes the baby, almost by instinct, and gives the burned-out parent a break.

***Don't blame each other when things go wrong.*** Try to keep sight of the fact that you are in this together, and that part of being a parent is being imperfect and making mistakes. If you go on an outing with the baby, whose responsibility is it to bring the baby bag? And when something important is forgotten, like the pacifier or a change of diaper, do you turn on each other like savages, pointing fingers and placing blame? It's bad enough having a cranky baby; cranky parents aren't going to help the situation.

***Give up trying to be "right."*** If either partner feels the need to be right, then the couple can wind up criticizing each other all day long because they need to defend their own positions. Childbirth and life with a newborn are often quite different from what you expected. You can have the best laid plans and find that what you have to deal with is entirely different. Trying to force reality to meet your fantasies is a waste of time and energy. It doesn't work if you try to be "right," to set up some kind of rigid plan and fit reality into it. Let go of your grievances and focus on what got you to the point of parenthood: love for each other, shared goals, and so on.

***Flexibility is a key to harmony.*** Couples whose relationships are successful, and who are harmonious as parents, tend to be flexible with each other. They are not harsh and judgmental. They allow their partner to love the baby in his/her own way. They also give each other the room to make mistakes. This creates an environment in which you can all grow as individuals and a family.

***Generosity of spirit and mutual respect go a long way.*** An important attitude to develop is respect for each other's commitments, whether it's a board meeting or a shuffleboard game. It helps if you're on the same wavelength about a fundamental aspect of parenthood, which is the belief that you are sharing a life's work. If you don't both have this philosophy, then one person becomes the martyr, the one who is "holier." Instead of being generous about juggling your plans, or about baby-sitting while your spouse takes off, these issues can become a test of wills. One of you may accuse the other, "It was your responsibility to arrange the baby-sitter.'' One of you may claim that you need more private or recreational time. One of you may feel you deserve more because you had a tough week. Parenthood shouldn't be a contest—you're supposed to be on the same team!

## PRACTICAL ASPECTS OF SHARED CARE

*Make a weekly schedule together.*   Pick a night of the week, perhaps Sunday, when you will regularly sit down together and plan out the week ahead. Each of you should write down your own and your partner's appointments so that you don't make conflicting plans. You can try to weigh the relative importance of the commitments you've made and which ones can be most easily changed if needed (although be careful that this doesn't develop into a contest over whose plans are more important). Just because you've made a weekly plan together does not mean that it is written in stone. Some dates and appointments are made to be changed, just as rules are made to be broken.

*Revise your weekly strategy and rotate the schedule.* Who will take responsibility for which chores, in and outside the house? Which of you is in charge of arranging the baby care? Do you want to take turns making those plans, or does it work out better for one of you to always have that job? There are a few ways to parcel out time and chores: one of you can do certain chores for a while and then rotate, or you can divide the week and each do three days at a time.

*Weekends are especially important.*   Decide together what tasks or pleasures are the most important to you. Learn to strike a balance between structured time and loose time. If you aren't especially good at taking it easy when there's a lot to be done, you might even have to block out ''do-nothing'' time. Remember to schedule time for yourselves as a couple, even if it's only 3 hours on Sunday.

*Certain jobs may be easier or more pleasant for one parent.*   Ideally, the partner who does a thing best should do it. In some relationships you find that the areas of expertise or ease mesh nicely: a couple agrees that one of them will cook while the other does the bookkeeping. If at all possible, neither of you should have to do anything that you really despise doing. Both of you should get as much pleasure as possible from child rearing and not feel that certain tasks are a "punishment"!

***There is no "best" parent for the job.*** However, you can't just absolve yourself from a dislikable job. There are several household and baby chores that can be generally considered "no-gratification jobs." Tasks that neither of you wants to do should be shared, unless, like Tom Sawyer, you can find a sucker to do them.

***Your different temperaments may affect the division of labor.*** One of you is probably by nature a more responsible, organized type of person. Often this difference between a man and woman was part of what attracted them to each other and creates a balance between them. But don't allow the person who naturally assumes responsibility to overtake the other, or to let him/her off the hook about carrying a fair share. Eventually you'll feel resentful; the responsible person will feel overwhelmed and the other may feel left out or pushed aside.

## SHARING BABY CARE

***Sharing baby care is an act of love.*** When you both participate in caring for your child, you aren't just nurturing the baby, you are showing love to each other. It also reinforces positive feelings about your partner's ability to be nurturant. Even something as simple as planning your child's future is a statement of your commitment to each other.

***The father may want to take off a week when the baby is born.*** Taking a week's paternity leave may be easier in some professions than in others, but it's worth the effort for a man who desires it. It can be great for you to share an experience that can bond the three of you together as a family. It often happens that the mother automatically puts herself in charge, and feels she has to direct both household and infant-care tasks. If you want to get your sharing off to a good start, try to avoid clichéd role playing.

***Both of you need basic baby-care skills.*** Regardless of what division of labor you work out, both parents are going to feel better about themselves and more comfortable in their new roles if they know the practical basics of caring for an infant. Even if you expect to have full-time help, taking care of your baby's basic needs is part of infant-parent bonding.

***You might try role reversal for a day.*** A new mother may find that her spouse is insensitive to her daily travails with infant care—and he probably will be until he experiences it first hand. If a new father is having trouble being supportive and compassionate toward his wife's role as primary caregiver for their baby, why not let him take over for a day? One day can give you only a preview, but hands-on experience can at least help you appreciate the frustrations and exhaustion of caring for a child and your wife's need for support and help.

***Reversing roles may be necessary but it's not a punishment.*** Do not look at role reversal as a power play: it is not a chance for a woman to "get back" at her partner. She will need to show you where all the baby's supplies are kept and make a list of the schedule for feeding, bathing, and so on. She should also let you know any special hints she has picked up in what works to calm the baby.

Role reversal will probably be tough for a man, but it is a lot easier than inconclusive arguments and negotiations about his lack of involvement in baby care. Anger and tempers may erupt between you in this exercise, but it's better than repressing those same feelings. A father will probably be a wreck the first time, but at least he'll understand his wife's daily life. For some fathers it may be the only way they can fully understand the demands of caring for an infant. Without reversing roles a father may not feel as responsible for baby care as the mother—and both of you must accept that responsibility even if you don't have a 50-50 share of tasks.

*A woman may force the baby on his father.* Some mothers make the mistake of trying to shove the child down his father's throat. You may be so eager for your husband to be an equal partner in parenting that you try to force bonding on him. Beware of your own enthusiasm and the strength of your personality, because your attempts may backfire and drive a new father in the opposite direction. Even a man who loves and feels attached to his baby does not want his wife's ideas of fatherhood forced on him, nor her schedule of how involved he should be.

*Dividing care can result in a nonsexist child.* If a father shares at least some real part of baby care, it means that he doesn't become just an evening visitor to his children, but part of their lives. Also, it can mean that you raise a child who is more equally attached to both his mother and father, which is a bonus for your entire family.

*Men can gain the most from sharing baby care.* A father's role has been historically limited. For some men it can be hard to enter the domestic realm, but once they get there they love it. The bond between a father and his child can be especially enriching. It can give a new meaning to your life, which may have been primarily focused on getting ahead, ambition, financial pressures, and so forth.

Kids can bring out the nurturant, physical, pleasurable aspects of yourself. The first time you actually release these emotions may be with your child. Loving and hugging a child feels good—a small child returns love wholeheartedly. How can you measure what you gain from sharing in your baby's care? A child needs you and loves you. The special feelings, the simple contentment, the highs and lows, are a gift that you share with your child and partner.

*Shared care can give a man a new identity.* Being a hands-on father can show you an aspect of yourself besides your earning power. You will get love and respect—from your wife as well as from your child—for being a caring, loving father. A child will not view an involved father as an absent, distant disciplinarian. And the more involved a father is, the better his understanding of his child will be, which can only make their relationship stronger.

***A man can be humbled by participating in baby care.*** Being forced—or being eager—to take an active parenting role can put you in touch with feelings you didn't know you had. Doing diapers and fixing bottles can give you a certain perspective on life and put you in touch with reality in a way that nothing else in your life may have done.

***A woman has to have some time off from mothering.*** A mother should not have responsibility for her baby 24 hours a day or the quality of her life—and the baby's—is sure to decline. If you don't have full-time help, then you should agree upon a prearranged time every evening (or three times a week) when the father takes over and the mother is off-duty. Although you can arrange for a sitter to do this, it can actually be nice for a father to know that he has this time with his child.

***Parents are putting out more than they're getting back.*** Especially with a newborn, you and your partner are giving more to the baby than you're receiving. You are working and nurturing in a situation where you aren't necessarily "getting fed" in return. This can lead to a feeling of competitiveness between you for the little time and energy that is left over after baby care, housework, and careers. One solution to avoid this conflict is if you're able to consciously decide to be real partners—which means cooperating for your mutual benefit.

***There can be a fundamental misconception about sharing care.*** There is a philosophical difference between shared care and a man who is just "helping out." If a man is only "chipping in" out of the goodness of his heart, then he has no genuine responsibility. This means that he can cop out on his contribution to child care because he's "too tired" or he's "had a hard day at work." This attitude suggests that neither of these excuses could apply to a woman who has been with the baby since 5 a.m. Of course a man needs a chance to unwind and recharge his batteries at the end of the day—but then so does a woman. The attitude of man as "helper" also means that he can put the burden on his wife to "remind me" to feed the baby (or dress her or play with her). It is unfair to put a woman in the position of having to beg or force her husband to participate in looking after their child and home.

*If a man is only "helping," it upsets the balance in your relationship.* If a man thinks of himself only as a helper, then his contribution to child care is a "gift" to his wife. This can alter the social exchange and balance of power in your marriage. Although you may not realize it, if a man's involvement is considered an act of charity, then a woman is constrained to have to return the favor in some way. A woman will have to reciprocate with sexual favors, by doing more chores, etc.

*The first months may be a honeymoon.* Some fathers look at the first months of the baby's life as a game of sorts. You may look at baby care as an amusing novelty. Once the fun wears off, you may consider yourself "off-duty" and return to your previous routine, but that isn't "cricket," as the saying goes. The baby is here to stay, and so is all the hard work that accompanies her. She is not a toy, and this isn't a game like "playing house."

*A man may be applauded by others for "helping."* Society may applaud a man who participates in child care, which can contribute to the possibility that he'll view his involvement as a gracious gesture. A woman can resent other people saying how lucky she is that her husband helps her, yet never is there a word of acknowledgment for what she does every day. A woman can get angry when she gets no credit for juggling the house, the child, and perhaps a career, whereas the man gets a pat on the back for every bottle he feeds the baby.

*A woman's resentment can spill over into the relationship.* If your husband is neither helpful nor compassionate about the work you have to do with a new baby, you can become resentful. Disenchantment with your mate for not pulling his weight can pollute your relationship. A woman who feels she isn't getting help or appreciation can withdraw from her spouse, either emotionally or sexually;

this can be the beginning of the end unless you catch it in time.

*A woman can be at fault for not asking properly for her husband's participation.*    It can be hard for some women to correct a man's impression of fathering as "lending a hand once in a while." You may be afraid to ask your husband for help if he comes home tired, which means you are validating the "old-fashioned" view of the bread-winner who comes home and plops down in front of the TV, waiting for dinner to be served.

If you do gather up the courage to ask your spouse to help, you may worry that your request will make him resent you. Instead of taking that risk, you might opt to do the work yourself—which means that you may wind up resenting him! If you can't be forthright and honest you run the risk of see-sawing between being a saint who tries to handle it all alone and feeling put upon and retreating in anger.

Your husband is not necessarily at fault; he is not a thoughtless villain. You might have hang-ups about a man sharing care; you may feel guilty or foolish about your feelings, but admit that you have them. You are going to have to talk about your conflicted feelings before they create ugly scenes and problems in your relationship.

*Men do deserve praise!*    Any man who makes the effort to mesh child care and his work deserves appreciative strokes. Any woman who doesn't understand that is missing the whole point of sharing care; after centuries of societal pressure excluding a man from the kitchen or nursery, your husband needs all the support you can muster to encourage his involvement. Even the most cooperative and generous man is going to feel burdened by taking on parenting responsibilities without role models. Your mate will withdraw if you don't give him respect for trying new habits and tasks without a precedent to follow. It would be quite natural for him to become defensive and give up if you also expect him to be strong and silent about the unfamiliar burdens to which he has to adjust.

*Calling your husband names is not recommended!* A woman is self-defeating if, in her frustration, she resorts to calling her husband pointless phrases like "male chauvinist." What does a woman accomplish if she reprimands her spouse for complaining about the difficulties of child care? What is the use of admonishing your husband? You are missing the point, sweetheart! You'll only have your righteous indignation and back issues of *Ms.* magazine to keep you company!

## A MAN CAN HAVE DIFFICULTIES SHARING CARE

*There is no social support for a father doing baby care.* A man who is caring for his child can feel isolated and lonely. A father does not have the female support network that a mother can automatically find. As a simple example of social attitudes toward a father who actively participates in child care, look what can await you if you take your child to the playground. You may find the mothers and nannies regarding you suspiciously—you are guilty until proven innocent. What would a "proper" man be doing in the park at 10 in the morning? Are you an out-of-work bum supported by a hardworking wife? Did you kidnap that child in the pram? It is not easy to break with social conventions.

*Some men are apprehensive about sharing child care.* You may feel frightened about caring for your baby because you feel unsure and unskilled as a father. In reaction to your insecurities you may fall back on the traditional male behavior that you saw when you were growing up. This early traditional socialization may surface when your baby is born, to the point that you may even feel awkward holding or kissing your infant. If your own father wasn't physically affectionate you may feel subconsciously disloyal to him by choosing another fathering style, or you just may feel awkward. One way to lessen your anxieties and help you feel comfortable is for you to try to be actively involved in choosing a pediatrician, in deciding about child care, and so on.

*Some men have deep problems with housework.* Most men feel awkward and unskilled about housework, but this is a natural discomfort that they overcome when they learn the ropes. Most men do not know what is involved in running a household: they aren't even going to think about it unless someone points out the various tasks and worries. However, you may be one of those men who has deeply ingrained notions of what a man is, and housework may seem like an imposition on your masculinity. You may not be able to accept the image of yourself pushing a vacuum cleaner or running the washing machine.

*There is a profile of men with the most problems about doing housework.* Helping around the house may be most difficult if you came from a traditional family and had a mother who gave you a very traditional upbringing. If you are a conservative, middle-aged man, who is used to having his needs looked after automatically (and who is surrounded by friends with the same world view), you're not going to jump right into dusting. You also are probably not going to learn the intricacies of loading a dishwasher properly if you are a man who takes financial responsibility seriously and puts most of his energy and time (mental and physical) into his career.

*There are some standard male excuses for not sharing care.* The following are excuses that men use to extricate themselves from participating in child rearing and house management. Be forewarned that none of these is a valid excuse and you should feel embarrassed for stooping so low!

---

INVALID MALE EXCUSES FOR NOT SHARING CARE

- "I help more than most men."
- "I did a lot the first few months."
- "I have more outside demands and less time and energy for the kid."
- "Women are more naturally suited to this stuff."
- "I'm not any good at baby care." ("The diaper always falls off when I do it," etc.)
- "The baby is better with you." ("He cries less, you know how to soothe him better," etc.)

# THE HORRIBLE "H" WORD: HOUSEWORK

As Joan Rivers has pointed out, housework is a waste of time—you dust and scrub and polish, then six months later you have to turn around and do it all over again! Once you have a baby, there is so much more to do that you have to find a way to share the chores and also rethink your priorities about what actually needs doing.

## HOUSEWORK AND YOUR RELATIONSHIP

*Housework is the biggest cause of marital fights.* Some surveys have shown that household chores cause not only domestic arguments but even violence. The studies show that often the more housework a man does, the more fights the couple has over this issue.

*Men and women have a different outlook about chores.* Male and female expectations about household maintenance are usually quite different, but a baby can change that. Until you have a child, it is usually assumed that running the house is a woman's responsibility. However, some new division of labor is forced upon you when you become parents. Old presumptions are shaken up and it can be a shock to the new father, especially if he's a man with a traditional outlook on what the woman is "supposed" to do.

*Fully shared housework is very rare.* Many new mothers continue to do the majority of household chores, even though they might wish their partner would help them. These women find that it's easier to shoulder most of the work because this eliminates the hassles that arise when they try to get their husband's participation.

*Some kind of negotiation is necessary.* When there is a child involved, there is so much more to do, and therefore to divide between you. Because domestic chores increase dramatically with a newborn in the house, some new division of labor seems necessary.

*A **woman can resent having to ask for help.*** Although it would be nice if a man just pitched in on his own, things don't usually work that way. Yet there are new mothers who fill themselves with righteous indignation. This doesn't get the chores done nor does it help your relationship. If you allow yourself to get angry without expressing it appropriately, your negative emotions can create deeper problems in your relationship. A woman who is very angry can withhold sex, erupt into a tirade, go into a depression, or express her rage as irritability with the child.

Realistically, a woman usually has to ask her spouse (often more than once) for specific help with the baby and household. Even though a new mother may not be able to be straightforward in explaining her needs to her partner, she can get furious all the same if he doesn't participate in housework.

***The return home in the evening can be the most difficult part of the day.*** Re-entry into the house can be stressful for career parents. Here are some suggestions on ways to make your return home more pleasant:

1. Concentrate on unwinding and trying to relax on the way home.
2. Establish a routine that the parent who gets home last has 15 minutes to him/herself upon arrival—to open the mail, freshen up, change clothes, etc.
3. The parent who gets home earlier and deals with the initial onslaught deserves extra time alone in the evening or on the weekend.
4. Do not take business calls at home. Use an answering machine to screen calls so that you only pick up those that are truly urgent.

***Beware the "6 o'clock syndrome."*** A sure way to end the day poorly and get the evening off to a bad start is to become a victim of the "6 o'clock syndrome." This phenomenon occurs when you are home alone all day with your child—as evening approaches, your patience and energy wear thin. You begin to count the minutes until your husband gets home—not because you're dying to see him, but because he is the emergency relief shift.

Your unsuspecting spouse makes the mistake of walking through the front door. You hand the baby to him like a hot potato and storm out of the room, declaring, "Take him, I can't stand this another minute!" If he makes the further mistake of being later than usual, you'll probably blast him for that, too, in your frustration. All new parents should be alert to the 6 o'clock syndrome and do everything they can to protect themselves from it.

## DEVELOP NEW ATTITUDES TOWARD HOUSEWORK

**Chores can overtake your life.** If you allow housework to take a disproportionate part of your time and energy, this may mean you're sacrificing quality in your relationship for quality in floor care. You may find that you're both racing around the house, ignoring each other in your hurry to accomplish chores.

**What really "needs" to be done?** Many of us feel compelled to maintain a certain standard of housekeeping because of ideas that were implanted in us, usually by our mothers. Your expectations can be the cause of some ugly scenes between you unless you're willing to stop and evaluate what really needs doing and what is obsessive or neurotic in your housekeeping (like drying all the spots off glasses, constantly fluffing pillows on the couch, etc.). Basically, what is important from a practical, hygienic point of view is that bathrooms and the kitchen should be really clean—living areas can be as dusty or cluttered as you can tolerate.

**Make a list of household chores.** Decide as a team effort which tasks are really necessary and how often you really need to do them. Eliminate nonessential chores, then divide your list according to each of your abilities and schedule. Remember: 50-50 is not your goal and there is no universal yardstick on what is a fair division of tasks. Fairness is whatever the two of you agree upon, given your individual relationship.

***Integrate parental and household duties.*** If you can decide on a comfortable way to juggle the demands of parenting and house maintenance, you may be able to get twice as many chores accomplished. Sharing care can also give you a chance for individual time alone with baby; for example, one of you can say, "I'll run the vacuum cleaner while you take the baby for a stroll."

***A compulsive housewife may impose her standards on her spouse.*** (Although some men are fanatically particular about cleanliness, etc., this is usually a female problem so I am addressing it as such.) The transition to parenthood is not the time for compulsive house cleaning, but some women have a hard time accepting this. If your wife compulsively does things around the house and also confronts you with chores that she wants done, get her to slow down for a moment. Tell her that it doesn't bother you (the clothes, dishes, windows, etc.). A compulsive housekeeper may finally become tired enough to get the point and let go of some of her compulsions.

***Rethink how you approach and execute housework.*** Don't look at cleaning your house as something you spend the day doing. Reorient yourself so that you can view house cleaning as a series of small jobs. Redefine a job by its parts: rather than feeling frustrated that you cannot manage to clean an entire room, break it into its components. Clean the oven one day, the floor the next, put dishes or handwashables to soak, and then read or feed your baby.

You can also do many tasks with the baby. You can dust or vacuum with your baby in a sling or backpack. You can keep her near you in an infant seat while you're paying bills, letter writing, cooking, or sewing.

***A man has to develop self-confidence.*** Most men are not brought up knowing how to do even the most rudimentary household tasks. There are some women who want their husbands to do half the housekeeping—but on their terms, their way. Needless to say, a man will withdraw from a woman who sabotages his efforts at being an involved father or helping at home. Simply by attempting to get involved in the home and hearth a man is challenging personally ingrained habits and social traditions. It is going to take guts and hard work to cut a new path through the woods and a man needs to be encouraged, not undermined, by his partner.

*A woman can have a psychological investment in her role as housewife.* You may feel that your identity is so closely tied to motherhood that you can't give any of it to your husband. Some women cannot comfortably share housekeeping (or infant care) because reducing their performance in that role undermines their self-image. A woman may feel threatened if she can't count on housework and baby care as her domain.

*A woman may feel the house is her kingdom.* If a mother and housewife feels possessive about her parenting role, she may become dominant and bossy about the house and child. Even a woman with a career may get at best only token help from her husband if she is not willing to delegate responsibility to him in their home.

*The "right" way to do a job.* Without realizing it, you often expect your partner to do things your way. Unfortunately, you may not stop to consider that your mate has also lived a number of years on this planet and has ideas of his/her own on "how" to do a task. In case you had not considered this, there can be two "best" ways to raise a child or do a household task. It really isn't necessary to debate every decision with the hope of converting your spouse to your method.

*Don't look upon your spouse as a trainee in your style.* If you find yourself compiling a list of complaints about the "imperfect" way that your mate does certain things, consider this: your partner probably has a list, too! Try this: do things your own way, don't try to impose your style on your mate, and don't check up on him/her. Live and let live is an attitude that can take you a long way together.

*You can learn from each other.* A woman's "chauvinism" about the home is no different from a man who thinks that anything to do with a car is purely a man's territory. But if you regard yourselves as a team, you can exchange ideas and information in a positive way.

- Answer questions without a superior attitude or critical tone.
- Let your partner do things his/her own way.
- Don't supervise or breathe down his/her neck and interfere.
- Doing something "well enough" is good enough. Nothing has to be done your way, or as well as you do—simply "doing," being involved, is what counts.

## TWO-CAREER COUPLES

### CAN YOU HAVE IT ALL?

***You're not going to be constantly happy.*** We know that it's possible for a couple to both have jobs and raise a family, but it's not humanly possible to enjoy all of it all the time. When both parents have jobs, it means that their roles as parents and workers are blurred, blended, and perhaps enriched.

Two-career couples have the potential for fuller, more satisfying lives, but at the same time something has to give. If you both work it probably means that you have to forfeit some other possibilities in your personal life. A full-time parent does not have the benefits you enjoy by working in the outside world. In order to be working parents you may have to give up leisure time, personal gratification, or even some of the order and peace you would have wanted in your lives.

***Over-achievement is a dangerous American goal.*** Our culture applauds people who attempt to be super-achievers in their lives. This social attitude can translate as pressure on new parents if you expect yourselves to be "mega" in all your roles. It can undermine your happiness and self-confidence if you attempt to be super-successful parents, super-successful workers, and have super-successful kids.

***Two careers require a balancing act.*** As a family in which both parents work you're going to have to focus on how to balance parenting, your jobs, and your personal relationship. For many new parents it often seems that the baby comes first, at least in their emotions, while their careers (which may require the most time) take second place. The equation seems to work out so that they give the lowest priority to the needs of their relationship. You have to focus on protecting your relationship and the precious little time that you have for each other.

***Do both of you share the same priorities?*** New parents probably won't have too many problems if both partners value their family life and careers ahead of their marital relationship. However, if one of you feels the loss of the intimacy with your spouse, it's vital to communicate those feelings as soon as you're aware of them.

***Both of you have to extend yourselves to make it work.*** As a couple you had ingrained habits before becoming parents. You also saw role models in your parents that can make it hard for you to adapt to newer ideas about two-career parents. Your expectations, based on what you learned in your family of origin, can make it difficult for you to adjust to the life you have chosen as working parents.

***You may both feel conflicted about having dual roles.*** A man may give verbal support to his wife's career. He may even be proud of his wife's achievements and the fact that she's juggling motherhood and career. However, underneath he may feel cheated and even worry that his child is being deprived. A mother can feel conflicted because although she needs help with the baby and even believes she deserves it, she may feel guilty asking for it.

## HOW TO FIND A BALANCE BETWEEN YOUR DUAL ROLES

***Make yourselves a top priority.*** Take a close look at how you spend your time. Are you making good choices? Are you devoting your time and energy to things that are necessary? The expression "A woman's work is never done" may have been coined by the first compulsive housewife who didn't know how to sit down and take a deep breath! A man or woman could assign themselves household chores and the list would never finish. If you suffer from this syndrome, then make another list for yourself: that list can consist of one item, call it "Time for each other." You need time to talk and listen to each other. That is an essential ingredient of a loving, intimate relationship and especially important for two-career parents.

***A lack of time for each other can be destructive.*** If you don't have enough time or energy for each other, it can lead to a lack of intimacy. Two-career parents can become so tired that they can't make love; they can become too preoccupied to make conversation; they can be so overwhelmed by the demands on them that they forget what it's like to just have fun.

***You may wind up feeling resentful.*** It's very common for working parents to feel overworked and underappreciated. If you aren't even aware of your resentment, you may wind up feeling hostility toward your partner which can surface at unexpected times. Try to remember that you have each made your choice to work while raising a child: it's not your partner's fault if it takes more out of you than you thought.

***Working parents could both use a "wife."*** Working parents who have to rush home in the evening and deal with their baby and household often indulge in a delicious daydream as they struggle with rush hour. Two-career parents may secretly wish for the luxury of having a loving "wife" greet them at the door. The fantasy of having your very own "wife" may seem too much to hope for: someone to cook delicious meals and keep the refrigerator filled with snacks, someone to amuse and encourage your baby, someone to keep the house tidy. What about the simple joy of someone asking, "How was your day?" . . . and really wanting to know!

## A MAN'S NEGATIVE ATTITUDE TOWARD
## A WORKING WIFE

*A man may not want to be part of a two-career couple.* Your husband may be opposed to your working outside the home once you have a baby. For men whose early socialization was very traditional, they may have conservative prejudices against a mother who works. These prejudices can surface when the baby is born. Intellectually these men may acknowledge that a woman has the "right" to work, but emotionally they may be uncomfortable with the idea that their child does not have a full-time mother.

*A working mother can feel terrible without her husband's support.* A mother who works undoubtedly already feels some measure of guilt about being away from her child. In addition you may find that your husband is unhappy about your career and/or puts pressure on you to stop working. Your partner's negative response can create distress for you and stress between the two of you.

*The father should get involved in child-care decisions.* One way for a working mother to feel less pressure, and for the new father to feel more comfortable about his wife's working, is for him to share decisions about the child's care. If a man is involved in his child's care he becomes an active participant and shares responsibility for choices about child rearing.

*It falls on a woman's shoulders to improve her mate's attitude.* Many men simply assume and expect their wives to drop everything else when their baby is born. Society, and often their own mothers, have taught them that. A woman may have given indications that she would dedicate herself entirely to motherhood, but when the baby is born she may find that she wants to continue working. It becomes a woman's responsibility to help her husband adjust and accept this change in plans.

Marriage is a contract, and a woman is renegotiating some of the terms of that contract if she wants to change her husband's expectations of her role. If your husband is passively unhelpful, or actively opposed to your career, you are the one who's going to have to raise this issue in order to resolve his opposition.

***A career mother should be careful in approaching a resentful husband.*** I do not intend to make a sexist comment when I suggest that a man who is threatened and/ or confused should be treated with kid gloves. Outdated or sexist as this may sound, it's still pretty valid advice. You will accomplish a great deal more if you think through how and when to approach your mate about topics that are potentially explosive.

***Appeal to the positive, not the negative.*** You don't want the subject of your working to become a power issue. You don't want to debate whose work is more important or lucrative. Neither do you want to put your husband on the defensive nor to back yourself into a corner.

It is not a great idea for you to be hostile, demanding, or confrontational even if you have good reason to be angry at your husband for his lousy attitude toward your desire to work. Try to approach him in a nonthreatening way about his resistance to you as a working mother. For instance, appeal to your husband on the basis that you know he wants you to be happy and personally fulfilled and that your career allows you that. Do not blame him, be manipulative, or attack him. Comments like "I'm not your mother, so don't expect me to be a martyr for my child like she was for you" will only be counterproductive.

***A man may not feel comfortable helping around the house.*** Even though you both have jobs, your husband may still not feel at ease sharing household maintenance with you. His attitudes are based on a combination of his own upbringing, his age and that of the child(ren), his work situation and ambitions for the future, his sense of his own success or failure, and his sense of his own masculinity. Your reaction to your husband's attitude will be partially based on how great your desire is to be out of the house and how much your income is needed. There is the additional factor that your career might threaten him because your husband needs to feel important, or even central, in your life.

*The woman has to be the "bigger man" to get her husband to participate.* If you want to get your reluctant husband to carry some of the load with the baby or household tasks, your only chance is to rise above the situation and encourage him. Even though it may not be fair that you do lots of things that he takes for granted, he's going to need positive feedback from you to motivate him.

*A man won't participate if his wife is a ball-buster.* If a woman criticizes her husband, he'll probably stop making the effort to be involved. Many new mothers cut their husbands off at the knees: they say they want the father to help but then are critical about the way that he performs the task. A woman may want to feel that the child and home are a joint responsibility, and not that her husband deigns to help every so often. But by criticizing him, she drives him away.

*Is criticism shorthand for something else?* Beware that a woman who criticizes the way her husband does chores or handles the baby may be doing so to disguise a personal complaint. For example, is your annoyance with the way your husband puts away the diapers really a way of saying, "I want more affection"?

*Guilt can make you tense about your new roles.* Two-career couples usually suffer from more guilt and strain than families where only one parent works. Your feelings of guilt may be a result of feeling inadequate as parents. A man can criticize his wife's part-time mothering, and she can complain about his earning power or lack of interest in the baby, but these are probably reactions to the conflicted emotions that working parents often have to juggle.

### WHAT IF THE WOMAN'S CAREER IS MORE SUCCESSFUL?

*A man may say that he is proud of his wife's success.* A man can be pleased by his wife's professional accomplishments, but often he is able to acknowledge her success only on an intellectual level. Emotionally, a man may feel conflicted if his wife's career outstrips his.

*A man may feel that his wife's success makes him a failure.*   Your wife's accomplishments may make you feel small. If your wife suddenly has more success financially than you do, or she gains more status or visibility in her work, you may experience her success as your failure. In our society, it is usually assumed that in a two-career family the man's career will be the dominant one.

*There may be less time for a man with a successful wife.*   If your wife's achievements leave less time for you and your child(ren), it can make you resentful. You may also feel diminished if your wife's success occupies a lot of her time because there will be that much less for you.

*Some men cannot accept a less prominent position.*   Depending on your age, your background, and the kind of work that you and your wife do, you may be unable to gracefully accept the position of being less successful in your work. You may have these feelings and not understand them, which can be destructive in a more subtle way.

*The wife should not just assume that everything is fine.*   Just because your husband has not said anything about his feelings, do not go on the assumption that he isn't having any difficulty with your success. A relationship can be destroyed if both partners don't make an effort to recognize these potential problems. Talking together before, during, and after the woman achieves her greater salary or status can help diffuse the situation for new parents.

*A woman may be afraid of success.*   You may worry about your relationship and what will happen if you surpass your husband's success level. Talking with your mate about these issues is the best way to prevent them from reaching a blow-up. The following are some of the fears that a woman can have about how her success will affect her relationship:

* Will your husband be resentful or leave you?
* Will he become competitive and combative?
* Will you feel guilty about having less time for him?

• Will your feelings toward him change: will you admire or respect him less?

### SUGGESTIONS ON HOW TO AVOID OVERLOAD

*Make a list of what doesn't feel right.*   Both partners should make a list of how they are feeling overloaded as two-career parents. List what you think has gone wrong in your management of parenting and careers.

*Make a list of what doesn't need doing.*   When your job is especially stressful or demanding, make a list of the things that you don't really need to do at home. Equally, if there is a lot of pressure at home, either of you can try to find ways temporarily to lighten the load at your job. During periods of pressure there are certain errands and household chores that can wait for a while—maybe a *long* while— (maybe until your baby finishes high school!).

*Get out of the house.*   When things become overwhelming, try to make arrangements so that you can get away, together or separately, if only for a short break. Do nothing for an hour or two, take a break from all the pressures and demands. "Wasting time" as a novelty can be very good for the mental health of two-career parents who have every minute planned.

*Don't place blame for your discontent or frustration.*   Don't make the mistake of saying that "life would be fine" if it weren't for: your spouse, his/her job, your spouse's boss, your spouse's business trips, your mortgage, the baby, your in-laws, etc. When two-career couples feel overwhelmed (which happens to full-time parents also) it is destructive to place blame on any one element of your complicated life. Being parents with two careers is a difficult, exhausting job—you miss the point if you think along the lines that "life would be easy if it weren't for . . ."

# 16

# Problems with the baby

This chapter—Problems with the Baby—is a mixed bag. It covers everything from an infant's physical and emotional difficulties to problems you may have with your own attitudes toward your child. However, these problems are not outlined from the point of view of the child and her needs. The focus in this chapter continues the theme of the book, which is to examine the effect on your marriage of difficulties with the baby.

Whenever problems with your baby are getting you down, imagine the roles reversed in about 40 years. As difficult as a colicky baby may be, just think of what *you* will be like when you're a crotchety old parent! With any luck, your child will show you some of the loving patience that you extend to her now. Think of treating your baby as you hope she'll treat you some day.

## A BABY OF THE "WRONG" SEX

*You may be devastated by the gender of your baby.* Although it's not the baby's fault, a "wrong sex" baby can seem like a terrible problem to a parent who is disappointed. If either one of you is overinvested in wanting a boy or girl, it can be a big strain on the relationship if you don't get what you want.

***Don't pretend you don't care when you do.*** It is essential that you admit to yourself and your partner how much the baby's gender matters to you. In the long run, being honest about your feelings (even if you are embarrassed or guilty about them) will create fewer problems than repressing your negative emotions.

Although we've all heard the cliché "All I want is a healthy baby," there are some parents who put a very high premium on their child's gender. In fact, to such a parent it can seem as though the baby is "defective" by being the wrong sex.

***Most men want a boy.*** If this is true of you and you have a daughter (or a second daughter), it's better for you and your family if you can voice this disappointment to your wife. You may be pleasantly surprised to find that you feel very close to your little girl and have a strong desire to protect and care for her. If you bury your unhappiness, it can repress the positive emotions you might have had. By voicing your sadness or anger, it can free you to love your daughter. Once you've allowed yourself to express your negative feelings, you may be pleased to discover that they begin to dissipate.

***Some mothers feel uncomfortable with a baby boy.*** You may wonder how to handle a boy and feel awkward at first. You may be self-conscious about cleaning his genitals or seeing masturbation, which is common and harmless. Don't worry: with time you'll be able to relax and enjoy your son.

***Your desire for a child of a specific sex can affect your marriage.*** Your unhappiness about the baby's gender can make your spouse feel s/he has let you down. It will help to discuss this openly so that neither of you is harboring secret grudges or guilts, which are obviously irrational.

If you have a strong desire for a same-sex baby because you suppose it will make you feel closer to the child, consider whether your imagined alliance with the baby will make your partner jealous or tense. If the baby is the "wrong" sex, will you shy away from creating that closeness just because you didn't get what you wanted?

***Why does the baby's gender matter so much to you?***
One way to overcome your powerful feelings about your baby's gender is to understand some of the conscious or hidden reasons that make you feel so strongly about getting the "right" gender. (Of course this doesn't apply to the expectant couple with three sons who are praying for a girl. Any mother would be eager to finally have a chance to buy a smocked party dress after years of buying only overalls!)

---

**REASONS FOR WANTING A SAME-SEX BABY**

- You expect it will be easier to understand the child
- You think your sameness will guarantee a close relationship
- You want the child to achieve what you hoped for yourself and didn't accomplish
- Your relationship with your same-sex parent was better

---

**REASONS FOR WANTING AN OPPOSITE-SEX BABY**

- The child will give you less competition for your partner's love and attention
- Fear of getting too close to the child: you think you'll stay more separate from an opposite-sex child
- Less possibility that you'll repeat patterns you had with your own parents
- Your relationship was better with the opposite-sex parent

## PARENTS' EMOTIONAL PROBLEMS WITH THE BABY

***Unrealistic expectations may be at the center of some problems.*** You may not have had a good idea of how a newborn really looks or behaves. Advertisements show an adorable, cooing five-month-old, the typical Gerber Baby, but if that's what you expect, you may be in for a big shock. Most newborns usually don't look too great; they also don't laugh or even respond to your smile. Their repertoire is often limited just to grimacing, eating, and sleeping.

Unrealistic expectations about how much time and effort a baby requires have been covered in other sections of the book, but it's worth mentioning the concept of "the 2 a.m. feeding" because you may wonder if you have a problem with your child. You may have thought that the night feeding would be quick: you'd get up, feed the baby, and sleep through the rest of the night. But realistically, the baby has to be changed, gets fussy, dilly-dallies in eating (whether breast or bottle), dirties his diaper again after you change it, and then may stay awake for several hours. If you aren't prepared for this fairly normal routine, you can perceive it as a problem with your baby.

***You may not experience love at first sight.*** Many new parents do not feel instantaneous love for their baby. This doesn't have to be a problem if you don't allow it to be. Love is something that develops gradually. You would not be alone if you didn't experience deep love for your baby until she began to show pleasure in response to the care and attention you give her. If you aren't in love with the baby at first, be patient. When the baby smiles and seems to enjoy and recognize you, a stronger relationship may develop.

Don't feel guilty or too disappointed if love takes longer than you expected. A father may need even more time to develop close feelings to the baby if he's away all day. This process of falling in love with your infant is not a problem unless you imagine that it is.

## THE "FUNNY-LOOKING KID" ("FLK") SYNDROME

***Some parents have trouble relating to an "FLK."***
Some babies are what you might call funny-looking; they
have physical characteristics such as ears that stick out, a
strangely shaped head or nose, or a birthmark. Pediatricians
sometimes use the term "FLK" to refer to such kids. Some
parents react in a radical way to such "imperfections." If
you have an FLK, you might consider it a blow to your ego,
a reflection on your own perfection or attractiveness. Perhaps some parents feel that having an FLK means that they
are an FLA (adult)!

***The image of the Gerber Baby can trip you up.***   It
can be dangerous to have a mental image only of a cherubic
gorgeous baby like the ones in the magazines: it can mean
that your dreams are shattered if you have an FLK. The
difference between your expectations and the way your
baby actually looks in the beginning can make you doubt
the child entirely. You may wonder whether such a disap-
pointing-looking child will let you down in other hopes
you may have for her. Never mind that this sounds superficial; for some parents these feelings can be truly disturbing.

***FLK can interfere with bonding.***   If you are uncomfortable with how your child looks, it can block the powerful positive emotions that you had anticipated having.
You may discover that the surge of parental love just isn't
there. This lack of feeling can lead you to question yourself
as a parent. For these reasons, having an FLK can also contribute to postpartum depression.

***Deep attachments take a long time.***   Think about how
you and your spouse fell in love; even if it was love-at-first-
sight, that can't be what's held you together. In the same
way, your child's physical appearance will become less important to you as you get to know him as a person. You
and your mate may have shocked each other in turning out
differently from what you first expected, yet love can grow
even with disappointments and surprises. You can become
a good parent in the same way. Your pleasure and pride in

the baby, and your feeling of closeness to him, will grow as you spend time together and discover each other.

However, if in a few weeks you or your partner still don't feel especially connected to the baby, then something isn't right. This doesn't mean you're a bad person or an unfit parent. It just means that your dreams and fantasies were so shattered by the surprise of how your baby looked that it's still getting in the way of making an attachment. This is an issue you have to confront and solve with your spouse, or with professional help, as soon as possible. The longer you delay in bonding, you can have greater difficulties forming a close attachment to your baby.

## SERIOUS PHYSICAL PROBLEMS WITH THE BABY

*Any illness can affect your adjustment to parenthood.*   Even the possibility that your child is sick, or the fear that she might be, can become overwhelming when added to the inherent pressures of being new parents. Illness can interfere with your bonding process to the baby or even with your marital relationship.

*It's too easy for parents to forget each other.*   When all the attention and energy is directed to the sick child, a couple can lose sight of each other. You may overlook each other's feelings because there is such intense focus on the baby. Both of you need each other's love and understanding, especially when you have a handicapped child or one who is hospitalized for a long time.

*Your reactions will probably follow a pattern.*   Several generalizations can be made about what many new parents experience when their baby is premature, handicapped, hospitalized, or dies. The first difficulty is usually one of accepting the problem: the delay in your acceptance is because you have to reconcile your expectations and the reality that you face. It is common for parents to want to escape upsetting news about their baby.

*The initial reaction is usually shock.*   The shock that your baby has a problem will probably be closely followed

by disbelief and denial of the bad news. It is common for a
parent then to experience guilt and anger. The guilt may be
because you might have done something during the pregnancy or delivery that you think caused the problem. Then
you'll probably feel anger. You may turn your rage toward
your mate—s/he is the closest person to you, and therefore
the "safest" person with whom you can act out your anger.
All these emotions can be an additional strain on your marriage.

***Your parents may be of no help at all.*** Some grandparents react in a way that may disappoint you. Your parents or in-laws may behave as though the baby was their
own and **they** are the ones in need of comfort and support.
You may be surprised to discover that you have to take care
of the grandparents, and not vice-versa. You may have anticipated leaning on the grandparents' shoulders, but instead you have to be strong for them.

## DEALING WITH A BABY WITH COLIC

***Colic is not a disease.*** The only universal symptom of
colic is crying: the baby is normal before and after the crying. One definition of true colic is that, in the absence of
any phy  ' problem, a baby cries inconsolably for several
hours at  me. The crying is often accompanied by screaming, a re   face,  nd drawing up of the legs. There is often
gas or abdomin . pain, but not always.

***Don't blame yourselves.*** Colic is not caused by tension
in the home. If you aren't breast-feeding, don't feel guilty.
Nursing is not a guarantee against colic. However, other
people may mistakenly assume that your baby's colic is a
sign that you're mismanaging your parental duties, which
can be an additional pressure on you. Take heart: you are
not doing anything to cause the crying. As you've probably
discovered, there's not much you can do to stop it, either!
(Although you may want to try some of the soothing suggestions later in this section.)

***The colic can become more important than the
baby.*** It may be hard for you to focus on your baby and

enjoy him when all he seems to do is cry. Colic can become
the focal point for the parents and the people around them,
which can rob all of you of the pleasures of your infant.
It's possible to waste a lot of time and energy trying to
figure out "why" the baby cries so much. Talking to parents with easy children may only make you feel worse,
without solving anything.

*Colic can seem worse than it is.*   Because the baby's
screams and wails can be so piercing, it may seem worse to
you than it actually is. Try timing the crying spells, both
how long they last and how much time there is between
them. This can give you a better perspective, since 10 minutes of screaming can feel like an eternity. It may give you
the strength to carry on if you know that most colic goes
away at six weeks to three months of age.

*You must have a supportive pediatrician.*   You need
a doctor who will give your baby a really thorough examination to rule out any possible physical problems that could
account for the crying. Once that is out of the way, you
need the doctor's emotional support just as much as his/her
medical expertise. A pediatrician's attitude toward the parents of a colicky baby can have a profound influence on
how they perceive their own competence. A doctor can
help bolster your confidence as parents, which can be undermined by your baby's colic.

   If you become really worried about the crying, you
might talk to your pediatrician about spending part of a day
in his/her office. That way the doctor can see for him/herself how your baby behaves.

*Colic can create tremendous tension between you.*
When all the facts are in, it seems that most colicky babies
thrive. It's the parents who are in real trouble—they become anxious, tired, tense, and resentful! Coping with a
colicky baby can be a terrible strain on new parents, who
are struggling as it is with all the normal burdens of the
transition to parenthood. Most new parents are not prepared for their child's misery and they're frustrated by their
inability to alleviate her suffering.

   The strain on your marriage can come from expecting the impossible. A father often expects that a mother's touch will work to soothe the baby. A mother often expects her husband to soothe **her** when none of her touching does a bit of good to calm the baby. You may both feel that you're failing each other, and letting the baby down at the same time.

Admit to yourselves how lousy you feel. If you try to fake it and put on a cheerful face, it can make it difficult for your spouse to express negative feelings. Also, putting up a front creates another strain on you and your marriage.

*Get out of the house.*    Escape is standard advice for the parents of a colicky baby. The more time you have away from the baby's crying, the better you'll be able to cope with it when you're there. if you get too strung-out about it, you can't do yourself or the baby any good. Get out as much as possible, but don't be surprised if you aren't able to unwind or you imagine that you can still hear the crying.

*Find other parents with the same problem.*    Misery loves company, and it was never truer than with a screaming baby. If you participate in the usual type of postpartum group, it may make you uncomfortable to be there with your crying baby. If there's even one other colicky baby in the group you might want to consider going off and forming your own wailing duo with the other parent! Otherwise, you can ask your pediatrician for the name of other couples with a colicky baby and get in touch to see if they want to compare notes and lick their wounds with you.

*Do not let your baby "cry it out."*    You should not be afraid of "spoiling" your baby—a tiny infant has no concept of doing something to get attention. He is crying out of real distress and you should do everything in your power to try to make his life less painful. "Crying it out" is cruel for a baby with colic: crying causes a baby to swallow air, which can create more gas and discomfort. It can also frighten a child in pain to be left uncomforted for a long period of time.

Doctors have found that babies cry less often and for a shorter time if someone responds to them promptly. Crying is an essential form of communication for an infant; for a baby in pain, it is a crucial lifeline. If your pediatrician tells you to leave a colicky baby to cry, you should seriously consider changing doctors.

*There are many remedies for colic.* You can try any or all of these suggestions, although you should get your pediatrician's approval first. Whatever you do, don't give up. None of these remedies may work and then suddenly one day, one of them will make a difference.

---

### THINGS NEVER TO DO WITH A COLICKY BABY

- Don't leave a crying baby uncomforted
- Don't put sugar on a pacifier: it can lead to cavities in future teeth
- Don't put honey on a pacifier before a child is a year old: it can cause food poisoning
- Don't give alcohol: it can cause death or damage a baby's liver or brain
- Do not give any medication (unless a pediatrician orders it)

---

### FEEDING REMEDIES FOR COLIC

- Sucking allows the baby to comfort herself: a thumb or pacifier is fine; do not prohibit sucking
- Hold upright during and after feedings: may aid digestion and help burp up gas
- Don't offer extra milk after feeding: digesting more food can create more gas
- Feed smaller amounts more often so there's less to digest each feeding
- Weak herbal teas can help: camomile, fennel, peppermint, or comfrey may soothe
- Plain warm water in a bottle can soothe: it warms the stomach but doesn't require digestion
- Drop cow's milk products from her diet (and from your own if you're nursing). Substances in cow's milk can sometimes cause allergic reactions

### PHYSICAL REMEDIES TO SOOTHE COLIC

- Swaddling, especially wrapping securely in a warmed receiving blanket
- Rocking, walking
- Roll carriage back and forth over a bump
- Wear the baby in frontpack during the day
- Take the baby for a car ride
- Relax yourself—your tension can increase tension in baby, while your calm state of mind can help soothe her
- Speak softly, move slowly, handle the baby gently to help relax both of you
- Tilt the crib mattress so the baby's head is higher than her stomach, which can allow gravity to help action of the colon where gas may be trapped
- Warming the baby can ease intestinal spasms: give a warm bath, then wrap in a warm towel
- Place tummy down on warm (NOT HOT) water bottle covered with a towel, or face down with wrapped bottle in the middle of his back (NOTE: stay with the baby so the bottle doesn't unwrap and allow the hotter rubber to touch him)
- Place a loosely rolled diaper under the baby's tummy
- Press the baby's stomach on your lap and rhythmically rub or massage his back
- Is the room comfortable for sleep? Is it too hot, cold, or bright? Try a lamb's-wool pad over or under the crib sheet.
- Try music: soothing, or with a strong beat, or recording of a mother's heartbeat or ocean, etc.
- Visual stimulation for distraction: hang a mobile over the crib, or take the baby for a walk or drive

# DEALING WITH A PREMATURE INFANT

*Hospitals are intimidating.*   New parents usually feel overwhelmed by the hospital when they visit their child. A good way to combat this feeling is to learn as much as you can about the methods of care in a neonatal intensive-care unit (NCU). You also should feel free to call the hospital day or night for news of your child.

The best way to learn is to ask questions. Because the NCU can be very busy and intense, you'll have to pick the right moment to talk to a member of the staff who has time for you. Don't expect to learn everything about hospital procedures right away. As your anxiety level is high, you may have trouble comprehending or remembering what you are told; it can help to write down the answers. You can also ask your questions more than once, if necessary, and ask them of more than one caregiver if you aren't sure about the answer.

*You may feel unnecessary.*   It's possible to feel you are superfluous to your baby, compared to all the high-tech equipment and specially trained staff in the NCU. In fact, as parents you are the most important members of the team working to help your baby get well enough to leave the hospital. Don't doubt that—no one else will ever be your baby's Mom and Dad.

*If your baby's chances are "iffy," it can be a greater strain.*   Your fear that the baby may not survive can retard bonding and attachment. This is a natural response but you should discuss your baby's condition and prognosis with your pediatrician so you know whether you are being realistic or over-cautious. It's important, in any case, to give your baby a name, and tell the staff so that they can also call her by her name.

*Get to know your baby.*   It is important for you just to sit by your baby's isolette, watching, talking, and touching if possible. With the procedures that are done and the staff that changes with every shift, you are the only constant in your little baby's life.

There are ways you can help with her care, especially if you can develop a rapport with a supportive nursing staff. You can make sure the breathing and feeding tubes are correctly positioned and not irritating the baby, that the sheets are smooth and not rubbing her skin, that her mouth is moist, her diaper is clean, and most important of all, that she's getting as much touching as possible. You might also want to bring a small toy or music box (anything that the staff can sterilize) to put in her isolette.

***Breast-feeding can be great for you and the baby.*** If your child isn't yet strong enough to suck, you can express your breast milk every three hours and give it in a bottle. If a premature baby has the strength, many professionals encourage you to nurse every day (or as much as possible) in the hospital. This will maintain your milk supply, gives him antibodies, and minimizes your separation while giving him physical nurturing.

***Stay united with your spouse.*** There is so much strain on the parents of a preemie that it's easy to let the stress pull you apart. However, you will both be experiencing many of the same feelings and can be a comfort to each other. Some common feelings for parents of a preemie are: anger, exhaustion, anxiety, guilt, lack of appetite, and hostility toward the hospital staff and/or friends and relatives.

It may be easier for you to deal with these feelings if you can remain close to each other. Frequent visits to the baby can also help, especially if you participate in caring for him while you're there. Also, there are parent support groups for parents of preemies that can help you to identify, express, and resolve your feelings.

***You may blame yourselves for the prematurity.*** It is common for parents to blame some activity of pregnancy (working, sex, social activities) for their baby's premature arrival. None of that is true, but knowing the facts may not be enough to stop you from blaming yourselves. Yet self-destructive guilt must be controlled in order for you to make a healthy attachment to the child and get on with your lives.

If a new mother continues to torture herself with questions that begin with "What if . . . ?" or with "Why didn't I . . . ?", she is creating big problems for herself. By doing this, you will build a self-image of guilt and failure. This will add tension and make mothering more difficult, perhaps even affecting the quality of the care you can give to your baby.

***Taking the preemie home is stressful.*** Most parents still view their premature baby as frail and disease-prone, even if he looks healthy and is thriving. Doctors say that once a child is ready to leave the hospital he usually doesn't require special care. Still, if either of you is not convinced of that, you may be tense and worried, which can create additional stress in your relationship.

***Expect your baby to be slow in developing.*** Experts say that it takes about two years for a preemie to "catch up" developmentally. It can be a greater effort and take more time for him to learn to drink from a cup, eat unassisted, walk, and climb than a full-term child. If both parents accept this, then neither of them will be over-anxious about the baby's development. If either of you worries and makes an issue of this, it may create tension in the family and can eventually turn your child into an over-cautious, anxious person.

***There can be long-term problems with preemies.***
Some premature babies have learning difficulties, impaired hearing, or physical clumsiness. There is no way to know if your child will be affected in any of these areas, and worrying about it isn't going to help anyone. Put your energy into helping the baby develop in a loving, understanding, unpressured way. If either of you is terribly worried or anxious about the future, talk to your pediatrician about it rather than letting your fears run wild. If you don't feel the doctor is giving you the reassurance or information you need, then change pediatricians.

# DEALING WITH A HOSPITALIZED BABY

***Leaving your baby in the hospital is stressful.*** Having to leave your newborn in the hospital when you check out, or to readmit her once you've gone home, causes tremendous strain. First of all, you may feel anxious because you don't understand all the medical procedures. The hospital is a bureaucracy, a closed system which you may have to break through (not entirely different than it may have been for your delivery). You may have to be persevering and assertive to get answers about your baby from the hospital. This is something a couple can do as a team.

***Consent forms are standard.*** Don't be frightened when you are given consent forms to sign for your baby. This doesn't mean that the procedures they have to do are serious or dangerous. It is routine to request consent forms for X-rays, blood tests, examinations, etc. To alleviate some of your fears, you might try to locate someone on the hospital staff—a nurse or intern, perhaps—who can find the time to talk to you about your child's condition and care.

***You don't have to be separated from your child.*** When your baby is in the hospital and you can't care for her or protect her from pain, your sense of helplessness can be overwhelming. Although the hospital may try to keep you at a distance, you have legal rights to be at your child's side. By law you are allowed to be with your child during tests, procedures, and if she has surgery to be present for the administration of anesthesia and in the recovery room.

Obviously you have to use common sense and not interfere with medical procedures just because you feel protective toward your baby. Yet you don't have to relinquish all control, either. If you see your child experiencing any discomfort, don't be afraid to alert the hospital staff.

***Rooming-in is possible at many children's hospitals.*** Ask for rooming-in if it's available at your hospital. If not, sleep rooms for parents are sometimes offered.

If you are breast-feeding, it should be possible to nurse your child in the hospital. This should be possible even if he has an I.V., as long as he is permitted fluids by mouth. It is also possible for the hospital to administer your breast milk with a pump.

***Separation from your baby is sometimes necessary.*** If your baby is really sick when he is born, he must be kept in the intensive-care nursery. A seriously ill newborn can't room-in with his mother, nor can they bring him to you at the scheduled feeding times. This separation can increase your feeling of loss, of being different from other mothers, and it can increase your tendency to detach emotionally.

***Visit the baby in the NCU.*** It's most important that both of you visit your baby in the nursery. From the parents' point of view, the more time you can spend with the baby, the more it will increase your feeling of attachment to him. But visiting is probably even more important for the baby's sake. Because of his isolation, he needs a great deal of love and attention. He may need mothering and fathering even more than you feel the need to give it. A supportive nurse can show you how it is possible to hold a baby even with a nasal tube or an I.V.

Visiting the baby in the intensive-care nursery can be emotionally wrenching when you have to leave and go back home to the baby's empty nursery. If the mother is still in the hospital herself and there is no NCU there, the baby may be transferred to another hospital. This can make you feel even worse because you can't see the child to reassure yourself he's okay. Your husband can visit the baby and you can get the phone number of the NCU to stay in touch. Better yet, if you're feeling all right postpartum, ask for a discharge as soon as possible so you can visit.

***Guilt and self-blame are pointless.*** Regardless of the cause of your baby's hospitalization, it is useless to blame yourself. It won't help the situation if you punish yourself for anything you may have done to contribute to your child's condition. Some parents go so far as to blame themselves for choosing a particular doctor or hospital that may have had some part in the child's illness. This kind of *mea culpa* attitude is counterproductive: blaming yourself can have an adverse effect on the way you deal with your child and handle the situation.

*Your baby's condition is not a reflection on you.*
"What did I do to cause this?" is a fairly common response
to having a sick child. "What's wrong with me for creating
a child like this?" is another normal reaction to a child born
with serious problems. It is natural to try to find a "reason"
for tragic or unfortunate incidents—looking for answers
may be a way for you to soothe some of your pain. Eventually each parent has to find his/her own way to come to
terms with the problem.

*It's okay not to suffer 24 hours a day.* You may feel
it's terribly unfair for your child to be in the hospital while
you're on the outside, eating, laughing, and being active.
There's a tendency to feel guilty about your good health
and freedom. You may also feel bad when you forget your
child for a moment and enjoy yourself.

## COPING WITH A HANDICAPPED CHILD

*We all expect "perfect" babies.* All of us want to have
perfect-looking, wonderfully behaved kids with perfect
brains. You may feel you've failed if you don't produce a
child who fits the bill. It may appear as though what has
gone wrong—your imperfect baby—is a reflection on you
or your abilities.

It's probably not realistic to attempt to prevent such
feelings, or to stop them when they start. However, you
and your partner can make a pact with each other not to
indulge in self-damaging thoughts. Rather than diverting
positive energy into painful, self-destructive thoughts about
yourselves, you can agree to do whatever you can to help
your child be the best she possibly can.

*You may feel embarrassed in public.* If your child's
handicap is apparent to other people, you may be uncomfortable about taking him out in public. So on top of the
guilt and self-blame you may already feel, you may also be
self-conscious about dealing with the stares and comments
of outsiders. These are normal feelings, but having this embarrassment about your child's condition can make you feel
even more guilty.

*You'll go through recognizable emotional stages.*
1. **DENIAL:** You may have trouble accepting your baby's situation and integrating the reality. This can make you feel isolated. Your partner is probably having similar feelings so you should try to talk about them.

2. **DOUBTS:** You will wonder, what is your baby's future? How did you contribute to the problem? Are you going to be able to care for the child? What are your options? Even if the doctors can give you a definite prognosis, these doubts can still besiege you—if the diagnosis is unclear, the uncertainty can plague you.

3. **DEPRESSION:** You may get depressed because of feelings of self-doubt, guilt, and helplessness.

4. **ANGER:** Anger can be healthy because it is a way out of the passivity of depression, but you have to be careful about when and where you express your hostility. If you don't watch out, your anger can wind up aimed at your partner, your child, or the professionals who may be helping you.

*Get as much medical information as you can.* Educate yourselves by asking every question you can of your pediatrician and any specialists to whom s/he sends you. Write down your questions (and the answers you get) because it's hard to remember everything when your anxiety level is high. Also, both parents probably can't go to every appointment. If you don't go, you can give your partner a list of questions you'd like to ask.

*Make notes and keep a file of information you collect.* Keep a file of important names, or of people who have been helpful, with their phone numbers. Next to their names you can jot down the suggestions, advice, or referrals that they offered. Although this may not be your usual style of doing things, it can really help you remember. It's unlikely that you'll be able to keep everything straight in your head when it comes to seeking help for your handicapped child; you'll be surprised how the names and information accumulate. There may also be contradictory or confusing advice. If you have it in writing, it can help you to do the best you can for your child.

*Get second opinions whenever possible.* Do not hesitate to get second, third or fourth opinions from professionals who specialize in the area of your child's handicap. Often there is a fair amount of personal opinion in medical diagnosis. Also, so much is being discovered all the time that you should leave no stone unturned.

*Get all the help you can.* Outside support is especially necessary for first-time parents who have a handicapped child. You need to acknowledge the problems and decide how you are going to cope with your situation. Before you can even begin dealing with it, the first step is to assess and accept your child's condition. Support groups of parents who have similarly afflicted children may be your best bet. In order to find out where such groups exist in your area, you can check the library or health department for your local Easter Seal Society, health services, or speech therapists (pathologists).

*You'll need time away from home.* The parents of a handicapped child have a special need to find time alone together. In addition to all the demands of new parenthood, you have the stress and strain of your child's situation. It may help defuse some of those pressures if you can make time to resume some of the pre-baby activities that you enjoyed together.

## THE DEATH OF A BABY

*Losing your baby can bond you or drive you apart.* The gut-wrenching tragedy of having your baby die puts a strain on your marriage in ways you may not have anticipated. You may expect your spouse to react to the baby's death in the same way that you do—and feel disappointed or resentful if your partner's way of coping is quite different from yours. The way that you handle this tragedy between yourselves can mean the difference between strengthening or weakening your marriage.

***Communication is essential.*** If you don't tell each other what you're thinking and feeling, there are bound to be misunderstandings. Friction between you is the last thing you need at this difficult time. A man may believe that society dictates he should be strong for his wife and not express his grief. Of course this isn't wise, because feelings that are bottled up will eventually explode. At this time of extreme stress you both need each other's understanding and support.

***You need to grieve.*** Each parent will react in his/her own way to the baby's death. It's important to go through the grieving process, but it's just as important not to impose on your spouse your idea of what mourning "should" be. Allow yourself to cry if you feel like it, but if you don't feel like crying don't worry about it. The same goes for your partner. Everyone has their own timing in getting in touch with feelings and coming to terms with them.

***Insomnia and loss of appetite are normal.*** It is natural to have sleeping problems (inability to fall asleep, awaking and being unable to fall back to sleep) or nightmares after a baby's death. You may also lose your appetite. It's important for your health to force yourself (or your mate) to have frequent small amounts of nutritious, easily digested food.

***You may be unable to stay in the house alone.*** For some mothers it is very hard, perhaps impossible, to be at home alone after a baby's death. It takes time to adjust to the horrible reality of losing your child. For a few weeks after the death, you might want to ask a friend or relative to stay overnight or at least spend a few hours with you every day.

***Your mind may play tricks on you.*** You may not be able to concentrate on anything or remember things. You may think you hear a baby crying in another room. These and other similar problems will undoubtedly pass as time goes on. If the problems are really disturbing you, you might want to seek professional help.

*A baby's death is a big strain on a marriage.* When your baby dies, you are bombarded with emotions—guilt, anger, and blame among them. Both you and your partner are hurting. One of you can be so involved in your own grief that you forget your spouse's feelings. Make every effort to reach out and comfort each other.

*Be aware of other people's feelings.* This is a time to be gentle not only with yourself and your mate, but also with the various people around you who will all have their own difficulties in coping with your terrible loss. If there are other children in your family, they need to express their feelings, too. It's important to treat children and their feelings the same way you hope others will treat you. Sometimes a child who didn't want a sibling can feel responsible and guilt-ridden if the baby dies. Talking can relieve some of those feelings. Other children need to know that the baby has died and is buried, otherwise they may have fantasies and nightmares about what happened to the baby's body. *Learning to Say Good-by* is a good book on this subject (see *Bibliography*).

*Professional caregivers may feel awkward.* It is hard for doctors, nurses, and other professionals to deal with tragedies. They have their own guilts, fears, and emotional constrictions. Don't misinterpret any aloofness you may feel from professionals as meaning they are uncaring or cold. Also, some of them may make thoughtless remarks that upset you—you may want to let them know they've been insensitive, but don't overreact. They are only human beings, doing the best job they can in a difficult situation. You may feel less judgmental toward professionals if you imagine yourself in their shoes, having to find the words to talk to parents in your situation.

*People may avoid the subject of the baby's death.* Well-meaning people may try not to talk about your loss; however, that usually is not helpful. Part of the healing process in a tragedy like losing a baby is if friends and relatives can express sympathy to you and encourage you to talk about your feelings. An intimate friend may want to reach out but may admit to you, "I don't know what to say." If it's someone you feel comfortable with, you might say, "Just let me cry with you." Expressing feelings can relieve some of the pain.

***People may stay away from you.***   You may experience an extreme and painful feeling of isolation if friends or relatives don't call or visit after your baby dies. Don't imagine that no one cares. People are probably avoiding you out of respect for your privacy, but even more likely because they are at a loss about how to approach you.

    If you have the strength to do it, call the people you care most about and tell them you need to be with them. People may be shunning you because they don't want to "upset" you. But part of the healing process for a couple is to talk about their tragedy. Tell your friends that talking and tears are part of mourning, and that it's good for you to express your feelings with them.

***Sudden Infant Death Syndrome (SIDS) is a special problem.***   SIDS is a fatal condition of apparently healthy children (more often males) who die between two and six months of age. After you recover from the shock of losing your seemingly normal baby, there can be a further emotional price tag. It is common for parents to blame themselves when their baby dies of SIDS, and it's unfortunately not uncommon for others to blame them, too. It can be a great help to contact the National SIDS Foundation for information and support, at 310 South Michigan Avenue, Chicago, IL 60604.

***Contact parent support groups.***   Sharing your feelings and practical advice with other parents who have suffered similar tragedies can ease your burden. It can help you to learn how other people have coped with their personal and social lives, the remarks and attitudes of outsiders, and so on. By sharing your experience, you may discover how much better you're doing than you may have realized.

***What if your newborn is expected to die and lives?***
This situation can cause parents mixed emotions, which can be very confusing. You have adjusted to the infant's immi-

nent death and even begun to mourn in advance. If your newborn then recovers unexpectedly, you have to shift gears. Don't be surprised or worried if it takes time and effort to establish your bond with your child. That attachment has been delayed because the baby's precarious condition encouraged you to detach yourself emotionally.

## A BABY WITH A DIFFICULT TEMPERAMENT

*Several factors determine whether your child has a difficult temperament.* If your child has what is clinically considered a difficult temperament, this doesn't mean there is anything wrong with her. The factors mentioned here are simply an indication that your baby is "not average." What this usually means is that she may require more from you as parents, and may put more of a strain on you as a couple.

---

**FACTORS TO CONSIDER ABOUT A CHILD'S TEMPERAMENT**

- Energy level
- Sensitivity level
- Reaction to new experiences
- Adjustability to change
- Distractability
- Moods

---

*Certain issues will be problematic for such children.* If your child does have a difficult temperament, you'll probably find several issues (sleep, feeding, special fears and dependencies, being at risk for accidents) that will illuminate the baby's particular temperament. The following chart can give you an idea of signs of emotional distress in a child that may be symptomatic of temperamental problems.

---

**SYMPTOMS OF TEMPERAMENTAL DIFFICULTIES**

- Unusually high or low activity levels
- Oversensitivity
- Slow adjustment to something new
- Frequently upset by separations
- Persistent crying
- Frequent waking and fussing at night
- Trouble falling asleep

---

*If you're unprepared, the problems can magnify.* If what you expected your baby to be like doesn't fit the temperamentally "not average" child you have, it can exacerbate the situation. You may have imagined that your child would be "normal": moderately active and quick to adjust to change in her environment. But you may have an infant who is very very quiet and slow to adjust—or she may be energetic, persistent, and undistractable when she has her mind on something. Her difficult temperament may seem even more so if you didn't allow for these possibilities.

*Parents must not blame themselves.* It is unfortunately natural for some parents to believe that it must be their fault if they have a baby who is temperamentally difficult. Not only is this an unnecessary (and irrational) burden on yourselves as parents, but it also paints your child in a negative light. In the act of "blaming" yourself for his style, you are subtly redefining the baby's natural disposition as "unfavorable": an energetic kid becomes "bad," a quiet child is "weak," or a slow-adjusting child is redefined as "dependent."

*There is a myth: relaxed parents = relaxed child.* The concept that parents are responsible for their baby's difficult temperament is hogwash, like so many other creaky old myths! It is also a destructive and misleading notion. Of course, it is wonderful if the parents don't take things too seriously and can roll with the punches of the first few weeks of the baby's life. However, just because you are relaxed parents, it doesn't necessarily mean your child will be relaxed.

A child has inborn physical and temperamental characteristics over which a parent has no control. A baby may be irritable and uncomfortable for reasons all his own, which you may not even understand. There may be things you can do to soothe him, but that's quite different from imagining that something you've done has made the child that way in the first place. Your baby is not a reflection of you. He is a separate person, with his own problems and pleasures.

Of course, it's true that a baby does pick up signals and cues from the way you touch and relate to him. But since each child has a unique way of acting and reacting, the way that you interact with him is not the cause of his personal style. If you let yourself think that your baby's fussiness and tenseness are your fault, you will probably get tense yourself and be less able to handle the situation calmly and objectively.

*A personality different from yours may disappoint you.* You may have expected that your child would have a temperament similar to your own, or at least compatible with yours. But if your infant is not in sync with your personal rhythm—let's say you're a high-energy, active person and you have a low-key baby who sleeps a lot—it can create problems. And these problems can spill over into your marital relationship.

If an "emotional fit" is lacking between you and your child, it can cause you ever-increasing stress and tension if you struggle to cope with a personality that may be the opposite of your own. Maybe you mistakenly keep hoping that if you work at it hard enough, you can get on the same "wavelength" with the baby. In fact, you are two separate individuals who will need time to understand and accept each other.

You may feel you are somehow inadequate as a parent if you can't naturally be tuned in to your child. You may think you have failed as a parent just because it requires a lot of effort for you to get in sync with the baby and be responsive to her. These are subjects you might want to discuss with your spouse (or other intimate, trustworthy friends, relatives, or a therapist). If you can become aware of the demands you're making on yourself and the child, you may be able to let go of some of those preconceived notions. Your child needs the room to develop into her own person, with her own abilities and potential, unencumbered by any of your expectations.

***Your baby may be what is called "irritable."*** This is not a criticism or value judgment, it is an assessment of a baby's personal style. An "irritable" baby is considered one who is cranky, who may be hard to warm up to, and might not like being cuddled.

It can be helpful to the parents of such a baby to know that there is nothing wrong with him, or them. Such babies tend to cause some degree of frustration for their parents. If your pediatrician or other professional suggests that you have a baby who is irritable, it allows you to be prepared for his difficult temperament. It can be easier on you if you try to look on the bright side of having an irritable infant. Think of it this way: at least you don't have a passive child, one who is nonresponsive or always asleep! Rather than thinking of your "irritable" baby in negative terms, try to emphasize the positive aspect: you have a child who is alert, interactive, and a challenge.

***"Hard-to-soothe" babies can be difficult.*** Studies have shown that babies who are unpredictable or inconsistent in their sleeping, eating, or elimination patterns will probably be hard to soothe. If your child is slow to adjust to changes, then each new situation in her life can be upsetting and make her cranky. A "hard-to-soothe" baby is often one whose "internal clock" doesn't yet seem to be set, therefore external stimuli upset her more. A baby can be hard to soothe because of her innate temperament. For other babies, they may become temporarily hard to soothe at five to six months, because of shots, teething, tiring outings, or other sensory overload.

***What can you do for a "hard-to-soothe" baby?*** When your baby is upset, you may be able to deactivate her oversensitive "touchiness" by surrounding her with familiar things. It can also help if you provide a fairly consistent schedule for the child. "On demand" feeding and sleeping are not recommended for hard-to-soothe babies, especially those that still haven't settled into a consistent daily pattern by five or six months of age. A lack of schedule can make a child like this even harder to soothe. She needs your help with external consistency in her daily schedule since she can't yet do it for herself.

***Limit visitors and outings if your baby is temperamentally difficult.*** It is hard to establish a routine for your child, and keep it, if there are a lot of interruptions in the baby's day. Other people may not understand the way that you have chosen to deal with your child, or recognize the special pressures you have. If you allow other people to have an opinion or get involved in handling your child, it can overstimulate the baby or make you feel guilty or tense.

If you take the child on a lot of outings, it can disrupt the calm and stable routine that you have worked to establish at home. A sensitive child can be upset by seeing too many new faces. On outings she may be overwhelmed by the noise, confusion, and changing physical conditions outside your home. You might want to wait until the baby is more settled herself before you help her learn to handle the world.

***Your needs as parents are especially important.*** Children with difficult temperaments demand a great deal from their parents and put extra pressure on a marriage. You need support and guidance so that this stress doesn't hurt your relationship or create emotional problems between you and your child.

Your need for sleep will be particularly high because you need so much strength and patience to deal with the baby. Anyone who hasn't slept enough will tend to be more irritable—if you have an irritable baby, you can't afford the luxury of being moody yourself! Getting out of the house can also relieve some of the pressure on you. It can be helpful even if you only get out briefly and interact with other adults by doing something as simple as grocery shopping.

***How do you two react to the baby and each other?*** Try to look at what your automatic responses are when either of you is under pressure. Your reactions may contribute—in either a positive or a detrimental way—to the situation of having a temperamentally difficult baby. When you are up against the wall, do you react by withdrawing, becoming frantic, nasty, blaming yourself, or turning on others?

The way you react can push automatic buttons in your partner. For example, if a woman cries, it can often make her husband feel helpless or impotent, even if he is not the cause of her emotions. If a man gets angry, his wife may feel personally blamed even though the anger isn't directed at her. If you are aware of this, you can modify your reactions or help change your spouse's response.

A difficult child can cause a negative interaction between his parents. If the baby's crying or irritability affects either of you by turning you against each other or the baby, allow some breathing room. Get away and take a break, even if it's only to walk around the block.

***Share your negative feelings with each other.*** A difficult child can stir up many emotions in his parents; your anger can give way to feeling sad, lonely, inadequate, hopeless, or fearful. You may feel there's no safe place to direct your anger or ventilate your other emotions. But rather than directing your feelings **at** each other or the baby, you can share them **with** each other. You can decide together on the approach you want to take to the child, which also helps you to avoid the common occurrence of blaming yourself or your partner for the baby's problems.

## THE NINTH MONTH CAN BE DIFFICULT

***The ninth month of the baby's life can be a particularly difficult time in your lives.*** It's a tough age for the baby, who may be clinging and also may be at her most demanding, troublesome, active, or fussy. Because many parents find that the time around the baby's sixth month is one of the nicest stages, the problems of the ninth month can come as even more of a shock.

***You may feel resentful and then guilty.*** For many parents, by the time their child is around nine months old they are finally adjusting to being a parent and feeling they know their child. If your baby suddenly becomes difficult at this point, it can make you angry or irritable. For some parents, it can be very disturbing to feel negative emotions toward their baby. If you think that the child "knows" that you've had these resentments, you may then feel guilty.

*A mother may have the ninth-month blues.* If you have a career that you've returned to, you may already be feeling conflicted or guilty about being a working mother. The baby's clinging to Mommy at this stage can make you feel even worse. If you don't have a job then you may be feeling ready to get out of the house, to have time for yourself and interests other than motherhood. It's quite natural to feel tired of being around the baby all the time; you may even want to experience the novelty of being a couple again with your husband!

*A nursing mother goes through changes.* If you're still nursing, you may menstruate for the first time around the ninth month. It can be unpleasant to have your period for the first time in 18 months. Also, for many women breast-feeding reduces their sex drive. If it hasn't driven him crazy yet, your husband may be getting tired by now of having his sexual desires take a back seat to the baby's nutritional needs.

*The ninth month can be burdensome to the father.* This can be a stage at which there are more demands on a father. Just when you may have thought you were off the hook, the increased demands that the baby makes on your wife affect you, too. After the pressures and adjustments of new fatherhood, you may be ready just about now to back off of fathering for a little and throw yourself into work or play. Yet this may be a time when your wife needs your support more than ever.

## SEPARATION ANXIETY

*Separation anxiety is normal, but separation is necessary.* At some point a small child (and his parents) will suffer some degree of anxiety when they are separated. However, you and your child have to learn to cope with your going out, whether it be leaving the room the child is in or leaving the house. It is important that you don't curtail your normal schedule or deny yourself excursions without the child.

***Separation anxiety can be "cured" by separation.***
The more opportunities your child has to experience separation anxiety, the better he'll learn to cope with it and resolve his fears. It can help you to handle the situation if you recognize that the baby is confused by your leaving and needs reassurance. The only way a child can truly come to terms with separation anxiety is if his parents consistently leave and consistently return. The pattern of going and returning will impress on the child that parents can disappear and reappear. Some experts feel that this is a concept that a child can't fully assimilate until he's around three-and-a-half years old.

***There are different degrees of anxiety.*** A child will not be constantly terrified every time you leave the house or room. Some days she'll be more upset than others. It's a process she has to work through; if you are calm and consistent she will overcome her fears eventually. If your child is profoundly disturbed by a separation, she will need special support from you. You might want to hold her while rocking her to sleep, lay her on her stomach while rubbing her back, or whatever special soothing you know works with her.

***There are various forms of separation anxiety.***
When a child is going through this stage of development, there are other forms of separation anxiety: naps, bedtime, and/or the parents being in another room. Bedtime problems are especially evident at this time. The baby may just need the comfort of knowing that you are nearby. The sound of your voice can let her know that you are there. If you feel you have to go into the child's room to comfort her, leave as soon as she is calm.

Many experts recommend that you don't respond to every whimper the child makes; she has to learn patience and tolerance. You aren't doing her any favor by jumping up the instant that she cries. Child development experts postulate that a child has to experience the discomfort of anxiety as an aspect of real life—it is part of the way that she learns how the world works and how to develop tolerance.

***Do not take the child into your bed.*** If your child is suffering separation anxiety at naptime or bedtime, it is no solution to take the baby into bed with you. All you're doing is delaying the inevitable moment of truth when the child discovers that the umbilical cord is cut and he is, in fact, separate from you. Although you may be tempted to take the baby into your bed because that will shut him up and you'll get more sleep, it is only a temporary solution. A child has to learn to behave independently of his parents.

***Never leave the child with a sitter when he's asleep.***
If your child is already going through a phase of separation anxiety, it can be very disturbing for him to awaken to a strange face. It may cause him to have nightmares if you do so. Instead, it is recommended that you wake the child up to say goodbye to him before you go out. You should do this even if you dread an emotional parting scene. Experts say that you should awaken the baby, tell him you're going out, and that you'll be back soon.

## A BABY WITH SLEEPING PROBLEMS

***A baby with sleeping problems means parents with sleeping problems.*** If your child isn't sleeping, at least one of you isn't either, which can create havoc for you personally and for your marriage. If your baby awakens during the night, then you have to catch up on sleep at other times. It is critical that you try to take a nap during the day if your sleep is constantly interrupted during the night. The more rest you get, the better you can cope with parenthood and the other demands on you.

***Sleep deprivation is a serious problem for adults.***
Being deprived of sleep can cause irritability, paranoid thinking, and visual hallucinations. Broken sleep affects "rapid eye movement" (REM) sleep and deep sleep cycles. Sleep is necessary in order for you to dream, store information, relax your nerves, and process the day's emotions—all this is vital for your mind and body to revitalize

for the following day. Sleep deprivation also affects the neuroendocrine system by disturbing circadian rhythms, which are the day-night, light-dark, wake-sleep cycles that all animals have. These are natural biological rhythms that are necessary for normal functioning. The accumulation of consecutive nights without sleep can lead to total collapse.

***Sleep deprivation is harmful for the baby, too.*** Exhaustion can affect a child's physical and intellectual development. When he is no longer an infant, your child's dependence on you for sleep during the night can lead to problems in independence and self-esteem. It may also mean that your child may suffer from sleep problems later in life. Establishing good sleep habits early is important for all of you.

***This won't last forever.*** Try to keep a perspective if you have a baby who won't sleep during the night. First-time parents can have a hard time reminding themselves that this is a temporary problem for a limited period of time. New parents often think their child will never settle down and that they will never get a full night's sleep again. If it makes you feel any better, be assured that **he** will and **you** will!

If you are the parent who has awakened and is pacing the floor at 3 a.m. with your squalling baby, there are two things you might remember. One is that life isn't always going to be like this. The other is that it is not your sleeping spouse's fault that the baby is awake!

***Is one of you sleeping in the baby's room?*** Sleeping with the baby instead of with each other sets a dangerous precedent in your relationship. You may think this is a good solution to having to get up for a child who awakens during the night: it may actually seem easier to sleep next to the crib than having to get up and go into the baby's room. But what you may think you're gaining in convenience, you may be losing in the privacy and intimacy of sharing a bed with your mate.

There are child-care experts who suggest sleeping next to the baby's crib for a night or two, with specific recommendations on how to handle the baby when he wakes. However, there are couples who decide that they'll take turns sleeping in the baby's room for weeks or months at a time. This is not considered healthy or helpful for a child's development, but the concern of this book is your marriage. If you choose not to sleep with your spouse, it is going to have some effect on your relationship. This is not a decision to make without stopping to think and talk about it. If you choose your child over your partner, then it may be time to look at your role and your child's place in your life and marital relationship.

***What is a "normal" sleep pattern for a baby?*** Some child-care books state that a newborn sleeps for 20 or more hours per day. Depending on your child's personal sleep habits, you may think your baby has a sleeping problem if she doesn't sleep that much. But many babies sleep for 8 hours or less. Some take cat naps, others sleep in long blocks of time. As a rule of thumb, newborns average about 16 hours of sleep a day; by the time they are three to five months of age most babies average about 14 hours of sleep every day.

***Most babies do not sleep through the night.*** We've all heard about the perfect little angel that slept through the night from the moment he came home, but those babies are the exception. Most infants are physiologically unable to sleep through the entire night. They have difficulty establishing a regular sleep cycle and need three to four months to develop the pattern of sleeping through the night. In the early weeks, some babies sleep only two to three hours at any given time.

***Differentiation between night and day takes time.*** Within the first month of life there is no definite rhythm or pattern to most babies' sleep/wake cycles. Within a couple of months, many babies have learned the difference between night and day and have established a sleep cycle accordingly. However, new studies show that sustained night sleep usually doesn't come before a baby is three to four months old.

**What influences a baby's sleep patterns?** Three primary factors affect sleep in an infant. A child's emotional, social, and neurological development affect her sleep habits, as does her environment. Another factor is her individual temperament—especially active or irritable babies may stay awake for long stretches. These periods of awakeness may seem even longer to you if your child is one who cries, fusses, and is hard to comfort.

*Going to sleep at a particular time is a skill that must be learned.* Some babies learn and accept a bedtime earlier and more easily than others. Often infants with certain temperamental factors fuss less and get to sleep sooner. These are usually babies who are consistent, who are predictable in their behavior patterns, or who are quieter, less energetic, or more adaptable. Children who are considered temperamentally difficult—who are energetic or slow to adapt to change—may find it harder to stop being involved in their discovery of the world around them and settle down for sleep.

*Sleep problems are normal at five to nine months.* One survey showed that nearly 50 percent of the parents with babies this age found problems with getting the child to sleep. However, if your child hasn't settled into an easy sleep routine by this point it is probably the result of habit. Common habits that a baby can develop by this age which interfere with going to sleep are: the inability to fall asleep alone, sleeping in the parents' bed, wanting to feed during the night, or wanting attention in the night.

*Waking or fussing during the night can be a problem.* Many five- to six-month-olds awaken at night, especially very active babies who are sensitive. They can wake themselves with their own motion and then be unable to fall back to sleep on their own. Many children don't yet have a consistent sleep pattern so they haven't learned how to get back to sleep without fussing. This doesn't mean that there's anything wrong with you or your baby—it will fall into place eventually.

*There are things you can do to encourage a baby to sleep.* The first thing you can do is get a book called *Help-*

*ing Your Child Sleep Through the Night* (see the *Bibliography*). This is one of the best books I've seen on the subject, addressing the problem in a clear, compassionate, and logical way. Since a baby with sleep problems can have such a profound affect on his parents' ability to sleep themselves, I am mentioning just a few suggestions that may help. Consulting with your pediatrician is, of course, one.

To deal with a baby that wakens during the night and can't get back to sleep, you can try keeping her awake later at night or keeping her awake more during daylight hours. However, most babies' internal clocks are self-regulated and manipulation may not work. You can also postpone the baby's last night feeding until you're ready to go to sleep or try waking her for an extra feeding before you go to bed.

Pacifiers, cuddly toys, and milk can help. With some babies, it can also help to let them cry themselves back to sleep, although that can be more harsh for some babies than others. Eventually your baby will learn to sleep all night. If you try to speed up her learning process but are unsuccessful, then don't fight it. Adjust your own habits for a while so that you catch a nap in the afternoon and catch old movies on TV late at night.

***There are ways to help an active baby get to sleep.*** If your baby is awake because he is temperamentally difficult—because he is very active and doesn't want to slow down—try gently holding her down and massaging her. If you have a baby who gets tired at different, unpredictable times, then your task is to teach her your schedule. Putting her to bed every night at the same time will help her to learn.

If your baby has trouble making the transition from waking to sleeping, try rocking her before bed and nursing her right before bedtime. These are things that mothers have done for centuries to make babies sleepy, but there is a scientific basis for it. Milk contains tryptophan, a natural sleep-inducing agent; also, rhythmic motions like rocking help create the right brain-wave patterns for sleep.

***Naps are not absolutely necessary for every child.*** Daytime naps are important for many children but there is nothing sacred about naptime—it depends on how a child does without one. Some active kids breeze through the day without a nap and stay cheery until their bedtime. Other children fall apart by dinnertime if they haven't napped. Others again are unpredictable: they can be fine without a nap one day and then be a basket-case the next time they miss their rest time.

Children who resist taking a nap and fight their tiredness to the bitter end—torturing themselves and everyone around them—are the ones who may need a structured naptime the most. You may have to put your child down repeatedly or just leave him to cry and fuss. If your baby is like this, you need to be firm so that he can get some rest and spare all of you the hysterical scenes of an overtired child.

## CRYING

*A hard-to-soothe baby can be tough to take.* Having a crying, hard-to-console baby can be a trying experience. It can be frustrating and exhausting to have a child who arches her back and cries even louder when you try to hold and cuddle her. Parents often blame themselves. There is nothing wrong with you. There's also probably nothing wrong with your baby, although it's a good idea to have the pediatrician check her out anyway.

Many babies have irritable natures—it is not their fault or yours. Many of these infants become bright, engaging children. Personality traits that can be hard to take in an infant can become more charming and endearing as the child grows.

*Outsiders' reactions can be unpleasant.* You may find that when your baby is crying, strangers give you dirty looks—raised eyebrows or nonverbal glares. The implication seems to be that the crying is your fault or that it's a terrible burden for them and you should be able to stop it. Some outsiders are irritated, others are sympathetic, many give useless advice.

As a new mother, you may already be unsure of whether you're doing the right thing with your child. You may already be anxious and blaming yourself for the baby's discomfort; strangers can make you feel worse. You might want to try saying something to these people like "I'm doing the best I can to soothe my baby. If you have any suggestions, I'd appreciate your help." Even if you get an earful you'd rather not hear, at least you'll have them on your side!

***Handling the crying can create conflict between the parents.*** Managing your baby's crying can become a bone of contention between you. You may feel incompetent as parents. A crying baby can make you feel intensely frustrated, angry, and impotent. Sometimes all you can do is be there for the baby, try to comfort and soothe her, and let her know she's not alone in the world.

***Picking up the baby will not spoil the child.*** Although there is disagreement on this subject (and you and your partner may not agree) many experts believe that until the end of the first year a child does not have sufficient understanding of the effects of his behavior to cry on purpose to get attention.

Some development experts maintain that an infant's crying is a request for assistance. They contend that if you do not respond to the baby, you may be teaching him to cry even more since his initial efforts at communicating were not effective.

***Leaving the baby to cry may be necessary.*** Letting the baby "cry it out" can be very difficult. You may feel guilty or fear you are hurting the child. However, if you've done all you can to soothe him, then putting him down may be better than communicating your frustration and tension to him. Each set of parents has to build their own special understanding with the baby, and he with them, learning each other's likes, dislikes, and personal style of expression.

***Some parents try to keep their baby from crying.*** This is an odd attitude to take toward crying, since it is a normal and natural part of a baby's life. Pain, frustration, etc., are part of life, and crying is the baby's way of expressing himself.

*Crying is normal, necessary, and often without cause.* There is a myth floating around that all babies are born placid and content and that any disruption of this calm by crying is the mother's fault. Research has proven this to be wrong. Crying is considered part of the baby's process of learning to cope with the world, and each does it in her own way.

There is often no apparent physical cause for a baby's crying, and it is unrelated to the quality of mothering the child receives. Crying is normal, although the range is great. Some babies cry very little and are extremely easy to soothe. Others cry a great deal and cannot be easily calmed or comforted. Both extremes are normal.

*Regular evening crying is very common.* Crying at the end of the day may serve a purpose for the baby to let off steam or unwind. Some studies show that a baby may become irritable and cry because of her mother's end-of-the-day fatigue, or, in the case of breast-feeding, because milk supply is reduced at that time.

*There is interesting new research on crying.* A recent study showed that crying reaches a peak of nearly 3 hours a day when the baby is four to six weeks old. The amount of crying then seems to drop rapidly and stabilize to less than 1 hour per day by 12 weeks of age. The researchers postulate that this results from internal and external stimuli acting on the baby, which decreases as the nervous system's controlling mechanisms develop to keep the child from being excessively aroused by outside stimuli. The study also showed that crying is more common in the evening hours.

### NORMAL PHYSICAL REASONS
### FOR CRYING

• COLIC If your child suffers from colic (see the earlier section in this chapter), then she will undoubtedly be crying a great deal. If you have a baby who cries a lot, you may be a parent who is relieved to know it's because of colic—you don't have to be continually concerned about the physical cause for the crying. Colic will pass harmlessly, eventually.

• TENSION  Prolonged and intense crying can create tension in a baby or be a way of releasing it. A baby may unwind and get rid of excess energy this way.

• HUNGER  Depending on your baby's age and weight, she may get hungry every 2 to 4 hours. She will cry from hunger. She may also cry from her previous feeding, if it was poorly digested and has given her a bit of a tummy ache.

• OVERFEEDING  If your baby puts her fist in her mouth or makes sucking movements, you may give her a bottle because you think it means she is hungry. If a bottle gets you peace and quiet from the infant then you may be tempted to feed her constantly, which among other problems may give her indigestion and cause more crying. As a yardstick, if a couple of hours have not passed since she last ate, then just give her a pacifier or a bottle of water to satisfy her desire to suckle.

• PHYSICAL DISCOMFORTS  A newborn's little body may not be functioning smoothly for a while. He may have a rash, allergy, or other physical irritation. Keep a sharp eye for such discomforts and talk to your pediatrician about unusual symptoms. The baby may also cry because he feels cold: either a wet diaper or undressing him can cause a sudden change in his body temperature, to which some babies are more sensitive than others.

• OVERSTIMULATION  The importance of stimulating infants is often overstressed in child development books. Some babies cannot tolerate too much playing, noise, or new people and experiences. A baby's circuits can overload and she cries. This can happen from activity around her, or if she's very sensitive even from her own thrashing around. If your baby is wound up, very alert, and crying a lot, then try giving her some private quiet time for herself.

• **OVERTIREDNESS** Each child needs a different amount of rest and has different needs for falling asleep—some can do so in the midst of a dinner party, others need darkness and quiet. Intensely active babies can have trouble unwinding and relaxing enough to sleep. If a baby has had a lot of stimulating play, it can be hard for him to settle down; if you give him more handling and noise to soothe him, it can make it even worse. Be aware of your child's sleeping patterns and avoid frantic periods in which the baby can get so overtired that he has trouble unwinding.

## SUGGESTIONS FOR SOOTHING A CRYING BABY

• **RELAX YOURSELF** If you are tired and tense (as a result of your crying baby), the infant will probably pick up your signals and get more irritable himself. At that point you will get overwhelmed and lose your perspective and patience. It can be very hard to cool off at moments like this. If you have any chance to leave the baby with some-one else, even for 5 minutes, you may be able to go for a walk or take a tea or beer break.

Your patience and relaxation can make all the differ-ence. Once a baby's crying has reached a fever pitch, both you and the baby may get too tense to be easily soothed unless you can step back and take a deep breath. Try to visualize letting go of your tension while helping the baby release hers. Once you have calmed yourself, you'll be bet-ter able to help your child.

• **BROADEN YOUR SOOTHING TACTICS** Don't rely just on holding and feeding the baby as your only ways of soothing him. The child will become dependent on these comforts and not accept others. Patterns you establish early on can become limiting for you and the child. Try to tune in to the baby and pick up his signals: try changing his po-sition, giving him a rub on the back, a little song, music box, or a favorite toy.

• **SWADDLING** This has been very effective over the centuries and in many cultures. It gives the baby warmth and the comforting stimulation of constant touch. It also reduces the baby's movements, like kicking or other random activities that can overstimulate the child.

• SUCKING  A baby can be soothed by sucking because it relaxes movements of the large intestine and the major muscles. Sucking is a baby's inborn natural ability to calm herself. You can use a pacifier or a bottle of warm water. NOTE: The first time that you use a pacifier or nipple it may be a good idea to boil it five or six times before use, discarding the water each time. This can eliminate any nitrosamines that may remain from the manufacturing process.

• ROCKING, CUDDLING  Holding and rocking your child provide constant rhythmic stimulation which can reduce other sensory input and relax the baby's body. Changing the baby's position can help, for instance, holding her straight up looking over your shoulder.

• RHYTHM AND SOUND  Rhythmic noises can be soothing to a baby. Household machines often work wonders; sometimes it can work to put a baby nearby when you are using the vacuum cleaner. Some parents find it helps if they put something inside the clothes dryer and put the baby in an infant seat on top while it's running (obviously staying next to the child so there's no chance of him falling).

• VISUAL STIMULATION  You might want to try experimenting with colorful pictures, musical mobiles, or other objects hanging over the crib which reflect light. By trying things you may find an object that is just right to catch your baby's attention and soothe her.

• MOTION  A ride in the car, a carriage ride, or a walk in a backpack can help some babies. Just rocking the carriage back and forth with your foot while you read or talk on the phone can often do the same trick.

• DON'T OVERDO IT  Your efforts may boomerang if you attempt too many comforting techniques at one time.

Instead of calming the baby, your efforts may actually stimulate him.

• **A BABY GROWS AND CHANGES**   As a baby develops, her responses change. The techniques you try now may not work to soothe her, but may be great later. Don't push too hard with a tactic that isn't working, but don't give up on it, either. Try again in a few weeks or months.

• **PARENTS' ANONYMOUS**   You or your partner may get so frustrated and angry about your baby's crying that you feel you can understand people who batter their children. Just the guilt of thinking these thoughts may make it worthwhile for you to make a telephone call to a parents' anonymous group. It can help you to feel good about yourself as a parent if you seek help in facing up to negative feelings, especially since at some point your emotions could become uncontrollable and turn into actions.

# Bibliography

LIVE-IN CHILD CARE, Barbara Binswanger and Betsy Ryan (Doubleday/Dolphin, New York, 1986)

EXPECTANT FATHERS, Sam Bittman and Sue Rosenberg Zalk, (Ballantine Books, New York, 1978)

OURSELVES AND OUR CHILDREN, Boston Women's Health Book Collective (Random House, New York, 1978)

IS THERE SEX AFTER MARRIAGE?, Carol Botwin (Little, Brown, Boston, 1985)

THE FAMILY LIFE CYCLE, eds. Elizabeth A. Carter and Monica McGoldrick (Gardner Press, New York, 1980)

HELP FOR DEPRESSED MOTHERS, Barbara Ciaramitaro (Charles Franklin Press, Edmonds, WA 1978)

STRESS AND THE HEALTHY FAMILY, Dolores Curran (Harper and Row, New York, 1985)

HELPING YOUR CHILD SLEEP THROUGH THE NIGHT, Joanne Cuthbertson and Susei Schevill (Doubleday, New York, 1985)

SOONER OR LATER, Pamela Daniels and Kathy Weingarten (W.W. Norton, New York, 1982)

THE NEW MOTHERCARE, Lynn Delli Quadri and Kati Breeckenridge (Jeremy Tarcher, Inc., Los Angeles, 1978, 1984)

COUPLES WITH CHILDREN, Randy and Virginia DeLuca (Warner Books, New York, 1981)

THE MARRIAGE AND FAMILY EXPERIENCE, Christine DeVault, Bryan Strong, Rebecca Reynolds, and Murray Suid (West Publishing Co., New York, 1979)

THE NEW MOTHER SYNDROME, Carol Dix, (Doubleday, New York, 1985)

STRESSFUL LIFE EVENTS, eds. Barbara and Bruce Dohrenwald (John Wiley & Sons, New York, 1974)

HOW TO STAY TWO WHEN BABY MAKES THREE, Marsha Dorman and Diane Klein (Prometheus Books, New York, 1984)

PREPARATION FOR PARENTHOOD, Donna Ewy (New American Library, New York, 1985)

SIBLINGS WITHOUT RIVALRY, Adele Faber and Elaine Mazlish (Avon Books, New York, 1988)

BETWEEN GENERATIONS: THE SIX STAGES OF PARENTHOOD, Ellen Galinsky (Times Books, New York, 1981)

THE SECOND NINE MONTHS, Judith Gansberg and Arthur Mostel (Tribeca Communications, New York, 1984)

TECHNIQUES OF FAMILY THERAPY, Jay Haley and Lynn Hoffman (Basic Books, New York, 1967)

BECOMING PARENTS, Sandra Sohn Jaffe and Jack Viertel (Atheneum, New York, 1979)

AND BABY MAKES THREE, Carol Kanter (Harper and Row, New York, 1983)

SURVIVING THE CRISIS OF MOTHERHOOD, Paula Kollstedt (St. Anthony Messenger Press, Cincinnati, 1981)

CONFLICT AND POWER IN MARRIAGE: EXPECTING THE FIRST CHILD, Ralph LaRossa (Sage Publications, Beverly Hills, 1977)

TRANSITION TO PARENTHOOD, Ralph and Maureen LaRossa (Sage Publications, Beverly Hills, 1981)

MARRIAGE AND THE FAMILY, Marcia and Thomas Laswell (D.C. Heath & Co., Boston, 1982)

LEARNING TO SAY GOOD-BY, Eda LeShan (Avon Books, New York, 1978)

CHILD INFLUENCES ON MARITAL AND FAMILY INTERACTION, eds. Richard Lerner and Graham Spanier (Academic Press, New York, 1978)

THE COMPLETE POSTPARTUM GUIDE, Diane Lynch-Fraser (Ballantine Books, New York, 1983)

THROUGH THE MOTHERHOOD MAZE, Sanford J. Matthews and Maryann B. Brinley (Doubleday, New York, 1982)

HANDBOOK OF SEXOLOGY, III: PROCREATION AND PARENTHOOD, eds. John Money and Herman Mustaph (Elsevier, New York, 1977)

THE WORKING PARENTS SURVIVAL GUIDE, Sally Wendkos Olds (Bantam Books, New York, 1983)

ANSWERS FOR NEW PARENTS, Howard and Joy Osofsky (Walker & Co., New York, 1980)

THE PRIVATE LIFE OF PARENTS, Roberta Plutzik and Maria Laghi (Everest House, New York, 1983)

WHEN TWO BECOME THREE: THE COUPLE'S BOOK OF PREGNANCY, Janice Presser (Doubleday, New York, 1984)

SURVIVING FAMILY LIFE, Sonya Rhodes and Joslean Wilson (G. P. Putnam, New York, 1981)

WHAT NOW? A HANDBOOK FOR NEW PARENTS, Mary Lou Rozdilsky and Barbara Banet (Scribners, New York, 1972, 1975)

THE SUPERWOMAN SYNDROME, Marjorie Shaevitz (Warner Books, New York, 1984)

THE MOTHER TO MOTHER BABY CARE BOOK, Barbara Sills and Jeanne Henry (Avon Books, New York, 1980)

FAMILY STRENGTHS, eds. Nick Stinnett, Barbara Chesser, John DeFrain, and Patricia Knaub (University of Nebraska Press, Lincoln, NE, 1980)

NEW PARENTHOOD: THE FIRST SIX WEEKS, Cecelia Worth (McGraw-Hill, New York, 1985)

## Books on Adoption

ADOPTION: PARENTHOOD WITHOUT PREGNANCY, Charlene Canape (Avon Books, New York, 1987)

THE ADOPTION RESOURCE BOOK, Lois Gilman (Harper & Row, New York, 1984)

OUR CHILD: PREPARATION FOR PARENTING IN ADOPTION, Carol Hallenbeck (Our Child Press, Wayne, PA, 1984)

AN ADOPTOR'S ADVOCATE, Patricia Johnstone (Perspectives Press, Fort Wayne, IN, 1984)

RAISING ADOPTED CHILDREN, Lois Melina (Harper & Row, New York, 1986)

# The Appendices

## APPENDIX I: Parenting Organizations

ALABAMA
Family Resource Center
2914 Linden Avenue
Birmingham, AL 35209
(205) 870-1717

ARIZONA
Parenting Plus
4628 North 17th Street, G119
Phoenix, AZ 85016
(602) 274-3652

CALIFORNIA
Pregnancy to Parenthood
  Family Center, Inc.
1010 Sir Francis Drake Blvd.
Kentfield, CA 94904
(415) 456-6466

Parenting Center
Stephen S. Wise Temple
15500 Stephen Wise Drive
Los Angeles, CA 90024
(213) 476-8561

Parents Anonymous of
  California
7120 Franklin Avenue
Los Angeles, CA 90046
(213) 876-0933

Child Rearing Education and
  Counseling Program
Children's Health Council
700 Willow Road
Palo Alto, CA 94304
(415) 326-5530

Early Childhood Mental
  Health Program
3701 Barrett Avenue
Richmond, CA 94805
(415) 236-3104

Parents Adjusting to
  Parenting
5911 Lana Drive
San Diego, CA 92117
(619) 560-6890

San Diego Family
P.O. Box 23965
San Diego, CA 92123
(619) 541-1162

Children's Council of
  San Francisco
3896 24th Street
San Francisco, CA 94114
(415) 647-0778

Family Support Network
150 College Avenue
San Francisco, CA 94112
(415) 333-4891

Parents Place
Jewish Family and
  Children's Services
3272 California Street
San Francisco, CA 94118
(415) 563-1041

Apple Parenting Center
70 Skyview Terrace
San Rafael, CA 94903
(415) 492-0720

Great Beginnings
Marin Jewish Community
  Center
200 North San Pedro Road
San Rafael, CA 94903
(415) 479-2000

Parent Support Network
Family Service Agency
817 de la Vina
Santa Barbara, CA 93101
(805) 965-1001

Postpartum Education
  for Parents (PEP)
927 N. Kellogg Avenue
Santa Barbara, CA 93111
(805) 964-2009

National Family Life
  Education Network
1700 Mission Street, Suite 203
Santa Cruz, CA 95060
(408) 429-9822

A Place for Parents, Inc.
2019 14th Street
Santa Monica, CA 90405
(213) 452-3823

California Parenting Institute
1212 College Avenue
Santa Rosa, CA 95404

Center for Improvement
  of Child
Caring, Inc.
11331 Ventura Blvd, Suite 103
Studio City, CA 91604
(818) 980-0903

Parenting Resources
250 El Camino Real, Suite 111
Tustin, CA 92680
(714) 669-8100

FLORIDA
The Family Center
Nova University
3301 College Avenue
Ft. Lauderdale, FL 33314
(305) 475-7670

Family Education and
Enrichment Center
6750 Sunset Drive
Miami, FL 33143
(305) 665-9987

Having Babies After 30
8955 S.W. 87th Court, Suite
200
Miami, FL 33176
(305) 666-4000

ILLINOIS
Erickson Institute
Advance Study in
Child Development
25 West Chicago Avenue
Chicago, IL 60610
(312) 280-7302

Family Resource Coalition
230 North Michigan Avenue,
Suite 1625
Chicago, IL 60601
(312) 726-4750

Parental Stress Services, Inc.
59 East Van Buren, #1618
Chicago, IL 60605
(312) 427-1161

Parenting: Your Child
from One to Six
Resurrection Hospital, Health
Promotion & Wellness
7435 West Talcott
Chicago, IL 60631
(312) 794-6044

Three General Project
2710 West Devon Avenue,
Room 211
Chicago, IL 60659
(312) 274-1324

Family Life Program
First Congregational Church
1047 Curtiss
Downers Grove, IL 60515
(312) 968-0527

Parenthesis Parent Child
Center
405 South Euclid
Oak Park, IL 60302
(312) 848-2227

Parent/Child Network
NI-ASPO
P.O. Box 784
Tinley Park, IL 60477
(312) 799-6851

Parent and Childbirth
Education Society (FACES)
P.O. Box 213
Western Springs, IL 60558
(312) 246-5502

INDIANA
P.R.O. Parents
1526 Redwing Drive
Evansville, IN 47715
(812) 477-5139

Parenting Guidance Center
Earlham Heights Presbyterian
Church
1625 West Main
Richmond, IN 47274
(317) 962-4902

KANSAS
McPherson Family Life Center
224 South Maple
McPherson, KS 67450
(316) 241-6603

KENTUCKY
Family & Children's Agency
of Metro. Louisville
1115 Garvin Place
Louisville, KY 40203
(502) 583-1741

LOUISIANA
The Parenting Center
Children's Hospital
200 Henry Clay Avenue
New Orleans, LA 70118
(504) 895-3574

Westbank Parenting Center
Westbank Center for
Psychotherapy
4601 Patterson Road
New Orleans, LA 70114
(504) 364-1632

MARYLAND
Frederick County Family
Life Center
Evangelical Lutheran Church
35 East Church Street
Frederick, MD 21701
(301) 663-9217

MASSACHUSETTS
The Parent Connection
1210 Massachusetts
Arlington, MA 02174
(617) 641-2229

COPE
37 Clarendon Street
Boston, MA 02115
(617) 357-5594

Newborn Support Service
104 Summit Avenue
Brookline, MA 02146
(617) 232-5344

Maternal & Child Health
Center
2464 Massachusetts Avenue
Cambridge, MA 02140
(617) 864-9343

Boston Association for
Childbirth Education (BACE)
184 Savin Hill Avenue
Dorchester, MA 02125
(617) 244-5102

Family Connection
4256 Washington Street
Roslindale, MA 02131
(617) 323-0300

MICHIGAN
Parents Supporting Parents
Kent County Health
Department
700 Fuller, NE
Grand Rapids, MI 49503
(616) 247-1373

MINNESOTA
Bloomington-Richfield Family
Center
8900 Portland Avenue S.
Bloomington, MN 55420
(612) 887-9239

Eden Prairie Parent Center/
Edina
Family Parent Center
Edina Community Center
5701 Normandale Road
Edina, MN 55424
(612) 927-9721, x52

Internal Childbirth Education
Association (ICEA)
8635 Fremont Avenue South
Minneapolis, MN 55420

Minnesota Early Learning
  Design (MELD)
123 North 3rd Street
Minneapolis, MN 55401
(612) 332-7563

New Parents Project
123 East Grant Street,
  Suite 612
Minneapolis, MN 55403
(612) 870-4488

Bloomington-Richfield
  Family Center
7001 Elliot Avenue S.
Richfield, MN 55423
(612) 861-1887

Parents Are Important
  in Rochester (PAIIR)
Northrop Community Services
815 NW Second Avenue
Rochester, MN 55901

MISSISSIPPI
Parent Child Program
Cary Christian Health Center
Box 57
Cary, MA 39054

MISSOURI
The Family Center . . .
  A Growing Place
School District of Clayton
7423 Wellington Way
Clayton, MO 63105
(314) 726-2550

Early Education Program
Ferguson-Florissant School
  District
1005 Waterford Drive
Florissant, MO 63033
(314) 838-9761

Affton-Lindbergh Early
  Childhood Education
Affton & Lindbergh School
  District
12225 Eddie & Park Road
St. Louis, MO 63127
(314) 842-3050

NEW HAMPSHIRE
The Children's Place
Concord Parents & Children,
  Inc.
P.O. Box 576
Concord, NH 03301
(603) 224-9920

NEW JERSEY
The Mothers' Center
P.O. Box 7
Scotch Plains, NJ 07076-0007

NEW YORK
Riverdale Neighborhood
  House
5521 Mosholu Avenue
Bronx, NY 10471
(212) 549-8100

Effective Parenting
  Information for Children
  (EPIC)
103 Bacon Hall, 1300
  Elmwood
Buffalo, NY 14222
(716) 884-4064

Parent-Child Workshop
Middle Country Public
  Library
101 Eastwood Blvd.
Centereach, NY 11720
(516) 585-9393

Parenting Center
Central Queens YM-YWHA
67-09 108th Street
Forest Hills, NY 11375
(212) 268-5011

The Parent Center
Day Care Council of
   Westchester
West Hyatt Avenue
Mt. Kisco, NY 10549
(914) 666-8215

Mother and Child Center
11 Wilmot Road
New Rochelle, NY 10804
(914) 834-1798

Early Childhood Resource and
   Information Center
New York Public Library
66 Leroy Street
New York, NY 10014
(212) 929-0815

Family Focus, Inc.
1370 Lexington Avenue
New York, NY 10128
(212) 410-0035

Family Life Education
Federation of Jewish
   Philanthropies
120 West 57th Street
New York, NY 10019
(212) 582-9100

Father Focus
204 West 20th Street
New York, NY 10011
(212) 316-1414

Maternity Center Association
48 East 92nd Street
New York, NY 10128
(212) 369-7300

The Parent & Child
   Consultation Service
20 West 64th Street
New York, NY 10023
(212) 877-8700

Parent Guidance Workshops
180 Riverside Drive
New York, NY 10024
(212) 787-8883

Parenting Center
92nd Street YM & YWHA
1395 Lexington Avenue
New York, NY 10028
(212) 427-6000

Skool for Parents
Lenox Hill Hospital
100 East 77th Street
New York, NY 10021
(212) 794-4510

Parent Resource Center
Flower Hill School
99 Campus Drive
Port Washington, NY 11050
(516) 883-4000, x230

Parents' Place, Inc.
3 Carhart Avenue
White Plains, NY 10605
(914) 948-5187

OHIO
Family Place
Jewish Community Center
3305 Mayfield Road
Cleveland, OH 44118
(216) 382-4000

OKLAHOMA
The Infant Center
Junior League of Oklahoma
815 NE 15th Street
Oklahoma City, OK 73104
(405) 271-8063

PENNSYLVANIA
The Fathers' Center
120 West Lancaster Avenue
Ardmore, PA 19003
(215) 649-6400

Parent Resource Association
Parent Resource Center
Box 2111
Jenkintown, PA 19046
(215) 576-7961

Parent Resource Association
Kent and Fernbrook Roads
Wyncote, PA 19095
(215) 576-7691

RHODE ISLAND
Child and Family Services of
   Newport County
24 School Street
Newport, RI 02840
(401) 849-2300

TEXAS
Dallas Assoc. for Parent
   Education (DAPE)
13551 North Central Exp., #12
Dallas, TX 75243
(214) 699-0420

Parents of Prematures
Houston Organization
   for Parent Education (HOPE)
3311 Richmond, #330
Houston, TX 77098
(713) 524-3089

VIRGINIA
The Family Center
Alexander Community Y
418 South Washington Street
Alexandria, VA 22314
(703) 549-1111

WISCONSIN
Aid Association for
   Lutherans
4321 North Ballard Road
Appleton, WI 54919
(414) 734-5721

Family Enhancement Program
605 Spruce Street
Madison, WI 53715
(608) 256-3890

Parent Education
Milwaukee Dept. of
   Social Services
1220 West Vliet Street
Milwaukee, WI 53205
(414) 289-6461

United Cerebral Palsy of
   Southeastern Wisconsin
152 West Wisconsin Avenue
Milwaukee, WI 53203
(414) 272-4500

Parents Place
336 Wisconsin Avenue
Waukesha, WI

CANADA
Pacific Postpartum Support
   Society
888 Burrand Street
Vancouver, B.C. V6Z 1X9
(604) 689-9994

## APPENDIX II: NEWSLETTERS AND PUBLICATIONS

NEW WAYS TO WORK
149 Ninth Street
San Francisco, CA 94103

NATIONAL INFORMATION
   CENTER FOR
   HANDICAPPED CHILDREN
   & YOUTH (NICHCY)
P.O. Box 1492
Washington, D.C. 20013
(703) 522-3332

GROWING CHILD
Dunn & Hargitt
22 North Second Street
P.O. Box 1100
Lafayette, IN 47902
(317) 423-2624

GROWING PARENT
Dunn & Hargitt
22 North Second Street
P.O. Box 1100
Lafayette, IN 47902
(317) 423-2624

THE BOSTON PARENTS'
   PAPER
P.O. Box 1777
Boston, MA 02130
(617) 522-1515

PRACTICAL PARENTING
18326 Minnetonka Blvd.
Deephaven, MN 55391
(612) 475-1505

MOTHERING PUBLICATIONS
   INC.
P.O. Box 8410
Sante Fe, NM 87504
(505) 984-8116

WORKING PARENTS'
   FORUM
Center for Family &
   Community Education, Inc.
P.O. Box 4505
New Windsor, NY 12550
(914) 565-4061

CHILDBIRTH EDUCATOR
575 Lexington Avenue
New York, NY 10022
(212) 752-0775

MOTHERS TODAY
441 Lexington Avenue
New York, NY 10017
(212) 867-4820

PARENTGUIDE MAGAZINE
Two Park Avenue, Suite 2012
New York, NY 10016
(212) 213-8840

MOTHER'S CHOICE
107 S. Main Street
Hendersonville, NC 28739

THE NEWSLETTER OF
   PARENTING
803 Church Street
Honesdale, PA 18431
(717) 253-1080

# APPENDIX III: ADOPTIVE PARENTS' GROUPS

ARIZONA
Adoptive Parents' Education
   Program
P.O. Box 32114
Phoenix, AZ 85064
(602) 957-2896

CALIFORNIA
Post Adoption Center for
   Education and Research
   (PACER)
477-15th Street, #200
Oakland, CA 94612

Post Adoption Center for
   Education and Research
2255 Ygnacio Valley Road,
   Suite L
Walnut Creek, CA 94598

DISTRICT OF COLUMBIA
National Committee for
   Adoption
1346 Connecticut Avenue
   N.W. #326
Washington, DC 20036

IDAHO
Adopted Child
P.O. Box 9362
Moscow, ID 83843

KENTUCKY
Family and Children's Agency
   of Metropolitan Louisville
1115 Garvin Place
P.O. Box 3775
Louisville, KY
(502) 583-1741

MARYLAND
Families Adopting Children
   Everywhere (FACE)
P.O. Box 28058
Northwood Station
Baltimore, MD 21239

Family Building Associates,
   Inc.
11419 Rokeby Avenue
Kensington, MD 20895
(301) 942-1218

MASSACHUSETTS
Open Door Society of
   Massachusetts, Inc.
19 Omaha Avenue
Northboro, MA 01532

MINNESOTA
OURS, INC. (Organization for
   United Response)
3307 Hwy. 100 North
Minneapolis, MN 55422
(612) 535-4829

NEW YORK
The Center for Adoptive
   Families, Inc.
67 Irving Place
New York, NY 10003
(212) 420-8811

VERMONT
Parents for Private Adoption
P.O. Box 7
Pawlet, VT 05761

VIRGINIA
North American Council on
   Adoptable Children
413 Duck Street
Alexandria, VA 22314

## APPENDIX IV:
## NATIONAL ORGANIZATIONS FOR CHILD ABUSE

CHILDHELP NATIONAL CHILD ABUSE HOTLINE (800) 422-4453. 24-hour professional help for crisis situations and also recommendations for long-term treatment and support.

NATIONAL CENTER FOR MISSING AND EXPLOITED CHILDREN 1835 K Street, N.W., Washington, DC, 20006 (202) 634-9821. Referrals and information for parents and professionals on detection, prevention, and treatment of child abuse.

PARENTS UNITED INTERNATIONAL P.O. Box 952, San Jose, CA 95108 (408) 280-5055. Coalition of 160 community groups dealing with child sexual abuse.

## APPENDIX V:
## REGIONAL RESOURCE CENTERS
## ON CHILDREN AND YOUTH SERVICES

There are 10 regional centers which provide resources and technical assistance for families. These centers draw on federal, state, and local organizations to offer information on adoption and parenting in your region.

New England Resource Center for Children and Families
Judge Baker Guidance Center
295 Longwood Avenue
Boston, MA 02115

Region II Resource Center on Children and Youth
Cornell University
Family Life and Development Center
College of Human Ecology
Ithaca, NY 14853

Region III Resource Center for Children, Youth and Families
Virginia Commonwealth University
School of Social Work
1001 West Franklin Street
Richmond, VA 23284

Southeastern Regional Resource Center for Children and Youth
University of Tennessee
School of Social Work
1838 Terrance Avenue
Knoxville, TN 37996

Region V Resource Center on
Children and Youth Services
University of Wisconsin-
Milwaukee
School of Social Welfare
P.O. Box 786
Milwaukee, WI 53201

Region VI Regional Resource
Center for Children, Youth
and Families
University of Texas at Austin
School of Social Work
Austin, TX 78712

Region VII Children, Youth
and Family Center
University of Iowa
Institute of Child Behavior and
Development
Oakdale Campus
Iowa City, IA 52319

Region VIII Family Resource
Center
University of Denver
Graduate School of Social
Work
Denver, CO 80208

Region IX Consolidated
Resource Center for
Children & Youth Service
California State University at
Los Angeles
5151 State University Drive
Los Angeles, CA 90032

Northwest Resource Center
for Children, Youth and
Families
University of Washington
School of Social Work
4101 15th Avenue N.E.
Seattle, WA 98185

## APPENDIX VI: NEW WAYS TO WORK

New Ways to Work (NWW) is a nonprofit work resource organization based in San Francisco. Founded in 1972, NWW has been a pioneer in promoting a wide range of new work schedules, which can be especially important for parents who want to adjust their careers to spend time with their child. "Job sharing" is one of the primary options that NWW has promoted: two people voluntarily sharing the responsibilities of one full-time position with salary and benefits pro-rated. NWW can provide you with information and assistance on a number of other work time options as well, including voluntary reduced work plans, permanent part-time employment, work sharing, sabbaticals, leaves, flextime, and compressed work week. Fifteen community organizations around the country belong to the Network for Work Time Options and can provide you with assistance.

## Network for Work Time Options

CALIFORNIA
Flexible Career Associates
P.O. Box 6701
3704 State Street
Santa Barbara, CA 93111

New Ways to Work
149 Ninth Street
San Francisco, CA 94103

COLORADO
Alliance on Alternative Work
  Strategy
c/o Judy L. Henke
5121 S. Ironton
Denver, CO 80111

INDIANA
Continuing Education Center
IU-Purdue
1317 W. Michriver Street
Indianapolis, IN 46223

MAINE
Nancy Viehmann
Pier Road, Box 78
Cape Porpoise, ME 04014

MICHIGAN
Work Options Resource
  Center
Michigan Dept. of Labor
State Secondary Complex
7150 Harris Drive, Box 30015
Lansing, MI 48909

MINNESOTA
CHART
Wesley Temple Building
123 E. Grant Street
Minneapolis, MN 55403

NEW YORK
CATALYST
14 East 60th Street
New York, NY 10022

OHIO
RESOURCE: Careers
1258 Euclid Ave.
Cleveland, OH 44115

PENNSYLVANIA
Center for Flexible
  Employment
P.O. Box 1054
Langhorne, PA 19047

Work Time Options
966 Summer Place
Pittsburgh, PA 15213

TEXAS
Austin Women's Center
Women's Employment Adv.
  Prog.
2700 S. First Street
Austin, TX 78704

UTAH
Phoenix Institute
1800 S.W. Temple, Suite 211
Salt Lake City, UT 84115

VIRGINIA
APTP/Washington Chapter
Flow General Building
7655 Old Springhouse Road
McLean, VA 22102

WASHINGTON
FOCUS
509 Tenth Avenue, E.
Seattle, WA 98102

CANADA
WORK WELL
#521-620 View Street
Victoria, B.C.
Canada V8W 1J6

# Index